A Neurocomputational Perspective

Dave Coone
Pittsburgh
20/6/92

A Neurocomputational Perspective

The Nature of Mind and the
Structure of Science

Paul M. Churchland

A Bradford Book
The MIT Press
Cambridge, Massachusetts
London, England

First MIT Press paperback edition, 1992
© 1989 Massachusetts Institute of Technology

This book was set in Palatino by Asco Trade Typesetting Ltd., Hong Kong, and printed and bound in the United States of America.

Library of Congress Cataloguing-in-Publication Data

Churchland, Paul M., 1942–
  A neurocomputational perspective: the nature of mind and the
structure of science/Paul M. Churchland.

    p.   cm.
  Bibliography: p.
  Includes index.
  ISBN 0-262-03151-5 (HB), 0-262-53106-2 (PB)
  1. Intellect. 2. Consciousness. 3. Cognition. 4. Neural
computers. 5. Science—Philosophy. 6. Psychology—
Philosophy. 7. Science and psychology. I. Title.
BF431.C48   1989
128'.1—dc20   89-9398
                                                  CIP

For Mark and Anne,
two lamps against the darkness

Contents

Preface

The single most important development in the philosophy of mind during the past forty years has been the emerging influence of the philosophy of science. Issues that had been the special province of metaphysicians and philosophers of language came increasingly to be seen as issues of the same sort as those found elsewhere in our scientific history. The questions surrounding the nature of mind and consciousness have slowly come to be represented as empirical questions, high level perhaps, but solvable eventually by the methods of theoretical science. The seminal thinkers who launched the philosophy of mind on this dramatic new course—Feigl, Smart, Sellars, and Feyerabend spring immediately to mind—were also and without exception first-rate philosophers of science. Since then it has hardly been possible to do any systematic work in the philosophy of mind, or even to understand the debates, without drawing heavily on themes, commitments, or antecedent expertise drawn from the philosophy of science.

Examples of this infusion are close at hand. The nature of explanation in general and of psychological explanations in particular became an issue central to philosophers of mind because the conceptual framework with which we conceive of ourselves (as creatures with beliefs, desires, and other mental states) came to be seen as a common-sense explanatory *theory*—"folk psychology"—a theory that enables each of us to predict and explain the behavior of the other humans that surround us. This made an issue in turn of the status of theoretical entities (Are mental states real?), the nature of cross-theoretic identities (Are mental states identical with brain states?), and the criteria for intertheoretic reduction (Could folk psychology itself eventually be explained in turn by a deeper and more neurobiological theory of human nature?).

Ontological concerns were joined by epistemological concerns. Whether our noninferential knowledge must always be laden with prior theoretical commitments became a further focus of dispute because the apparent authority of *introspection* was by this means called into question (Can one know by sheer introspection that the mind is distinct from the brain?), and because it held out the intriguing possibility of conceptual change even at the introspective level (Might one learn to introspect, to be "directly aware" of, one's own neurochemical and neurocomputational states?).

Even the highly abstract issue of the desirability of an ultimately *unified* science of Nature has become a bone of fierce contention among philosophers of mind. This is because the pressure on folk psychology to find an integrated place within such a unified explanatory scheme, or else be thrown on the scrap heap of history, will be a function of how high a value we place on the unity of science. Philosophers such as Jerry Fodor, Donald Davidson, and Dan Dennett, in their quite different ways (namely, positive disunity in science, conceptual dualism, and selective instrumentalism), place a sharply restricted value on unity and thus feel able to claim a separate and autonomous place for folk psychology safe from the advancing tide of natural science. Other philosophers, such as W. V. Quine, Patricia Churchland, Cliff Hooker, and myself, place a very high value on unity, and thus insist that folk psychology cannot be protected indefinitely from having to meet the obligations that all acceptable theories must ultimately meet. Either it must be successfully reduced (to a matured cognitive neurobiology, for example), perhaps undergoing some modification in the process. Or it must be displaced by a better theory, one that does cohere with the rest of our growing scientific corpus.

In these ways, and in others, problems in the philosophy of mind have found themselves systematically reconstructed as problems in the philosophy of science. This infusion of information from a highly developed area of philosophy has transformed the philosophy of mind by placing it within a new and more general context of important questions and plausible answers, and more important still, by placing it firmly in contact with ongoing developments in the adjacent natural sciences. The essays in part 1 of this volume constitute one journey through the major problems in the philosophy of mind, one attempt to bring the most important results in the philosophy of science to bear on them. They also attempt to apply the most recent results in computational neuroscience and connectionist AI to the many problems at hand. The problem of subjective sensory qualia is salient here, as is the the problem of mental representation. Both have been central to philosophical discussions about the nature of mind, and both have been sharply illuminated by recent developments in physiological psychology and cognitive neurobiology.

Though published independently over a period of seven years, the essays of part 1 constitute an unfolding argument for a unified materialist position concerning the mind. The first and earliest of the essays here assembled, "Eliminative Materialism and the Propositional Attitudes" (1981a), picks up on a theme that concluded my 1979 book. That theme urges the need for a new cognitive kinematics and correlative dynamics, one that is radically different from the venerable sentence-crunching paradigm common to folk psychology, orthodox cognitive science, and conventional AI. The new kinematics and dynamics, I argued, should be drawn from, or inspired by, the emerging sciences of the brain, and I there presumed to sketch some general features that the new cognitive paradigm should display (pp. 17–18). At the time I would have guessed that a new paradigm meeting the stated conditions was at least twenty-five years away, and probably more like fifty.

In this I was wrong, for in fact it already existed and had existed, at least in stick-figure form, since the late fifties. By 1959 F. Rosenblatt had developed the Perceptron paradigm of vector-to-vector transformations in a parallel network of neuronlike processing units. These artificial networks could learn to recognize patterns by the repeated presentation of similar examples. Unfortunately, that paradigm did not catch on, and for two decades it was almost forgotten—its resources pursued by only a small handful of researchers: a few within neuroscience and even fewer within AI. It stumbled as it left the starting blocks partly because of the limited success of its earliest networks, partly because of some slightly overstated but widely influential criticisms by M. Minsky and S. Papert (1969), but mostly because of the simultaneous eclipse of this immature paradigm by the very real virtues of conventional general-purpose computers and the more immediate rewards of program-writing AI. The AI profession flocked enthusiastically to this nonbiological alternative, and the neural-network approach faded to invisibility.

Within two years of the 1981a paper Patricia Churchland and I were fortunate to stumble across this obscure vector-transformation-in-a-parallel-network model during our meanders through the field of neuroscience. Specifically, Andras Pellionisz and Rodolfo Llinas had developed a theoretical model of the cerebellum that showed us how such a massively parallel system could solve complex problems in motor control and sensorimotor coordination. But we, as they, could see that its potential applications were much broader. Some computer simulations of sensorimotor coordination on my own modest machine deepened my acquaintance with its virtues, and the paper

"Some Reductive Strategies in Cognitive Neurobiology" was written with some excitement in the spring of 1984.

That paper provides a detailed articulation of something I had been arguing for and seeking since 1971: a genuine alternative cognitive paradigm, one firmly grounded in neuroscience, one that might eventually be developed so as to reduce or displace the sentential paradigm of folk psychology. Most of my work since 1984 has been aimed at exploring that promise. But the account in that paper also has a major lacuna. It outlines no procedures by which the relevant networks can *arrive* at the specific configurations necessary to execute their cognitive achievements. It contains, that is, no account of functional plasticity, or *learning*.

That piece of the puzzle was still missing as, in the fall of 1984, I left the University of Manitoba to join the philosophy department at the University of California, San Diego, and became a member of the campus cognitive-science faculty. This interdisciplinary group of perhaps two dozen scholars held a weekly seminar organized mainly by David Rumelhart. There I discovered something I had not appreciated before arriving. The vector-transformation-by-parallel-network paradigm had been a topic of research among UCSD's cognitive scientists for several years, and suspicion of the orthodox sentential approaches to modeling the mind was already widespread in that group. Moreover, during that first year or so Rumelhart, Hinton, and Williams (1986a) perfected an important generalization of Rosenblatt's original learning algorithm, the simple delta rule. Their *generalized delta rule*, or *back propagation algorithm* as it is often called, would train multilayered artificial networks to perform almost any vector-to-vector transformation, given repeated exposure to many instances of the transformation desired.

The full significance of that algorithm was only dimly appreciated at its initial articulation (late in 1980), even by its authors. It was biologically unrealistic for starters. It was computationally intensive and hence rather slow in execution. And for a wide variety of problems it was not expected to be reliable at getting anywhere close to an optimal solution. On the first two points the worries were well founded. But on the third point the worries proved to be exaggerated. Experience in training diverse networks on many different problems showed the back-propagation algorithm to be a relentlessly efficient and highly reliable means of finding excellent solutions over a wide range of problems. Though it was not the only learning algorithm that had been developed, it quickly became the technology of choice nationwide for training various networks to see what they could and could not do.

They could do, it began to seem, just about anything. They could perform sensorimotor coordination, direct gaze accurately despite changes in head position, recognize subtle similarities among sonar returns, pronounce well-articulated speech from printed text, recognize three-dimensional shapes independently of the angle of illumination, parse sentences into grammatical types, recognize voiced phonemes, predict the folding of protein molecules, correctly recognize colors across changes in illumination, and so forth. And they did all of this by learning from a store of relevant examples. The practical necessity of *simulating* the relevant parallel networks within conventional serial computers imposed limits on how large the model networks could be, since the number of computationally active synaptic connections explodes as roughly the square of the number of neuronal units in the network. And a further limit was imposed by the necessity of computing thousands of adjustments for each of these many connections during the course of training with the backpropagation algorithm. Even so, networks of a few hundred units were readily simulated, and they proved to be capable, after training, of some quite arresting displays of cognitive sophistication.

The questions then became, Just how are these networks doing all this? How do they manage to find unity and structure in the chaos and diversity of their sensory inputs? What forms of representation are being generated inside them? Why do some networks learn better than others on the same training corpus? Fortunately, simulated networks, unlike biological brains, can easily be tweaked into giving up their hidden secrets. One need not insert microelectrodes one by one and blindly into a mass of fragile cells. One can write the simulation program to read out on command the simultaneous and undegraded microbehavior of entire populations of artificial neurons.

Here the results are highly intriguing, and to the eye of a philosopher of science they are very revealing. Almost immediately one could begin to see lessons that bear directly and systematically on issues central to the philosophy of science: the nature of theories, the theory-ladenness of perception, the nature of conceptual unification, the virtues of theoretical simplicity, the nature of paradigms, the kinematics of conceptual change, the character of abductive inference, and the nature of explanatory understanding (see especially the discussions in chapters 9, 10, and 11).

This brings me to the second major theme of this volume. I began this preface by detailing how it is no longer possible to do major work in the philosophy of mind without drawing on themes from the philosophy of science and the several sciences of the mind-brain. I wish now to suggest that the instruction and information has begun to flow vigorously in the opposite direction. Very shortly it will no longer be possible to do major work in the philosophy of science without drawing on themes from the philosophy of mind and from the related disciplines of computational neuroscience, cognitive psychology, and connectionist AI.

The detailed grounds for this claim are to be found in the essays of part 2, especially in chapters 9 to 11, but the basic sketch is quickly given. First, the relevant theme from the philosophy of mind is the view that the sentential kinematics of folk psychology is but a commonsense *theory*, and almost certainly a *false* theory, at least as an account of the basic kinematics of cognitive creatures generally. Second, the relevant theme from cognitive neurobiology and connectionst AI is that the basic kinematics of cognitive creatures is a kinematics not of sentences but of high-dimensional activation vectors being transformed into other such vectors by passing through large arrays of synaptic connections. A new kinematics for cognitive activity is already here. Dynamical alternatives (for learning) are under active exploration, and results directly relevant to the nature of scientific inquiry can already be discerned. It is the primary aim of this volume to bring those results to the attention of the philosophy-of-science community.

Though the results are unexpected and to some extent destructive of orthodoxy, I expect them to be given a fair hearing by the relevant community, since a crucial precedent has already been set. The relevance, to theories about the nature of science, of the actual *history* of human scientific inquiry is something that has been conceded by the bulk of the community for well over a decade. On the whole, this has been a healthy development. The more empirical constraints we can place on any theoretical enterprise, the better, and the philosophy of science is no exception. The infusion I am recommending is more of the same. But the empirical data are drawn not from history or sociology: they are drawn from the brain and from those artificial systems that model the salient microstructural and microfunctional features of the brain. Moreover, the data are accompanied by some promising new theory about the nature of cognition. Suitably developed, that theory may help us find a new coherence in the scattered issues that make up the philosophy of science, new solutions to old philosophical problems, and new possibilities for the enterprise of science itself. There is no guarantee that this will happen, but the gathering case is assembled in part 2 of this volume.

Almost all of the essays here collected were written as independent pieces, and almost all should be intelligible as such. Certain strong threads connect them, however, and certain sequences are salient.

The quick tour through the major themes of the volume would focus on chapters 1, 5, and 6 from part 1, and chapters 9, 10 and 11 from part 2.

The research here presented was supported by a grant from the Institute for Advanced Study, by a grant from the Social Sciences and Humanities Research Council of Canada, by a sabbatical leave from the University of Manitoba, and by the University of California, San Diego. Turning finally to individuals, I am pleased to be able to thank Larry Jordan, David Zipser, Terry Sejnowski, David Rumelhart, Francis Crick, Rodolfo Llinas, Andras Pellionisz, Philip Kitcher, Stephen Stich, and Patricia Churchland. Without their wise and generous company to draw on, I could never have written the later papers in this volume, and would never have been able to complete the argument begun in the earlier papers. Thanks in large measure to them, I have a coherent story to tell.

La Jolla, California, 1988

PART I

The Nature of Mind

Chapter 1

Eliminative Materialism and the Propositional Attitudes

Eliminative materialism is the thesis that our commonsense conception of psychological phenomena constitutes a radically false theory, a theory so fundamentally defective that both the principles and the ontology of that theory will eventually be displaced, rather than smoothly reduced, by completed neuroscience. Our mutual understanding and even our introspection may then be reconstituted within the conceptual framework of completed neuroscience, a theory we may expect to be more powerful by far than the commonsense psychology it displaces, and more substantially integrated within physical science generally. My purpose in this paper is to explore these projections, especially as they bear on (1) the principal elements of commonsense psychology: the propositional attitudes (beliefs, desires, etc.), and (2) the conception of rationality in which those elements figure.

This focus represents a change in the fortunes of materialism. Twenty years ago emotions, qualia, and "raw feels" were held to be the principal stumbling blocks for the materialist program. With these barriers dissolving (Feyerabend 1963a; Rorty 1965; Churchland 1979), the locus of opposition has shifted. Now it is the realm of the intentional, the realm of the propositional attitude, that is most commonly held up as being both irreducible to and ineliminable in favor of anything from within a materialist framework. Whether and why this is so, we must examine.

Such an examination will make little sense, however, unless it is first appreciated that the relevant network of commonsense concepts does indeed constitute an empirical theory, with all the functions, virtues, *and perils* entailed by that status. I shall therefore begin with a brief sketch of this view and a summary rehearsal of its rationale. The resistance it encounters still surprises me. After all, common sense has yielded up many theories. Recall the view that space has a pre-

This paper first appeared in the *Journal of Philosophy* 78 (1981), no. 2.

ferred direction in which all things fall, that weight is an intrinsic feature of a body, that a force-free moving object will promptly return to rest, that the sphere of the heavens turns daily, and so on. These examples are clear, perhaps, but people seem willing to concede a theoretical component within common sense only if (1) the theory and the common sense involved are safely located in antiquity, and (2) the relevant theory is now so clearly false that its speculative nature is inescapable. Theories are indeed easier to discern under these circumstances. But the vision of hindsight is always 20/20. Let us aspire to some foresight for a change.

1 Why Folk Psychology Is a Theory

Seeing our commonsense conceptual framework for mental phenomena as a theory brings a simple and unifying organization to most of the major topics in the philosophy of mind, including the explanation and prediction of behavior, the semantics of mental predicates, action theory, the problem of other minds, the intentionality of mental states, the nature of introspection, and the mind-body problem. Any view that can pull this lot together deserves careful consideration.

Let us begin with the explanation of human (and animal) behavior. The fact is that the average person is able to explain, and even predict, the behavior of persons with a facility and success that is remarkable. Such explanations and predictions standardly make reference to the desires, beliefs, fears, intentions, perceptions, and so forth, to which the agents are presumed subject. But explanations presuppose laws—rough and ready ones, at least—that connect the explanatory conditions with the behavior explained. The same is true for the making of predictions, and for the justification of subjunctive and counterfactual conditionals concerning behavior. Reassuringly, a rich network of commonsense laws can indeed be reconstructed from this quotidian commerce of explanation and anticipation; its principles are familiar homilies; and their sundry functions are transparent. We understand others, as well as we do, because we share a tacit command of an integrated body of lore concerning the lawlike relations holding among external circumstances, internal states, and overt behavior. Given its nature and functions, this body of lore may quite aptly be called "folk psychology." (I shall examine a handful of these laws presently. For a more comprehensive sampling of the laws of folk psychology, see P. M. Churchland 1979. For a detailed examination of the laws that underwrite action explanations in particular, see P. M. Churchland 1970.)

This approach entails that the semantics of the terms in our familiar mentalistic vocabulary is to be understood in the same manner as the semantics of theoretical terms generally: the meaning of any theoretical term is fixed or constituted by the network of laws in which it figures. (This position is quite distinct from logical behaviorism. I deny that the relevant laws are analytic, and it is the lawlike connections generally that carry the semantic weight, not just the connections with overt behavior. But this view does account for what little plausibility logical behaviorism did enjoy.)

More important, the recognition that folk psychology is a theory provides a simple and decisive solution to an old skeptical problem, the problem of other minds. The problematic conviction that another individual is the subject of certain mental states is not inferred deductively from his behavior, nor is it inferred by inductive analogy from the perilously isolated instance of one's own case. Rather, that conviction is a singular *explanatory hypothesis* of a perfectly straightforward kind. Its function, in conjunction with the background laws of folk psychology, is to provide explanations/predictions/understanding of the individual's continuing behavior, and it is credible to the degree that it is successful in this regard over competing hypotheses. In the main, such hypotheses are successful, and so the belief that others enjoy the internal states comprehended by folk psychology is a reasonable belief.

Knowledge of other minds thus has no essential dependence on knowledge of one's *own* mind. Applying the principles of our folk psychology to our behavior, a Martian could justly ascribe to us the familiar run of mental states, even though his own psychology were very different from ours. He would not, therefore, be "generalizing from his own case."

As well, introspective judgments about one's own case turn out not to have any special status or integrity anyway. On the present view, a spontaneous introspective judgment is just an instance of an acquired habit of conceptual response to one's internal states, and the integrity of any particular response is always contingent on the integrity of the acquired conceptual framework (theory) in which the response is framed. Accordingly, one's *introspective* certainty that one's mind is the seat of beliefs and desires may be as badly misplaced as was the classical man's *visual* certainty that the star-flecked sphere of the heavens turns daily.

Another conundrum is the intentionality of mental states. The "propositional attitudes," as Russell called them, form the systematic core of folk psychology, and their uniqueness and anomalous logical properties have inspired some to see here a fundamental contrast with anything that mere physical phenomena might conceivably display. The key to this matter lies again in the theoretical nature of folk psychology. The intentionality of mental states here emerges not as a mystery of nature, but as a structural feature of the concepts of folk psychology. Ironically, those same structural features reveal the very close affinity that folk psychology bears to theories in the physical sciences. Let me try to explain.

Consider the large variety of what might be called "numerical attitudes" appearing in the conceptual frameworks of physical science: '. . .has a mass$_{kg}$ of n', '. . .has a velocity$_{m/s}$ of n', '. . .has a temperature$_K$ of n', and so forth. These expressions are predicate-forming expressions: when one substitutes a singular term for a number into the place held by 'n', a determinate predicate results. More interesting, the relations between the various "numerical attitudes" that result are precisely the relations between the numbers "contained" in those attitudes. More interesting still, the argument place that takes the singular terms for numbers is open to quantification. All this permits the expression of generalizations concerning the lawlike relations that hold between the various numerical attitudes in nature. Such laws involve quantification over numbers, and they exploit the mathematical relations holding in that domain. Thus, for example,

(1) $(x)(f)(m)[((x$ has a mass of $m)$ & $(x$ suffers a net force of $f))$ $\supset (x$ accelerates at $f/m)]$.

Consider now the large variety of propositional attitudes: '. . .believes that p', '. . .desires that p', '. . .fears that p', '. . .is happy that p', etc. These expressions are predicate-forming expressions also. When one substitutes a singular term for a proposition into the place held by 'p', a determinate predicate results, e.g., '. . .believes that Tom is tall'. (Sentences do not generally function as singular terms, but it is difficult to escape the idea that when a sentence occurs in the place held by 'p', it is there functioning as or like a singular term. More on this below.) More interesting, the relations between the resulting propositional attitudes are characteristically the relations that hold between the propositions "contained" in them, relations such as entailment, equivalence, and mutual inconsistency. More interesting still, the argument place that takes the singular terms for propositions is open to quantification. All this permits the expression of generalizations concerning the lawlike relations that hold among propositional attitudes. Such laws involve quantification over propositions, and they exploit various relations holding in that domain. Thus, for example,

(2) $(x)(p)[(x$ fears that $p) \supset (x$ desires that $\sim p)]$

(3) $(x)(p)[((x$ hopes that $p)$ & $(x$ discovers that $p))$
      $\supset (x$ is pleased that $p)]$

(4) $(x)(p)(q)[((x$ believes that $p)$ & $(x$ believes that (if p then $q)))$
      $\supset$ (barring confusion, distraction, etc., x believes that $q)]$

(5) $(x)(p)(q)[((x$ desires that $p)$ & $(x$ believes that (if q then $p))$
      & $(x$ is able to bring it about that $q))$
      $\supset$ (barring conflicting desires or preferred means,
      x brings it about that $q)]$.

(If we stay within an objectual interpretation of the quantifiers, perhaps the simplest way to make systematic sense of expressions like ⌐x believes that p⌐ and closed sentences formed therefrom is just to construe whatever occurs in the nested position held by 'p', 'q', etc. as there having the function of a singular term. Accordingly, when the standard connectives occur between terms in that nested position, they must be construed as there functioning as operators that form compound singular terms from other singular terms, and not as sentence operators. The compound singular terms so formed denote the appropriate compound propositions. Substitutional quantification will of course underwrite a different interpretation, and there are other approaches as well. Especially appealing is the prosentential approach of Grover, Camp, and Belnap 1975. But the resolution of these issues is not vital to the present discussion.)

Finally, the realization that folk psychology is a theory puts a new light on the mind-body problem. The issue becomes a matter of how the ontology of one theory (folk psychology) is, or is not, going to be related to the ontology of another theory (completed neuroscience); and the major philosophical positions on the mind-body problem emerge as so many different anticipations of what future research will reveal about the intertheoretic status and integrity of folk psychology.

The identity theorist optimistically expects that folk psychology will be smoothly *reduced* by completed neuroscience, and its ontology preserved by dint of transtheoretic identities. The dualist expects that it will prove *ir*reducible to completed neuroscience, by dint of being a nonredundant description of an autonomous, nonphysical domain of natural phenomena. The functionalist too expects that it will prove irreducible, but on the quite different grounds that the internal economy characterized by folk psychology is not, in the last analysis, a law-governed economy of natural states but an abstract organization of functional states, an organization instantiable in a variety of quite different material substrates. It is therefore irreducible to the principles peculiar to any one of them.

Finally, the eliminative materialist too is pessimistic about the prospects for reduction, but his reason is that folk psychology is a radically inadequate account of our internal activities, too confused and too defective to win survival through intertheoretic reduction. On his view, it will simply be displaced by a better theory of those activities.

Which of these fates is the real destiny of folk psychology, we shall attempt to divine presently. For now the point to keep in mind is that we shall be exploring the fate of a theory, a systematic, corrigible, speculative *theory*.

2   Why Folk Psychology Might (Really) Be False

Since folk psychology is an empirical theory, it is at least an abstract possibility that its principles are radically false and that its ontology is an illusion. With the exception of eliminative materialism, however, none of the major positions takes this possibility seriously. None of them doubts the basic integrity or truth of folk psychology (FP), and all of them anticipate a future in which its laws and categories are conserved. This conservatism is not without some foundation. After all, FP does enjoy a substantial amount of explanatory and predictive success. And what better grounds for confidence in the integrity of its categories?

What better grounds indeed. Even so, the presumption in favor of FP is spurious, born of innocence and tunnel vision. A more searching examination reveals a different picture. First, we must reckon not only with the successes of FP but also with its explanatory failures and with their extent and seriousness. Second, we must consider the long-term history of FP, its growth, fertility, and current promise of future development. And third, we must consider what sorts of theories are *likely* to be true of the etiology of our behavior, given what else we have learned about ourselves in recent history. That is, we must evaluate FP with regard to its coherence and continuity with fertile and well-established theories in adjacent and overlapping domains—with evolutionary theory, biology, and neuroscience, for example—because active coherence with the rest of what we presume to know is perhaps the final measure of any hypothesis.

A serious inventory of this sort reveals a very troubled situation, one which would evoke open skepticism in the case of any theory less familiar and dear to us. Let me sketch some relevant detail. When one centers one's attention not on what FP can explain, but on what it cannot explain or fails even to address, one discovers that there is a great deal. As examples of central and important mental phenomena that remain largely or wholly mysterious within the framework of FP, consider the nature and dynamics of mental illness, the faculty of creative imagination, or the ground of intelligence differences between individuals. Consider our utter ignorance of the nature and psychological functions of sleep, that curious state in which a third of one's life is spent. Reflect on the common ability to catch an outfield fly ball on the run, or hit a moving car with a snowball. Consider the internal construction of a three-dimensional visual image from subtle differences in the two-dimensional array of stimulations in one's respective retinas. Consider the rich variety of perceptual illusions, visual and otherwise. Or consider the miracle of memory, with its lightning capacity for relevant retrieval. On these and many other mental phenomena, FP sheds negligible light.

One particularly outstanding mystery is the nature of the learning process itself, especially where it involves large-scale conceptual change, and especially in its prelinguistic or entirely nonlinguistic form (as in infants and animals), which is by far the most common form in nature. FP is faced with special difficulties here, since its conception of learning as the manipulation and storage of propositional attitudes founders on the fact that how to formulate, manipulate, and store a rich fabric of propositional attitudes is itself something that is learned, and is only one among many acquired cognitive skills. FP would thus appear constitutionally incapable of even addressing this most basic of mysteries. (A possible response here is to insist that the cognitive activity of animals and infants is linguiformal in its elements, structures, and processing right from birth. J. A. Fodor [1975] has erected a positive theory of thought on the assumption that the innate forms of cognitive activity have precisely the form here denied. For a critique of Fodor's view, see P. S. Churchland 1978.)

Failures on such a large scale do not yet show that FP is a false theory, but they do move that prospect well into the range of real possibility, and they do show decisively that FP is *at best* a highly superficial theory, a partial and unpenetrating gloss on a deeper and more complex reality. Having reached this opinion, we may be forgiven for exploring the possibility that FP provides a positively misleading sketch of our internal kinematics and dynamics, one whose success is owed more to selective application and forced interpretation on our part than to genuine theoretical insight on FP's part.

A look at the history of FP does little to allay such fears, once raised. The story is one of retreat, infertility, and decadence. The presumed domain of FP used to be much larger than it is now. In primitive cultures, the behavior of most of the elements of nature were understood in intentional terms. The wind could know anger, the moon jealousy, the river generosity, the sea fury, and so forth. These were not metaphors. Sacrifices were made and auguries undertaken to placate or divine the changing passions of the gods. Despite its sterility, this animistic approach to nature has dominated our history, and it is only in the last two or three thousand years that we have restricted FP's literal interpretation to the domain of the higher animals.

Even in this preferred domain, however, both the content and the success of FP have not advanced sensibly in two or three thousand years. The FP of the Greeks is essentially the FP we use today, and we are negligibly better at explaining human behavior in its terms than was Sophocles. This is a very long period of stagnation and infertility for any theory to display, especially when faced with such an enormous backlog of anomalies and mysteries in its own explanatory domain. Perfect theories, perhaps, have no need to evolve. But FP is profoundly imperfect. Its failure to develop its resources and extend its range of success is therefore darkly curious, and one must query the integrity of its basic categories. To use Imre Lakotos's terms, FP is a stagnant or degenerating research program and has been for millennia.

Explanatory success to date is, of course, not the only dimension in which a theory can display virtue or promise. A troubled or stagnant theory may merit patience and solicitude on other grounds, for example, on grounds that it is the only theory or theoretical approach that fits well with other theories about adjacent subject matters, or the only one that promises to reduce to, or to be explained by, some established background theory whose domain encompasses the domain of the theory at issue. In sum, it may rate credence because it holds promise of theoretical integration. How does FP rate in this dimension?

It is just here, perhaps, that FP fares poorest of all. If we approach *Homo sapiens* from the perspective of natural history and the physical sciences, we can tell a coherent story of the species' constitution, development, and behavioral capacities that encompasses particle physics, atomic and molecular theory, organic chemistry, evolutionary theory, biology, physiology, and materialistic neuroscience. That story, though still radically incomplete, is already extremely powerful, outperforming FP at many points even in its own domain. And it is deliberately and self-consciously coherent with the rest of our developing world picture. In short, the greatest theoretical synthesis in the history of the human race is currently in our hands, and parts of it already provide searching descriptions and explanations of human sensory input, neural activity, and motor control.

But FP is no part of this growing synthesis. Its intentional categories stand magnificently alone, without visible prospect of reduction to that larger corpus. A successful reduction cannot be ruled out, in my view, but the explanatory impotence and long stagnation of FP inspire little faith that its categories will find themselves neatly reflected in the framework of neuroscience. On the contrary, one is reminded of how alchemy must have looked as elemental chemistry was taking form, how Aristotelian cosmology must have looked as classical mechanics was being articulated, or how the vitalist conception of life must have looked as organic chemistry marched forward.

In sketching a fair summary of this situation, we must make a special effort to abstract from the fact that FP is a central part of our current *Lebenswelt*, and serves as the principal vehicle of our interpersonal commerce. For these facts provide FP with a conceptual inertia that goes far beyond its purely theoretical virtues. Restricting ourselves to this latter dimension, what we must say is that FP suffers explanatory failures on an epic scale, that it has been stagnant for at least twenty-five centuries, and that its categories appear (so far) to be incommensurable with, or orthogonal to, the categories of the background physical science whose long-term claim to explain human behavior seems undeniable. Any theory that meets this description must be allowed a serious candidate for outright elimination.

We can, of course, insist on no stronger conclusion at this stage. Nor is it my concern to do so. We are here exploring a possibility, and the facts demand no more, and no less, than that it be taken seriously. The distinguishing feature of the eliminative materialist is that he takes it very seriously indeed.

3   Arguments against Elimination

Thus the basic rationale of eliminative materialism: FP is a theory, and quite probably a false one; let us attempt, therefore, to transcend it.

The rationale is clear and simple, but many find it uncompelling. It will be objected that FP is not, strictly speaking, an *empirical* theory; that it is not false, or at least not refutable by empirical considerations; and that it ought not or cannot be transcended in the fashion of a defunct physical theory. In what follows I shall examine these objections as they flow from the most popular and best founded of the competing positions in the philosophy of mind: functionalism.

An antipathy toward eliminative materialism arises from two distinct threads running through contemporary functionalism. The first thread concerns the *normative* character of FP, or at least of that central core of FP that treats of the propositional attitudes. FP, some will say, is a characterization of an ideal, or at least a praiseworthy, mode of internal activity. It outlines not only what it is to have and process beliefs and desires, but also (and inevitably) what it is to be rational in their administration. The ideal laid down by FP may be imperfectly achieved by empirical humans, but this does not impugn FP as a normative characterization. Nor need such failures seriously impugn FP even as a descriptive characterization, for it remains true that our activities can be both usefully and accurately understood as rational *except* for the occasional lapse due to noise, interference, or other breakdown, which defects empirical research may eventually unravel. Accordingly, though neuroscience may usefully augment it, FP has no pressing need to be displaced, even as a descriptive theory; nor could it be replaced, *qua* normative characterization, by any descriptive theory of neural mechanisms, since rationality is *defined over* propositional attitudes like beliefs and desires. FP, therefore, is here to stay.

Daniel Dennett has defended a view along these lines. (He defended it most explicitly in 1981, but this theme of Dennett's goes all the way back to his 1971.) And the view just outlined gives voice to a theme of the property dualists as well. Karl Popper and Joseph Margolis both cite the normative nature of mental and linguistic activity as a bar to their penetration by any descriptive/materialist theory (Popper 1972; Popper and Eccles 1978; Margolis 1978). I hope to deflate the appeal of such moves below.

The second thread concerns the *abstract* nature of FP. The central claim of functionalism is that the principles of FP characterize our internal states in a fashion that makes no reference to their intrinsic nature or physical constitution. Rather, they are characterized in terms of the network of causal relations they bear to one another and to sensory circumstances and overt behavior. Given its abstract specification, that internal economy may therefore be realized in a nomically heterogeneous variety of physical systems. All of them may differ, even radically, in their physical constitution, and yet at another level they will all share the same nature. This view, says Fodor, "is compatible with very strong claims about the ineliminability of mental language from behavioral theories" (1968, p. 116). Given the real possibility of multiple instantiations in heterogeneous physical substrates, we cannot eliminate the functional characterization in favor of any theory peculiar to one such substrate. That would preclude our being able to describe the (abstract) organization that any one instantiation shares with all the others. A functional characterization of our internal states is therefore here to stay.

This second theme, like the first, assigns a faintly stipulative character to FP, as if the onus were on the empirical systems to instantiate faithfully the functional organization that FP specifies, instead of the onus being on FP to describe faithfully the internal activities of a naturally distinct class of empirical systems. This impression is enhanced by the standard examples used to illustrate the claims of functionalism: mousetraps, valve lifters, arithmetical calculators, computers, robots, and the like. These are artifacts, constructed to fill a preconceived bill. In such cases, a failure of fit between the physical system and the relevant functional characterization impugns only the former, not the latter. The functional characterization is thus removed from empirical criticism in a way that is most unlike the case of an empirical theory. One prominent functionalist, Hilary Putnam, has argued outright that FP is not a corrigible empirical theory at all (Putnam 1964, pp. 675, 681ff). Plainly, if FP is construed on these models, as regularly it is, the question of its empirical integrity is unlikely ever to pose itself, let alone receive a critical answer.

Although fair to some functionalists, the preceding is not entirely fair to Fodor. On his view the aim of psychology is to find the *best* functional characterization of ourselves, and what that is remains an empirical question. Also, his argument for the ineliminability of mental vocabulary from psychology does not pick out current FP in particular as ineliminable. It need claim only that *some* abstract functional characterization must be retained, some articulation or refinement of FP perhaps.

His estimate of eliminative materialism remains low, however. First, Fodor plainly thinks that there is nothing fundamentally or interestingly wrong with FP. On the contrary, FP's central conception of cognitive activity—as consisting in the manipulation of propositional attitudes—turns up as the central element in Fodor's own theory of the nature of thought (1975). And second, there remains the point that, whatever tidying up FP may or may not require, it cannot be displaced by any naturalistic theory of our physical substrate, since it is the abstract functional features of the internal states that make a person, not the chemistry of his substrate.

All of this is appealing. But almost none of it, I think, is right. Functionalism has too long enjoyed its reputation as a daring and avant-garde position. It needs to be revealed for the shortsighted and reactionary position it is.

4   *The Conservative Nature of Functionalism*

A valuable perspective on functionalism can be gained from the following story. To begin with, recall the alchemists' theory of inanimate matter. We have here a long and variegated tradition, of course, not a single theory, but our purposes will be served by a gloss.

The alchemists conceived the "inanimate" as entirely continuous with animated matter in that the sensible and behavioral properties of the various substances are due to the ensoulment of baser matter by various spirits or essences. These nonmaterial aspects were held to undergo development, just as we find growth and development in the various souls of plants, animals, and humans. The alchemist's peculiar skill lay in knowing how to seed, nourish, and bring to maturity the desired spirits enmattered in the appropriate combinations.

On one orthodoxy, the four fundamental spirits (for "*inanimate*" matter) were named "mercury," "sulfur," "yellow arsenic," and "sal ammoniac." Each of these spirits was held responsible for a rough but characteristic syndrome of sensible, combinatorial, and causal properties. The spirit mercury, for example, was held responsible for certain features typical of metallic substances: their shininess, liquefiability, and so forth. Sulfur was held responsible for certain residual features typical of metals, and for those displayed by the ores from which running metal could be distilled. Any given metallic substance was a critical orchestration principally of these two spirits. A similar story held for the other two spirits, and among the four of them a certain domain of physical features and transformations was rendered intelligible and controllable.

The degree of control was always limited, of course. Or better, such prediction and control as the alchemist possessed was owed more to the manipulative lore acquired as an apprentice to a master than to any genuine insight supplied by the theory. The theory followed, more than it dictated, practice. But the theory did supply some rhyme to the practice, and in the absence of a developed alternative it was sufficiently compelling to sustain a long and stubborn tradition.

The tradition had become faded and fragmented by the time the elemental chemistry of Lavoisier and Dalton arose to replace it for good. But let us suppose that it had hung on a little longer—perhaps because the four-spirit orthodoxy had become a thumb-worn part of everyman's common sense—and let us examine the nature of the conflict between the two theories and some possible avenues of resolution.

No doubt the simplest line of resolution, and the one that historically took place, is outright displacement. The dualistic interpretation of the four essences—as immaterial spirits—will appear both feckless and unnecessary given the power of the corpuscularian taxonomy of atomic chemistry. And a reduction of the old taxonomy to the new will appear impossible, given the extent to which the comparatively toothless old theory cross-classifies things relative to the new. Elimination would thus appear the only alternative—*unless* some cunning and determined defender of the alchemical vision had the wit to suggest the following defense.

Being "ensouled by mercury," or "sulfur," or either of the other two so-called spirits, is actually a *functional* state. The first, for example, is defined by the disposition to reflect light, to liquefy under heat, to unite with other matter in the same state, and so forth. And each of these four states is related to the others, in that the syndrome for each varies as a function of which of the other three states is also instantiated by the same substrate. Thus the level of description comprehended by the alchemical vocabulary is abstract: *various* material substances, suitably "ensouled," can display the features of a metal, for example, or even of gold specifically. For it is the total syndrome of occurrent and causal properties that matters, not the corpuscularian details of the substrate. Alchemy, it is concluded, comprehends a level of organization in reality that is distinct from, and irreducible to, the organization found at the level of corpuscularian chemistry.

This view might have had considerable appeal. After all, it spares alchemists the burden of defending immaterial souls that come and go; it frees them from having to meet the very strong demands of a naturalistic reduction; and it spares them the shock and confusion of outright elimination. Alchemical theory emerges as basically all right! Nor need the alchemists appear too obviously stubborn or dogmatic in this. Alchemy as it stands, they concede, may need substantial tidying up, and experience must be our guide. But we need not fear its naturalistic displacement, they remind us, since it is the peculiar orchestration of the syndromes of occurrent and causal properties that makes a piece of matter gold, not the idiosyncratic details of its corpuscularian substrate. A further circumstance would have made this claim even more plausible. For the fact is, the alchemists *did* know how to make gold, in this relevantly weakened sense of 'gold', and they could do so in a variety of ways. Their "gold" was never as perfect, alas, as the "gold" nurtured in nature's womb, but what mortal can expect to match the skills of nature herself?

What this story shows is that it is at least possible for the constellation of moves, claims, and defenses characteristic of functionalism to constitute an outrage against reason and truth, and to do so with a plausibility that is frightening. Alchemy is a terrible theory, well deserving of its complete elimination, and the defense of it just explored is reactionary, obfuscatory, retrograde, and wrong. But in historical context, that defense might have seemed wholly sensible, even to reasonable people.

The alchemic example is a deliberately transparent case of what might be called "the functionalist stratagem," and other cases are easy to imagine. A cracking good defense of the phlogiston theory of combustion can also be constructed along these lines. Construe being highly phlogisticated and being dephlogisticated as functional states defined by certain syndromes of causal dispositions; point to the great variety of natural substrates capable of combustion and calxification; claim an irreducible functional integrity for what has proved to lack any natural integrity; and bury the remaining defects under a pledge to contrive improvements. A similar recipe will provide new life for the four humors of medieval medicine, for the *archeus* or vital essence of premodern biology, and so forth.

If its application in these other cases is any guide, the functionalist stratagem is a smoke screen for the preservation of error and confusion. Whence derives our assurance that in contemporary journals the same charade is not being played out on behalf of FP? The parallel with the case of alchemy is in all other respects distressingly complete, right down to the parallel between the search for artificial gold and the search for artificial intelligence!

Let me not be misunderstood on this last point. Both aims are worthy aims: thanks to nuclear physics, artificial (but real) gold is finally within our means, if only in submicroscopic quantities, and artificial (but real) intelligence eventually will be. But just as the careful orchestration of superficial syndromes was the wrong way to produce genuine gold, so may the careful orchestration of superficial syndromes be the wrong way to produce genuine intelligence. Just as with gold, what may be required is that our science penetrate to the underlying *natural* kind that gives rise to the total syndrome directly. (See chapters 5 and 9 to 11.)

In summary, when confronted with the explanatory impotence, stagnant history, and systematic isolation of the intentional idioms of FP, it is not an adequate or responsive defense to insist that those idioms are abstract, functional, and irreducible in character. For one thing, this same defense could have been mounted with comparable plausibility no matter *what* haywire network of internal states our folklore had ascribed to us. And for another, the defense assumes essentially what is at issue: it assumes that it is the intentional idioms of FP, plus or minus a bit, that express the *important* features shared by all cognitive systems. But they may not. Certainly it is wrong to assume that they do, and then argue against the possibility of a materialistic displacement on grounds that it must describe matters at a level that is distinct from the important level. This just begs the question in favor of the older framework.

Finally, it is very important to point out that eliminative materialism is strictly *consistent* with the claim that the essence of a cognitive system resides in the abstract functional organization of its internal states. The eliminative materialist is not committed to the idea that the correct account of cognition *must* be a naturalistic account, though he may be forgiven for exploring the possibility. What he does hold is that the correct account of cognition, whether functionalistic or naturalistic, will bear about as much resemblance to FP as modern chemistry bears to four-spirit alchemy.

Let us now try to deal with the argument, against eliminative materialism, from the normative dimension of FP. This can be dealt with rather swiftly, I believe.

First, the fact that the regularities ascribed by the intentional core of FP are predicated on certain logical regularities among propositions is not by itself grounds for claiming anything essentially normative about FP. To draw a relevant parallel, the fact that the regularities ascribed by the classical gas law are predicated on arithmetical relations between numbers does not imply anything essentially normative about the classical gas law. And logical relations between propositions are as much an objective matter of abstract fact as are arithmetical relations between numbers. In this respect, the law

(4) $(x)(p)(q)[((x$ believes that $p)$ & $(x$ believes that (if p then $q)))$
$\supset$ (barring confusion, distraction, etc., x believes that $q)]$

is entirely on a par with the classical gas law

(6) $(x)(P)(V)(\mu)[((x$ has a pressure $P)$
& $(x$ has a volume $V)$ & $(x$ has a quantity $\mu))$
$\supset$ (barring very high pressure or density,
x has a temperature of $PV/\mu R)]$.

A normative dimension enters only because we happen to *value* most of the patterns ascribed by FP. But we do not value all of them. Consider

(7) $(x)(p)[((x$ desires with all his heart that $v)$
& $(x$ learns that $\sim p))$
$\supset$ (barring unusual strength of character,
x is shattered that $\sim p)]$.

Moreover, and as with normative convictions generally, fresh insight may motivate major changes in what we value.

Second, the laws of FP ascribe to us only a very minimal and truncated rationality, not an ideal rationality as some have suggested. The rationality characterized by the set of all FP laws falls well short of an ideal rationality. This is not surprising. We have no clear or finished conception of ideal rationality anyway; certainly the ordinary man does not. Accordingly, it is just not plausible to suppose that the explanatory failures from which FP suffers are due primarily to human failure to live up to the standards it provides. Quite to the contrary, the conception of rationality it provides appears limping and superficial, especially when compared with the dialectical complexity of our scientific history or with the ratiocinative virtuosity displayed by any child.

Third, even if our current conception of rationality—and more generally, of cognitive virtue—is largely constituted within the sentential/propositional framework of FP, there is no guarantee that this framework is adequate to the deeper and more accurate account of cognitive virtue that is clearly needed. Even if we concede the categorial integrity of FP, at least as applied to language-using humans, it remains far from clear that the basic parameters of intellectual virtue are to be found at the categorial level comprehended by the propositional attitudes. After all, language use is something that is learned, by a brain already capable of vigorous cognitive activity; language use is acquired as only one among a great variety of learned manipulative skills; and it is mastered by a brain that evolution has shaped for a great many functions, language use being only the very latest and perhaps the least of them. Against the background of these facts, language use appears as an extremely peripheral activity, as a biologically idiosyncratic mode of social interaction that is mastered thanks to the versatility and power of a more basic mode of activity. Why accept, then, a theory of cognitive activity that models its elements on the elements of human language? And why assume that the fundamental parameters of intellectual virtue are, or can be defined over, the elements at this superficial level?

A serious advance in our appreciation of cognitive virtue would thus seem to *require* that we go beyond FP, that we transcend the poverty of FP's conception of rationality by transcending its propositional kinematics entirely, by developing a deeper and more general kinematics of cognitive activity, and by distinguishing within this new framework which of the kinematically possible modes of activity are to be valued and encouraged (as more efficient, reliable, productive, or whatever). Eliminative materialism does not imply the end of our normative concerns. It implies only that they will have to be re-constituted at a more revealing level of understanding, the level that a matured neuroscience will provide. [Added in 1989: The beginnings of such a reconstruction can be found in chapter 10, pp. 220–223.]

What a theoretically informed future might hold in store for us, we shall now turn to explore. Not because we can foresee matters with any special clarity, but because it is important to try to break the grip on our imagination held by the propositional kinematics of FP. As far as the present section is concerned, we may summarize our conclu-sion as follows. FP is nothing more and nothing less than a culturally entrenched theory of how we and the higher animals work. It has no special features that make it empirically invulnerable, no unique func-tions that make it irreplaceable, no special status of any kind what-soever. We shall turn a skeptical ear then, to any special pleading on its behalf.

5   Beyond Folk Psychology

What might the elimination of FP actually involve: not just the com-paratively straightforward idioms for sensation, but the entire appar-atus of propositional attitudes? That depends heavily on what neuroscience might discover and on our determination to capitalize on it. Here follow three scenarios in which the operative conception of cognitive activity is progressively divorced from the forms and categories that characterize natural language. If the reader will in-dulge the lack of actual substance, I shall try to sketch some plausible form.

First, suppose that research into the structure and activity of the brain, both fine-grained and global, finally does yield a new kinema-tics and correlative dynamics for what is now thought of as cognitive activity. The theory is uniform for all terrestrial brains, not just hu-man brains, and it makes suitable conceptual contact with both evolu-tionary biology and nonequilibrium thermodynamics. It ascribes to us at any given time a set or configuration of complex states that are specified within the theory as figurative "solids" within a four- or five-dimensional phase space. [Added in 1989: This guess has proved to be very timid. The relevant cognitive statespaces typically have hundreds, thousands, or even millions of distinct dimensions, and their partitioning into hypersolids is correspondingly complex. See chapter 9.] The laws of the theory govern the interaction, motion, and transformation of these "solid" states within that space, and also their relations to whatever sensory and motor transducers the system possesses. As with celestial mechanics, the exact specification of the "solids" involved and the exhaustive accounting of all dynamically relevant adjacent solids is not practically possible, for many reasons, but here too it turns out that the obvious approximations we fall back on yield excellent explanations/predictions of internal change and external behavior, at least in the short term. As for long-term activity, the theory provides powerful and unified accounts of the learning process, the nature of mental illness, and variations in character and intelligence across the animal kingdom as well as across individual humans.

Moreover, it provides a straightforward account of "knowledge," as traditionally conceived. According to the new theory, any declarative sentence to which a speaker would give confident assent is merely a one-dimensional *projection*—through the compound lens of Wernicke's and Broca's areas onto the idiosyncratic surface of the speaker's language—a one dimensional projection of a four- or five-dimensional solid that is an element in his true kinematical state. (Recall the shadows on the wall of Plato's cave.) Being projections of that inner reality, such sentences do carry significant information regarding it and are thus fit to function as elements in a communication system. On the other hand, being *sub*dimensional projections, they reflect but a narrow part of the reality projected. They are therefore *un*fit to represent the deeper reality in all its kinematically, dynamically, and even normatively relevant aspects. That is to say, a system of propositional attitudes, such as FP, must inevitably fail to capture what is going on here, though it may reflect just enough superficial structure to sustain an alchemylike tradition among folk who lack a better theory. From the perspective of the newer theory, however, it is plain that there simply are no law-governed states of the kind FP postulates. The real laws governing our internal activities are defined over different and much more complex states and configurations, as are the normative criteria for developmental integrity and intellectual virtue.

A theoretical outcome of the kind just described may fairly be counted as a case of the elimination of one theoretical ontology in favor of another, but the success here imagined for systematic neuroscience need not have any sensible effect on common practice. Old ways die hard, and in the absence of some practical necessity, they may not die at all. Even so, it is not inconceivable that some segment of the population, or all of it, should become intimately familiar with the vocabulary required to characterize our kinematical states, learn the laws governing their interactions and behavioral projections, acquire a facility in their first-person ascription, and displace the use of FP altogether, even in the marketplace. The demise of FP's ontology would then be complete.

We may now explore a second and rather more radical possibility. Everyone is familiar with Chomsky's thesis that the human mind or brain contains innately and uniquely the abstract structures for learning and using specifically human natural languages. A competing hypothesis is that our brain does indeed contain innate structures, but that those structures have as their original and still primary function the organization of perceptual experience, with the administration of linguistic categories being an acquired and additional function for which evolution has only incidentally suited them. (Richard Gregory has defended such a view in his 1970b.) This hypothesis has the advantage of not requiring the evolutionary saltation that Chomsky's view would seem to require, and there are other advantages as well. But these matters need not concern us here. Suppose, for our purposes, that this competing view is true, and consider the following story.

Research into the neural structures that fund the organization and processing of perceptual information reveals that they are capable of administering a great variety of complex tasks, some of them showing a complexity far in excess of that shown by natural language. Natural languages, it turns out, exploit only a very elementary portion of the available machinery, the bulk of which serves far more complex activities beyond the ken of the propositional conceptions of FP. The detailed unraveling of what that machinery is and of the capacities it has makes it plain that a form of language far more sophisticated than "natural" language, though decidedly alien in its syntactic and semantic structures, could also be learned and used by our innate systems. Such a novel system of communication, it is quickly realized, could raise the efficiency of information exchange between brains by an order of magnitude, and would enhance epistemic evaluation by a comparable amount, since it would reflect the underlying structure of our cognitive activities in greater detail than does natural language.

Guided by our new understanding of these internal structures, we manage to construct a new system of verbal communication entirely distinct from natural language, with a new and more powerful combinatorial grammar over novel elements forming novel combinations with exotic properties. The compounded strings of this alternative system—call them "*Übersätze*"—are not evaluated as true or false, nor are the relations between them remotely analogous to the relations of entailment, etc., that hold between sentences. They display a different organization and manifest different virtues.

Once constructed, this "language" proves to be learnable, it has the power projected, and in two generations it has swept the planet. Everyone uses the new system. The syntactic forms and semantic categories of so-called "natural" language disappear entirely. And with them disappear the propositional attitudes of FP, displaced by a more revealing scheme in which (of course) "*Übersatzenal* attitudes" play the leading role. FP again suffers elimination.

This second story, note, illustrates a theme with endless variations. There are possible as many different "folk psychologies" as there are possible differently structured communication systems to serve as models for them.

A third and even stranger possibility can be outlined as follows. We know that there is considerable lateralization of function between the two cerebral hemispheres, and that the two hemispheres make use of the information they get from each other by way of the great cerebral commissure, the corpus callosum, a giant cable of neurons connecting them. Patients whose commissure has been surgically severed display a variety of behavioral deficits that indicate a loss of access by one hemisphere to information it used to get from the other. However, in people with callosal agenesis (a congenital defect in which the corresponding cable is simply absent), there is little or no behavioral deficit, which suggests that the two hemispheres have learned to exploit the information carried in other, less direct pathways connecting them through the subcortical regions. This suggests that even in the normal case a developing hemisphere *learns* to make use of the information the cerebral commissure deposits at its doorstep. What we have, then, in the case of a normal human, is two physically distinct cognitive systems (both capable of independent function) responding in a systematic and learned fashion to exchanged information. And what is especially interesting about this case is the sheer amount of information exchanged. The cable of the commissure consists of roughly 200 million neurons (Gazzaniga and LeDoux 1975), and even if we assume that each of these fibers is capable of one of only two possible states each second (a most conservative estimate), we are looking at a channel whose information capacity is greater than 2×10^8 binary bits per second. Compare this to the less than 500 bits/second capacity of spoken English.

Now, if two distinct hemispheres can learn to communicate on so impressive a scale, why shouldn't two distinct brains learn to do it also? This would require an artificial "commissure" of some kind, but let us suppose that we can fashion a workable transducer for implantation at some site in the brain that research reveals to be suitable, a transducer to convert a symphony of neural activity into (say) microwaves radiated from an aerial in the forehead, and to perform the reverse function of converting received microwaves back into neural activation. Connecting it up need not be an insuperable problem. We simply trick the normal processes of dendritic arborization into growing their own myriad connections with the active microsurface of the transducer.

Once the channel is opened between two or more people, they can learn (*learn*) to exchange information and coordinate their behavior with the same intimacy and virtuosity displayed by your own cerebral hemispheres. Think what this might do for hockey teams, and ballet companies, and research teams! If the entire population were thus fitted out, spoken language of any kind might well disappear completely, a victim of the "Why crawl when you can fly?" principle. Libraries become filled not with books, but with long recordings of exemplary bouts of neural activity. These constitute a growing cultural heritage, an evolving "Third World," to use Karl Popper's term. But they do not consist of sentences or arguments.

How will such people understand and conceive of other individuals? To this question I can only answer, "In roughly the same fashion that your right hemisphere 'understands' and 'conceives of' your left hemisphere: intimately and efficiently, but not propositionally!"

These speculations, I hope, will evoke the required sense of untapped possibilities, and I shall in any case bring them to a close here. Their function is to make some inroads into the aura of inconceivability that commonly surrounds the idea that we might reject FP. The felt conceptual strain even finds expression in an argument to the effect that the thesis of eliminative materialism is incoherent since it denies the very conditions presupposed by the assumption that it is meaningful. I shall close with a brief discussion of this very popular move.

As I have received it, the *reductio* proceeds by pointing out that the statement of eliminative materialism is just a meaningless string of marks or noises, unless that string is the expression of a certain *belief*, and a certain *intention* to communicate, and a *knowledge* of the grammar of the language, and so forth. But if the statement of eliminative materialism is true, then there are no such states to express. The statement at issue would then be a meaningless string of marks or noises. It would therefore *not* be true. Therefore, it is not true. Q.E.D.

The difficulty with any nonformal *reductio* is that the conclusion against the initial assumption is always no better than the material assumptions invoked to reach the incoherent conclusion. In this case the additional assumptions involve a certain theory of meaning, one that presupposes the integrity of FP. But formally speaking, one can as well infer, from the incoherent result, that this (Gricean) theory of meaning is what must be rejected. Given the independent critique of FP leveled earlier, this would even seem the preferred option. But in any case, one cannot simply assume this particular theory of meaning without begging the question at issue, namely, the integrity of FP.

The question-begging nature of this move is most graphically illustrated by the following analog, which I owe to Patricia S. Churchland (1981). The issue here, placed in the seventeenth century, is whether there exists such a substance as *vital spirit*. At the time, this substance was held, without significant awareness of real alternatives, to be what distinguished the animate from the inanimate. Given the monopoly enjoyed by this conception, given the degree to which it was integrated with many of our other conceptions, and given the magnitude of the revisions any serious alternative conception would require, the following refutation of any antivitalist claim would be found instantly plausible.

> The antivitalist says that there is no such thing as vital spirit. But this claim is self-refuting. The speaker can expect to be taken seriously only if his claim cannot. For if the claim is true, then the speaker does not have vital spirit and must be *dead*. But if he is dead, then his statement is a meaningless string of noises, devoid of reason and truth.

The question-begging nature of this argument does not, I assume, require elaboration. To those moved by the earlier argument, I commend the parallel for examination.

The thesis of this paper may be summarized as follows. The propositional attitudes of folk psychology do not constitute an unbreachable barrier to the advancing tide of neuroscience. On the contrary, the principled displacement of folk psychology is not only richly possible; it represents one of the most intriguing theoretical displacements we can currently imagine.

Chapter 2

Functionalism, Qualia, and Intentionality

Functionalism—construed broadly as the thesis that the essence of our psychological states resides in the abstract causal roles they play in a complex economy of internal states mediating environmental inputs and behavioral outputs—seems to us to be free from any fatal or essential shortcomings. Functionalism-on-the-hoof is another matter. In various thinkers this core thesis is generally embellished with certain riders, interpretations, and methodological lessons drawn therefrom. With some of the more prominent of these articulations we are in some disagreement, and we shall turn to discuss them in the final section of this paper. Our primary concern, however, is to *defend* functionalism from a battery of better-known objections widely believed to pose serious or insurmountable problems even for the core thesis outlined above. In sections 1 and 2 we shall try to outline what form functionalism should take in order to escape those objections.

1 Four Problems concerning Qualia

'Qualia' is a philosopher's term of art denoting those intrinsic or monadic properties of our sensations discriminated in introspection. The quale of a sensation is typically contrasted with its causal, relational, or functional features, and herein lies a problem for functionalism. The quale of a given sensation—pain, say—is at best contingently connected with the causal or functional properties of that state, and yet common intuitions insist that this quale is an essential element of pain, on some views, *the* essential element. Functionalism, it is concluded, provides an inadequate account of our mental states.

Before addressing the issues in greater detail, let us be clear about what the functionalist need not deny. He need not and should not deny that our sensations have intrinsic properties, and he should

This paper was coauthored with Patricia S. Churchland. It first appeared in *Philosophical Topics* (1981), no. 1.

agree that those properties are the principal means of our introspective discrimination of one kind of sensation from another. What he is committed to denying is that any particular quale is *essential* to the identity of any particular type of mental state. Initially they may seem to be essential, but reflection will reveal that they do not have, and should not be conceded, that status. In what follows we address four distinct but not unrelated problems. Each problem is manageable on its own, but if they are permitted to band together for collective assault, the result is rather confusing and formidable, in the fashion of the fabled Musicians of Bremen. With the problems separated, our strategy will be to explain and exploit the insight that intrinsic properties per se are no anathema to a functionalist theory of mental states.

A.   The problem of inverted/gerrymandered qualia
This problem is just the most straightforward illustration of the general worry that functionalism leaves out something essential. The recipe for concocting the appropriate intuitions runs thus. Suppose that the sensations having the quale typical of pain in you play the functional role of pleasure sensations in someone else, and the quale typical of pleasure sensations in you are had instead by the sensations that have the functional role of pain in him. Functionally, we are to suppose, the two of you are indistinguishable, but his pleasure/pain qualia are simply inverted relative to their distribution among your own sensations, functionally identified. A variation on the recipe asks us to imagine someone with an inverted distribution of the color qualia that characterize your own visual sensations (functionally identified). He thus has (what you would introspectively identify as) a sensation of red in all and only those circumstances where you have a sensation of green, and so forth.

These cases are indeed imaginable, and the connection between quale and functional syndrome is indeed a contingent one. Whether it is the quale or the functional syndrome that determines type identity *qua* psychological state, we must now address. The intuitions evoked above seem to confound functionalist pretensions. The objection to functionalism is that when the inversion victim has that sensation whose functional properties indicate pleasure, *he is in fact feeling pain*, functional properties notwithstanding; and that when the victim of a spectrum inversion says, "I have a sensation of green" in the presence of a green object, *he is in fact having a sensation of red*, functional properties notwithstanding. So far as type identity of psychological states is concerned, the objection concludes, sameness of qualitative character dominates over sameness of functional role.

Now there is no point in trying to deny the possibilities just outlined. Rather, what the functionalist must argue is that they are better described as follows. "Your pains have a qualitative character rather different from that of his pains, and your sensations-of-green have a qualitative character rather different from that of his sensations-of-green. Such internal differences among the same psychological states are neither inconceivable nor even perhaps very unusual." That is to say, the functionalist should concede the juggled qualia, while continuing to reckon type identity in accordance with functional syndrome. This line has a certain intuitive appeal of its own, though rather less than the opposing story, at least initially. How shall we decide between these competing intuitions? By isolating the considerations that give rise to them and examining their integrity.

The "pro-qualia" intuitions, we suggest, derive from two main sources. To begin with, all of us have a strong and entirely understandable tendency to think of each type of psychological state as constituting a *natural kind*. After all, these states do play a vigorous explanatory and predictive role in everyday commerce, and the commonsense conceptual framework that comprehends them has all the features and functions of a sophisticated empirical theory (see Sellars 1956; P. M. Churchland 1979). To think of pains, for example, as constituting a natural kind is to think of them as sharing an *intrinsic nature* that is common and essential to *every* instance of pain. It is understandable then, that the qualitative character of a sensation, the only nonrelational feature to which we have access, should present itself as being that essential element.

Our inclination to such a view is further encouraged by the fact that one's introspective discrimination of a sensation's qualitative character is far and away the most immediate, most automatic, most deeply entrenched, and (in isolation) most authoritative measure of what sensations one has. In one's own case, at least. the functional features of one's sensations play a minor role in one's recognition of them. It is as if one had special access to the intrinsic nature of any given type of sensation, an access that is independent of the purely contingent and causal features that constitute its functional role.

Taken conjointly, these considerations will fund very strong intuitions in favor of qualia as *the* determinants of type identity for psychological states. But though natural enough, the rationale is exceptionally feeble on both points.

Take the first. However accustomed or inclined we are to think of our psychological states as constituting natural kinds, it is vital to see that it is not a semantic or a conceptual matter, but an objective *empirical* matter, whether or not they do. Either there is an objective intrinsic nature common to all cases of, e.g., pain, as it occurs in humans, chimpanzees, dogs, snakes, and octopuses, or there is not. And the fact is, the functionalist can point to some rather persuasive considerations in support of the view that there is not. Given the physiological and chemical variety we find in the nervous systems of the many animals that feel pain, it appears very unlikely that their pain states have a common physical nature underlying their common functional nature (see Putnam 1971). It remains possible that they all have some intrinsic *non*physical nature in common. But dualism is profoundly implausible on sheer evolutionary grounds. (Briefly, the evolutionary process just *is* the diachronic articulation of physical matter and energy. If we accept an evolutionary origin for ourselves, then our special capacities must be construed as the capacities of one particular articulation of matter and energy. This conclusion is confirmed by our increasing understanding of the nervous system, of both its past evolution and its current regulation of behavior.) In sum, the empirical presumption *against* natural-kind status for psychological states is substantial. We should not place much trust, therefore, in intuitions born of an uncritical prejudice to the contrary. Such intuitions may reflect ordinary language more or less faithfully, but they beg the question against functionalism.

The facts of introspection provide no better grounds for thinking that sensations constitute natural kinds, or for reckoning qualia as their constituting essences. That the qualitative character Q of a psychological state S should serve as the standard ground of S's introspective discrimination is entirely consistent with Q's being a nonessential feature of S. The black and yellow stripes of a tiger serve as the standard ground on which tigers are visually discriminated from other big cats, but the stripes are hardly an essential element of tigerhood: there are albino tigers as well as the very pale Himalayan tigers. The telling question here is this: why should the qualia of our familiar psychological states be thought any different? We learn to pick out those qualia in the first place, from the teeming chaos of our inner lives, only because the states thus discriminated are also the nexus of various generalizations connecting them to other inner states, to environmental circumstances, and to overt behaviors of interest and importance to us. Had our current taxonomy of introspectible qualia been *un*successful in this regard, we would most certainly have thrown it over, centered our attention on different aspects of the teeming chaos within, and recarved it into a different set of similarity classes, a set that *did* display its objective integrity by its many nomic connections, both internal and external. In short, the internal world comes precarved into observational kinds no more than does the external world, and it is evident that the introspective taxonomies into which we eventually settle are no less shaped by considerations of explanatory and causal coherence than are the taxonomies of external observation.

It is therefore a great irony, it seems to us, that anyone should subsequently point to whatever qualia our introspective mechanisms have managed tenuously to fix upon as more or less usable indicators of nomologically interesting states, and claim *them* as constituting the *essence* of such states. It is, of course, distantly possible that our mechanisms of introspective discrimination have lucked onto the constituting essences of our psychological states (assuming, contrary to our earlier discussion, that each type *has* a uniform natural essence), but a priori that seems about as likely as that the visual system lucked onto the constituting essence of tigerhood when it made black-on-yellow stripes salient for distinguishing tigers.

It seems very doubtful, therefore, that the type identity of any psychological state derives from its sharing in any uniform natural essence. Moreover, even if it does so share, it seems entirely unlikely that introspection provides any special access to that essence. Consequently, this beggars the intuition that sustains the inverted-qualia objections.

The preceding investigation into the weight and significance of factors determining type identity of psychological states does more than that, however. It also enriches the competing intuition, namely, that the type identity of psychological states is determined by functional characteristics. To repeat the point made earlier, since the taxonomy of observational qualia constructed by the questing child *follows* the discovered taxonomy of states as determined by interesting causal roles, it is evident that sameness of functional role dominates over differences in qualitative character, so far as the type identity of psychological states is concerned. That a single category, united by functional considerations, can embrace diverse and disparate qualitative characters has a ready illustration, ironically enough, in the case of pain.

Consider the wide variety of qualia willfully lumped together in common practice under the heading of pain. Compare the qualitative character of a severe electric shock with that of a sharp blow to the kneecap; compare the character of hands dully aching from making too many snowballs with the piercing sensation of a jet engine heard at very close range; compare the character of a frontal headache with the sensation of a scalding pot grasped firmly. It is evident that what unites sensations of such diverse characters is the similarity in their functional roles. The sudden onset of any of them prompts an involuntary withdrawal of some sort. Our reaction to all of them is immediate dislike, and the violence of the dislike increases with the intensity and duration of the sensation. All of them are indicators of physical trauma of some kind, actual or imminent. All of them tend to produce shock, impatience, distraction, and vocal reactions of familiar kinds. Plainly, it is these collected causal features that unite the class of painful sensations, not some uniform quale, invariant across cases. (For a general account of the intentionality of sensations, in which qualia also retreat into the background, see P. M. Churchland 1979, chapter 2.)

The converse illustration is provided by states having a uniform or indistinguishable qualitative character, states that are nevertheless distinguished by us according to *differences* in their functional roles. For example, our emotions have a certain qualitative character, but it is often insufficient to distinguish which of several emotions should be ascribed. On a particular occasion, the felt knot in one's soul might be mild sorrow, severe disappointment, or gathering despair, and which of these it is—really is—would depend on the circumstances of its production, the rest of one's psychological state, and the consequences to which it tends to give rise. Its type identity need not be a mystery to its possessor—he has introspective access to some of the context that embeds it—but the identification cannot be made on qualitative grounds alone. Similarly, a therapist may be needed, or a thoughtful friend, to help you distinguish your decided unease about some person as your hatred for him, envy of him, or simple fear of him. The *felt* quality of your unease may be the same for each of these cases, but its causes and effects would be significantly different for each. Here again, functional role is the dominant factor in the type identity of psychological states.

The reason that functional role dominates introspectible qualitative differences and similarities is not that the collected laws descriptive of a state's functional relations are analytically true, or that they exhaust the essence of the state in question (though, withal, they may). The reason is that the commonsense conceptual framework in which our psychological terms are semantically embedded is an *empirical theory*. As with theoretical terms generally, their changeable position in semantic space is fixed by the set of theoretical laws in which they figure. In the case of folk psychology, those laws express the causal relations that connect psychological states with one another, with environmental circumstances, and with behavior. Such laws need not be seen, at any given stage in our growing understanding, as *exhausting* the essence of the states at issue, but at any given stage they constitute the best-founded and most authoritative criterion available for identifying those states.

We conclude against the view that qualia constitute an essential element in the type identity of psychological states. Variations within a single type are both conceivable and actual. The imagined cases of qualia inversion are of interest only because they place directly at odds intuitions that normally coincide: the noninferential impulse of observational habit (i.e., qualia) against the ponderous background of theoretical understanding (i.e., functional role). However, the qualitative character of a sensation is a relevant mark of its type identity only when and only insofar as that character is the uniform concomitant of a certain repeatable causal syndrome. In the qualia-inversion thought experiments, that uniformity is broken. And consequently, so is the relevance of those qualia for judging type identity, at least insofar as they can claim a *uniform* relevance across people and across times.

B. *The problem of absent qualia*

The preceding arguments may settle the inverted-qualia problem, but the position we have defended is thought to raise in turn an even more serious problem for functionalism (see Block and Fodor 1972; Block 1978). If the particular quale a sensation has contributes nothing to its type identity, then what are we to say of a psychological system that is functionally isomorphic to us, but whose functional states have no qualia whatever? Surely such systems are possible (nomically as well as logically), runs the objection. Surely functionalism entails that such a system feels pain, warmth, and so on. But since its functional states have no qualitative character whatever, surely such a system *feels nothing at all*! Functionalism, accordingly, must be false.

This argument is much too glib in the contrast it assumes between functional features (which supposedly matter to functionalism) and qualitative character (which supposedly does not). As the functionalist should be the first to admit, our various sensations are introspectively discriminated by us on the basis of their qualitative character, and any adequate psychological theory must take this fact into account. How might functionalism do this? Straightforwardly. It must require of any state that is functionally equivalent to the sensation-of-warmth, say, that it have some intrinsic property or other whose presence is detectable by (that is, is causally sufficient for affecting) our mechanisms of introspective discrimination in such a way as to cause, in a conceptually competent creature, belief states such as the belief that it has a sensation-of-warmth. If these sorts of causal relations are not part of a given state's functional identity, then it fails to be a sensation-of-warmth on purely functional grounds. (Sydney Shoemaker makes much the same point in his 1975. We do not know if he will agree with the points that follow.)

So functionalism *does* require that sensations have an intrinsic property that plays a certain causal role. But it is admittedly indifferent as to precisely what that intrinsic property might happen to be for any given type of sensation in any given person. So far as functionalism is concerned, that intrinsic property might be the spiking frequency of the signal in some neural pathway, the voltage across a polarized membrane, the temporary deficit of some neurochemical, or the binary configuration of a set of direct-current pulses. So long as the property is one to which the mechanisms of introspective discrimination are keyed, the property fills the bill.

"But *these* are not qualia!" chorus the outraged objectors. Are they not indeed. Recall the characterization of qualia given on the first page of this chapter: "those intrinsic or monadic properties of our sensations discriminated in introspection." Our sensations are anyway token-identical with the physical states that realize them, so there is no problem in construing a spiking frequency of 60 hertz as an intrinsic property of a given sensation. And why should such a property, or any of the others listed, *not* be at the objective focus of introspective discrimination? To be sure, they would be *opaquely* discriminated, at least by creatures with a primitive self-conception like our own. That is to say, the spiking frequency of the impulses in a certain neural pathway need not prompt the noninferential belief, "My pain has a spiking frequency of 60 hertz"; it may prompt only the belief, "My pain has a searing quality." But withal, the property you opaquely distinguish as searingness may be precisely the property of having 60 hertz as a spiking frequency.

There are many precedents for this sort of thing in the case of the intrinsic properties of material objects standardly discriminable in observation. The redness of an object turns out to be a specific reflectance triplet for three critical wavelengths in the electromagnetic spectrum. The pitch of a singer's note turns out to be its frequency of oscillation in air pressure. The warmth of a coffee cup turns out to be the vibrational energy of its molecules. The tartness of one's lemonade turns out to be its high relative concentration of H^+ ions. And so forth.

These chemical, electromagnetic, and micromechanical properties have been briskly discriminated by us for many millennia, but only opaquely. The reason is that we have not possessed the concepts necessary to make more penetrating judgments, and our mechanisms of sensory discrimination are of insufficient resolution to reveal on their own the intricacies that were eventually uncovered by other means. Unambiguous perception of molecular kinetic energy, for example, would require a sensory apparatus capable of resolving down to about 10^{-10} meters, and capable of tracking particles having the velocity of rifle bullets, millions of them, simultaneously. Our sensory apparatus for detecting and measuring molecular kinetic energy is rather more humble, but even so, it connects us reliably with the parameter at issue. Mean molecular kinetic energy may not seem like an observable property of material objects, but most assuredly it is. (For a working-out of these themes in detail, see P. M. Churchland 1979.)

Similarly, spiking frequency may not seem like an introspectible property of sensations, but there is no reason why it should not be, and there is no reason why the epistemological story for the faculty of inner sense should be significantly different from the story told for outer sense. Qualia, therefore, are not an ineffable mystery, any more than colors or temperatures are. They are physical features of our psychological states, and we may expect qualia of some sort or other in any physical system that is sufficiently complex to be functionally isomorphic with our own psychology. The qualia of such a robot's states are not "absent." They are merely *unrecognized* by us under their physical/electronic descriptions, or as discriminated by the modalities of outer sense rather than inner sense.

We may summarize all of this by saying that the functionalist need not, and perhaps should not, attempt to deny the existence of qualia. Rather, he should be a realist about qualia—in particular, he should be a *scientific* realist.

It is important to appreciate that one can be reductionistic about qualia, as outlined above, without being the least bit reductionistic about the taxonomy of states appropriate to psychological theory. Once qualia have been denied a role in the type identity of psychological states, the path described is open. If this line on qualia is correct, then it vindicates Ned Block's prophecy (1978, p. 309) that the explication of the nature of qualia does not reside in the domain of psychology. On the view argued here, the nature of specific qualia will be revealed by neurophysiology, neurochemistry, and neurophysics.

C.   The problem of distinguishing states with qualia from states without

One could distinguish many differences between the sensations and the propositional attitudes, but one particular difference is of special interest here. A sensation-of-warmth, for example, has a distinct qualitative character, whereas the belief-that-Tom-is-tall does not. Can functionalism explain the difference?

Yes it can. The picture to be avoided here depicts sensations as dabbed with metaphysical paint, while beliefs remain undabbed and colorless. The real difference, we suggest, lies less in the objective nature of sensations and beliefs themselves than in the nature of the introspective mechanisms used to discriminate and identify the states of each class. This hypothesis requires explanation.

How many different types of sensation are there? One hundred? One thousand? Ten thousand? It is difficult to make an estimate, since most sensations are arrayed on a qualitative continuum of some sort, and it is to some extent arbitrary where and how finely the lines between different kinds are drawn. It is plain, however, that the number of distinct continua that we recognize, and the number of significant distinctions we draw within each, is sufficiently small that the brain can use the following strategy for making noninferential identifications of sensations.

Consider the various physical properties that, in you, are characteristic of the repeatable brain state that realizes a given sensation. Simply exploit whichever of those physical properties is accessible to your innate discriminatory mechanisms, and contrive a standard habit of conceptual response ("Lo, a sensation of warmth") to the property-evoked activation of those mechanisms. While this strategy will work nicely for the relatively small class of sensations, it will not work at all well for the class of beliefs, or for any of the other propositional attitudes. The reason is not that the brain state that realizes a certain belief *lacks* intrinsic properties characteristic of it alone. Rather, the reason is that there are far too many beliefs, actual and possible, for us to have any hope of being able to discriminate and identify all of them on such a one-by-one basis. The number of possible beliefs is at least a denumerable infinity, and the number of possible beliefs expressible in an English sentence of ten words or less is still stupendous. If we assume a vocabulary of 10^5 words for English, the number of distinct strings of ten words or less is 10^{50}. If we conservatively assume that only one string in every trillion trillion is grammatically and semantically well formed, this still leaves us over 10^{25} distinct sentences. Even if there were a distinct and accessible monadic property for each distinct belief state, therefore, the capacity of memory is insufficient to file all of them. Evidently the brain must use some more systematic strategy for discriminating and identifying beliefs, a strategy that exploits in some way the unique combinatorial structure of any belief.

But this is a very complex and sophisticated matter requiring the resources of our higher cognitive capacities, capacities tuned to the complex relational, structural, and combinatorial features of the domain in which the discriminations are made. Unlike the sensation case, no narrow range of stimulus-response connections will begin to characterize the mechanisms at work here.

Sensations and beliefs, accordingly, must be introspectively discriminated by entirely distinct cognitive mechanisms, mechanisms facing quite different problems and using quite different strategies for their solutions. Sensations are identified by way of their intrinsic properties; beliefs are identified by way of their highly abstract structural features. It should not be wondered at, then, that there is a subjective contrast in the nature of our awareness of each.

[Added in 1989: I must now express a loss of confidence in this argument. The problem is that sensations now appear to be decidedly more various than I had originally estimated and to have a much more intricate combinatorial structure than I had earlier supposed (see chapter 5, sec. 7). Accordingly, the contrasts on which the preceding argument places so much weight now appear spurious: what seemed a large difference in kind now seems a mere difference in degree.]

D.   The differentiation problem

This problem arises because we are occasionally able to discriminate between qualitatively distinct sensations where we are ignorant of any corresponding functional differences between them, and even where we are wholly ignorant of the causal properties of both of them, as when they are new to us, for example. These cases are thought to constitute a problem in that functional considerations should bid us count the states as type identical, whereas by hypothesis they are type distinct (see Block 1978, p. 300).

The objection has two defects. First, sheer ignorance of functional differences need not bind us to counting the sensations as functionally identical. The functionalist can and should be a realist about functional properties. Functional identities are not determined by what we do or do not know, but by what is actually out there in the world (or *in* there in the brain). Second, the objection begs the question against functionalism by assuming that a discriminable qualitative difference between two sensations entails that they are type distinct *qua* psychological states. We have already seen that this inference is wrong: pains display a variety of qualitative characters, but because of their functional similarities, they still count as pains.

In short, we can and do make discriminations among our sensations in advance of functional understanding. But whether the discriminations thus made mark a difference of any importance for the taxonomy of psychological theory is another question. In some cases they will; in other cases they will not. What decides the matter is whether those qualitative differences mark any causal or functional differences relevant to the explanation of psychological activity and overt behavior.

So long as introspectible qualia were thought to be ineffable, or epiphenomenal, or dualistic, or essential for type identity, one can understand the functionalist's reluctance to have anything to do with them. But once we have seen how the functionalist can acknowledge them and their epistemic role, within a naturalistic framework, the reluctance should disappear. For the taxonomy of states appropriate for psychological theory remains dictated entirely by causal and explanatory factors. Qualia are just accidental hooks of opportunity for the introspective discrimination of *dynamically* significant states.

2   The Problem of Nonstandard Realizations

Some of the issues arising here have already been broached in the subsection on absent qualia. However, novel problems arise as well, and organization is best served by a separate section. All of the problems here begin with the functionalist's central contention that the functional organization necessary and sufficient for personhood is an abstract one, an organization realizable in principle in an indefinite variety of physical systems. Such liberalism seems innocent enough when we contemplate the prospect of humanoid aliens, biomechanical androids, and electromechanical robots whose physical constitutions are at least rough parallels of our own. Who could deny that C3PO and R2D2—of *Star Wars* fame—are persons? But our liberal intuitions are quickly flummoxed when we consider bizarre physical systems that might nevertheless realize the abstract causal organization at issue, and such cases move one to reconsider one's generosity in the more familiar cases as well.

The following discussion will explore but two of these nonstandard "persons": Ned Block's "Chinese nation" (1978) and John Searle's "Chinese-speaking room" with the monolingual anglophone locked inside it (Searle 1980). Block is concerned with the absence of *qualia* from states posing as sensations, and Searle is concerned with the absence of *intentionality* from states posing as propositional attitudes.

A.   Qualia in the Chinese nation
Block's example will be examined first. He has us imagine a certain Turing machine T_m, which is realized in the population of China, as follows. Each citizen has a two-way radio link to a certain robotic device with sensory transducers and motor effectors. This robot is the

body of the simulated person, and it interacts with its collective brain as follows. It sends a sensory input message I_j to every single citizen and subsequently receives a motor output message O_i from exactly one citizen. Which citizen sends what output is determined as follows.

Overhead from a satellite some state letter S_k is displayed in lights for all to see. For each possible state letter S_k there is permanently assigned a distinct subset of the population. In the rare event when S_k is displayed *and* input I_j is received, one person in the S_k group, a person to whom I_j has been assigned, performs the following pre-assigned task. She sends to the robot the unique output message O_i antecedently assigned to her for just this occasion, radios the satellite to display the state letter S_p antecedently assigned to her for just this occasion, and then subsides, waiting for the next opportunity to do exactly the same thing in exactly the same circumstances.

As organized above, each citizen realizes exactly one square of the machine table that specifies T_m. (A machine table is a matrix or checkerboard with state letters heading the columns and input letters heading the rows. Any square is the intersection of some S_k and I_j, and it specifies an output O_i and a shift to some state S_p, where possibly $p = k$. See figure 2.1.) Block asks us to assume that T_m adequately simulates your own functional organization. One is likely to grant him this, since any input-output function can in principle be realized in a suitable Turing machine. In pondering an apparently fussy detail, Block wonders, "How many homunculi are required?" and answers, "Perhaps a billion are enough; after all, there are only about a billion neurons in the brain" (p. 278). Hence his choice of China as the potential artificial brain. (Block underestimates here. The number of neurons in the brain exceeds 100 billion.)

Finally, Block finds it starkly implausible to suppose that this nationwide realization of T_m has states with a qualitative character like pains, tastes, and so on. It is difficult not to agree with him. His homunculi do not even interact with one another, save indirectly through the satellite state letter and even less directly through the adventures of the robot body itself. The shimmering intricacies of one's inner life are not to be found here.

The way to avoid this criticism of functionalism is just to insist that any subject of beliefs and sensations must not only be Turing equivalent to us (that is, produce identical outputs given identical inputs); it must be *computationally* equivalent to us as well. That is, it must have a system of inner states whose causal interconnections mirror those in our own case. This is not an arbitrary restriction. Folk psychology is, and scientific psychology should be, realistic about our mental states,

DISTINCT INTERNAL STATES

DISTINCT INPUTS

	S_1	S_2	......	S_k
I_1	Do O_{17}, then go to state S_5	Do O_8, then go to state S_2		Do O_1, then go to state S_{18}
I_2	Do O_{10}, then go to state S_6	Do O_3, then go to state S_{13}		etc.
⋮				
I_j	Do O_{12}, then go to state S_{27}	etc.		etc.

Figure 2.1
A Turing machine table. The machine is always in some one or other internal state S_n represented by one of the vertical columns. When it receives an input I_m, it executes the instructions in the specific square where the S_n column and the I_m row intersect, and then it waits for the next input.

and mere parity of gross behavior does not guarantee parity of causal organization among the states that produce it. The computational organization displayed in the Chinese-nation Turing machine is not even distantly analogous to our own. If it were analogous to our own, worries about absent qualia could be handled as outlined in the subsection about absent qualia above. That is, we could insist that the qualia are there all right, but are unrecognized by us under their physical descriptions.

There is a further reason why it is not arbitrary to insist on a computational organization more along the lines of our own, and we may illustrate it by examining a further defect in Block's example. It is demonstrable that no T_m realized as described in the population of China could possibly simulate your input-output relations. There are not nearly enough Chinese for this job, not even *remotely* enough. In fact, a spherical volume of space centered on the Sun and ending at

Pluto's orbit packed solidly with cheek-to-cheek Chinese (roughly 10^{36} homunculi) would still not be remotely enough, as I shall show.

Since it is realized on a one-man/one-square basis, the Chinese T_m can have at most 10^9 distinct possible outputs, and at most $10^9/S$ distinct possible inputs, where S is the total number of distinct state letters. That is, T_m has rather less than 10^9 possible inputs. How many distinct possible inputs characterize your own functional organization? Since the present argument requires only a lower limit, let us consider just one of your retinas. The surface of your retina contains roughly 10^8 light-sensitive cells, which we shall conservatively assume to be capable of only two states: stimulated and unstimulated. Good eyesight has a resolution limit of about one foot at a distance of a mile, or slightly less than one arc-minute, and this angle projected from the lens of the eye subtends about six microns at the retina. This is roughly the distance between the individual cells to be found there, so it is evident that individual cells, and not just groups, can serve as discriminative atoms, functionally speaking.

If we take distinct stimulation patterns in the set of retinal cells as distinct inputs to the brain, it is evident that we are here dealing with 2 to the (10^8)th power distinct possible inputs. This is an appallingly large number. Since $2^{332} \approx 10^{100}$ (a googol), $2^{10^8} \approx 10^{30,000,000}$ distinct possible inputs from a single retina! Since a one-man/one-square Turing machine must have at least as many homunculi as possible inputs, any such realization adequate to the inputs from a single retina would require no less than $10^{30,000,000}$ distinct homunculi. However, there are only about 10^{80} distinct atoms in the accessible universe. Small wonder the Chinese nation makes an unconvincing simulation of our inner lives. Plainly, we should never have acquiesced in the premise that a Turing machine thus realized could even begin to simulate your overall functional organization. The Chinese robot body can have at most a mere 30 binary input sensors, since $2^{30} \approx 10^9$, and the number of distinct inputs cannot exceed 10^9.

This argument does not depend on inflated estimates concerning the retina or its input to the brain. (It might be objected, for example, that retinal cell stimulation is not independent of the state of its immediate neighbor cells, or that the optic nerve has only 800,000 axons.) If your retina contained only 332 discriminatory units, instead of 10^8, the number of distinct inputs would still be 2^{332}, or roughly 10^{100}: ninety-one orders of magnitude beyond the capacity of the Chinese nation, and twenty orders of magnitude beyond the atoms in the universe. Nor have we even begun to consider the other dimension of the required machine table: the range of states, S, of the brain that receives these inputs, a brain which has at least 10^{11}

distinct cells in its own right, each with about 10^3 connections with other cells. Our estimate of the number of distinct states of the brain must be substantially in excess of $10^{30,000,000}$, our number for the retina.

Our conclusion is that *no* brute-force, one-device/one-square realization of a Turing machine constructible in this universe could even begin to simulate your input-output organization. Even the humblest of creatures are beyond such simulation. An unprepossessing gastropod like the sea slug *Aplysia californica* has well in excess of 332 distinct sensory cells, and thus is clearly beyond the reach of the crude methods at issue. This does not mean that the human input-output relations cannot be represented by an abstract Turing machine T_m. What it does mean is that any *physical* machine adequate to such simulation *must* have its computational architecture and executive hardware organized along lines vastly different from, and much more unified and efficient than, those displayed in Block's example. That example, therefore, is not even remotely close to being a fair test of our intuitions. Quite aside from the question of qualia, the Chinese Turing machine couldn't simulate an earthworm.

This weakness in the example is not adequately made up by allowing, as Block does at one point (p. 284), that each homunculus might be responsible for a wide range of inputs, each with corresponding outputs. On this modification, each homunculus would thus realize, dispositionally, many machine-table squares simultaneously. Suppose, then, that we make each Chinese citizen responsible for one billion squares peculiar to him (this was the size of the original T_m). This raises the number of distinct inputs processable by the system to 10^9 citizens $\times$ 10^9 squares $= 10^{18}$ possible inputs, still well short of the $10^{30,000,000}$ we are striving for.

Well, how many squares much each citizen realize if the nation as a whole *is* to instantiate some Turing machine adequate to handle the required input? The answer is, of course, $10^{(30,000,000 - 9)}$ squares each. But how will each homunculus-citizen handle this awesome load? *Not* by being a simple one-device/one-square Turing machine in turn, as we have already seen. No physical simulation adequate to your input-output relations, therefore, can avoid having the more unified and efficient modes of computational organization alluded to in the preceding paragraphs, even if they show up only as modes of organization of its various subunits. That is, any successful simulation of you must somewhere display a computational-executive organization that is a much more plausible home for qualitative states than Block's example would suggest. [Added in 1989: A good example of a more plausible home is the vector coding and parallel distributed processing arrangment discussed in chapter 5.|

But can a number of distinct persons or near persons collectively constitute a further person? Apparently so, since the system consisting of your right hemisphere and your left hemisphere (and your cerebellum and thalamus and limbic system, etc.) seems to do precisely that. Further attempts to construct homunculi-headed counterexamples to functionalism should perhaps bear this fact in mind.

The argument of the preceding pages does not, of course, show that the specific details of *our* computational organization are essential to achieving the informational capacity required. And this raises a question we might have asked anyway: if we do require of any subject of sensations, beliefs, and so forth, that it be functionally equivalent to us in the strong sense of "computationally equivalent," do we then not run the opposite danger of allowing too *few* things to count as sites of genuine mentality? (See again Block 1978, p. 310ff, on species chauvinism.) If we restrict the application of the term "mentality" to creatures having sensations, beliefs, intentions, etc., we shall indeed have become too restrictive. Yet the functionalist need not pretend that our internal functional organization exhausts the possible kinds of mentality. He need only claim that our kind of internal functional organization is what constitutes a psychology of *beliefs, desires, sensations,* and so forth. He is free to suggest that an alien functional organization, comparable only in sophistication to our own, could constitute an alien psychology of quite different internal states. We could then speak of Martian mentality, for example, as well as of human mentality.

Still, it might be wondered, what is the shared essence that makes both of us instances of the now more general term "mentality"? There need be none, beyond the general idea of a sophisticated control center for complex behavior. One of the functionalist's principal theses, after all, is that there are no natural essences to be found in this domain. If he is right, it is folly to seek them. And in any case, it is question begging to demand that he find them.

On the other hand, there may yet prove to be some interesting natural kind of which both we and the Martian are variant instances: some highly abstract thermodynamic kind, perhaps. In that case, orthodox functionalism would be mistaken in one of its purely negative theses. On this matter, see the final section of this essay.

B. Intentionality in the Chinese room
Let us now turn to John Searle's worries about meaning and intentionality. The states at issue here are beliefs, thoughts, desires, and

the rest of the propositional attitudes. On the functionalist's view, the type identity of any of these states is determined by the network of relations it bears to the other states and to external circumstances and behavior. In the case of the propositional attitudes, those relations characteristically reflect a variety of logical and computational relations among the propositions that the attitudes "contain." We can thus at least imagine a computer of sufficient capacity programmed so as to display an economy of internal states whose interconnections mirror those in our own case. The simulation would create the required relational order by exploiting the logical and computational relations defined over the formal/structural/combinatorial features of the individual propositional states.

Searle has no doubt that such a simulation could, in principle, be constructed. His objection to functionalism is that the states of such a system would nevertheless lack real meaning and intentionality: "No purely formal model will ever be sufficient by itself for intentionality because the formal properties are not by themselves constitutive of intentionality" (Searle 1980, p. 422). His reasons for holding this position are illustrated in the following thought experiment.

Imagine a monolingual anglophone locked in a room with a substantial store of sequences of Chinese symbols, and a set of complex transformation rules, written in English, for performing operations on sets and sequences of Chinese symbols. The occupant periodically receives a new sequence of Chinese symbols through a postal slot. He applies his transformation rules dutifully to the ordered pair <new sequence, old store of sequences>, and they tell him to write out a further sequence of Chinese symbols, which he sends back out through the postal slot.

Now, unknown to the occupant, the large store of sequences embodies a rich store of information on some one or more topics, all written in Chinese. The new sequences sent through the door are questions and comments on those topics. The transformation rules are a cunningly devised program designed to simulate the thought processes and conversational behavior of a native speaker of Chinese. The symbol sequences the occupant sends out are "responses" to the queries and comments received. We are to suppose that the transformation rules are well devised, and that the simulation is as convincing as you please, considered from the outside.

However convincing it is, says Searle, it remains plain that the room's occupant does not understand Chinese: he applies transformation rules, and he understands those rules, but the sequences of Chinese symbols are meaningless to him. Equally clear, claims Searle, is that the *entire system* of the room plus its contents does not understand Chinese either. Nothing here understands Chinese, save those sending and receiving the messages, and those who wrote the program. No computational state or output of that system has any meaning or intentionality save as it is interpretively imposed from without by those who interact with it.

However, concludes Searle, this system already contains everything relevant to be found in the physical realization of any purely formal program. If meaning and intentionality are missing here, they will be missing in any such attempt to simulate human mental activity. Instantiating a program cannot be a sufficient condition of understanding,

> because the formal symbol manipulations by themselves don't have any intentionality; they are quite meaningless; they aren't even *symbol* manipulations, since the symbols don't symbolize anything. In the linguistic jargon, they have only a syntax but no semantics. Such intentionality as computers appear to have is solely in the minds of those who program them, those who send in the input and those who interpret the output. (p. 422)

The set of commentaries published in the same issue provides many useful and interesting criticisms of Searle's argument and of his conclusions as well. The critical consensus is roughly as follows. If the system of the room plus contents were upgraded so that its conversational skills extend beyond a handful of topics to include the entire range of topics a normal human could be expected to know; and if the system were supplied with the same inductive capacities we enjoy; and if the "belief store" were integrated in the normal fashion with some appropriately complex goal structure; and if the room were causally connected to a body in such a fashion that its inputs reflected appropriate sensory discriminations and its outputs produced appropriate behavior; *then* the system of the room plus contents jolly well *would* understand Chinese, and its various computational states— beliefs that *p*, desires that *q*—would indeed have meaning and intentionality in the same way as with a normal Chinese speaker.

Searle is quite willing to consider upgradings of the kind described—he attempts to anticipate them in his paper—but he is convinced they change nothing relevant to his case. As it emerges clearly in his Author's Response (pp. 450–456), of central importance to his argument is the distinction between

> cases of what I will call *intrinsic intentionality*, which are cases of actual mental states, and what I will call *observer-relative ascrip-*

tions of intentionality, which are ways that people have of speaking about entities figuring in our activities but lacking intrinsic intentionality. [The latter] are always dependent on the intrinsic intentionality of the observers. (pp. 451–452)

Examples of the latter would be the words and sentences of one's native tongue. These have meaning and intentionality, allows Searle, but only insofar as they bear certain relations to our beliefs, thoughts, and intentions—states with intrinsic intentionality. A simulation of human mentality grounded in a formal program may yield states having this derivative observer-relative brand of intentionality, concedes Searle, but they cannot have intrinsic intentionality. And since they lack a feature essential to genuine mental states, they cannot be genuine mental states, and to that extent the simulation must be a failure.

As we see it, this criticism of functionalism is profoundly in error. It is a mistake to try to meet it, however, by continuing with the strategy of trying to upgrade the imagined simulation in hopes of finally winning Searle's concession that at last its states have achieved intrinsic intentionality. The correct strategy is to argue that our own mental states are just as innocent of "intrinsic intentionality" as are the states of any machine simulation. On our view, all ascriptions of meaning or propositional content are relative (in senses to be explained). The notion of "intrinsic intentionality" makes no more empirical sense than does the notion of position in absolute space. We shall try to explain these claims.

There are basically just two ways in which one can assign propositional content to the representational states of another organism. An example of the first is the translation of a foreign language. An example of the second is the calibration of an instrument of measurement or detection.

In the case of translation, one assigns specific propositional contents to the alien representations because one has found a general mapping between the alien representations and our own such that the network of formal and material inferences holding among the alien representations closely mirrors the same network holding among our own representations. Briefly, their collected representations display an *intensional structure* that matches the intensional structure displayed by our own.

The story is essentially the same when we are assigning propositional content to an alien's thoughts, beliefs, etc. It matters naught whether the alien's representation is overt, as with a sentence, or covert, as with a belief. We assign a specific content, *p*, to one of the alien's representations on the strength of whatever assurances we have that his representation plays the same abstract inferential role in his intellectual (computational) economy that the belief-that-*p* plays in ours. And what goes for aliens goes also for one's brothers and sisters.

This is not to say that the representational states of other humans have content only insofar as others interpret them in some way. After all, the set of abstract relations holding among the representations in someone's intellectual economy is an objective feature intrinsic to that person. But it does mean that the content, call it the *translational content*, of any specific representation of his *is a matter of the inferential/ computational relations it bears to all the rest of his representations*. There can be no question of an isolated state or token possessing an intrinsic translational content; it will have a specific translational content only if, and only insofar as, it enjoys a specific set of relations to the other elements in a *system* of representations.

Contrast translational content with what is naturally termed *calibrational content*. The repeatable states of certain physical systems are more or less reliable indicators of certain features of their environment, and we may assign content (e.g., "The temperature is 0° C") to such states (e.g., a certain height in a column of red alcohol) on the strength of such empirical connections. This goes for the human system as well. The various states we call "perceptual beliefs" can be assigned contents in this same manner: as a function of what environmental circumstance standardly triggers their occurrence. In fact, if a system has any systematic responses to its environment at all, then calibration can take place even where translation cannot, either because the system simply lacks the internal economy necessary for translational content or because the intensional structure of that economy is incommensurable with our own. Furthermore, calibrational content may regularly *diverge* from translational content, even where translational content is possible. Consider a tribal utterance that calibrates as "There is thunder," but which translates as "God is shouting"; or one that calibrates as "This man has a bacterial infection," but which translates as "This man is possessed by a pink demon."

Accordingly, Searle is right to resist the suggestion that merely hooking up the room system, via some sensors, to the outside world would supply a unique meaning or content to the room's representational states. Genuine mental states do indeed have a content or intentionality that is independent of, and possibly quite different from, their straightforward calibrational content. That independent intentionality is their *translational content*.

But this content falls well short of being the "intrinsic intentionality" Searle imagines our states to have. Translational content is not environmentally determined, nor is it observer-relative, but it is most certainly a *relational* matter, a matter of the state's inferential/computational relations within a system of other such states. Accordingly, it is entirely possible for translational content to be possessed by the states of a machine—as the realization of a purely formal program.

What more than this Searle imagines as fixing the content of our mental states, we are unable to surmise. He floats the distinction between intrinsic intentionality and other kinds of intentionality by means of illustrative examples only (p. 451); he hazards no palpable account of what intrinsic intentionality consists in; and the intuitions to which he appeals can be explained in less mysterious ways, as outlined above. To conclude, there simply is no such thing as intrinsic intentionality, at least as Searle conceives it. Functionalists need not be concerned, then, that computer simulations of human mentality fail to display it.

We complete this section by underscoring a contrast. In the first half of this section we conceded to the critic of functionalism that our mental states have qualia, but we argued that the states of a machine simulation could have them as well. In this second half we have conceded to the critic of functionalism that the states of certain machine simulations must lack intrinsic intentionality. But we insist that our own states are devoid of it as well.

3   Functionalism and Methodology

Despite the defenses offered above, we do wish to direct certain criticisms against functionalism. The criticisms are mainly methodological rather than substantive, however, and we shall here provide only a brief summary, since they have been explained at length elsewhere.

A.   Conceptual conservatism
No functionalist will suppose that the functional organization recognized in the collected lore of folk psychology exhausts the functional intricacies that make up our internal economy. All will agree that folk psychology represents only a partial, and in some respects even a superficial, grasp of the more complex organization that empirical psychology will eventually unravel. Even so, there is a decided tendency on all sides to suppose that, so far as it goes, folk psychology is essentially correct in the picture that it paints, at least in basic outlines. Empirical psychology will add to it, and explain its principles, many expect, but almost no one expects it to be overthrown or transmogrified by such research.

This sanguine outlook is not unique to functionalists, but they are especially vulnerable to it. Since the type identity of mental states is held to reside not in any shared physical or other natural essences, but in the structure of their causal relations, there is a tendency to construe the generalizations connecting them as collectively *stipulating* what it is to be a belief, a desire, a pain, and so forth. Folk psychology is thus removed from the arena of empirical criticism. This is unfortunate, since the "denaturing" of folk psychology does not change its epistemic status as a speculative account of our internal workings. Like any other theory, it may be radically false, and like any other deeply entrenched theory, its falsity is unlikely to be revealed without a vigorous exploration of that possibility.

A functionalist can, of course, accept these points without danger to what is basic in his position. Nevertheless, they are worth making for two reasons. First, eliminative materialism is not a very widespread opinion among adherents of functionalism, despite being entirely consistent with their view. And second, there are very good reasons for doubting the integrity of folk psychology in its central structures as well as in its peripheral details (See P. M. Churchland 1979, chapter 5, and 1981a; P. S. Churchland 1980a, 1980b; and Stich 1983).

B.   Top down versus bottom up

Given that the essence of our psychological states resides in the set of causal relations they bear to one another, etc., and given that this abstract functional organization can be realized in a nomically heterogeneous variety of substrates, it is fair enough that the functionalist should be more interested in that abstract organization than in the machinery that realizes it. With the science of psychology, it is understanding the "program" that counts; an understanding of such hardwares as may execute it is secondary and inessential.

This much is fair enough, but so long as we are so profoundly ignorant of our functional organization as we are at present, and ignorant of where to draw the line between "hardware" and "program" in organisms, we cannot afford to be so indifferent to the neurosciences as the preceding rationale might suggest. If we wish to unravel the functional intricacies of our internal economy, one obvious way to go about this is to unravel the intricacies of the physical system that executes it. This bottom-up approach is not the only approach we might follow, but it does boast a number of advantages: it is very strongly empirical; it is not at all constrained by the preconceptions of folk psychology; it has the capacity to force surprises on us; it permits a nonbehavioral comparison of cognitive differences

across species; it enjoys direct connections with evolutionary etholo-
gy; and at least in principle it *can* reveal the functional organization
we are looking for.

Neuroscience is an awkward and difficult pursuit, however, and
there is an overwhelming preference among philosophers, psychologists, and artificial-intelligence researchers for a more top-down
approach: hypothesize functional systems (programs) and test them
against our molar behavior, as conceived within common sense. This
is entirely legitimate, but if the functionalist is moved by the argument from abstraction to ignore or devalue the bottom-up approach,
his methodology is dangerously conservative and one-sided. (We
have discussed these shortcomings at length in P. S. Churchland
1980a, 1980c; and in P. M. Churchland 1981a, 1982, 1980.)

C. Reductionism
Thanks to the argument from abstraction, functionalists tend to be
strongly antireductionist. They deny that there can be any general
characterization of what makes something a *thinker* that is expressible
in the language of any of the physical sciences. Given the variety of
possible substrates (biological, chemical, electromechanical) that
could realize a thinking system, it is difficult not to agree with them.
But it does not follow, from multiple instantiability per se, that no
such general characterization is possible. It follows only that the required characterization cannot be expressed in the theoretical vocabulary peculiar to any one of the available substrates. It remains entirely possible that there is a level of physical description sufficiently
abstract to encompass all of them, and yet sufficiently powerful to
fund the characterization required.

As it happens, there is indeed a physical theory of sufficient generality to encompass the activity of all of these substrates, and any
others one might think of. The theory is thermodynamics—the
general theory of energy and entropy. It has already supplied us with
a profoundly illuminating characterization of what the nineteenth
century called "vital activity," that is, of the phenomenon of *life*. And
it is far from unthinkable that it might do the same for what this century calls "mental activity" (for a brief exploration of these ideas, see
P. M. Churchland 1982). The theoretical articulation of such a characterization would be a very great achievement. It would be unfortunate if the search for it were impeded by the general conviction that it is
impossible, a conviction born of the antireductionist urgings of a
false orthodoxy among functionalists.

Chapter 3

Reduction, Qualia, and the Direct Introspection
of Brain States

Do the phenomenological or qualitative features of our sensations constitute a permanent barrier to the reductive aspirations of any materialistic neuroscience? I here argue that they do not. Specifically, I wish to address the recent antireductionist arguments posed by Thomas Nagel (1974), Frank Jackson (1982), and Howard Robinson (1982). And I wish to explore the possibility of human subjective consciousness within a conceptual environment constituted by a matured and successful neuroscience.

If we are to deal sensibly with the issues here at stake, we must approach them with a general theory of scientific reduction already in hand, a theory motivated by and adequate to the many instances and varieties of interconceptual reduction displayed *elsewhere* in our scientific history. With an independently grounded account of the nature and grounds of intertheoretic reduction, we can approach the specific case of subjective qualia free from the myopia that results from trying to divine the proper conditions on reduction by simply staring long and hard at the problematic case at issue.

1 Intertheoretic Reduction

We may begin by remarking that the classical account of intertheoretic reduction (Nagel 1961) now appears to be importantly mistaken, though the repairs necessary are quickly and cleanly made. Suppressing nicities, we may state the original account as follows. A new and more comprehensive theory *reduces* an older theory just in case the new theory, when conjoined with appropriate correspondence rules, logically entails the principles of the older theory. (The point of the correspondence rules or "bridge laws" is to connect the disparate ontologies of the two theories; often these are expressed as identity statements, such as $Temperature = mv^2/3k$.) Schematically,

This essay first appeared in the *Journal of Philosophy* 82, no. 1 (January 1985).

T_N & (correspondence rules)

logically entails

T_O.

Difficulties with this view begin with the observation that most reduced theories turn out to be, strictly speaking and in a variety of respects, *false*. (Real gases don't really obey $PV = \mu RT$, as in classical thermodynamics; the planets don't really move in ellipses, as in Keplerian astronomy; the acceleration of falling bodies isn't really uniform, as in Galilean dynamics; etc.) If reduction is *deduction*, *modus tollens* would thus require that the premises of the new reducing theories (statistical thermodynamics in the first case, Newtonian dynamics in the second and third) be somehow false as well, in contradiction to their assumed truth.

This complaint can be temporarily deflected by pointing out that the premises of a reduction must often include, not just the new reducing theory, but also some limiting assumptions or counterfactual boundary conditions (such as that the molecules of a gas have only mechanical energy, or that the mass of the planets is negligible compared to the sun's, or that the distance any body falls is negligibly different from zero). Falsity in the reducing premises can thus be conceded, since it is safely confined to those limiting or counterfactual assumptions.

This defense will not deal with all cases of falsity, however, since in some cases the reduced theory is so radically false that some or all of its ontology must be rejected entirely, and the "correspondence rules" connecting that ontology to the newer ontology therefore display a problematic status. Newly conceived features cannot be identical with, nor even nomically connected with, old features, if the old features are illusory and uninstantiated. For example, relativistic mass is not identical with Newtonian mass, nor even coextensive with it, even at low velocities. Nevertheless, the reduction of Newtonian by Einsteinian mechanics is a paradigm of a successful reduction. For a second example, neither is caloric-fluid-pressure identical with, nor even coextensive with, mean molecular kinetic energy. But an overtly *fluid* thermodynamics (i.e., one committed to the existence of "caloric") still finds a moderately impressive reduction within statistical thermodynamics. In sum, even theories with a *nonexistent* ontology can enjoy reduction, and this fact is problematic on the traditional account at issue.

Cases like these invite us to give up the idea that what gets deduced in a reduction is the theory to be reduced. A more accurate, general, and illuminating schema for intertheoretic reduction is as follows:

T_N & limiting assump. & boundary cond.

logically entails

I_N (a set of theorems of (restricted) T_N),
e.g., $(x)(Ax \supset Bx)$,
    $(x)((Bx \text{ \& } Cx) \supset Dx)$,

which is relevantly isomorphic with

T_O (the older theory),
e.g., $(x)(Jx \supset Kx)$,
    $(x)((Kx \text{ \& } Lx) \supset Mx)$.

That is to say, a reduction consists in the deduction, within T_N, not of T_O itself, but rather of a roughly equipotent *image* of T_O, an image still expressed in the vocabulary proper to T_N. The correspondence rules play no part whatever in the deduction. They show up only later, and not necessarily as material-mode statements, but as mere ordered pairs: $<Ax, Jx>$, $<Bx, Kx>$, $<Cx, Lx>$, $<Dx, Mx>$. Their function is to indicate which term substitutions in the image I_N will yield the principles of T_O. The older theory, accordingly, is never deduced; it is just the target of a relevantly adequate *mimicry*. Construed in this way, a correspondence rule is entirely consistent with the assumption that the older predicate it encompasses has no extension whatever. This allows that a true theory might reduce even a substantially false one.

The point of a reduction, according to this view, is to show that the new or more comprehensive theory contains explanatory and predictive resources which parallel, to a relevant degree of exactness, the explanatory and predictive resources of the reduced theory. The intra-theoretic deduction (of I_N within T_N) and the intertheoretic mapping (of T_O into I_N) jointly constitute a fell-swoop demonstration that the older theory can be displaced wholesale by the new without significant explanatory or predictive loss. (This sketch of intertheoretic reduction is drawn from P. M. Churchland 1979, section 11. For a more detailed account, see Hooker 1981.)

Material-mode statements of identity can occasionally be made, of course. We do wish to assert that visible light = electromagnetic waves between 0.35 μm and 0.75 μm, that sound = atmospheric compression waves, that temperature = mean molecular kinetic energy, and that electric current = net motion of charged particles. But a correspondence rule does not itself make such a claim. At best, it records the fact that the new predicate applies in all those cases where its

T_O-doppelgänger predicate was normally *thought* to apply. On this view, full-fledged *identity* statements are licensed by the comparative *smoothness* of the relevant reduction (i.e., the limiting assumptions or boundary conditions on T_N are not wildly counterfactual, all or most of T_O's principles find close analogues in I_N, etc.). This smoothness permits the comfortable assimilation of the old ontology within the new, and thus allows the old theory to retain all or most of its ontological integrity. *It is smooth intertheoretic reductions that motivate and sustain statements of cross-theoretic identity, not the other way around.*

The preceding framework allows us to frame a useful conception of reduction for specific *properties*, as opposed to entire theories, and it allows us to frame a useful conception of the contrary notion of "emergent" properties. A property F, postulated by an older theory or conceptual framework T_O, is reduced to a property G in some new theory T_N just in case

(1) T_N reduces T_O,

(2)   'F' and 'G' are correspondence-rule paired in the reduction, and

(3)   the reduction is sufficiently smooth to sustain the ontology of T_O and thus to sustain the identity claim 'F-ness = G-ness'.

Intuitively, and in the material mode, this means that F-ness reduces to G-ness just in case the causal powers of F-ness (as outlined in the laws of T_O) are a subset of the causal powers of G-ness (as outlined in the laws of T_N).

Finally, a property F will be said to be an *emergent* property (relative to T_N) just in case

(1) F is definitely real and instantiated,

(2) F is cooccurrent with some feature or complex circumstance recognized in T_N, but

(3) F cannot be *reduced* to any property postulated by or definable within T_N.

Intuitively, this will happen when T_N does not have the resources adequate to define a property with all of the causal powers possessed by F-ness. Claims about the emergence of certain properties are therefore claims about the relative poverty in the resources of certain aspirant theories. Having outlined these notions, we shall turn to address substantive questions of emergence and irreducibility in a few moments.

(A word of caution is perhaps in order here, since the expression 'emergent property' is often used in two diametrically opposed senses. In scientific contexts, one frequently hears it used to apply to what might be called a "network property," a property that appears exactly when the elements of some substrate are suitably organized, a property that *consists in* the elements of that substrate standing in certain relations to one another, a set of relations that collectively sustain the set of causal powers ascribed to the "emergent" property. In this innocent sense of 'emergent', there are a great many emergent properties, and quite probably the qualia of our sensations should be numbered among them. But in philosophical contexts one more often encounters a different sense of 'emergent', one that implies that an emergent property does *not* consist in any collective or organizational feature of its substrate. The first sense positively implies reducibility; the second implies *ir*reducibility. It is emergence in the second sense that is at issue in this paper.)

Before we continue, several points about reduction need to be emphasized. The first is that in arguing for the emergence of a given property F relative to some theory T_N, it is not sufficient to point out that the existence or appearance of F-ness cannot be deduced from T_N. It is occasionally claimed, for example, that the objective features of warmth or blueness must be irreducibly emergent properties, since however much one bends and squeezes the molecular theory concerning H_2O, one cannot deduce from it that water will be *blue*, but only that water will scatter electromagnetic radiation at such and such wavelengths. And however much one wrings from the mechanics of molecular motion, one cannot deduce from it that a roaring hearth will be *warm*, but only that its molecules will have such and such a mean kinetic energy and will collectively emit electromagnetic radiation at longish wavelengths.

These premises about nondeducibility are entirely true, but the conclusion against reducibility does not follow. It is a serious mistake to make even *in*direct deducibility (i.e., deducibility with the help of correspondence rules) a requirement on successful reduction, as we saw at the beginning of this section. And there are additional reasons why it would be even more foolish to insist on the much stronger condition of direct deducibility. For example, formal considerations alone guarantee that, for any predicate 'F' not already in the proprietary lexicon of the aspirant reducing theory T_N, no statements whatever involving 'F' (beyond tautologies and other trivial exceptions) will be deducible from T_N. The deducibility requirement would thus trivialize the notion of reduction by making it impossible for *any* conceptual framework to reduce any other distinct conceptual framework. Even temperature, that paradigm of a successfully reduced property, would be rendered irreducible, since the term 'temperature' does not appear in the lexicon of statistical mechanics.

There is a further reason why the demand for direct deducibility is too strong. The fact is, it is an historical accident that we humans currently use precisely the conceptual framework we do use. We might have used any one of an infinite number of other conceptual frameworks to describe the observable world, each one of which could have been roughly adequate to common experience, and many of which would be roughly isomorphic (each in its different way) with some part of the correct account that a utopian theory will eventually provide. Accordingly, we can legitimately ask of a putatively correct theory of a given objective domain that it account for the phenomena in (that is, function successfully in) that domain. But we cannot insist that it also be able to predict how this, that, or the other conceptually idiosyncratic human culture is going to *conceive* of that domain. That would be to insist that the new theory do *predictive cultural anthropology* for us, as well as mechanics, or electromagnetic theory, or what have you. The demand that molecular theory directly entail *our* thermal or color concepts is evidently this same unreasonable demand.

All we can properly ask of a reducing theory is that it have the resources to conjure up a set of properties whose nomological powers/roles/features are systematic *analogues* of the powers/roles/features of the set of properties postulated by the old theory. Since both theories presume to describe the same empirical domain, these systematic nomological parallels constitute the best grounds there can be for concluding that both theories have managed to latch onto the *same* set of objective properties. The hypothesized identity of the properties at issue explains why I_N and T_O are taxonomically and nomically parallel: they are both at least partially correct accounts of the very same objective properties. I_N merely frames that account within a much more penetrating conceptual system—that of T_N.

Moreover, it is to be expected that existing conceptual frameworks will eventually be reduced or displaced by new and better ones, and those in turn by frameworks better still, for who will be so brash as to assert that the feeble conceptual achievements of our adolescent species comprise an exhaustive account of anything at all? If we put aside this conceit, then the only alternatives to intertheoretic reduction are epistemic stagnation or the outright elimination of old frameworks as wholly false and illusory.

2   *Theoretical Change and Perceptual Change*

Esoteric properties and arcane theoretical frameworks are not the only things that occasionally enjoy intertheoretic reduction. Observable properties and commonsense conceptual frameworks can also enjoy smooth reduction. Thus, being a middle-A sound is identical with being an oscillation in air pressure at 440 hertz; being red is identical with having a certain triplet of electromagnetic reflectance efficiencies; being warm is identical with having a certain mean level of microscopically embodied energies, and so forth.

Moreover, the relevant reducing theory is capable of replacing the old framework not just in contexts of calculation and inference. *It should be appreciated that the reducing theory can displace the old framework in all of its observational contexts as well.* Given the reality of the property identities just listed, it is quite open to us to begin framing our spontaneous perceptual reports in the language of the more sophisticated reducing theory. It is even desirable that we begin doing this, since the new vocabulary observes distinctions which are in fact within the discriminatory reach of our native perceptual systems, though those objective distinctions go unmarked and unnoticed from within the old framework. We can thus make more penetrating use of our native perceptual equipment. Such displacement is also desirable for a second reason: the greater inferential or computational power of the new conceptual framework. We can thus make better inferential *use* of our new perceptual judgments than we made of our old ones.

It is difficult to convey in words the enormity of such perceptual transformations and the naturalness of the new conceptual regime once established. A nonscientific example may help to get the initial point across.

Consider the enormous increase in discriminatory skill that spans the gap between an untrained child's auditory apprehension of a symphony, and the same person's apprehension of the same symphony forty years later, when hearing it in his capacity as conductor of the orchestra performing it. What was before a seamless voice is now a mosaic of distinguishable elements. What was before a dimly apprehended tune is now a rationally structured sequence of distinguishable and identifiable chords supporting an appropriately related melody line. The matured musician hears an entire world of structured detail, concerning which the child is both dumb and deaf.

Other modalities provide comparable examples. Consider the practiced and chemically sophisticated wine taster, for whom the category "red wine" used by most of us divides into a network of fifteen or twenty distinguishable elements: ethanol, glycol, fructose, sucrose, tannin, acid, carbon dioxide, and so forth, whose relative concentrations he can estimate with accuracy. Or consider the astronomer, for whom the speckled black dome of her youth has become a visible abyss, scattering nearby planets, yellow dwarf stars, blue and red giants, distant globular clusters, and even a remote galaxy or two, all discriminable as such and locatable in three-dimensional space with her unaided (repeat: *unaided*) eye.

In each of these cases, what is finally mastered is a conceptual framework—whether musical, chemical, or astronomical—a framework that embodies far more wisdom about the relevant sensory domain than is immediately apparent to untutored discrimination. Such frameworks are characteristically a cultural heritage, pieced together over many generations, and their mastery supplies a richness and penetration to our sensory lives that would be impossible in their absence. (The role of theory in perception and the systematic enhancement of perception through theoretical progress are examined at length in P. M. Churchland 1979, sections 1 through 6.)

Our *introspective* lives are already the extensive beneficiaries of this phenomenon. The introspective discriminations we make are for the most part learned; they are acquired with practice and experience, often quite slowly. And the specific discriminations we learn to make are those it is useful for us to make. Generally, those are the discriminations that others are already making, the discriminations embodied in the psychological vocabulary of the language we learn. The conceptual framework for psychological states that is embedded in ordinary language is a modestly sophisticated theoretical achievement in its own right, and it shapes our matured introspection profoundly. If it embodied substantially *less* wisdom in its categories and connecting generalizations, our introspective apprehension of our internal states and activities would be much diminished, though our native discriminatory mechanisms remain the same. Correlatively, if folk psychology embodied substantially *more* wisdom about our inner nature than it actually does, our introspective discrimination and recognition could be very much *greater* than it is, though our native discriminatory mechanisms remain unchanged.

This brings me to the central positive suggestion of this paper. Consider now the possibility of learning to describe, conceive, and introspectively apprehend the teeming intricacies of our inner lives within the conceptual framework of a matured neuroscience, a neuroscience that successfully reduces, either smoothly or roughly, our commonsense folk psychology. Suppose we trained our native mechanisms to make a new and more detailed set of discriminations, a set that corresponded not to the primitive psychological taxonomy of ordinary language, but to some more penetrating taxonomy of states drawn from a completed neuroscience. And suppose we trained ourselves to respond to that reconfigured discriminative activity with judgments that were framed, as a matter of course, in the appropriate concepts from neuroscience. (I believe it was Paul K. Feyerabend and Richard Rorty who first identified and explored this suggestion. See Feyerabend 1963a and Rorty 1965. This occurred in a theoretical environment prepared largely by Sellars 1956. The idea has been explored more recently in P. M. Churchland 1979 and in chapter 1 above.)

If the examples of the symphony conductor (who can hear the Am7 chords), the enologist (who can see and taste the glycol), and the astronomer (who can see the temperature of a blue giant star) provide a fair parallel, then the enhancement in our introspective vision could approximate a revelation. Dopamine levels in the limbic system, the spiking frequencies in specific neural pathways. resonances in the nth layer of the occipital cortex, inhibitory feedback to the lateral geniculate nucleus, and countless other neurophysical nicities could be moved into the objective focus of our introspective discrimination, just as Gm7 chords and Adim chords are moved into the objective focus of a trained musician's auditory discrimination. We will of course have to *learn* the conceptual framework of a matured neuroscience in order to pull this off. And we will have to *practice* its non-inferential application. But that seems a small price to pay for the quantum leap in self-apprehension.

All of this suggests that there is no problem at all in conceiving the eventual reduction of mental states and properties to neurophysiological states and properties. A matured and successful neuroscience need only include, or prove able to define, a taxonomy of kinds with a set of embedding laws that faithfully mimics the taxonomy and causal generalizations of *folk* psychology. Whether future neuroscientific theories will prove able to do this is a wholly empirical question, not to be settled a priori. The evidence for a positive answer is substantial and familiar, and it centers on the growing explanatory success of the several neurosciences.

But there is negative evidence as well; I have even urged some of it myself (1981a). My negative arguments there center on the explanatory and predictive poverty of folk psychology, and they question whether it has the categorial integrity to *merit* the reductive preservation of its familiar ontology. That line suggests substantial revision or outright elimination as the eventual fate of our mentalistic ontology. The qualia-based arguments of Nagel, Jackson, and Robinson, however, take a quite different line. They find no fault with folk psychology. Their concern is with the explanatory and descriptive poverty of any possible *neuroscience*, and their line suggests that emergence is the correct story for our mentalistic ontology. Let us now examine their arguments.

3   Thomas Nagel's Arguments

For Thomas Nagel, it is the phenomenological features of our experiences, the properties or *qualia* displayed by our sensations, that constitute a problem for the reductive aspirations of any materialistic neuroscience. In his classic position paper (1974), I find three distinct arguments in support of the view that such properties will never find any plausible or adequate reduction within the framework of a matured neuroscience. All three arguments are beguiling, but all three, I shall argue, are unsound.

The first argument
What makes the proposed reduction of mental phenomena different from reductions elsewhere in science, says Nagel, is that

> it is impossible to exclude the phenomenological features of experience from a reduction, in the same way that one excludes the phenomenal features of an ordinary substance from a physical or chemical reduction of it—namely, by explaining them as effects on the minds of human observers. (1974, p. 437)

The reason it is impossible to exclude them, continues Nagel, is that the phenomenological features are essential to experience, and to the subjective point of view. But this is not what interests me about this argument. What interests me is the claim that reductions of various substances elsewhere in science *exclude the phenomenal features of the substance.*

This is simply false, and the point is extremely important. The phenomenal features at issue are those such as the objective redness of an apple, the warmth of a coffee cup, and the pitch of a sound. These properties are not excluded from our reductions. Redness, an objective phenomenal property of apples, is identical with a certain wavelength triplet of electromagnetic reflectance efficiencies. Warmth, an objective phenomenal property of objects, is identical with the mean level of the objects' microscopically embodied energies. Pitch, an objective phenomenal property of a sound, is identical with its oscillatory frequency. These electromagnetic and micromechanical properties, out there in the objective world, are genuine phenomenal properties. Despite widespread ignorance of their dynamical and microphysical details, it is these objective physical properties to which everyone's perceptual mechanisms are keyed.

The reductions whose existence Nagel denies are in fact so complete that one can already displace entirely large chunks of our commonsense vocabulary for observable properties, and learn to frame one's perceptual judgements directly in terms cf the reducing theory. The mean kinetic energy (KE) of the molecules in this room, for example, is currently about 6.2×10^{-21} joules. The oscillatory frequency of this sound (I here whistle C one octave above middle C) is about 524 hertz. And the three critical electromagnetic reflectance efficiencies (at 0.45, 0.53, and 0.63 μm) of this white piece of paper are all above 80 percent. These microphysical and electromagnetic properties can be felt, heard, and seen, respectively. Our native sensory mechanisms can easily discriminate such properties, cne from another, and their presence from their absence. They have been doing so for millennia. The "resolution" of these mechanisms is inadequate, of course, to reveal the microphysical details and the extended causal roles of the properties thus discriminated. But they are abundantly adequate to permit the reliable discrimination of the properties at issue. (See my 1979, sections 2 through 6. See also Paul and Patricia Churchland 1981b, pp. 128–130 [this volume, chapter 2, pp. 30–31].)

On this view, the standard perceptual properties are not "secondary" properties at all, in the standard sense that implies that they have no real existence save *inside* the minds of human observers. On the contrary, they are as objective as you please, with a wide variety of objective causal properties. Moreover, it would be a mistake even to *try* to "kick the phenomenal properties inwards," since that only postpones the problem of reckoning their place in nature. We shall only confront them again later as we address the place in nature of mental phenomena. And as Nagel correctly points out, the relocation dodge is no longer open to us once the problematic properties are already located within the mind.

Nagel concludes from this that subjective qualia are unique in being immune from the sort of reductions found elsewhere in science. I draw a very different conclusion. The *objective* qualia (redness, warmth, etc.) should never have been "kicked inwards to the minds of observers" in the first place. They should be confronted squarely, and they should be reduced where they stand: *out*side the human observer. As we saw, this can and has in fact been done. If objective phenomenal properties are so treated, then subjective qualia can be confronted with parallel forthrightness, and can be reduced where *they* stand: *in*side the human observer. So far then, the external and the internal cases are not different: they are parallel after all.

The second argument
A second argument urges the point that the intrinsic character of experiences, the qualia of sensations, are essentially accessible from

only a single point of view, the subjective point of view of the experiencing subject. The properties of physical brain states, by contrast, are accessible from a variety of entirely objective points of view. We cannot hope adequately to account for the former, therefore, in terms of properties appropriate to the latter domain. (see Nagel 1974, pp. 442–444.)

This somewhat diffuse argument appears to be an instance of the following argument.

(1)   The qualia of my sensations are directly known by me, by introspection, as elements of my conscious self.

(2)   The properties of my brain states are *not* directly known by me, by introspection, as elements of my conscious self.

∴ (3)   The qualia of my sensations ≠ the properties of my brain states.

And perhaps there is a second argument here as well, a complement to the first:

(1)   The properties of my brain states are known-by-the-various-external-senses, as having such and such physical properties.

(2)   The qualia of my sensations are *not* known-by-the-various-external-senses, as having such and such physical properties.

∴ (3)   The qualia of my sensations ≠ the properties of my brain states.

The argument form here is apparently

(1) Fa

(2) $\sim Fb$

∴ (3) $a \neq b$.

Given Leibniz's Law and the extensional nature of the property F, this is a valid argument form. But in the examples at issue, F is obviously not an extensional property. The fallacy committed in both cases is amply illustrated in the following parallel arguments.

(1)   Hitler is widely recognized as a mass murderer.

(2)   Adolf Schicklgruber is *not* widely recognized as a mass murderer.

∴ (3)   Hitler ≠ Adolf Schicklgruber.

or,

> (1) Aspirin is known by John to be a pain reliever.
>
> (2) Acetylsalicylic acid is *not* known by John to be a pain reliever.
>
> ∴ (3) Aspirin ≠ acetylsalicylic acid.

or, to cite an example very close to the case at issue,

> (1) Temperature is known by me, by tactile sensing, as a feature of material objects.
>
> (2) Mean molecular kinetic energy is *not* known by me, by tactile sensing, as a feature of material objects.
>
> ∴ (3) Temperature ≠ mean molecular kinetic energy.

The problem with all of these arguments is that the "property" ascribed in premise (1) and witheld in premise (2) consists only in the subject item's being *recognized, perceived,* or *known* as something, *under some specific description or other.* Such apprehension is not a genuine feature of the item itself, fit for divining identities, since one and the same subject may be successfully recognized under one description (e.g., 'qualia of my mental state'), and yet fail to be recognized under another, equally accurate, coreferential description (e.g., 'property of my brain state'). In logician's terms, the propositional function, 'x is known (perceived, recognized) by me, as an F' is one of a large number of *intensional contexts* whose distinguishing feature is that they do not always retain the same truth value through substitution of a coreferential or coextensive term for whatever holds the place of 'x'. Accordingly, that such a context (i.e., the one at issue) should show a difference in truth value for two terms 'a' and 'b' (i.e., 'qualia of my sensations' and 'property of my brainstates') is therefore hardly grounds for concluding that 'a' and 'b' cannot be coreferential or coextensive terms! (I believe it was Richard Brandt and Jaegwon Kim (1967) who first identified this fallacy specifically in connection with the identity theory.)

This objection is decisive, I think, but it does not apply to a different version of the argument, which we must also consider. It may be urged that one's brain states are more than merely not (yet) known by introspection: they are not know*able* by introspection under any circumstances. In correspondence, Thomas Nagel has advised me that what he wishes to defend is the following *modalized* version of the argument.

> (1) My mental states are knowable by me by introspection.

(2)   My brain states are *not* knowable by me by introspection.

∴ (3)   My mental states ≠ my brain states.

Here Nagel will insist that being knowable by me by introspection is a genuine relational property of a thing, and that this version of the argument is free of the intensional fallacy discussed above.

And so it is. But now the reductionist is in a position to insist that the argument contains a false premise: premise (2). At the very least, he can insist that (2) begs the question. For if mental states are indeed identical with brain states, then it is really brain states that we have been introspecting all along, though without appreciating their fine-grained nature. And if we can learn to think of and recognize those states under their familiar mentalistic descriptions—*as all of us have*—then we can certainly learn to think of and recognize them under their more penetrating neurophysiological descriptions. Brain states, that is, are indeed know*able* by introspection, and Nagel's argument commits the same error instanced below.

(1)   Temperature is knowable by tactile sensing.

(2)   Mean molecular kinetic energy is *not* knowable by tactile sensing.

∴ (3)   Temperature ≠ mean molecular kinetic energy.

Here the conclusion is known to be false. Temperature is indeed mean molecular kinetic energy. Since the argument is valid, it must therefore have a false premise. Premise (2) is clearly the stinker. Just as one can learn to feel that the summer air is about 70°F, or 21°C, so one can learn to feel that the mean KE of its molecules is about 6.2×10^{-21} joules, for whether we realize it or not, that is the property our native discriminatory mechanisms are keyed to. And if one can come to know, by feeling, the mean KE of atmospheric molecules, why is it unthinkable that one might come to know, by introspection, the states of one's brain? (What would that feel like? It would feel exactly the same as introspecting the states of one's mind, since they are one and the same states. One would simply employ a different and more penetrating conceptual framework in their description.)

One must be careful, in evaluating the plausibility of Nagel's second premise, to distinguish it from the second premise of the very first version of the argument, the version that commits the intensional fallacy. My guess is that Nagel has profited somewhat from the ambiguity here. For in the first version, both premises are true. And in the second version, the argument is valid. Neither version, however, meets both conditions.

The matter of introspecting one's brain states will arise once more in the final section of this paper. For now, let us move on.

The third argument
The last argument here is the one most widely associated with Nagel's paper. The leading example is the (mooted) character of the experiences enjoyed by an alien creature such as a bat. The claim is that, no matter how much one knew about the bat's neurophysiology and its interaction with the physical world, one could still not know, nor perhaps even imagine, what it is like to be a bat. Even total knowledge of the physical details still leaves something out. The lesson drawn is that the reductive aspirations of neurophysiology are doomed to dash themselves, unrealized, against the impenetrable keep of subjective qualia. (see Nagel 1974, pp. 438ff.)

This argument is almost identical to an argument put forward in a recent paper by Frank Jackson (1982). Since Jackson's version deals directly with humans, I shall confront the problem as he formulates it.

4 Jackson's Knowledge Argument

Imagine a brilliant neuroscientist named Mary who has lived her entire life in a room that is rigorously controlled to display only various shades of black, white, and grey. She learns about the outside world by means of a black/white television monitor, and being brilliant, she manages to transcend these obstacles. She becomes the world's greatest neuroscientist, all from within this room. In particular, she comes to know everything there is to know about the physical structure and activity of the brain and its visual system, of its actual and possible states.

But there would still be something she did *not* know, and could not even imagine, about the actual experiences of all the other people who live outside her black/white room, and about her possible experiences were she finally to leave her room: the nature of the experience of seeing a ripe tomato, what it is like to see red or have a sensation-of-red. Therefore, complete knowledge of the physical facts of visual perception and its related brain activity *still leaves something out*. Hence, materialism cannot give an adequate reductionist account of all mental phenomena.

To give a conveniently tightened version of this argument,

   (1) Mary knows everything there is to know about brain states and their properties.

(2) It is not the case that Mary knows everything there is to know about sensations and their properties.

Therefore, by Leibniz's Law,

(3) Sensations and their properties ≠ brain states and their properties

It is tempting to insist that we here confront just another instance of the intensional fallacy discussed earlier, but Jackson's defenders (e.g., Campbell 1983) insist that 'knows *about*' is a perfectly transparent, entirely extensional context. Let us suppose that it is. We can, I think, find at least two other shortcomings in this sort of argument.

The first shortcoming
This defect is simplicity itself. 'Knows about' may be transparent in both premises, but it is not *univocal* in both premises. (David Lewis [1983] and Laurence Nemirow [1980] have both raised this same objection, though their analysis of the ambiguity at issue differs from mine.) Jackson's argument is valid only if 'knows about' is univocal in both premises. But the kind of knowledge addressed in premise (1) seems pretty clearly to be different from the kind of knowledge addressed in (2). Knowledge in (1) seems to be a matter of having mastered a set of sentences or propositions, the kind one finds written in neuroscience texts; whereas knowledge in (2) seems to be a matter of having a representation of redness in some prelinguistic or sublinguistic medium of representation for sensory variables, or to be a matter of being able to *make* certain sensory discriminations, or something along these lines.

Lewis and Nemirow plump for the "ability" analysis of the relevant sense of 'knows about', but they need not be so narrowly committed, and the complaint of equivocation need not be so narrowly based. As my alternative gloss illustrates, other analyses of 'knowledge by acquaintance' are possible, and the charge of equivocation will be sustained so long as the type of knowledge invoked in premise (1) is distinct from the type invoked in premise (2). Importantly, they do seem very different, even in advance of a settled analysis of the latter.

In short, the difference between a person who knows all about the visual cortex but has never enjoyed a sensation of red, and a person who knows no neuroscience but knows well the sensation of red, may reside not in *what* is respectively known by each (brain states by the former, qualia by the latter), but rather in the different *type* of knowledge each has of *exactly the same thing*. The difference is in the manner of the knowing, not in the nature of the thing(s) known. If one replaces the ambiguous occurrences of 'knows about' in Jackson's argument with the two different expansions suggested above, the resulting argument is a clear *non sequitur*.

(a) Mary has mastered the complete set of true propositions about people's brain states.

(b) Mary does *not* have a representation of redness in her prelinguistic medium of representation for sensory variables.

Therefore, by Leibniz's Law,

(c) The redness sensation ≠ any brain state.

Premises (a) and (b) are compossible, even on a materialist view. But they do not entail (c).

In sum, there are pretty clearly more ways of "having knowledge" than having mastered a set of sentences. And nothing in materialism precludes this. The materialist can freely admit that one has "knowledge" of one's sensations in a way that is independent of the scientific theories one has learned. This does not mean that sensations are beyond the reach of physical science. *It just means that the brain uses more modes and media of representation than the simple storage of sentences.* And this proposition is pretty obviously true: almost certainly the brain uses a considerable variety of modes and media of representation, perhaps hundreds of them. Jackson's argument, and Nagel's, exploit this variety illegitimately: both arguments equivocate on 'knows about'.

This criticism is supported by the observation that, if Jackson's form of argument were sound, it would prove far too much. Suppose that Jackson were arguing not against materialism, but against dualism: against the view that there exists a nonmaterial substance—call it 'ectoplasm'—whose hidden constitution and nomic intricacies ground all mental phenomena. Let our cloistered Mary be an "ectoplasmologist" this time, and let her know$_1$ (by description) everything there is to know about the ectoplasmic processes underlying vision. There would still be something she did not know$_2$ (by acquaintance): what it is like to see red. Dualism is therefore inadequate to account for all mental phenomena.

This argument is as plausible as Jackson's, and for the same reason: it exploits the same equivocation. But the truth is, such arguments show nothing, one way or the other, about how mental phenomena might be accounted for.

The second shortcoming
There is a further shortcoming with Jackson's argument, one of profound importance for understanding one of the most exciting consequences to be expected from a successful neuroscientific account of
mind. I draw your attention to the assumption that even a utopian
knowledge of neuroscience *must* leave Mary hopelessly in the dark
about the subjective qualitative nature of sensations not yet enjoyed.
It is true, of course, that no sentence of the form '*x* is a sensation-of-
red' will be deducible from premises restricted to the language of
neuroscience. But this is no point against the reducibility of phenomenological properties. As we saw in section 1, direct deducibility
is an intolerably strong demand on reduction, and if this is all the
objection comes to, then there is no objection worth addressing.
What the defender of emergent qualia must have in mind here, I
think, is the claim that Mary could not even *imagine* what the relevant
experience would be like, despite her exhaustive neuroscientific
knowledge, and hence, that she must still be missing certain crucial
information.

This claim, however, is simply false. Given the truth of premise (1),
premise (2) seems plausible to Jackson, Nagel, and Robinson only
because none of these philosophers has adequately considered how
much one might know if, as premise (1) asserts, one knew *everything*
there is to know about the physical brain and nervous system. In
particular, none of these philosophers has even begun to consider the
changes in our introspective apprehension of our internal states that
could follow upon a wholesale revision in our conceptual framework
for our internal states.

The fact is, we can indeed imagine how neuroscientific information
would give Mary detailed information about the qualia of various
sensations. Recall our earlier discussion of the transformation of
perception through the systematic reconceptualization of the relevant
perceptual domain. In particular, suppose that Mary has learned to
conceptualize her inner life, even in introspection, in terms of the
completed neuroscience we are to imagine. So she does not identify
her visual sensations crudely as 'a sensation-of-black', 'a sensation-
of-grey', or 'a sensation-of-white'; but rather identifies them more
revealingly as various spiking frequencies in the nth layer of the occipital cortex (or whatever). If Mary has the relevant neuroscientific
concepts for the sensational states at issue (namely, sensations-of-
red), but has never yet been *in* those states, she may well be able to
imagine being in the relevant cortical state, and imagine it with substantial success, even in advance of receiving external stimuli that
would actually produce it.

One test of her ability in this regard would be to give her a stimulus that would (finally) produce in her the relevant state (namely, a spiking frequency of 90 hertz in the gamma network: a "sensation-of-red" to us), and see if she can identify it correctly *on introspective grounds alone*, as 'a spiking frequency of 90 hertz, the kind a tomato would cause'. It does not seem to me to be impossible that she should succeed in this, and do so regularly on similar tests for other states, conceptualized clearly by her, but not previously enjoyed.

This may seem to some an outlandish suggestion, but the following will show that it is not. Musical chords are auditory phenomena that the young and unpracticed ear hears as undivided wholes, discriminable one from another, but without elements or internal structure. A musical education changes this, and one comes to hear chords as groups of discriminable notes. If one is sufficiently practised to have absolute pitch, one can even name the notes of an apprehended chord. And the reverse is also true: if a set of notes is specified verbally, a trained pianist or guitarist can identify the chord and recall its sound in auditory imagination. Moreover, a really skilled individual can construct, in auditory imagination, the sound of a chord he may never have heard before and certainly does not remember. Specify for him a relatively unusual one—an F♯9th*add*13th for example—and let him brood for a bit. Then play for him three or four chords, one of which is the target, and see if he can pick it out as the sound that meets the description. Skilled musicians can do this. Why is a similar skill beyond all possibility for Mary?

Ah, it is tempting to reply, musicians can do this only because chords are audibly structured sets of elements. Sensations-of-color are not.

But neither did chords seem, initially, to be structured sets of elements. They also seemed to be undifferentiated wholes. Why should it be unthinkable that sensations-of-color possess a comparable internal structure, unnoticed so far, but awaiting our determined and informed inspection? Jackson's argument, to be successful, must rule this possibility out, and it is difficult to see how he can do this *a priori*, especially since there has recently emerged excellent empirical evidence to suggest that *our sensations-of-color are indeed structured sets of elements*.

The Retinex theory of color vision recently proposed by Edwin Land (1977) represents any color apprehendable by the human visual system as being uniquely specified by its joint position along three vertices—its reflectance efficiencies at three critical wavelengths, those wavelengths to which the retina's triune cone system is selectively responsive. Since colors are apprehended by us, it is a good hypothesis that those three parameters are represented in our visual systems, and that our sensations-of-color are in some direct way determined by them. Sensations-of-color may turn out literally to *be* three-element chords in some neural medium! In the face of all this, I do not see why it is even briefly plausible to insist that it is utterly impossible for a conceptually sophisticated Mary accurately to imagine, and then reliably pick out, color sensations she has not previously enjoyed. We can already foresee how it might actually be done.

The preceding argument does not collapse the distinction (between knowledge by description and knowledge by acquaintance) urged earlier in the discussion of equivocation. But it does show that the "taxonomies" that reside in our prelinguistic media of representation can be profoundly shaped by the taxonomies that reside in the linguistic medium, especially if one has had long practice at the observational discrimination of items that answer to those linguistically embodied categories. This is just a further illustration of the plasticity of human perception.

I do not mean to suggest, of course, that there will be no limits to what Mary can imagine. Her brain is finite, and its specific anatomy will have specific limitations. For example, if a bat's brain includes computational machinery that the human brain simply lacks (which seems likely), then the subjective character of *some* of the bat's internal states may well be beyond human imagination. Clearly, however, the elusiveness of the bat's inner life here stems not from the metaphysical "emergence" of its internal qualia, but only from the finite capacities of our idiosyncratically human brains. Within those sheerly structural limitations, our imaginations may soar far beyond what Jackson, Nagel, and Robinson suspect, if we possess a neuroscientific conceptual framework that is at last adequate to the intricate phenomena at issue. (See especially chapter 5, section 7, and chapter 9, section 4.)

I suggest, then, that those of us who prize the flux and content of our subjective phenomenological experience need not view the advance of materialistic neuroscience with fear and foreboding. Quite the contrary. The genuine arrival of a materialist kinematics and dynamics for psychological states and cognitive processes will constitute not a gloom in which our inner life is suppressed or eclipsed, but rather a dawning, in which its marvellous intricacies are finally *revealed*—most notably, if we apply ourselves, in direct self-conscious introspection.

Chapter 4

Knowing Qualia: A Reply to Jackson

In a recent paper concerning the direct introspection of brain states (1985b) I leveled three criticisms against Frank Jackson's "knowledge argument." At stake was his bold claim that no materialist account of mind can possibly account for all mental phenomena. Jackson has replied to those criticisms in his 1986. It is to those replies, and to the issues that prompted them, that the present chapter is directed.

1 The Persistent Equivocation

Jackson concedes the criticism I leveled at my own statement of his argument—specifically, that it involves an equivocation on 'knows about'—but he insists that my reconstruction does not represent the argument he wishes to defend. I accept his instruction, and turn my attention to the summary of the argument he provides at the bottom of page 293. Mary, you will recall, has been raised in innocence of any color experience, but has an exhaustive command of neuroscience.

(1) Mary (before her release) knows everything physical there is to know about other people.

(2) Mary (before her release) does not know everything there is to know about other people (because she *learns* something about them on her release).

∴ (3) There are truths about other people (and herself) which escape the physicalist story.

Regimenting further, for clarity's sake, yields the following.

(1) $(x)[(Hx \,\&\, Px) \supset Kmx]$

(2) $(\exists x)[Hx \,\&\, \sim Kmx]$ (viz., "what it is like to see red")

∴ (3) $(\exists x)[Hx \,\&\, \sim Px]$

Here m = Mary; $Kyx = y$ knows about x; $Hx = x$ is about persons; $Px = x$ is about something physical in character; and x ranges over "knowables," generously construed so as not to beg any questions about whether they are propositional or otherwise in nature.

Thus expressed, the argument is formally valid: the salient move is a *modus tollens* that applies the second conjunct of premise (2), '$\sim Kmx$', to the waiting consequent of premise (1), 'Kmx'. The questions now are whether the premises are jointly true, and whether the crucial notion 'Kmx' is univocal in both of its appearances. Here I am surprised that Jackson sees any progress at all with the above formulation, since I continue to see the same equivocation found in my earlier casting of his argument.

Specifically, premise (1) is plausibly true, within Jackson's story about Mary's color-free upbringing, only on the interpretation of 'knows about' that casts the object of knowledge as something propositional, as something adequately expressible in an English sentence. Mary, to put it briefly, gets 100 percent on every written and oral exam; she can pronounce on the truth of any given sentence about the physical characteristics of persons, especially the states of their brains. Her "knowledge by description" of physical facts about persons is without lacunae.

Premise (2), however, is plausibly true only on the interpretation of 'knows about' that casts the object of knowledge as something non-propositional, as something inarticulable, as something that is non-truth-valuable. What Mary is missing is some form of "knowledge by acquaintance," acquaintance with a sensory character, prototype, or universal, perhaps.

Given this prima facie difference in the sense of 'knows about', or the kind of knowledge appearing in each premise, we are still looking at a prima facie case of an argument invalid by reason of equivocation on a critical term. Replace either of the 'K's above with a distinct letter, as acknowledgment of the ambiguity demands, and the inference to (3) evaporates. The burden of articulating some specific and unitary sense of 'knows about', and of arguing that both premises are true under that interpretation of the epistemic operator, is an undischarged burden that still belongs to Jackson.

It is also a *heavy* burden, since the resources of modern cognitive neurobiology already provide us with a plausible account of what the difference in the two kinds of knowledge amounts to, and of how it is possible to have the one kind without the other. Let me illustrate with a case distinct from that at issue, so as not to beg any questions.

Any competent golfer has a detailed representation (perhaps in his cerebellum, perhaps in his motor cortex) of a golf swing. It is a *motor* representation, and it constitutes his "knowing how" to *execute* a proper swing. The same golfer will also have a discursive representation of a golf swing (perhaps in his language cortex, or in the neighboring temporal and parietal regions), which allows him to describe a golf swing or perhaps draw it on paper. The motor and the discursive representations are quite distinct. Localized brain trauma, or surgery, could remove either one while sparing the other. Short of that, an inarticulate golf champion might have a superb representation of the former kind, but a feeble representation of the latter kind. And a physicist or sports physiologist might have a detailed and penetrating representation of the mechanics of a good swing, and yet be unable to duff the ball more than ten feet because he lacks an adequate *motor* representation, of the desired behavioral sequence, in the brain areas that control his limbs. Indeed, if our physicist is chronically disabled in his motor capacities, he may have no motor representation of a golf swing whatsoever. In one medium of representation, his representational achievements on the topic may be complete; while in another medium of representation, he has nothing.

A contrast between "knowing how" and "knowing that" is one already acknowledged in common sense, and thus it is not surprising that some of the earliest replies to Jackson's argument (Nemirow 1980; Lewis 1983) tried to portray its equivocation in these familiar terms, and tried to explicate Mary's missing knowledge solely in terms of her missing some one or more *abilities* (to recognize red, to imagine red, etc.). While the approach is well motivated, this binary distinction in types of knowledge barely begins to suggest the range and variety of different sites and types of internal representation to be found in a normal brain. There is no reason why we must be bound by the crude divisions of our prescientific idioms when we attempt to give a precise and positive explication of the equivocation displayed in Jackson's argument. And there are substantial grounds for telling a somewhat different story concerning the sort of nondiscursive knowledge at issue. Putting caution and qualification momentarily aside, I shall tell such a story.

In creatures with trichromatic vision (i.e., with three types of retinal cone), color information is coded as a pattern of spiking frequencies across the axonal fibers of the parvocellular subsystem of the optic nerve. That massive cable of axons leads to a second population of cells in a central body called the lateral geniculate nucleus (LGN), whose axonal projections lead in turn to the several areas of the visual cortex at the rear of the brain's cerebral hemisperes, to V1, V2, and ultimately to V4, which area appears to be especially devoted to the processing and representation of color information (Zeki 1980; Van Essen and Maunsell 1983; Hubel and Livingstone 1987). Human cognition divides a smooth continuum of color inputs into a finite number of prototypical categories. The laminar structure at V4 is perhaps the earliest place in the processing hierarchy to which we might ascribe that familiar taxonomy. A creature competent to make reliable color discriminations has there developed a representation of the range of familiar colors, a representation that appears to consist in a specific configuration of weighted synaptic connections meeting the millions of neurons that make up area V4.

That configuration of synaptic weights partitions the "activation space" of the neurons in area V4: it partitions that abstract space into a structured set of subspaces, one for each prototypical color. Inputs from the eye will each occasion a specific pattern of activity across these cortical neurons, a pattern or vector that falls within one of those subspaces. In such a pigeon holing, it now appears, does visual recognition of a color consist (see chapters 5 and 9 for the general theory of information processing here appealed to). This recognition depends upon the creature possessing a prior representation—a learned configuration of synapses meeting the relevant population of cells—that antecedently partitions the creature's visual taxonomy so it can respond selectively and appropriately to the flux of visual stimulation arriving from the retina and LGN.

This distributed representation is not remotely propositional or discursive, but it is entirely real. All trichromatic animals have one, even those without any linguistic capacity. It apparently makes possible the many abilities we expect from color-competent creatures: discrimination, recognition, imagination, and so on. Such a representation is presumably what a person with Mary's upbringing would lack, or possess only in stunted or incomplete form. Her representational space within the relevant area of neurons would contain only the subspace for black, white, and the intervening shades of gray, for the visual examples that have shaped her synaptic configuration were limited to these. There is thus more than just a clutch of abilities missing in Mary: there is a complex representation—a processing framework that deserves to be called "cognitive"—that she either lacks or has in reduced form. There is indeed something she "does not know." Jackson's premise (2), we may assume, is thus true on these wholly materialist assumptions.

These same assumptions are entirely consistent with the further assumption that elsewhere in Mary's brain—in the language areas, for example—she has stored a detailed and even exhaustive set of discursive, propositional, truth-valuable representations of what goes on in people's brains during the experience of color, a set she has brought into being by the exhaustive reading of authoritative texts in a completed cognitive neuroscience. She may even be able to explain her own representational deficit, as sketched above, in complete neurophysical detail. Jackson's premise (1), we may thus assume, is also true on these wholly materialist assumptions.

The view sketched above is a live candidate for the correct story of sensory coding and sensory recognition. But whether or not it is true, it is at least a logical possibility. Accordingly, what we have sketched here is a consistent but entirely *physical* model (i e., a model in which Jackson's conclusion is false) in which both of Jackson's premises are true under the appropriate interpretation. They can hardly entail a conclusion, then, that is inconsistent with physicalism. Their compossibility, on purely physicalist assumptions, resides in the different character and the numerically different medium of representation at issue in each of the two premises. Jackson's argument, to refile the charge, equivocates on 'knows about'.

2   Other Invalid Instances

An argument form with one invalid instance can be expected to have others. This was the point of a subsidiary objection in my 1985b paper: if valid, Jackson's argument, or one formally parallel, would also serve to refute the possibility of *substance dualism*. I did not there express my point with notable clarity, however, and I accept responsibility for Jackson's quite missing my intention. Let me try again.

The basic point is that the canonical presentation of the knowledge argument, as outlined on p. 67 above, would be just as valid if the predicate term 'P' were everywhere replaced by 'E'. And the resulting premises would be just as plausibly true if

(1)   'E' stood for 'is about something ectoplasmic in character' (where 'ectoplasm' is an arbitrary name for the dualist's nonphysical substance), and

(2)   the story is altered so that Mary becomes an exhaustive expert on a completed *ectoplasmic* science of human nature.

The plausibility would be comparable, I submit, because a long discursive lecture on the objective, statable, law-governed properties of ectoplasm, whatever they might be, would be exactly as useful, or use*less*, in helping Mary to *know-by-acquaintance* "what it is like to see red," as would a long discursive lecture on the objective, statable, law-governed properties of the physical matter of the brain. Even if substance dualism were true, therefore, and ectoplasm were its heroic principal, an exactly parallel "knowledge argument" would "show" that there are some aspects of consciousness that must forever escape the *ectoplasmic* story. Given Jackson's antiphysicalist intentions, it is at least an irony that the same form of argument should incidentally serve to blow substance dualism out of the water.

Though I am hardly a substance dualist (and neither is Jackson), I do regard substance dualism as a theoretical possibility, one that might conceivably succeed in explicating the psychological ontology of common sense in terms of the underlying properties and law-governed behavior of the nonmaterial substance it postulates. And I must protest that the parallel knowledge argument against substance dualism would be wildly unfair, and for the very same reason that its analogue against physicalism is unfair: it would equivocate on 'knows about'. It would be no more effective against dualism than it is against materialism.

The parallel under examination contains a further lesson. If it works at all, Jackson's argument works against physicalism not because of some defect that is unique to physicalism; *it works because no amount of discursive knowledge, on any topic, will constitute the nondiscursive form of knowledge that Mary lacks.* Jackson's argument is one instance of an indiscriminately *antireductionist* form of argument. If it works at all, an analog will work against any proposed reductive, discursive, objective account of the nature of our subjective experience, no matter what the reducing theory might happen to be. I see this as a further symptom of the logical pathology described earlier. Since the argument "works" for reasons that have nothing essential to do with physicalism, it should "work" against the explanatory aspirations of other ontologies as well. And so it "does." The price of embracing Jackson's argument is thus dramatically higher than first appears. For it makes any scientific account of our sensory experience entirely impossible, no matter what the ontology employed.

3   A Genuinely Nonequivocal Knowledge Argument

We can appreciate the equivocation more deeply if we explore a version of Jackson's argument that does *not* equivocate on 'knows about'. The equivocation can quickly be closed, if we are determined to do so, and the results are revealing. Given that the problem is a variety in the possible forms of knowing, let us simply rewrite the argument with suitable quantification over the relevant forms of knowing. The first premise must assert that, for any knowable x, and for any form f of knowledge, if x is about humans and x is physical in character, then Mary knows(f) about x. The second premise is modified in the same modest fashion, and the conclusion is identical. Canonically,

(1') $(x)(f)[(Hx \ \& \ Px) \supset K(f)mx]$

(2') $(\exists x)(\exists f)[Hx \ \& \sim K(f)mx]$

∴ (3') $(\exists x)[Hx \ \& \sim Px]$

This argument is also formally valid, and its premises explicitly encompass whatever variety there may be in forms of knowing. What can we say about its soundness?

Assume that Mary has had the upbringing described in Jackson's story, and thus lacks any knowledge-by-acquaintance with "what it is like to see red." Premise (2') will then be true, as and for the reasons that Jackson's story requires. What will be the truth value of premise (1') on these assumptions?

Premise (1') is now a very strong claim indeed, much stronger than the old premise (1), and a materialist will be sure to insist that it is false. The reason offered will be that, because of her deprived upbringing, Mary quite clearly *lacks* one form of knowledge of a certain physical aspect of people. Specifically, she lacks a proper configuration of synaptic connections meeting the neurons in the appropriate area of her visual cortex. She thus lacks an appropriately partitioned activation vector space across those neurons, and therefore has no representation, at that site, of the full range of sensory coding vectors that might someday come from the retina and the LGN. In other words, there is something physical about persons (their color sensations, or identically, their coding vectors in their visual pathways), and there is some form of knowledge (an antecendently partitioned prelinguistic taxonomy), such that Mary lacks that form of knowledge of that aspect of persons. Accordingly, premise (1') is false and the conclusion (3') is not sustained.

From a materialist's point of view, it is obvious that (1') will be false on the assumptions of Jackson's story. For that story denies her the upbringing that normally provokes and shapes the development of the relevant representation across the appropriate population of cortical neurons. And so, of course, there is a form of knowledge, of a physical aspect of persons, that Mary does not have. As just illustrated, the materialist can even specify that form of knowledge, and its objects, in neural terms. But this means that premise (1'), as properly quantified at last, is false. Mary does *not* have knowledge of everything physical about persons, in every way that is possible for her. (That is why premise (2') is true.)

There is, of course, no guarantee that the materialist's account of sensations and sensory recognition is correct (although the experimental and theoretical evidence for a view of this general kind continues to accumulate). But neither is Jackson in a position to insist that it must be mistaken. That would beg the very question at issue: whether sensory qualia form a metaphysically distinct class of phenomena beyond the scope of physical science.

To summarize, if we write a deliberately non-equivocal form of Jackson's argument, one that quantifies appropriately over all of the relevant forms of knowledge, then the first premise must almost certainly be false under the conditions of his own story. So, at any rate, is the materialist in a strong position to argue. Jackson's expressed hope for "highly plausible premises" is not realized in (1'). The original premise (1) was of course much more plausible. But it failed to sustain a valid argument, and it was plausible only because it failed to address all the relevant forms of knowledge.

4   Converting a Third-Person Account into a First-Person Account

My final objection to Jackson was aimed more at breaking the grip of the ideology behind his argument than at the argument itself. That ideology includes a domain of properties—the qualia of subjective experience—that are held to be metaphysically distinct from the objective physical properties addressed by orthodox science. It is not a surprise, then, on this view, that one might know all physical facts, and yet be ignorant of some domain of these nonphysical qualia. The contrast between what is known and what is not known simply reflects an antecedent metaphysical division in the furniture of the world.

But there is another way to look at the situation, one that finds no such division. Our capacity for recognizing a range of (currently) inarticulable features in our subjective experience is easily explained on materialist principles; the relevant sketch appears earlier in this essay and elsewhere in this volume (chapter 5, section 7). Our discursive inarticulation of those features is no surprise either, and signifies nothing about their metaphysical status (chapter 10, section 5). Indeed, that veil of inarticulation may itself be swept aside by suitable learning. What we are now able spontaneously to report about our internal states and cognitive activities need not define the limit on what we might be able to report, spontaneously and accurately, if we were taught a more appropriate conceptual scheme in which to express our discriminations. In closing, let me again urge on Jackson this exciting possibility.

The intricacies of brain function may be subjectively opaque to us now, but they need not remain that way forever. Neuroscience may appear to be defective in providing a purely "third-person account" of mind, but only familiarity of idiom and spontaneity of conceptual response are required to make it a "first-person account" as well. *What makes an account a "first-person account" is not the content of that account, but the fact that one has learned to use it as the vehicle of spontaneous conceptualization in introspection and self-description.* We all of us, as children, learned to use the framework of current folk psychology in this role. But it is entirely possible for a person or culture to learn and use some other framework in that role, the framework of cognitive neuroscience, perhaps. Given a deep and practiced familiarity with the developing idioms of cognitive neurobiology, we might learn to discriminate by introspection the coding vectors in our internal axonal pathways, the activation patterns across salient neural populations, and myriad other things besides.

Should that ever happen, it would then be obvious to everyone who had made the conceptual shift that a completed cognitive neuroscience would constitute not a pinched and exclusionary picture of human consciousness, one blind to the subjective dimension of self, as Jackson's argument suggests. Rather, it would be the vehicle of a grand reconstruction and expansion of our subjective consciousness, since it would provide us with a conceptual framework that, unlike folk psychology, is at last equal to the kinematical and dynamical intricacies of the world within. (See also chapter 1 of this volume, and Churchland 1979, section 16.)

Real precedents for such a reformation can be drawn from our own history. We did not lose contact with a metaphysically distinct dimension of reality when we stopped seeing an immutable, sparkle-strewn quintessential crystal sphere each time we looked to the heavens, and began to see instead an infinite space of gas and dust and giant stars structured by gravitational attractions and violent nuclear processes. On the contrary, we now see far more than we used to, even with the unaided eye. The diverse "colors" of the stars allow us to see directly their absolute temperatures. Stellar temperature is a function of stellar mass, so we are just as reliably seeing stellar masses. The intrinsic luminosity or brightness of a star is tightly tied to these same features, and thus is also visually available, no matter how bright or faint the star may appear from Earth. Apparent brightness is visually obvious also, of course, and the contrast between the apparent and the intrinsic brightnesses gives you the star's rough distance from Earth. In this way is the character and three-dimensional distribution of complex stellar objects in a volume of interstellar space hundreds of light years on a side made visually available to your unaided eyes from your own back yard, given only the right conceptual framework for grasping it, and observational practice in using that framework. From within the new framework, one finds a systematic significance in experiential details that hitherto went largely or entirely unnoticed (compare Feyerabend 1963b).

The case of inner space is potentially the same. We will not lose contact with a metaphysically distinct dimension of self when we stop introspecting inarticulable qualia, and start introspecting "instead" sensory coding vectors and sundry activation patterns within the vector spaces of our accessible cortical areas. As with the revolution in astronomy, the prospect is one we should welcome as metaphysically liberating, rather than deride as metaphysically irrelevant or metaphysically impossible.

Chapter 5

Some Reductive Strategies in Cognitive Neurobiology

A powerful conception of representation and computation—drawn from recent work in the neurosciences—is here outlined. Its virtues are explained and explored in three important areas: sensory representation, sensorimotor coordination, and microphysical implementation. It constitutes a highly general conception of cognitive activity that has significant reductive potential.

1 Introduction

The aim of this paper is to make available to philosophers an intriguing theoretical approach to representation and computation currently under exploration in the neurosciences. The approach is intriguing for at least three reasons. First, it provides a highly general answer to the question of how the brain might *represent* the many aspects of the world in which it lives. Later in the paper I shall explore that answer as it applies to a case familiar to philosophers: the case of the various subjective sensory qualia displayed in one's manifold of sensory intuition. There we shall find the outlines of a genuine neurobiological reduction of the familiar sensory qualia. This application is but one among many, however, as I shall also try to show. One important result is that diverse cases of representation, cases that appear to common sense as being entirely distinct in character, emerge as being fundamentally the same. The approach thus finds unity in diversity.

The second intriguing aspect concerns *computation*. The style of representation to be outlined lends itself uniquely well to a powerful form of computation, a form well suited to the solution of a wide variety of problems. One of them is a problem relatively unfamiliar to philosophers, the problem of sensorimotor coordination. However unfamiliar it may be, this problem is of fundamental importance to

This paper first appeared in *Mind* 95, no. 379 (July 1986).

cognitive theory, since the administration of appropriate behavior in the light of current experience is where intelligence has its raw beginnings. Since sensorimotor coordination is the most fundamental problem that any animal must solve, a means of solution coupled to a general account of representation must surely arouse our curiosity.

Third, the approach is intriguing in the way in which it embraces the mystery of the *microphysical organization* of the brain and the question of how its specific organization *implements* the representational and computational activities that the brain as a whole displays. Here too the approach finds empirical encouragement, for there are at least two major ways of physically implementing the abstract approach to representation and computation proposed, and each of them bears a suggestive resemblance to real neural structures displayed prominently throughout the empirical brain, namely, the laminar organization of the cerebral cortex and the dense orthogonal matrix of the cerebellar cortex.

Overall, the approach constitutes an unabashedly reductive strategy for the neuroscientific explanation of a variety of familiar cognitive phenomena. The propriety of such strategies is still, of course, a keenly debated issue within the philosophy of mind. Historically, this debate has been impoverished by the lack of any very impressive general *theories* from neurobiology, theories that promise actually to effect the neurobiological reduction of some familiar class of cognitive phenomena. At least, if such theories did exist in the outlying literature, they did not manage to make it into the philosophical debates. Given this absence of relevant theory, antireductionist arguments could and often did proceed simply by holding up some aspect of our cognitive life and asking the rhetorical question, "How could *this* ever be accounted for, or even addressed, by any possible story about the nuts and bolts of neurons?"

Such rhetorical questions unfairly exploit the feebleness of our imaginations, since a reply even remotely adequate to the phenomena is not something we can reasonably be expected to think up on demand. As it happens, however, potentially adequate replies have indeed emerged from recent work in cognitive psychology and cognitive neurobiology. Their existence, I believe, must soon shift our attention from the abstract issue of whether any such reduction is possible to the concrete issue of which of various alternative neurobiological theories truly provides the right reduction, and to its long-term consequences for our overall self-conception.

The basic idea, to be explained as we proceed, is that the brain represents various aspects of reality by a *position* in a suitable *state space*, and the brain performs computations on such representations by means of general *coordinate transformations* from one state space to another. These notions may seem arcane and forbidding, but the graphics below will demystify them very swiftly The theory is entirely accessible—indeed, in its simplest form it is *visually* accessible—even to the nonmathematical reader.

I was initially introduced to this theoretical approach by reading the provocative papers of the neuroscientists Andras Pellionisz and Rodolfo Llinas (1979, 1982, 1984, 1985). Their presentations are much more general and more penetrating than the sketch to be provided here. But for didactic reasons, discussion of their ground-breaking work will be postponed until the later sections of the paper. At the outset I wish to keep things as simple as possible.

We open our discussion, then, by confronting three apparently distinct puzzles:

- The mystery of how the brain *represents* the world, and how it performs *computations* on those representations
- The mystery of *sensorimotor coordination*
- The mystery of the brain's *microphysical organization*.

It is especially encouraging that these problems appear to admit of a simultaneous solution. Let us begin by addressing the third mystery, the microstructural mystery.

2 Laminar Cortex, Vertical Connections, and Topographic Maps

The outer surface of the brain's great cerebral hemispheres consists of a thin layer, the classical "grey matter," in which most of their neuronal cell bodies are located (see figure 5.1a). The remaining "white matter" consists primarily of long axons projecting from the cells in this layer to other parts of the brain. If one examines the internal structure of this wrinkled layer, one finds that it subdivides into further layers (see figure 5.1b). Human cortex has six of these layers. Other creatures display a different number, but the laminar pattern is standard.

These further layers are distinguished by the type and concentration of cells within each sublayer, and by the massive intralayer or "horizontal" projections within each sublayer. Moreover, these distinct layers are further distinguished by their proprietary inputs or outputs. The top several layers tend to have only inputs of one kind or another, from the sensory periphery, from other parts of the cortex, or from other parts of the brain. And the bottom layer seems invariably to be an output layer.

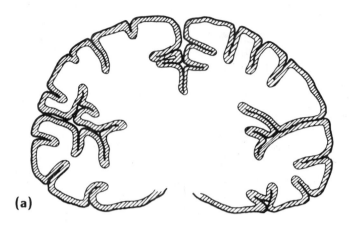

(a)

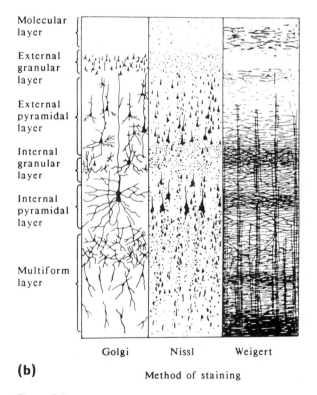

Molecular
layer

External
granular
layer

External
pyramidal
layer

Internal
granular
layer

Internal
pyramidal
layer

Multiform
layer

Golgi   Nissl   Weigert

(b)   Method of staining

Figure 5.1
(*a*) A cross-section of the cerebral hemispheres showing the outer gray layer, the cerebral cortex. (*b*) The internal laminar structure of the cortical layer, as revealed by three different stains. (*c*) Brodmann's areas

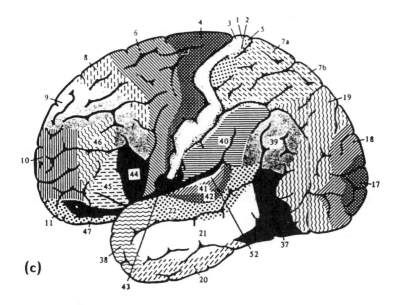

(c)

Finally, these distinct layers are systematically connected, in the fashion of nails struck through plywood, by large numbers of vertically oriented cells that permit communication between the several layers. These vertical cells conduct neuronal activity downwards, from the superficial input layers above to the output layer below.

If we now leave our microscopic edgewise perspective and look at the cortical sheet from the outside, we find that the cortical surface divides into a patchwork of smaller regions (see figure 5.1c). These areas are distinguished to some degree by differences in their laminar cytoarchitectures. An initial taxonomy, into what are called "Brodmann's areas" after their discoverer, is based on this criterion. These areas or subareas of these areas are of further interest because several of them plainly constitute *topographic maps* of some aspect of the sensory or motor periphery, or of some other area of the brain. For example, the neighborhood relations holding between the cells in a given layer of the visual cortex at the rear of the brain correspond to the neighborhood relations holding between the cells in the retina from which they receive inputs. The bundle of axonal projections from the retinal cells to the cortical cells preserves the topographic organization of the retinal cells. The surface of the primary visual cortex thus constitutes a topographic map of the retinal surface.

It is termed a 'topographic map' rather than simply a 'map' because the *distance* relations among retinal cells are generally *not* preserved. Typically, such maps are metrically deformed, as if they were made of rubber and then stretched in some fashion.

Many such maps have been identified. The so-called "visual cortex" (areas 17, 18) has already been mentioned. The upper layer of the somatosensory cortex (area 3) is a topographic map of the body's tactile surface. The lower layer of the motor cortex (area 4) is a topographic map of the body's muscle system. The auditory cortex (areas 41, 42) contains a topographic map of frequency space. And there are many other cortical areas, less well understood as to exactly what they map, but whose topographical re-presentation of distant structure is plain.

This general pattern of neural organization is not confined to the surface of the great cerebral hemispheres. As well, various nuclei of "grey matter" in the more central regions of the brain—for example, the superior colliculus, the hippocampus, and the lateral geniculate nucleus—display this same multilayered, topographically organized, vertically connected structure. Not *everything* does (the cerebellum, for example, is rather different, of which more later), but the pattern described is one of the major organizational patterns to be found in the brain.

Why *this* pattern? What is its functional or cognitive significance? What do these structures do, and how do they do it? We can approach a possible answer to these questions by addressing the second mystery, the problem of sensorimotor coordination.

3   Sensorimotor Coordination

Let me begin by suggesting that vertically connected laminar structures are one of evolution's simplest solutions to a crucial type of problem, one that any sensorimotor system beyond the most rudimentary must somehow solve. In order to appreciate this type of problem, let us consider a schematic creature of a deliberately contrived simplicity.

Figure 5.2b is a plan view of a crablike schematic creature (5.2a) with two rotatable eyes and an extendable arm. If this equipment is to be useful to the crab, the crab must embody some functional relationship, between its eye-angle pairs when an edible object is triangulated, and its subsequent shoulder and elbow angles, so that the arm can assume a position that makes contact with the edible target. Crudely, it must be able to grasp what it sees, wherever the seen object lies.

We can characterize the required arm/eye relationship as follows. First of all, let us represent the input (the pair of eye angles) by a point

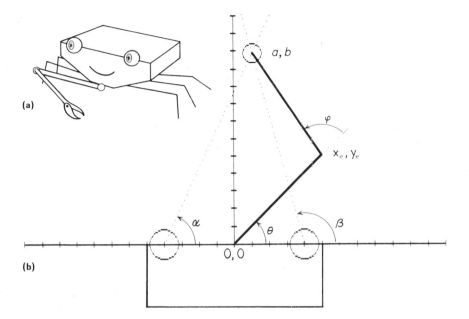

Figure 5.2

in a two-dimensional sensory-system coordinate space or *state space* (figure 5.3*a*). The output (the pair of arm angles) can be also be represented by an appropriate point in a separate two-dimensional *motor state space* (figure 5.3*b*).

We now need a function to take us from any point in the sensory state space to a suitable point in the motor state space, a function that will coordinate arm position with eye position in the manner described. (I here sketch the deduction of the relevant function so that its origin will not be a mystery, but the reader may leap past the algebra without any loss of comprehension. The only point to remember is that we are deducing a suitable function to take us from eye configurations to arm configurations.)

The two eye angles $<\alpha, \beta>$ determine two lines that intersect at the seen object. The coordinates (a, b) of that point (in *real* space) are given by

$$a = -4(\tan\alpha + \tan\beta)/(\tan\alpha - \tan\beta)$$
$$b = -8(\tan\alpha \cdot \tan\beta)/(\tan\alpha - \tan\beta)$$

The tip of the arm must make contact with this point. If we assume that both the forearm and the upper arm have a fixed length of 7 units, the elbow will therefore have to lie at the intersection of two

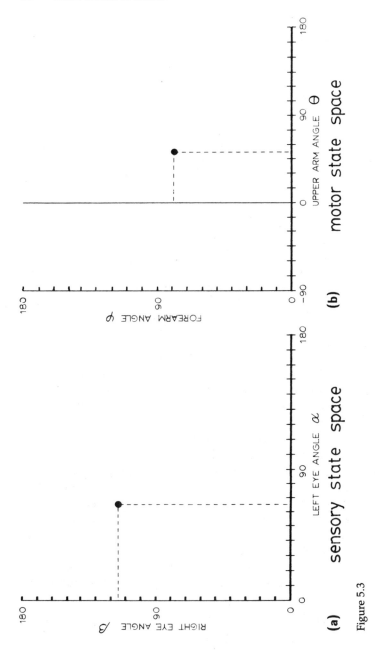

Figure 5.3

circles of radius 7 units: one centered at (a, b), and the other centered at $(0, 0)$, where the upper arm projects from the crab's body. If we solve for the relevant intersection, the real-space elbow coordinates (x_e, y_e) are given by

$$x_e = ((49 - ((a^2 + b^2)^2/4b^2) \cdot (1 - ((a^2/b^2)/((a^2/b^2) + 1))))^{1/2}$$
$$+ (((a/b) \cdot ((a^2 + b^2)/2b))/((a^2/b^2) + 1)^{1/2}))/((a^2/b^2) + 1)^{1/2}$$

$$y_e = (49 - x_e^2)^{1/2}$$

The three points in real space, (a, b), (x_e, y_e), $(0, 0)$, determine the position of the arm, whose upper arm and forearm angles $<\theta, \varphi>$ are finally given by

$$\theta = \tan^{-1}(y_e/x_e)$$
$$\varphi = 180 - (\theta - \tan^{-1}((b - y_e)/(a - x_e)))$$

These are the desired coordinates of the arm in motor state space. The reader will note that the assembled functions that yield them are rather tangled ones.

Tangled or not, if the crab is drawn on a computer screen such that its final arm position (drawn by the computer as output) is the specified function of its eye positions (entered by us as input), then it constitutes a very effective and well-behaved sensorimotor system, especially if we write the controlling program as follows.

Let the program hold the crab's arm folded against its chest (at $\theta = 0°$, $\varphi = 180°$), until some suitable stimulus registers on the fovea of both eyes. The arm is then moved from its initial state-space position $(0°, 180°)$ along a straight line in motor-state space, to its computed target position in motor-state space. This is the state-space position at which, in *real* space, the tip of the arm contacts the triangulation point of the eyes. This arrangement produces a modestly realistic system that reaches unerringly for whatever it sees anywhere within reach of its arm (figure 5.4a–d).

The algebraic representation of the crab's sensorimotor transformation, as represented in the six equations listed earlier, supplies no intuitive conception of its overall nature. A *geometrical* presentation is much more revealing. Let us therefore consider the projection of the active portion of the crab's sensory state space (figure 5.5a) onto the orthogonal grid of its motor state space (figure 5.5b), as imposed by the function under discussion. That is to say, for every point in the displayed sensory grid, we have plotted the corresponding arm-position within the motor grid.

Here we can see at a glance the distortion of the vertical and horizontal lines of sensory space, as projected onto motor space. The

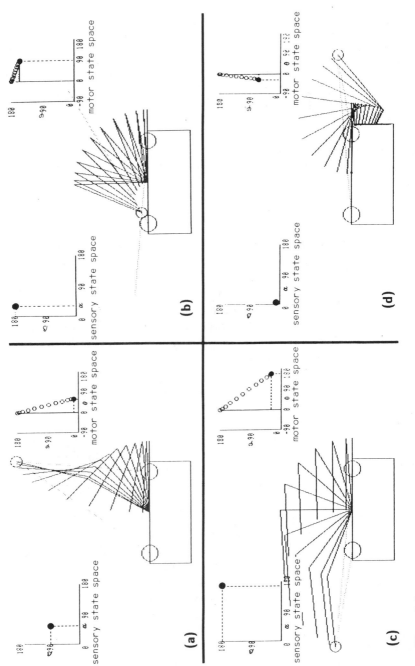

Figure 5.4
The crab's arm in action

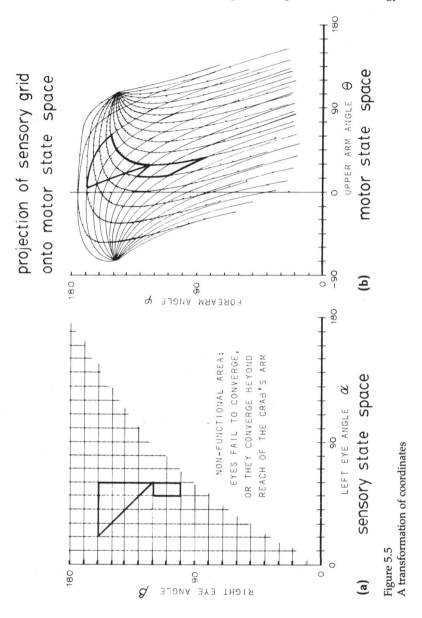

Figure 5.5
A transformation of coordinates

topological features of the sensory space are preserved, but its metrical properties are not. What we see is a systematic *transformation of coordinates*. (The heavy scored triangle and rectangle are drawn in solely to help the reader locate corresponding positions in the deformed and undeformed grids. Note also that the left border or β axis of figure 5.5a shrinks to the left radial point in figure 5.5b, and that the top border of figure 5.5a shrinks to the right radial point in figure 5.5b.)

4   Coordinate Transformation: Its Physical Implementation

The transformation described above sustains effective and realistic sensorimotor behavior. But how could a real nervous system possibly compute such a complex coordinate transformation? It is not realistic to expect it to compute this complex trigonometric function step by step as our computer simulation does. Nevertheless, given their sophisticated sensorimotor coordination, biological systems somehow *must* be computing transformations like these, and others more complex still. How might they do it?

Figure 5.5 suggests a surprisingly simple means. If we suppose that the crab contains internal representations of both its sensory state space and its motor state space, then the following arrangement will effect the desired transformation. Let the crab's sensory state space be represented by a physical grid of signal carrying fibers, a grid that is metrically deformed in real space in just the way displayed in figure 5.5b. Let its motor state space be represented by a second grid of fibers, in an undeformed orthogonal array. Position the first grid over the second, and let them be connected by a large number of short vertical fibers, extending from coordinate intersections in the sensory grid down to the nearest coordinate intersection in the underlying motor grid, as in figure 5.6.

Suppose that the fibers of the sensory grid receive input from the eyes' proprioceptive system, such that the position of each eye stimulates a unique fiber in the upper (deformed) grid. The left eye activates one fiber from the right radial point, and the right eye activates one from the left. Joint eye position will thus be represented by a simultaneous stimulation at the appropriate coordinate *intersection* in the upper grid.

Underneath that point in the upper map lies a unique intersection in the motor grid. Suppose that this intersecting pair of orthogonal motor fibres, when jointly activated, induces the arm to assume the position that is *appropriate* to the specific motor coordinate intersection where this motor signal originates.

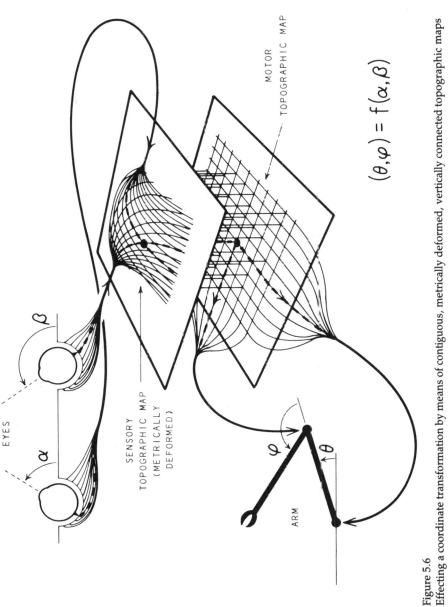

$$(\theta, \varphi) = f(\alpha, \beta)$$

Figure 5.6
Effecting a coordinate transformation by means of contiguous, metrically deformed, vertically connected topographic maps

Happily, the relative metrical deformations in the maps have placed in correspondence the appropriate points in the upper and lower maps. We need now suppose only that the vertical connections between the sensory grid and the motor grid function as *and* gates or threshold switches, so that a signal is sent down the vertical connection to the motor grid just in case the relevant sensory intersection point is simultaneously stimulated by both of its intersecting sensory fibres. Such a system will compute the desired coordinate transformations to a degree of accuracy limited only by the grain of the two grids and by the density of their vertical connections. I call such a system a "state-space sandwich."

Three points are worth noting immediately about the functional properties of such an arrangement. First, it will remain partially functional despite localized damage. A small lesion in either grid will produce only a partial dyskinesia (two permanent "shadows" of fiber inactivity downstream from the lesion), for which a shift of bodily position will usually compensate (by bringing the target's state-space position out of the shadow).

Indeed, we can do even better than this. Let the dimple on the back of the crab's schematic eye (figure 5.6) be replaced by a bar so as to stimulate not one proprioceptive cell, but rather a set of adjacent proprioceptive cells. The position of each eye will then be represented in the upper map by the activation of a *band* of fibers centered on the "correct" fiber. *Joint* eye position will then be registered in the upper layer by a distributed *area* of stimulation, an area centered on the "correct" point. This will cause a corresponding area of stimulation in the bottom grid, and thus a band of stimulation will be sent to each muscle. If the muscles are connected so as to assume a position appropriate to the "mean" fiber within that distributed signal, even if that specific fiber happens to be inactive, then an appropriate motor response will be forthcoming even if the sandwich has suffered the scattered loss of a great many cells. Such a system will be functionally persistent despite widespread cell damage. The quality of the sensorimotor coordination would be somewhat degraded under cell damage, but a roughly appropriate motor response would still be forthcoming.

Second, this system will be *very* fast, even with fibers with biological conduction velocities of between 10 and 100 meters per second. In a creature the size of a crab, in which the total conduction path is less than 10 centimeters, this system will yield a motor response in well under 10 milliseconds. In the crab simulation described earlier, my microcomputer (doing its trigonometry within the software) takes 20 times that interval to produce a motor response on screen, and its conduction velocities are on the order of the speed of light. Evidently, the massively parallel architecture of the state-space sandwich buys it a large advantage in speed, even with vastly slower components.

Third, the quality of the crab's coordination will not be uniform over its field of motor activity, since in the maximally deformed areas of the sensory grid, small errors in sensory registration produce large errors in the motor response (see again figure 5.5b). Accordingly, the crab is least well coordinated in the area close between its eyes, and to its extreme right and left.

All three of these functional properties are biologically realistic. And the sandwich appears biologically realistic in one further respect: it is relatively easy to imagine such a system being *grown*. Distinct layers can confine distinct chemical gradients, and can thus guide distinct morphogenetic processes. Accordingly, distinct topographic maps can appear in closely adjacent layers. But given that the maps are so closely contiguous, and given that they are appropriately deformed, the problem of connecting them up so as to produce a functional system becomes a trivial one: the solution is just to grow conductive elements that are roughly orthogonal to the layers.

Different creatures will have different means of locating objects, and different motor systems to effect contact with them, but all of them will face the same problem of coordinating positions in their sensory state space with positions in their motor state space, and the style of solution here outlined is evidently quite general in nature. In fact, the coordination of distinct biological subsystems by coordinate transformation is a matter that presumably extends far beyond the obvious case of basic sensorimotor coordination. The same strategy may also be useful, or even essential, in the execution of higher cognitive activities, as we shall see later on. The point to be emphasized here is that a state-space sandwich constitutes a simple and biologically realistic means for effecting *any* two-dimensional to two-dimensional coordinate transformation, whatever its mathematical complexity and whatever features—external or internal, abstract or concrete—the coordinate axes may represent to the brain. If the transformation can be graphed at all, a sandwich can compute it. The sensorimotor problem solved above is merely a transparent example of the general technique at work.

Beyond its functional realism, the system of interconnected maps in figure 5.6 is suggestively similar to the known *physical* structure of typical laminar cortex, including the many topographic maps distributed across the cerebral surface. In all of these areas, inputs address a given layer of cells, which layer frequently embodies a metrically deformed topographic map of something or other. And outputs leave the area from a different layer, with which the first layer enjoys massive vertical connections.

I therefore propose the hypothesis that the scattered maps within the cerebral cortex, and many subcerebral laminar structures as well, are all engaged in the coordinate transformation of points in one neural state space into points in another, by the direct interaction of metrically deformed, vertically connected topographic maps. Their mode of representation is state-space position, their mode of computation is coordinate transformation, and both functions are simultaneously implemented in a state-space sandwich.

[Added in 1989: The second and especially the third part of this hypothesis now seem almost certainly mistaken, at least as an account of the cerebral cortex. The cell population of a given layer in a given cortical area is indeed coding state-space positions, but more likely by means of the overall *pattern* of activation levels across the entire population of cells, rather than by the narrow spatial location of maximal cell activation. And the axonal projections from that layer into adjacent cell layers do indeed effect a transformation from one state-space to another, but more probably this is done by means of the matrix-multiplication style of transformation explained in section 6 below, rather than by the simple transfer of an activational hot-spot between mutually deformed maps. The topographic mappings so characteristic of many cortical areas now appear as the occasional artifacts of a deeper coding strategy, the high-dimensional vector coding explained in section 6 below. The discussion of this section remains instructive, however, as a possible account of areas like the superior colliculus, and as an illustration of the relevant computational ideas.]

I can cite not a single cerebral area for which this functional hypothesis is known to be true. The decoding of cortical maps is a business that has only begun. Clear successes can be numbered on the fingers of at most three or four hands, and they are generally confined to the superficial cortical layers. There is a major subcortical area, however, whose upper-level and lower-level maps have been at least partially decoded. This subcortical area does display the general pattern depicted in figure 5.6.

The *superior colliculus* is a phylogenetically very old laminar structure (figure 5.7a) located on the dorsal midbrain. Among other things, it sustains the familiar reflex whereby the eye makes an involuntary saccade so as to foveate (look directly at) any sudden change or movement that registers on the retina away from the foveal center. We have all had the experience of being in a darkened movie theater when someone down in the front row left suddenly ignites a match or

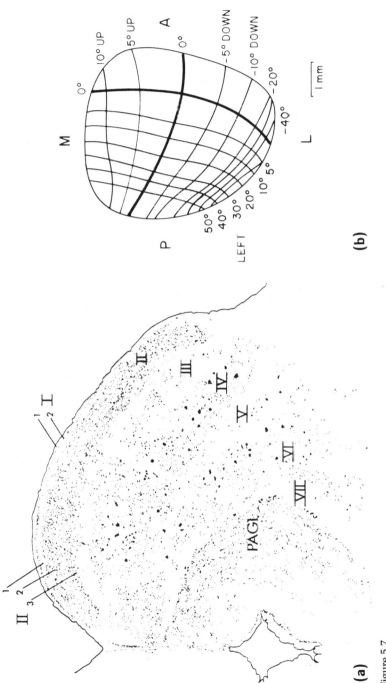

Figure 5.7
(*a*) A projection drawing of a Nissl-stained cross-section of cat superior colliculus illustrating laminar organization. Dots correspond to collicular neurons. From Kanaseki and Sprague 1974; reprinted with permission. (*b*) A retinotopic map, a metrically deformed topographic map of the visual hemifield, in rectangular coordinates, on the superficial layer of the right colliculus of the cat. M = medial; L = lateral; A = anterior; P = posterior. Adapted from Schiller 1984

lighter to light a cigarette. Every eye in the house makes a ballistic saccade to fixate this brief stimulus before returning to the screen. This is the colliculus at work. Appropriately enough, this is sometimes called the "visual grasp reflex."

In humans and the higher mammals the superior colliculus is a visual center secondary to the more important striate cortex (areas 17 and 18 on the Brodmann map) and located at the rear of the cerebral hemispheres, but in lower animals such as the frog or snake, which lack any significant cortex, the superior colliculus (or optic tectum, as it is called in them) is their principal visual center. It is an important center even for mammals, however, and it works roughly as follows.

The top-most layer of the superior colliculus (SC) receives projections directly from the retina, and it constitutes a metrically deformed topographic map of the retinal surface (figure 5.7b) (Schiller 1984; Goldberg and Robinson 1978; Cynader and Berman 1972; Gordon 1973). Vertical elements connect this layer to the deepest layer of the SC. These vertical connections appear to consist of a chain of two or three short interneurons descending stepwise through two intervening layers (Schiller 1984, p. 460, 466), of which more later. Also, the dendrites of some of the deep-layer neurons appear to ascend directly into the visual layer to make synaptic connections with visual cells (Mooney et al. 1984, p. 185). The neurons of the deepest layer project their output axons via two distinct nervous pathways, one of which leads eventually to the pair of extraocular muscles responsible for vertical eye movements, and the other of which leads eventually to the pair responsible for horizontal eye movements (Huerta and Harting 1984, p. 287).

Intriguingly, this underlying motor layer also embodies a topographic map, a map of a state space that represents changes in the contractile position of the ocular muscles (Robinson 1972, p. 1800). Microstimulation by an electrode at a given point in this deepest layer causes the eyes to execute a saccade of a characteristic size and direction, a saccade that moves the fovea into the position formerly occupied by that retinal cell that projects to *the immediately overlying visual cell in the top-most layer of the colliculus* (Robinson 1972; Schiller and Stryker 1972). In other words, the relative metrical deformations in the two maps have placed into correspondence the appropriate points in the upper and lower maps. (This means that the "deformation" seen in figure 5.7b should not of itself be taken as evidence for the state-space sandwich hypothesis. What is crucial is the deformation of the maps relative to each other.)

Finally, any sufficiently strong retinally produced stimulation in that top-most visual map is conveyed downward by the appropriate vertical elements to the motor map, where it produces a saccade of just the size and direction appropriate for foveating the external stimulus that provoked it. The superior colliculus thus appears to be an instance of both the structural and the functional pattern displayed in figure 5.6.

One might expect a biological sandwich to code the position of retinal stimulations with an *area* of stimulation in the upper map, rather than a single point, so as to be functionally persistent in the face of small lesions and scattered cell death, as explained earlier. Activity in the SC does display this pattern (McIlwain 1975; 1984, p. 268). The schematic model of figure 5.6 also predicts that the size and direction of the motor response induced by microstimulation at various points within the collicular sandwich will be a function solely of where in either map the stimulation occurs, and not of the magnitude of the stimulation nor of its vertical position between the two maps. Experimentation has already yielded this result (Robinson 1972; Schiller and Stryker 1972). The superior colliculus, it appears, is a real sensorimotor coordinate transformer of roughly the kind at issue. It foveates on changing or moving visual targets by essentially the same means whereby the schematic cortex of the crab reaches out for triangulated objects.

A word of caution is in order here, since the account just offered does not do justice to the full complexity of the superior colliculus. In mammals, especially the higher mammals, the SC is a tightly integrated part of a larger modulating system that includes inputs from the visual cortex and the frontal eye fields, and outputs to the neck muscles. The functional properties of the entire system are more varied and more subtle than the preceding account suggests, and the job of sorting them out is still underway (Mays and Sparks 1980; Schiller and Sandell 1983). The preceding is submitted as an account of the central or more primitive functions of the SC, at best.

With the examples of the crab's "cortex" and the superior colliculus in mind, it is appropriate to focus on the many other topographically organized, multilayered cortical areas scattered throughout the brain, and ask what coordinate transformations *they* might be effecting. Here it is very important to appreciate that the topographic maps we seek to decode need not, and generally will not, be maps of something anatomically obvious, such as the surface of the retina, or the surface of the skin. More often they will be maps of some *abstract* state space, whose dimensional significance is likely to be opaque to the casual observer, though of great functional importance to the brain. Two nice examples of such abstract maps are the map of *echo delays* in the bat's auditory cortex, and the map of *binaural disparities* in the owl's inferior colliculus (Konishi 1986).

In the case of the crab's schematic cortex, the angular state of an external system (the eyes) is directly mapped onto the angular state of another external system (the jointed arm). But in a creature of any complexity, we can expect a long chain or hierarchy of internal systems interacting with one another, systems that are maps of the output of other internal systems and whose output drives the activities of further internal systems. To understand such maps will require that we understand the function of the other maps in the overall system.

All of this suggests that the brain may boast many more topographic maps than have so far been identified or even suspected. Certainly the brain has a teeming abundance of topographically organized areas, and recent work has expanded the number of known sensory-related maps considerably (Merzenich and Kaas 1980; Allman et al. 1981). All of this further suggests that we will make better progress in trying to understand the significance of the many topographically organized cortical areas when we approach them as maps of abstract but functionally relevant state spaces.

There has been a tendency among neuroscientists to restrict the term "topographic map" to neural areas that mirror some straightforward aspect of the physical world or sensory system, such as the retina, or the surface of the skin. This is unfortunate, since there is no reason for the brain to show any such preference in what it constructs maps of. Abstract state spaces are just as mappable as concrete physical ones, and the brain surely has no advance knowledge of which is which. We should expect it, rather, to evolve maps of what is functionally significant, and that will frequently be an abstract state space.

5   Cortex with More than Two Layers

While we are discussing the biological reality of the laminar mechanism proposed, consider the objection that our model cortex has only two layers, whereas typical human cortex has six layers and, if we count fine subdivisions, perhaps eight or nine in some areas. What are they for?

There is no difficulty in perceiving a function for such additional layers. Let us return again to the superior colliculus, which illustrates one of many possibilities here. Between the visual and motor maps of the superior colliculus there are, in some creatures, one or two intermediate layers (see again figure 5.7). These appear to constitute an auditory map and/or a somatosensory map (a facial or whisker map), whose function is again to orient the eye's fovea, this time toward the source of sudden *auditory* and/or *somatosensory* stimulation (Goldberg and Robinson 1978). Not surprisingly, these intervening maps are each metrically deformed in such a fashion as to be in rough co-ordinate register with the motor map and hence with each other. Altogether, this elegant three- or four-layer topographic sandwich constitutes a *multimodal* sensorimotor coordinate transformer.

Multilayered structures have further virtues. It is plain that maps of several distinct modalities, suitably deformed and placed in collective register within a "club sandwich," provide a most effective means of cross-modal integration and comparison. In the SC, for example, this multimodal arrangement is appropriate to the production of a motor response to the *joint* receipt of faint but spatiotemporally coincident auditory and visual stimuli, stimuli that, in isolation, would have been *subthreshold* for a motor response. For example, a faint sound from a certain compass point may be too faint to prompt the eyes into a foveating saccade, and a tiny movement from a certain compass point may be similarly impotent, but if both the sound *and* the movement come from the same compass point (and are thus coded in the SC along the same vertical axis), then their simultaneous conjunction will indeed be sufficient to make the motor layer direct the eyes appropriately. This prediction is strongly corroborated by the recent results of Meredith and Stein (1985).

Further exploration reveals that multilayered sandwiches can subserve decidedly sophisticated cognitive functions. In an earlier publication on these matters (1986d), I have shown how a *three*-layer state-space sandwich can code, and project, the path of a moving object in such a fashion as to position the crab's arm to catch the moving target on the fly. Evidently, a multilayered cortex can offer considerable advantages.

6   Beyond State-Space Sandwiches

The examples studied above are uniform in having an input state space of only two dimensions and an output state space of only two dimensions. This allows the required coordinate transformation to be achieved by a contiguous pair of sheetlike maps. But what of cases where the subsystems involved each have more than two parameters? What of cases where the coordinate transformations are from an input space of n dimensions to an output space of m dimensions, where n and m are different and both greater than two? Consider, for example, the problem of coordinating the joint angles of a limb with three or more joints, and the problem of coordinating several such limbs with each other. Or consider the problem of coordinating the even larger number of muscles that collectively control such limbs. As soon as one examines the problems routinely faced and solved by real creatures, one appreciates that many of them are far more complex than can be represented by a simple two-dimensional to two-dimensional transformation.

Perhaps some of these more complex problems might be solved by dividing them into a set of smaller ones, problems that can be managed after all by a set of distinct two-dimensional state-space sandwiches, each addressing some slice or aspect of the larger problem (for some specific suggestions in this vein, see Ballard 1986). The predominance of laminar cortex in the brain certainly encourages speculation along these lines. But such solutions, even approximate ones, cannot in general be guaranteed. The brain badly needs some mechanism beyond the state-space sandwich if it is routinely to handle these higher-dimensional problems.

Pellionisz and Llinas have already outlined a mechanism adequate to the task, and have found impressive evidence of its implementation within the cerebellum. The cerebellum is the large structure at the rear of the brain just underneath the cerebral hemispheres. Its principal function, divined initially from lesion studies, is the coordination of complex bodily movements, such as would be displayed in preparing a dinner or in playing basketball. It displays a neural organization quite different from that of the cerebral hemispheres, an organization whose significance may be rendered transparent by the account of Pellionisz and Llinas.

To illustrate this more general mechanism for coordinate transformation, let us consider an input system of four dimensions whose inputs a, b, c, d, are transformed into the values x, y, z, of a three-dimensional output system. As before, the inputs and outputs can each be regarded as points in a suitable state space. Since they are n-tuples, each can also be regarded as a vector (whose base lies at the origin of the relevant state space and whose arrowhead lies at the point specified by the n-tuple).

A standard mathematical operation for the systematic transformation of vectors into vectors is matrix multiplication. Here it is the *matrix* that embodies or effects the desired coordinate transformation. To see how this works, consider the matrix of figure 5.8, which has four rows and three columns.

To multiply the input vector $<a, b, c, d>$ by this matrix, we multiply a times p_1, b times p_2, c times p_3, d times p_4, and then sum the four results to yield x. We then repeat the process with the second column

$$<a, b, c, d> \cdot \begin{bmatrix} p_1 & q_1 & r_1 \\ p_2 & q_2 & r_2 \\ p_3 & q_3 & r_3 \\ p_4 & q_4 & r_4 \end{bmatrix}$$

$$= <x, y, z>$$

Figure 5.8
Vector-to-vector transformation by matrix multiplication

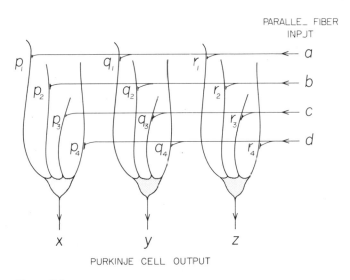

Figure 5.9
Effecting vector-to-vector transformations with a neural net

to yield y, and again with the third column to yield z. Thus results the output vector $<x, y, z>$.

This algebraic operation can be physically realized quite simply by the neural array of figure 5.9. The parallel input fibers at the right each send a train of electrochemical "spikes" toward the waiting dendritic trees. The numbers a, b, c, d represent the amount by which the momentary spiking frequency of each of the four fibers is above (positive number) or below (negative number) a certain baseline spiking frequency. The top-most input fiber, for example, synapses onto each of the three output cells, making a stimulatory connection in each case, one that tends to depolarize the cell body and make it send a spike down its vertical output axon. The output frequency of spike emissions for each cell is determined by the simple *frequency* of input stimulations it receives from all incoming synaptic connections, and by the *weight* or *strength* of each synaptic connection, which is determined by the placement of the synapses and by their cross-sectional areas. These strength values are individually represented by the coefficients of the matrix of figure 5.8. *The neural interconnectivity thus implements the matrix.* Each of the three cells of figure 5.9 "sums" the stimulation it receives, and emits an appropriate train of spikes down its output axon. Those three output frequencies differ from the background or baseline frequencies of the three output cells by positive or negative amounts, and these amounts correspond to the output vector $<x, y, z>$.

Note that with state-space sandwiches the coding of information is a matter of the spatial location of neural events. By contrast, with the matrix-multiplication style of computation under discussion, input and output variables are coded by sets of spiking frequencies in the relevant pathways. The former system uses spatial coding; the latter system uses frequency coding. But both systems are engaged in the coordinate transformation of state-space positions.

The example of figure 5.9 concerns a three-by-four matrix. But it is evident that neither the mathematical operation nor its physical realization suffers any dimensional limitations. In principle, a Pellionisz-Llinas connectivity matrix can effect transformations on state spaces of a dimensionality into the thousands and beyond.

The schematic architecture of figure 5.9 corresponds very closely to the style of microorganization found in the cerebellum (figure 5.10). (For an accessible summary of cerebellar architecture, see Llinas 1975). The horizontal fibers are there called 'parallel fibers', and they input from the higher motor centers. The bushy vertical cells are there called 'Purkinje cells', and they output through the cerebellar nucleus to the motor periphery. In fact, it was from the observation of the cerebellum's beautifully regular architecture, and from the attempt to re-create its functional properties by modeling its large-scale *physical* connectivity within a computer, that Pellionisz and Llinas (1979) were originally led to the view that the cerebellum's job is the systematic transformation of vectors in one neural hyperspace into vectors in another neural hyperspace.

Given that view of the problem, the tensor calculus emerges as the natural framework with which to address such matters, especially since we cannot expect the brain to limit itself to Cartesian coordinates. In the examples discussed so far, variation in position along any axis of the relevant state space is independent of variation along any of the other axes, but this independence will not characterize state spaces with nonorthogonal axes. Indeed, this generalization of the approach, to include non-Cartesian hyperspaces, is regarded by

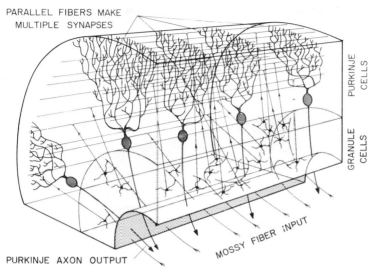

PARALLEL FIBERS MAKE
MULTIPLE SYNAPSES

PURKINJE
CELLS

GRANULE
CELLS

MOSSY FIBER INPUT

PURKINJE AXON OUTPUT

Figure 5.10
A schematic section of the cerebellum (cell population and fiber density reduced for clarity)

Pellionisz and Llinas as one of the most important features of their account, a feature that is essential to understanding all but the simplest coordination problems. Unfortunately, I cannot pursue this feature here.

Three final points about the neural matrix of figure 5.9. First, it need not be limited to computing linear transformations. The individual synaptic connections might represent any of a broad range of functional properties. They need not be simple multipliers. In concert then, they are capable of computing a large variety of nonlinear transformations. Second, a neural matrix will have the same extraordinary speed displayed by a state-space sandwich. And third, given large matrices and/or cell redundancy, such structures will also display a functional persistence despite the scattered loss of their cellular components.

These brief remarks do not do justice to the very extensive work of Pellionisz and Llinas, nor have I explored any criticisms. The reader must turn to the literature for deeper instruction. (For criticisms, see Arbib and Amari 1985. For a reply, see Pellionisz and Llinas 1985.) The principal lesson of this section is that the general functional schema being advanced in this paper—the schema of representation by state-space position, and computation by coordinate transformation—does not encounter implementational difficulties when the representational and computational task exceeds the case of two dimensions. On the contrary, the brain boasts neural machinery that is ideally suited to cases of very high dimensionality. We have, then, at least two known brain mechanisms for performing coordinate transformations: the state-space sandwich specifically for two-dimensional cases, and the neural matrix for cases of any dimensionality whatever.

7   The Representational Power of State Spaces

Discussion so far has been concentrated on the impressive *computational* power of coordinate transformations of state spaces and on the possible neural implementation of such activity. But it is important to appreciate fully the equally powerful *representational* capacity of neural state spaces. The global state of a complex system of n distinct variables can be economically represented by a single point in an abstract n-dimensional state space. And such a state-space point can be neurally implemented, in the simplest case, by a specific distribution of n spiking frequencies in a system of only n distinct fibres. Moreover, a state-space representation embodies the *metrical* relations between distinct possible positions within it, and thus embodies the representation of *similarity* relations between distinct items thus represented. Five examples will illustrate these claims, all of which may be real, and three of which pose problems familiar to philosophers.

The qualitative character of our sensations is commonly held to pose an especially intractible problem for any neurobiological reduction of mental states (see Nagel 1974; Jackson 1982; Robinson 1982). And it is indeed hard to see much room for reductive purchase in the subjectively discriminable but "objectively uncharacterizable" qualia present to consciousness.

Even so, a determined attempt to find order rather than mystery in this area uncovers a significant amount of expressible information. For example, we will all agree that the color qualia of our visual sensations arrange themselves on a continuum. Within this continuum of properties there are similarity relations (orange is similar to red), relative similarity relations (orange is more similar to red than to purple), and betweenness relations (orange is between red and yellow). There are also an indefinite number of distinct "paths" through continuously similar colors that will take us from any given color to a different color.

To this we can add that people who suffer one or another of the various types of color blindness appear to embody a significantly *reduced* continuum of color qualia, one reduced in at least partially specifiable ways (it fails to display a contrast between red and green, or between blue and yellow, etc.). This question of the relative variety of qualia displayed within a given modality raises the point that across the familiar five modalities there is noteworthy variation. For example, though the variety of discriminable color sensations is large, the variety of discriminable taste sensations is even larger, and the variety of discriminable smell sensations is larger still. Such variation reminds us further of the presumed variation across species, as instanced in the canine's extraordinary ability to discriminate, by smell alone, any one of the 3.5 billion people on the planet. One presumes that the canine's continuum of olfactory sensations is somehow much "larger" than a human's, in the sense of containing a greater variety of discriminable types of sensation.

Here, then, are some humdrum facts about the manifold(s) of subjective sensory qualia, facts which a reductive account of mind might attempt to explain. It must do this by reconstructing these facts, in some revealingly systematic way, in neurobiological terms. (For a general account of the nature of cross-theoretic identities and intertheoretic reductions, see chapter 3 and P. M. Churchland 1979.) This possibility will now be explored. For several of the relevant modalities, physiological and cognitive psychologists have already sketched the outlines of such an account, and state-space representations play a prominent role in all of them.

Consider first the abstract three-dimensional "color cube" proposed by Edwin Land (1977), within which every one of the many hundreds of humanly discriminable colors occupies a unique position or small volume (figure 5.11). Each axis represents the eye/brain's reconstruction of the *objective* reflectance of the seen object at one of the three wavelengths to which our cones are selectively responsive. Two colors are closely similar just in case their state-space positions within this cube are close to one another. And two colors are dissimilar just in case their state-space positions are distant. We can even speak of the degree of the similarity, and of the dimensions along which it is reckoned. (See also Zeki 1983.)

If the human brain does possess an internal implementation of such a state space, it has purchased a great deal of representational power at a very low price. For example, if our native discrimination along each axis of Land's color state space is only 10 distinct positions, then a ternary system should be able to represent fully 10^3 distinct colors. If anything, this underestimates our capacities, so the assumption of 10-unit axial discrimination is likely too low. In any case, there is no trouble accounting for our broad discriminatory powers: one's discrimination within Land's state space explodes as the

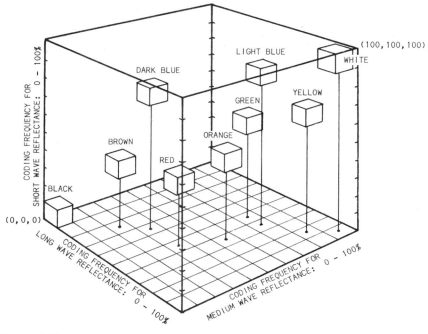

Figure 5.11
Color state space

third power of one's discrimination along each axis. And certainly our peripheral machinery tends to bear out the general hypothesis. All color perception arises from the inputs of exactly three kinds of retinal cones.

All of which suggests the hypothesis that a visual *sensation* of any specific color is literally identical with a specific triplet of spiking frequencies in some triune brain system. If this is true, then the similarity of two color sensations emerges as just the proximity of their respective state-space positions. Qualitative betweenness falls out as state-space betweenness. And, of course, there are an indefinite number of continuous state-space paths connecting any two state-space points. Evidently, we can reconceive the cube of figure 5.11 as an internal "qualia cube." Just think of each axis as representing the instantaneous activity level, or spiking frequency, of one of the three internal pathways for reflectance information.

Finally, if genetic misadventure should deprive a human of one of the standard three pathways, then that person's qualia space should collapse to one of three possible two-dimensional spaces according to which of the three axes is rendered inoperative. A specific and predictable deficit in color discrimination should accompany each loss. And so it does. There are three principal types of color blindness, each corresponding to the loss of one of the three types of cones in the retina. What we have here is the outline of a genuinely reductive account of one domain of sensory qualia.

Our gustatory system appears to exploit a similar arrangement, although here the dimensionality of the state space would appear to be four, since that is the number of distinct kinds of taste receptors in the mouth. Any humanly possible taste sensation, it is therefore conjectured, is a point somewhere within a four-dimensional gustatory state space. Or more literally, it is a quadruple of spiking frequencies in the four proprietary pathways carrying information from the gustatory receptors for distribution to the rest of the brain. If our discrimination along each axis is comparable to that within color space (10 or more units per axis), this means that the variety of different taste sensations will be greater than the variety of different color sensations by roughly an order of magnitude. And so it seems. This state-space approach to gustatory sensations appears in the neuroscience literature as the "across-fiber pattern theory" (Bartoshuk 1978; Smith 1983; Pfaff 1985).

This insight into gustatory space allows us to say something determinate about "what it is like" to be a rat, and a cat. Like humans, rats and cats are mammals, and they also possess a four channelled gustatory system. One difference merits mention, however. One of the four pathways—sometimes labelled the "bitter" pathway, since the four-value code for bitterness requires a high level of activity in that pathway—shows a different sensitivity across the three species. In rats, this pathway shows a narrower range of evocable activity (it is less discriminating) than it does in humans. In cats, it shows a wider range of activity (it is more discriminating).

Consider now the slight contrast, in humans, between the taste of sugar (sucrose) and the taste of saccharin. Sugar is generally preferred because saccharin has a faintly bitter aspect to it. The preceding information about rats and cats suggests that in rats this difference in respect of bitterness will be smaller than it is in humans, and that in cats the difference will be larger. Saccharin, that is, should taste rather more bitter to cats than it does to us. Or so the preceding would suggest. As it happens, the choice behavior of rats does not discriminate between sugar and saccharin: they will eat either indiscriminantly. Cats, by contrast, will eat sugar, but reject saccharin (Bartoshuk 1978).

An account of this same general kind may hold for our olfactory system, which has six or more distinct types of receptor. A six-dimensional space has greater volume still, and will permit even greater feats of discrimination. A six-dimensional space, at 10-unit axial discrimination, will permit the discrimination of 10^6 odors. And if we imagine only a seven-dimensional olfactory space, with only three times the human axial discrimination, which space a dog almost certainly possesses, then we are contemplating a state space with 30^7, or 22 billion, discriminable positions! With such a space, a canine's ability to distinguish by smell any one of the 3.5 billion people on the planet no longer presents itself as a mystery.

I have neither the space nor the understanding to discuss the complex case of auditory qualia, but here too a state-space approach is claimed to be illuminating (see Risset and Wessel 1982). Depending on the researchers and the modality involved, the state-space approach is variously called 'multivariate analysis', 'multidimensional scaling', 'across-fiber pattern coding', 'vector coding', and so forth. But these are all alternative incarnations of the same thing: state-space representations.

Evidently, this approach to understanding sensory qualia is both theoretically and empirically motivated, and it lends support to the reductive position advanced in chapter 3 on the ontological status of sensory qualia. In particular, it suggests an effective means of expressing the allegedly inexpressible. The "ineffable" pink of one's current visual sensation may be richly and precisely expressible as a 95Hz/80Hz/80Hz "chord" in the relevant triune cortical system. The "unconveyable" taste sensation produced by the fabled Australian health tonic Vegamite might be quite poignantly conveyed as a 85/80/90/15 "chord" in one's four-channeled gustatory system (a dark corner of taste-space that is best avoided). And the "indescribable" olfactory sensation produced by a newly opened rose might be quite accurately described as a 95/35/10/80/60/55 "chord" in some six-dimensional system within one's olfactory bulb.

This more penetrating conceptual framework might even displace the commonsense framework as the vehicle of intersubjective description and spontaneous introspection. Just as a musician can learn to recognize the constitution of heard musical chords, after internalizing the general theory of their internal structure, so may we learn to recognize, introspectively, the n-dimensional constitution of our subjective sensory qualia, after having internalized the general theory of *their* internal structure. This analogy has the further advantage of preempting the predictable response that such a reconception of the "internal world" would rob it of its beauty and peculiar identity. It would do so no more than reconceiving musical phenomena in terms of harmonic theory robs music of its beauty and peculiar identity. On the contrary, such reconception opens many aesthetic doors that would otherwise have remained closed.

The familiar "ineffable qualia" are continuous, I believe, with features that clearly do divide into components. Consider the human "module" for facial recognition. We apparently have one, since the specific ability to recognize faces can be destroyed by specific right parietal lesions. Here it is plausible to suggest that there is an internal state-space representation of perhaps 20 dimensions, each coding some salient facial feature such as nose length, facial width, etc. (Police Identi-kits attempt to exploit such a system, with some success.) Even if discrimination along each axis were limited to only 5 distinct positions, such a high-dimensional space would still have an enormous volume (5^{20} positions), and it would permit the discrimination and recognition of billions of distinct faces. It would also embody similarity relations, so that close relatives could be successfully grouped, and so that the same person could be reidentified in photos taken at different ages. Consider two photos of the young and the old Einstein. What makes them similar? They occupy proximate positions in one's facial state space.

Finally, let us turn to a motor example, and let us consider one's "body image," one's continuously updated sense of one's overall bodily configuration in space. That configuration is constituted by the simultaneous position and tension of several hundreds of muscles, and one monitors it all quite successfully, to judge from the smooth coordination of most of one's movements. How does one do it? With a high-dimensional state space, according to the theories of Pellionisz and Llinas, who ascribe to the cerebellum the job of computing appropriate transformations among high-dimensional codings of actual and intended motor circumstances, codings lodged in the input parallel fibers and the output Purkinje axons.

Some of the possibilities here can be evoked by a very simple example. Consider a highly complex and critically orchestrated periodic motion, such as occurs in feline locomotor activity (figure 5.12a). Consider now a three-dimensional joint-angle motor state space for the cat's hind limb, a space in which every possible configuration of that limb is represented by a point, and every possible movement is represented by a continuous path. The graceful step cycle of the galloping cat will be very economically represented by a closed loop in that joint-angle state space (figure 5.12b). If the relevant loop is specified or "marked" in some way, then the awesome task of coordinated locomotion reduces to a simple tracking problem: make your motor state-space position follow the path of that loop.

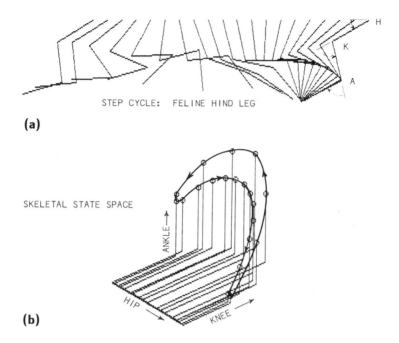

(a)

STEP CYCLE: FELINE HIND LEG

SKELETAL STATE SPACE

(b)

Figure 5.12
A state-space representation of complex locomotor activity

Whether anything in the brain answers to this suggestion is moot. But exploration of this technique, with the ultimate aim of using portable microcomputers as an artificial means of generating effective locomotor activity in paraplegics, is under way in the CNS Lab of Larry Jordan at the University of Manitoba.

Once we have taken the step beyond the cognitive significance of points in two-dimensional state space to the cognitive significance of *lines* and *closed loops* in *n*-dimensional state spaces, it seems possible that we will also find cognitive significance in *surfaces*, and *hypersurfaces*, and *intersections* of hypersurfaces, and so forth. What we have opening before us is a "geometrical," as opposed to a narrowly syntactic, conception of cognitive activity.

8 Concluding Remarks

We have seen how a representational scheme of this kind can account, in a biologically realistic fashion, for a number of important features of motor control, sensory discrimination, and sensorimotor coordination. But has it the resources to account for the so-called higher cognitive activities, as represented by *language use*, for example, and by our propositional knowledge of the world in general?

Conceivably, yes. One might try to find, for example, a way of representing "anglophone linguistic hyperspace" so that all grammatical sentences turn out to reside on a proprietary hypersurface within that hyperspace, with the logical relations between them reflected as spatial relations of some kind. I do not know how to do this, of course, but it holds out the possibility of an alternative to, or potential reduction of, the familiar Chomskyan picture.

As for the set of beliefs that is commonly supposed to constitute a person's knowledge, it may be that a geometrical representation of sentences will allow us to solve the severe problem of tacit belief (Dennett 1975; Lycan 1985). Just as a hologram does not "contain" a large number of distinct three-dimensional images, curiously arranged so as to present a smoothly changing picture of a real object as the hologram is viewed from different positions; so may humans not "contain" a large number of distinct beliefs, curiously arranged so as collectively to present a coherent account of the world.

Perhaps the truth is rather that in both cases a specific image or belief is just an arbitrary projection or "slice" of a deeper set of data structures, and the collective coherence of such sample slices is a simple consequence of the manner in which the global information is stored at the deeper level. It is not a consequence of, for example, the busywork of some fussy inductive machine applying inductive rules for the acceptance or rejection of discreet slices taken singly. Which means that, to understand learning, we may have to understand the forces that dictate directly the evolution of the global data structures at the deeper level.

These highly speculative remarks illustrate one direction of research suggested by the theory outlined in this paper. Just what are the abstract representational and computational capacities of a system of state spaces interacting by coordinate transformations? Can we use it to articulate models for the "higher" forms of cognitive activity? The theory also begs research in the opposite direction, toward the neurophysiology of the brain. Since the brain is definitely not a general-purpose machine in the way that a digital computer is, it may often turn out that, once we are primed to see them, the brain's localized computational tactics can simply be read off its microstructure. There is point, therefore, to studying that microstructure. (For an accessible review of cognitive neurobiology, see P. S. Churchland 1986.)

Taken jointly, the prodigous representational and computational capacities of a system of state spaces interacting by coordinate transformations suggest a powerful and highly general means of understanding the cognitive activities of the nervous system. Especially since the physical mechanisms appropriate to implement such a system are widespread throughout the brain.

Chapter 6

Folk Psychology and the Explanation of
Human Behavior

Folk psychology, insist some, is just like folk mechanics, folk thermo-dynamics, folk meteorology, folk chemistry, and folk biology. It is a framework of concepts, roughly adequate to the demands of every-day life, with which the humble adept comprehends, explains, pre-dicts, and manipulates a certain domain of phenomena. It is, in short, a folk *theory*. As with any theory, it may be evaluated for its virtues or vices in all of the dimensions listed. And as with any theory, it may be rejected in its entirety if it fails the measure of such evaluation. Call this the "theoretical view" of our self understanding.

Folk psychology, insist others, is radically unlike the examples cited. It does not consist of laws. It does not support causal explana-tions. It does not evolve over time. Its central purpose is normative rather than descriptive. And thus, it is not the sort of framework that might be shown to be radically defective by sheerly empirical find-ings. Its assimilation to theories is just a mistake. It has nothing to fear, therefore, from advances in cognitive theory or the neurosci-ences. Call this the "antitheoretical view" of our self understanding.

Somebody here is deeply mistaken. The first burden of this paper is to argue that it is the antitheoretical view that harbors most, though not all, of those mistakes. In the thirty years since the theoretical view was introduced (see especially Sellars 1956; Feyerabend 1963a; Rorty 1965; P. M. Churchland 1970, 1979; and chapter 1), a variety of objec-tions have been leveled against it. The more interesting of those will be addressed shortly. My current view is that these objections moti-vate no changes whatever in the theoretical view.

The second and more important burden of this paper, however, is to outline and repair a serious failing in the traditional expressions of the theoretical view, my own expressions included. The failing, as I see it, lies in representing one's commonsense understanding of hu-

An abridged version of this paper first appeared in *Proceedings of the Aristote-lian Society*, supplementary vol. 62 (1988).

man nature as consisting of *an internally stored set of general sentences*, and in representing one's predictive and explanatory activities as being a matter of *deductive inference* from those sentences plus occasional premises about the case at hand.

This certainly sounds like a major concession to the anti- theoretical view, but in fact it is not. For what motivates this reappraisal of the character of our self understanding is the gathering conviction that little or *none* of human understanding consists of stored sentences, not even the prototypically *scientific* understanding embodied in a practicing physicist, chemist, or astronomer. The familiar conception of knowledge as a set of propositional attitudes is itself a central aspect of the framework of folk psychology, according to the reappraisal at hand, and it is an aspect that needs badly to be replaced. Our self understanding, I continue to maintain, is no different in character from our understanding of any other empirical domain. It is speculative, systematic, corrigible, and in principle replaceable. It is just not so specifically *linguistic* as we have chronically assumed.

The speculative and replaceable character of folk psychology is now somewhat easier to defend than it was in the sixties and seventies, because recent advances in connectionist AI and computational neuroscience have provided us with a fertile new framework with which to understand the perception, cognition, and behavior of intelligent creatures. Whether it will eventually prove adequate to the task of replacing folk psychology remains to be seen, but the mere possibility of systematic alternative conceptions of cognitive activity and intelligent behavior should no longer be a matter of dispute. Alternatives are already in the making. Later in the paper I shall outline the main features of this novel framework and explore its significance for the issues here at stake. For now, let me acquiesce in the folk-psychological conception of knowledge as a system of beliefs or similar propositional attitudes, and try to meet the objections to the theoretical view already outstanding.

1   Objections to the Theoretical View

As illustrated in my 1970, 1979, and 1984, a thorough perusal of the explanatory factors that typically appear in our commonsense explanations of our internal states and our overt behavior sustains the quick "reconstruction" of a large number of universally quantified conditional statements, conditionals with the conjunction of the relevant explanatory factors as the antecedent and the relevant explanandum as the consequent. It is these universal statements that are supposed to constitute the "laws" of folk psychology.

A perennial objection is that these generalizations do not have the character of genuine causal/explanatory laws; rather, they have some other, less empirical status (e.g., that of normative principles or rules of language or analytic truths). Without confronting each of the many alternatives in turn, I think we can make serious difficulties for any objection of this sort.

Note first that the concepts of folk psychology divide into two broad classes. On the one hand, there are those fully intentional concepts expressing the various propositional attitudes, such as belief and desire. And on the other hand, there are those nonintentional or quasi-intentional concepts expressing all of the other mental states, such as grief, fear, pain, hunger, and the full range of emotions and bodily sensations. Where states of the latter kind are concerned, I think it is hardly a matter for dispute that the common homilies in which they figure are causal/explanatory laws. Consider the following.

- A person who suffers severe bodily damage will feel pain.
- A person who suffers a sudden sharp pain will wince.
- A person denied food for any length will feel hunger.
- A hungry person's mouth will water at the smell of food.
- A person who feels overall warmth will tend to relax.
- A person who tastes a lemon will have a puckering sensation.
- A person who is angry will tend to be impatient.

Clearly these humble generalizations, and thousands more like them, are causal/explanatory in character. They will and regularly do support simple explanations, sustain subjunctive and counterfactual conditionals, and underwrite predictions in the standard fashion. Moreover, concepts of this simple sort carry perhaps the major part of the folk-psychological burden. The comparatively complex explanations involving the propositional attitudes are of central importance, but they are surrounded by a quotidean whirl of simple explanations like these, all quite evidently of a causal/explanatory cast.

It won't do, then, to insist that the generalizations of folk psychology are on the whole nonempirical or noncausal in character. The bulk of them, and I mean thousands upon thousands of them, are transparently causal or nomological. The best one can hope to argue is that there is a central core of folk-psychological concepts whose explanatory role is somehow *discontinuous* with that of their fellows. The propositional attitudes, especially belief and desire, are the perennial candidates for such a nonempirical role, for explanations in their terms typically display the explanandum event as "rational." What shall we say of explanations in terms of beliefs and desires?

We should tell essentially the same causal/explanatory story, and for the following reason. Whatever else humans do with the concepts for the propositional attitudes, they do use them successfully to predict the future behavior of others. This means that, on the basis of presumed information about the current cognitive states of the relevant individuals, one can nonaccidentally predict at least some of their future behavior some of the time. But any principle that allows us to do this—that is, to predict one empirical state or event on the basis of another, logically distinct, empirical state or event—*has* to be empirical in character. And I assume it is clear that the event of my ducking my head is logically distinct both from the event of my perceiving an incoming snowball, and from the states of my desiring to avoid a collision and my belief that ducking is the best way to achieve this.

Indeed, one can do more than merely predict: one can control and manipulate the behavior of others by controlling the information available to them. Here one is bringing about certain behaviors by steering the cognitive states of the subject, by relating opportunities, dangers, or obligations relevant to that subject. How this is possible without an understanding of the objective empirical regularities that connect the internal states and the overt behaviors of normal people is something that the antitheoretical position needs to explain.

The confused temptation to find something special about the case of intentional action derives primarily from the fact that the central element in a full-blooded action explanation is a configuration of propositional attitudes in the light of which the explanandum behavior can be seen as sensible or rational, at least from the agent's narrow point of view. In this rational-in-the-light-of relation we seem to have some sort of supercausal *logical* relation between the explanans and the explanandum, which is an invitation to see a distinct and novel type of explanation at work.

Yet while the premise is true—there is indeed a logical relation between the explanandum and certain elements in the explanans—the conclusion does not begin to follow. Students of the subject are still regularly misled on this point, for they fail to appreciate that a circumstance of this general sort is *typical* of theoretical explanations. Far from being a sign of the nonempirical and hence nontheoretical character of the generalizations and explanations at issue, it is one of the surest signs available that we are here dealing with a high-grade theoretical framework. Let me explain.

The electric current I in a wire or any conductor is causally determined by two factors: it tends to increase with the electromotive force or voltage V that moves the electrons down the wire, and it tends to be reduced according to the resistance R the wire offers against their motion. Briefly, $I = V/R$. Less cryptically and more revealingly,

$$(x)(V)(R)[(x \text{ is subject to a voltage of } (V)) \text{ \& } (x \text{ offers a resistance of } (R))$$
$$\supset (\exists I)((x \text{ has a current of } (I)) \text{ \& } (I = V/R))]$$

The first point to notice here is that the crucial predicates—*has a resistance of (R)*, *is subject to a voltage of (V)*, and *has a current of (I)*—are what might be called "numerical attitudes": they are predicate-forming functors that take singular terms for numbers in the variable position. A complete predicate is formed only when a specific numeral appears in the relevant position. The second point to notice is that this electrodynamical law exploits a relation holding on the domain of numbers in order to express an important empirical regularity. The current I is the *quotient* of the voltage V and the resistance R, whose values will be cited in explanation of the current. And the third point to notice is that this law and the explanations it sustains are typical of laws and explanations throughout science. Most of our scientific predicates express numerical attitudes of the sort displayed, and most of our laws exploit and display relations that hold primarily on the abstract domain of numbers. Nor are they limited to numbers. Other laws exploit the abstract relations holding on the abstract domain of vectors, or on the domain of sets, or groups, or matrices. But none of this means they are nonempirical, or noncausal, or nonnomic.

Action explanations, and intentional explanations in general, follow the same pattern. The only difference is that here the domain of abstract objects being exploited is the domain of propositions, and the relations displayed are logical relations. And like the numerical and vectorial attitudes typical of theories, the expressions for the propositional attitudes are predicate-forming functors. *Believes that P*, for example, forms a complete predicate only when a specific sentence appears in the variable position P. The principles that comprehend these predicates have the same abstract and highly sophisticated structure displayed by our most typical theories. They just exploit the relations holding on a different domain of abstract objects in order to express the important empirical regularities comprehending the states and activities of cognitive creatures. That makes folk psychology a very interesting theory, perhaps, but it is hardly a sign of its being *nontheoretical*. Quite the reverse is true. (This matter is discussed at greater length in Churchland 1979, section 14, and 1981a, pp. 82–84.)

In sum, the simpler parts of folk psychology are transparently causal or nomic in character, and the more complex parts have the same sophisticated logical structure typical of our most powerful theories.

But we are not yet done with objections. A recurrent complaint is that in many cases the reconstructed conditionals that purport to be sample "laws" of folk psychology are either strictly speaking false, or they border on the trivial by reason of being qualified by various *ceteris paribus* clauses. A first reply is to point out that my position does not claim that the laws of folk psychology are either true or complete. I agree that they are a motley lot. My hope is to see them replaced entirely, and their ontology of states with them. But this reply is not wholly responsive, for the point of the objection is that it is implausible to claim the status of an entrenched theoretical framework for a bunch of "laws" that are as vague, as loose, and as festooned with *ceteris paribus* clauses as are the examples typically given.

I will make no attempt here to defend the ultimate integrity of the laws of folk psychology, for I have little confidence in them myself. But this is not what is required to meet the objection. What needs pointing out is that the "laws" of folk theories are *in general* sloppy, vague, and festooned with qualifications and *ceteris paribus* clauses. What the objectors need to do, in order to remove the relevant system of generalizations from the class of empirical theories, is to show that folk psychology is significantly *worse* in all of these respects than are the principles of folk mechanics, or folk thermodynamics, or folk biology, and so forth. In this they are sure to be disappointed, for these other folk theories are even worse than folk psychology (see McKloskey 1983). In all, folk psychology may be a fairly ramshackle theory, but a theory it remains. Nor is it a point against this that folk psychology has changed little or none since ancient times. The same is true of other theories near and dear to us. The folk physics of the twentieth century, I regret to say, is essentially the same as the folk physics of the ancient Greeks (McKloskey 1983). Our conceptual inertia on such matters may be enormous, but a theory remains a theory, however many centuries it may possess us.

A quite different objection directs our attention to the great many things beyond explanation and prediction for which we use the vocabulary and concepts of folk psychology. Their primary function, runs the objection, is not the function served by explanatory theories, but rather the myriad social functions that constitute human culture and commerce. We use the resources of folk psychology to promise, to entreat, to congratulate, to tease, to joke, to intimate, to threaten, and so on. (See Wilkes 1981, 1984).

The list of functions is clearly both long and genuine. But most of these functions surely come under the heading of control or manipulation, which is just as typical and central a function of theories as is either explanation or prediction, but which is not mentioned in the list of theoretical functions supplied by the objectors. Though the image may be popular, the idle musings of an impotent stargazer provide a poor example of what theories are and what theories do. More typically, theories are the conceptual vehicles with which we literally come to grips with the world. The fact that folk psychology serves a wealth of practical purposes is no evidence of its being non-theoretical. Quite the reverse.

Manipulation aside, we should not underestimate the importance for social commerce of the explanations and predictions that folk psychology makes possible. If one cannot predict or anticipate the behavior of one's fellows at all, then one can engage in no useful commerce with them whatever. And finding the right explanations for their past behavior is often the key to finding the appropriate premises from which to anticipate their future behavior. The objection's attempt to paint the functions of folk psychology in an exclusively nontheoretical light is simply a distortion born of tunnel vision.

In any case, it is irrelevant. For there is no inconsistency in saying that a theoretical framework should also serve a great many non-theoretical purposes. To use an example I have used before (1986b), the theory of *witches, demonic possession, exorcism,* and *trial by ordeal,* was also used for a variety of social purposes beyond strict explanation and prediction. For example, its vocabulary was used to warn, to censure, to abjure, to accuse, to badger, to sentence, and so forth. But none of this meant that demons and witches were anything other than theoretical entities, and none of this saved the ontology of demon theory from elimination when its empirical failings became acute and different conceptions of human pathology arose to replace it. Beliefs, desires, and the rest of the folk-psychological ontology all are in the same position. Their integrity, to the extent that they have any, derives from the explanatory, predictive, and manipulative prowess they display.

It is on the topic of explanation and prediction that a further objection finds fault with the theoretical view. Precisely what, begins the objection, is the observable behavior that the ontology of folk psychology is postulated to explain? Is it bodily behavior as *kinematically* described? In some cases, perhaps, but not in general, certainly, because many quite different kinematical sequences could count as the same intentional action, and it is generally the *action* that is properly the object of folk-psychological explanations of behavior. In general, the descriptions of human behavior that figure in folk-psychological explanations and predictions are descriptions that *already* imply perception, intelligence, and personhood on the part of the agent. Thus, it must be wrong to see the relation between one's psychological states and one's behavior on the model of theoretical states postulated to explain the behavior of some conceptually independent domain of phenomena (Haldane 1988).

The premise of this objection is fairly clearly true: a large class of behavior descriptions are not conceptually independent of the concepts of folk psychology. But this affords no grounds for denying theoretical status to the ontology of folk psychology. The assumption that it does reflects a naive view of the relation between theories and the domains they explain and predict. The naive assumption is that the concepts used to describe the domain to be explained must always be conceptually independent of the theory used to explain the phenomena within that domain. That assumption is known to be false, and we need look no farther than the special theory of relativity (STR) for a living counterexample.

The introduction of STR brought with it a systematic reconfiguration of all of the basic observational concepts of mechanics: spatial length, temporal duration, velocity, mass, momentum, etc. These are all one-place predicates within classical mechanics, but they are all replaced by two-place predicates within STR. Each ostensible "property" has turned out to be a *relation*, and each has a definite value only relative to a chosen reference frame. If STR is true, and since the early years of this century it has seemed to be, then one cannot legitimately describe the observational facts of mechanics save in terms that are drawn from STR itself.

Modern chemistry provides a second example. It is a rare chemist who does not use the taxonomy of the periodic table and the combinatorial lexicon of chemical compounds to describe both the observable facts and their theoretical underpinnings alike. For starters, one can just smell hydrogen sulphide, taste sodium chloride, feel any base, and identify copper, aluminum, iron, and gold by sight.

These cases are not unusual. Our theoretical convictions typically reshape the way we describe the facts to be explained. Sometimes it happens immediately, as with STR, but more often it happens after long familiarity with the successful theory, as is evidenced by the idioms casually employed in any working laboratory. The premise of the objection is true. But it is no point at all against the theoretical view. Given the great age of folk psychology, such conceptual invasion of the explanandum domain is only to be expected.

A different critique of the theoretical view proposes an alternative account of our understanding of human behavior. According to this view, one's capacity for anticipating and understanding the behavior of others resides not in a system of nomically embedded concepts, but rather in the fact that one is a normal person oneself, and can draw on one's own reactions, to real or to imagined circumstances, in order to gain insight into the internal states and the overt behavior of others. The key idea is that of empathy. One uses oneself as a simulation (usually imagined) of the situation of another and then extrapolates the results of that simulation to the person in question (see Gordon 1986; Goldman 1989).

My first response to this line is simply to agree that an enormous amount of one's appreciation of the internal states and overt behavior of other humans derives from one's ability to examine and to extrapolate from the facts of one's own case. All of this is quite consistent with the theoretical view, and there is no reason that one should attempt to deny it. One learns from every example of humanity one encounters, and one encounters oneself on a systematic basis. What we must resist is the suggestion that extrapolating from the particulars of one's own case is the fundamental ground of one's understanding of others, a ground that renders possession of a nomic framework unnecessary. Problems for this stronger position begin to appear immediately.

For one thing, if *all* of one's understanding of others is closed under extrapolation from one's own case, then the modest contents of one's own case must form an absolute limit on what one can expect or explain in the inner life and external behavior of others. But in fact we are not so limited. People who are congenitally deaf or blind know quite well that normal people have perceptual capacities beyond what they themselves possess, and they know in some detail what those capacities entail in the way of knowledge and behavior. People who have never felt profound grief, say, or love, or rejection, can nonetheless provide appropriate predictions and explanations of the behavior of people so afflicted. And so on. In general, one's immediately available understanding of human psychology and behavior goes substantially beyond what one has experienced in one's own case, either in real life or in pointed simulations. First-person experience or simulation is plainly not *necessary* for understanding the behavior of others.

Nor is it *sufficient*. The problem is that simulations, even if they motivate predictions about others, do not by themselves provide any explanatory understanding of the behavior of others. To see this, consider the following analogy. Suppose I were to possess a marvellous miniature of the physical universe, a miniature I could manipulate in order to simulate real situations and thus predict and retrodict the behavior of the real universe. Even if my miniature unfailingly provided accurate simulations of the outcomes of real physical processes, I would still be no further ahead on the business of *explaining* the behavior of the real world. In fact, I would then have two universes, both in need of explanation.

The lesson is the same for first-person and third-person situations. A simulation itself, even a successful one, provides no explanation. What explanatory understanding requires is an appreciation of the *general patterns* that comprehend the individual events in both cases. And that brings us back to the idea of a moderately general *theory*.

We should have come to that idea directly, since the empathetic account of our understanding of others depends crucially on one's having an initial understanding of oneself. To extrapolate one's own cognitive, affective, and behavioral intricacies to others requires that one be able to conceptualize and spontaneously to recognize those intricacies in oneself. But one's ability to do this is left an unaddressed mystery by the empathetic account. Self-understanding is not seen as a problem; it is other-understanding that is held up as the problem.

But the former is no less problematic than the latter. If one is to be able to apprehend even the *first-person* intricacies at issue, then one must possess a conceptual framework that draws all of the necessary distinctions, a framework that organizes the relevant categories into the appropriate structure, a framework whose taxonomy reflects at least the more obvious of the rough nomic regularities holding across its elements, even in the first-person case. Such a framework is already a theory.

The fact is, the categories into which any important domain gets divided by a learning creature emerge jointly with an appreciation of the rough nomic regularities that connect them. A nascent taxonomy that supports the expression of no useful regularities is a taxonomy that is soon replaced by a more insightful one. The divination of useful regularities is the single most dominant force shaping the taxonomies developed by any learning creature in any domain. And it is an essential force, even in perceptual domains, since our observational taxonomies are always radically underdetermined by our untrained perceptual mechanisms. To suppose that one's conception of one's *own* mental life is innocent of a network of systematic expectations is just naive. But such a network is already a theory, even before one addresses the issue of others.

This is the cash value, I think, of P. F. Strawson's insightful claim, now thirty years old, that to be in a position to pose any question about other minds, and to be in a position to try to construct arguments from analogy with one's own case, is already to possess at least the rudiments of what is sought after, namely, a general conception of mental phenomena, of their general connections with each other and with behavior (Strawson 1958). What Strawson missed was the further insight that such a framework is nothing other than an empirical theory, one justified not by the quasi-logical character of its principles, as he attempted unsuccessfully to show, but by its impersonal success in explaining and predicting human behavior at large. There is no special justificational story to be told here. Folk psychology is justified by what standardly justifies *any* conceptual framework: namely, its explanatory, predictive, and manipulative success.

This concludes my survey of the outstanding objections to the theoretical view outlined in the opening paragraph of the present chapter. But in defending this view there is a major difference between my strategy in earlier writings and my strategy here. In my 1970 paper, for example, the question was framed as follows: "Are action explanations *deductive-nomological* explanations?" I would now prefer to frame the question thus: "Are action explanations of the same general type as the explanations typically found in the sciences?" I continue to think that the answer to this second question is pretty clearly yes. My reasons are given above. But I am no longer confident that the deductive-nomological (D-N) model itself is an adequate account of explanation in the sciences or anywhere else.

The difficulties with the D-N model are detailed elsewhere in the literature, so I shall not pause to summarize them here. My diagnosis of its failings, however, locates the basic problem in its attempt to represent knowledge and understanding by sets of sentences or propositional attitudes. In this, the framers of the D-N model were resting on the basic assumptions of folk psychology. Let me close this paper by briefly exploring how we might conceive of knowledge, and of explanatory understanding, in a systematically different way. This is an important undertaking relative to the concerns of this chapter, for there is an objection to the theoretical view, as traditionally expressed, that seems to me to have some real bite. It is as follows.

If one's capacity for understanding and predicting the behavior of others derives from one's internal storage of thousands of laws or nomic generalizations, how is it that one is so poor at enunciating the laws on which one's explanatory and predictive prowess depends? It seems to take a trained philosopher to reconstruct them! How is it that children are so skilled at understanding and anticipating the behavior of humans in advance of ever acquiring the complex linguistic skills necessary to express those laws? How is it that social hunters such as wolves and lions can comprehend and anticipate each other's behavior in great detail when they presumably store no internal sentences at all?

We must resist the temptation to see in these questions a renewed motivation for counting folk psychology as special, for the very same problems arise with respect to any other folk theory you might care to mention: folk physics, folk biology, whatever. It even arises for theories in the highly developed sciences, since, as Kuhn has pointed out, very little of a scientist's understanding of a theory consists in his ability to state a list of laws. It consists, rather, in the ability to apply the conceptual resources of the theory to new cases, and thus to anticipate and perhaps manipulate the behavior of the relevant empirical domain. This means that our problem here concerns the character of knowledge and understanding in general. Let us finally address that problem.

2   An Alternative Form of Knowledge Representation

One alternative to the notion of a universal generalization about F is the notion of a *prototype* of F, a central or typical example of F which all other examples of F resemble, more or less closely, in certain relevant respects. Prototypes have certain obvious advantages over universal generalizations. Just as a picture can be worth a thousand words, so a single complex prototype can embody the same breadth of information concerning the organization of cooccurrent features that would be contained in a long list of complex generalizations. Furthermore, prototypes allow us a welcome degree of looseness that is precluded by the strict logic of a universal quantifier: not *all* Fs need be Gs, but the standard or normal ones are, and the nonstandard ones must be related by a relevant similarity relation to those that properly are G. Various theorists have independently found motive to introduce such a notion in a number of cognitive fields: they have been called 'paradigms' and 'exemplars' in the philosophy of science (Kuhn 1962), 'stereotypes' in semantics (Putnam 1970, 1975), 'frames' (Minsky 1981) and 'scripts' (Schank 1977) in AI research, and finally 'prototypes' in psychology (Rosch 1981) and linguistics (Lakoff 1987).

Their advantages aside, prototypes also have certain familiar problems. The first problem is how to determine just what clutch of elements or properties should constitute a given prototype, and the second problem is how to determine the metric of similarity along which closeness to the central prototype is to be measured. Though they pose a problem for notions at all levels, these problems are especially keen in the case of the so-called "basic" or "simple" properties, because common sense is there unable even to articulate any deeper constituting elements (for example, what elements "make up" a purple color, a sour taste, a floral smell, or the phoneme /ā/?). A final problem concerning prototypes is a familiar one: how might prototypes be effectively represented in a real cognitive creature?

This last question brings me to a possible answer, and to a path that leads to further answers. The relevant research concerns the operations of artificial neural networks, networks that mimic some of the more obvious organizational features of the brain. It concerns how they learn to recognize certain types of complex stimuli, and how they represent what they have learned. Upon repeated presentation of various real examples of the several features to be learned (F, G, H, etc.), and under the steady pressure of a learning algorithm that makes small adjustments in the network's synaptic connections, the network slowly but spontaneously generates a set of internal representations, one for each of the several features it is required to recognize. Collectively, those representations take the form of a set or system of similarity spaces, and the central point or volume of such a space constitutes the network's representation of a *prototypical F*, *G*, or *H*. After learning is completed, the system responds to any *F*-like stimulus with an internal pattern of neuronal activity that is *close to* the prototypical pattern in the relevant similarity space.

The network consists of an initial "sensory" layer of neurons, which is massively connected to a second layer of neurons. The sizes or "weights" of the many connections determine how the neurons at the second layer collectively respond to activity across the input layer. The neurons at the second layer are connected in turn to a third layer (and perhaps a fourth layer, etc., but I shall limit the discussion here to three-layer networks). During learning, what the system is searching for is a configuration of weights that will turn the neurons at the second layer into a set of *complex feature detectors*. We then want the neurons at the third or "output" layer to respond in turn to the second layer, given any *F*-like stimuli at the input layer, with a characteristic pattern of activity. All of this is achieved by presenting the network with diverse examples of *F*s, and slowly adjusting its connection weights in the light of its initially chaotic responses.

Such networks can indeed learn to recognize a wide variety of surprisingly subtle features: phonemes from voiced speech, the shapes of objects from grey-scale photos, the correct pronunciation of printed English text, the presence of metallic mines from sonar returns, and grammatical categories in novel sentences. Given a successfully trained network, if we examine the behavior of the neurons at the second or intermediate layer during the process of recognition, we discover that each neuron has come to represent, by its level of activity, some distinct aspect or dimension of the input stimulus.

Taken together, their joint activity constitutes a multidimensional analysis of the stimuli at the input layer. The trained network has succeeded in finding a set of dimensions, an *abstract space*, such that all more-or-less typical Fs produce a characteristic profile of neuronal activity across those particular dimensions, while deviant or degraded Fs produce profiles that are variously *close* to that central prototype. The job of the third and final layer is then the relatively simple one of distinguishing that profile-region from other regions in the larger space of possible activation patterns. In this way do artificial neural networks generate and exploit prototypes. It is now more than a suggestion that real neural networks do the same thing. (For a summary of these results and how they bear on the question of theoretical knowledge, see Churchland 1989a. For a parade case of successful learning, see Rosenberg and Sejnowski 1987. For the *locus classicus* concerning the general technique, see Rumelhart et al. 1986.)

Notice that this picture contains answers to all three of the problems about prototypes noted earlier. What dimensions go into a prototype of F? Those that allow the system to respond to diverse examples of F in a distinctive and uniform way, a way that reduces the error messages from the learning algorithm to a minimum. How is similarity to a prototype measured? By geometrical proximity in the relevant parameter space. How are prototypes represented in real cognitive creatures? By canonical activity patterns across an appropriate population of neurons.

Note also that the objective features recognized by the network can also have a temporal component: a network can just as well be trained to recognize typical *sequences* and *processes* as to recognize atemporal patterns. Which brings me to my final suggestion. A normal human's understanding of the springs of human action may reside not in a set of stored generalizations about the hidden elements of mind and how they conspire to produce behavior, but rather in one or more prototypes of the deliberative or purposeful process. To understand or explain someone's behavior may be less a matter of deduction from implicit laws, and more a matter of recognitional subsumption of the case at issue under a relevant prototype. (For a more detailed treatment of this view of explanation, the *prototype activation model*, see chapter 10.)

Such prototypes are no doubt at least modestly complex, and presumably they depict typical configurations of desires, beliefs, preferences, and so forth, roughly the same configurations that I have earlier attempted to express in the form of universally quantified sentences. Beyond this, I am able to say little about them, at least on this occasion. But I hope I have succeeded in making intelligible to you a novel approach to the problem of explanatory understanding in humans. This is an approach that is grounded at last in what we know about the brain. And it is an approach that ascribes to us neither reams of universally quantified premises, nor deductive activity on a heroic scale. Explanatory understanding turns out to be not quite what we thought it was, because cognition in general gets characterized in a new way. And yet explanatory understanding remains the same *sort* of process in the case of human behavior as in the case of natural phenomena generally. And the question of the *adequacy* of our commonsense understanding remains as live as ever.

3   Addendum: Commentary on Dennett

I focus here on one of the relatively few issues that still divide Dennett and me: the ontological status of intentional states. We both accept the premise that neuroscience is unlikely to find "sentences in the head," or anything else that answers to the structure of individual beliefs and desires. On the strength of this shared assumption, I am willing to infer that folk psychology is false, and that its ontology is chimerical. Beliefs and desires are of a piece with phlogiston, caloric, and the alchemical essences. We therefore need an entirely new kinematics and dynamics with which to comprehend human cognitive activity, one drawn, perhaps, from computational neuroscience and connectionist AI. Folk psychology could then be put aside in favor of this descriptively more accurate and explanatorily more powerful portrayal of the reality within. Certainly, it will be put aside in the lab and in the clinic, and eventually, perhaps, in the marketplace as well.

But Dennett declines to draw this eliminativist conclusion, despite his firm acceptance of the premise cited, and despite his willingness to contemplate unorthodox forms of cognitive theory. He prefers to claim a special status for the various intentional states, a status that will permit us to be "realists" about beliefs and desires despite their projected absence from our strict scientific ontology.

This impulse in Dennett continues to strike me as arbitrary protectionism, as ill motivated special pleading on behalf of the old and familiar. His initial rationale for exempting folk psychology from the usual scientific standards involved assigning it a purely instrumental

This note is a short commentary on Daniel C. Dennett's *Intentional Stance*. It first appeared in *Behavioral and Brain Sciences* 11 (1989), no. 3, under the title, "On the Ontological Status of Intentional States: Nailing Folk Psychology to Its Perch."

status, but this swiftly brought him all kinds of grief, as he himself explains (1987, pp. 71–72). Instrumentalism is first and foremost an *anti*realist position, hardly a welcome port given Dennett's aims, a fact Dennett now appreciates in more detail. Accordingly, his current rationale draws a much more narrowly focused analogy between intentional states and geometrical *abstracta* such as the centers of gravity, axes of rotation, equators, etc., that are postulated to such good effect in mechanics. As Dennett sees it, these latter are not real in the same sense that *concreta* like bricks and trees are real (you can't trip over them, for example), but they can reasonably be said to be real even so. Intentional states are real in this same sense, claims Dennett.

The reality of equators, centers, and rotational axes I am happy to grant. They are all places or loci of some sort that are decisively specifiable by reference to the shape or behavior of the relevant concrete object. But the alleged similarity of these items to beliefs, desires, and other intentional states escapes me entirely. In what respects are they similar, and why should they be grouped together in advance of the issue here at stake? That is, in advance of any hopes of finding an exculpatory status for intentional states?

Dennett is quick to point out that folk psychology has some nontrivial predictive power, especially in its central domain of normal human behavior, despite the lack of any neural *concreta* answering to the propositional attitudes. He emphasizes, quite correctly, that it is an objective fact about humans that a significant amount of their behavior is accurately predictable in intentional terms.

But I think he overvalues this fact wildly. We must not forget that all sorts of false theories, with wholly chimerical ontologies, can boast very impressive predictive power in various proprietary domains. But this buys their ontology no special status. It is an objective fact that much of the behavior of metals and ores is predictable in terms of the alchemical essences, that most of the behavior of the visible heavens is predictable in terms of nested crystal spheres, that much of the behavior of moving bodies is predictable in terms of impetus, and so forth. And yet there are no alchemical essenses, nor any crystal spheres, nor any impetuses. We could, of course, set about insisting that these three "things" are real and genuine after all, though mere *abstracta* to be sure. But none of us is tempted to salvage *their* reality by such a tortured and transparent ploy. Why should we be tempted in the case of the propositional attitudes?

This disagreement between us on the status of folk psychology dates from several letters now a full decade old. However, one point on which we then agreed was that neither of us could clearly imagine a systematic alternative to folk psychology. At the time I ascribed this inability to the natural poverty of our imaginations. Dennett was inclined to suspect a deeper reason. But since then the materials available to imagination have improved dramatically. The microstructure of the brain and the recent successes of connectionist AI both suggest that our principal form of representation is the high-dimensional activation vector, and that our principal form of computation is the vector-to-vector transformation, effected by a matrix of differently weighted synapses. In place of propositional attitudes and logical inferences from one to another, therefore, we can conceive of persons as the seat of vectorial attitudes and various nonlinear transformations from one vector to another. We can already see how such a vectorial system can do many of the things that humans and other animals do swiftly and easily, such as recognize faces and other highly complex stimuli, or control a complex body with both relevance and grace. The possibility of a real alternative now seems beyond dispute: we are already building it.

What remains an issue is how our familiar folk psychology will fare in light of what the new conception will reveal. Retention through reduction remains a real possibility, though the character of the theoretical developments just cited make this seem increasingly unlikely. If we rule out reduction, then elimination emerges as the only coherent alternative, Dennett's resistance notwithstanding.

In the end, Dennett's steadfast insistence that folk psychology is not just another a false theory, but rather an "abstract stance" of some kind, one with striking predictive powers, reminds me of the shopkeeper in the Monty Python sketch about the distraught customer trying to return a recently purchased but very dead parrot. Python fans will remember the shopkeeper's deliciously shifty-eyed insistence. "Naw, naw, it's not *dead*! It's just *resting*! It's just *pining* for the fiords!. . . Lovely *plumage*, the Norwegian Blue."

Chapter 7

Reductionism, Connectionism, and the Plasticity of Human Consciousness

It remains a matter of keen debate whether human nature in general, and the human sciences in particular, will ever be brought under the explanatory umbrella of the natural sciences. The resources of the latter continue to expand, and their accumulated successes reach ever closer to the domain of the former. Yet certain salient features of the human condition continue to elude naturalistic explanation, and they present themselves, to some eyes, as forever beyond that form of understanding.

My concern in this chapter is to examine one type of antinaturalist argument, a type that starts from the premise that human nature is both highly plastic and culturally configured. The first part of the challenge posed to naturalism is the claim that what constitutes a human consciousness is not just the intrinsic character of the creature itself, but also the rich matrix of relations it bears to the other humans, practices, and institutions of its embedding culture. A naturalistic account of human consciousness and behavior, insofar as it is limited to such things as the microscopic activities in an individual's brain, for example, cannot hope to capture more than a small part of what is explanatorily important.

The second part of the challenge arises directly from the first. Given that (possible) cultures are endlessly various, so also is "human nature." Human beings, unlike the objects of the natural sciences, are plastic in character. Moreover, humans are self-defining or self-constituting entities. As human cultures evolve, so also does the character of individual human consciousness. Simply put, there *is no* stable or lasting "human nature" that a reductive or naturalistic account might hope to explicate or capture. For this reason, the argument concludes, any such project must be misconceived from the outset.

This chapter is an abridged version of a paper that first appeared in *Cultural Dynamics* 1 (1988), no. 1.

This style of argument has a considerable history, but one of its clearest and most accessible contemporary exponents is Charles Taylor (1970, 1987). In what follows, I hope to reverse the antinaturalist, antireductionist conclusion of the argument. Yet this undertaking has a certain poignancy for me, since I accept both of the premises from which the argument proceeds. Indeed, in earlier writings (Churchland 1979, 1981a, 1985b) I have vigorously defended both the radical plasticity of the human mind, and the dramatic extent to which the character of human consciousness is determined by the cultural surround, specifically, by the ideological, linguistic, and practical surround. In this chapter I shall try to show how a naturalist can embrace the insights of the two premises cited, without compromising the possibility of a strongly naturalistic, and even reductionistic, science of human consciousness.

My strategy here is not merely critical, but positive. I propose to illustrate the weakness of the arguments cited above by outlining a recently developed theoretical and experimental approach to the phenomena of human cognition that is at once (a) naturalistic, (b) reductionistic, and (c) capable of explaining both the radical plasticity of human consciousness, and its intricate dependence on the extended cultural surround.

This new approach, called 'connectionism', resides at the interface of computational neuroscience, cognitive psychology, and artificial intelligence (AI). It represents a radical break with the approaches that have dominated all three of these disciplines for the last three decades. It even makes firm contact with some of the major themes of the continental tradition in philosophy, such as the inarticulate or nonpropositional character of the bulk of human knowledge, and the primacy of being an endlessly active agent in a world of practical exigencies. But it does *not* support the antinaturalist themes to be found in recent continental and analytical philosophies, as we are about to see. Let me begin with a brief introduction to the central concepts of this novel and very fertile approach. After we have seen the unusual properties displayed by connectionist systems, we shall return to the philosophical issues with which we began.

[I here ask the reader to turn to chapter 9, sections 3 and 4 (pp. 159–171), for the material on learning in brainlike networks. After reading that material, the present essay may be picked up below.]

Enough examples. You have seen something of what networks of this kind can do, and of how they do it. In both respects they contrast sharply with the kinds of representational and processing strategies that analytical philosophers, cognitive psychologists, and AI workers have traditionally ascribed to us (namely, sentencelike representations manipulated by formal rules.) You can see also why this theoretical and experimental approach has captured the interest of those who seek to understand how the microarchitecture of the biological brain produces the phenomena of human consciousness. Let us now return to philosophical issues.

1   The Plasticity Argument

We began this discussion with the objection that human consciousness is plastic, that it has no stable or essential character that a reductionist program might hope to capture, and that what character it does have derives mainly from the complex culture that surrounds it. Let us examine the first part first: the plasticity objection.

The plasticity of human nature is a problem for naturalistic and reductionistic theories only if they are unable to *explain* it. To explain our cognitive plasticity will require that the reductionist give an account of the underlying mechanisms that sustain such plasticity, the dimensions of variation along which change can occur, and the forces that can drive change from one cognitive configuration to another. The mere fact of conceptual plasticity is not a fatal problem for reductionists, since they are in no way committed to the idea that humans admit of only *one* cognitive configuration, only *one* style of consciousness. On the contrary, the radical plasticity of human nature is a major theme of some reductionist writers (P. M. Churchland 1979 and chapters 11 and 12 below).

But can a naturalistic theory have a realistic hope of ever explaining our plasticity? Certainly it can, and we may observe the outlines of a possible explanation in the approach detailed in chapter 9. According to that approach, one's basic cognitive apparatus consists of a very large network of interconnected units, which admits of variation in the weights of its myriad connections. The character of one's perception, one's cognition, and one's behavior is determined by the particular configuration of weights within that network. It is the many weights that determine what features in the world one responds to, which concepts one uses to process them, which values one embraces, and which range of behaviors one commands.

How much plasticity will this buy us? A spectacular amount. An almost incomprehensible amount. A typical human brain contains something close to 100 billion neurons. A typical neuron receives synaptic connections from roughly 3000 other neurons. A human brain, therefore, will typically contain something on the order of $10^{11} \times 10^3 = 10^{14}$ synaptic connections. Let us suppose, conservatively, that the weight of each connection can assume any 1 of only 10 possible values. Given these figures, how many distinct cognitive configurations can a human brain assume? Well, there are 10 possible weights for the first of its 10^{14} connections, times 10 possible weights for the second connection, times 10 for the third, and so on. The total number of distinct possible configurations is therefore $10^{10^{14}}$, or $10^{100,000,000,000,000}$. To get some idea of the size of this number, recall that the total number of elementary particles in the entire universe is generally estimated to be about 10^{87}.

To be sure, this measure of human plasticity is in one respect an overestimation, since many possible settings of the weights in a brain will not produce an "interestingly" functional creature. If we set all 10^{14} of the connection weights at zero, for example, the resulting creature would be useless, as would a creature with every weight set at maximum. Deletion of such cases will certainly reduce our estimate by several orders of magnitude, but we are still left with a spectacular number. Our measure is also an *under*estimation in at least one important respect. It assumes that connection weights represent the only dimension of variation. But real brains not only adjust their existing connection weights, they can and do grow millions of entirely new connections.

I will make no further attempt to fine tune this rough numerical estimate of the range of cognitive characters possible for humans. What is important here is that the number, whatever it is, is *very* large. Reductionists need not deny the plastic character of human consciousness. On the contrary, they are in an excellent position to explain it, conceivably in some detail.

2   The Cultural-Embedding Objection

This final objection begins with the claim that the features of the world that are maximally important for explaining the behavior of humans are not the simple ones that can be defined in the vocabulary of a naturalistic physics, but rather the much more subtle and complex features that constitute our social culture. One does indeed discriminate and respond to light, to warmth, to sound, and so forth. But one also discriminates and responds to the phonemes peculiar to one's language, to the meanings of its words, to the moral of a story, to the significance of gestures and facial expressions, to challenges and obligations and social opportunities, and to all of the intricacies that make up a functioning culture.

All of this is no doubt true. But again, these things are wholly consistent with a reductionist program for understanding the nature of human cognition. What the reductionist must do is explain how a physical system can come to address and manipulate such subtle and culturally configured features. While this is certainly a challenge, it no longer appears to be a problem in principle, for we have already seen how suitably trained networks can come to represent and discriminate features of great subtlety and abstraction.

What is important is that the network have a "teacher" of some appropriate sort, a teacher who can help to shape the character of its internal representations and the pattern of its environmental responses. We have seen how relatively simple networks can be trained to recognize complex and culturally-imposed auditory features like mine echoes and phonemes. We have seen (from chapter 9) how they can learn the highly irregular and highly context-sensitive transformation rules that are essential to the task of reading English text. And we have seen how they can be trained to recognize the endlessly variable three-dimensional structures of external objects from two-dimensional gray-scale pictures of them. In each case, the network is forced toward acknowledgment of some feature or domain of features selected from the infinity of possible features to which it might respond, and it is not an insuperable problem that the features at issue are complex, subtle, context sensitive, or stimulus transcendent. With suitable teaching, the network generates an internal representation of them regardless. This does not mean that the features addressed are magical, or superphysical, or beyond the realm of natural science. It just means that the simplest possible definition or representation of them may well be the entire configuration of the successfully trained network! Given a network of any nontrivial size, those representations can indeed be extraordinarily complex, but it is no part of the reductionist's program to deny this.

It therefore should not be a surprise that a human infant comes to recognize and respond to cultural features that resist definition in terms of notions like mass, charge, length, and so forth, because the most dominant "teacher" in the local environment is the culture into which the infant is born. The set of weights that constitutes a child's developing consciousness is continually being shaped by the linguistic, conceptual, and social surround. The developing brain comes to reflect the elements and structure of that surround in great detail. For that is what networks do. What shapes them is the stimuli they typically receive, and the subsequent corrections in their responses to which they are typically subject. Small wonder we become attuned to the categories of the culture that raises us.

This may sound like a major concession to the view that the most important factors in the explanation of human behavior are to be found at the cultural level rather than at the microphysical level. But to say this would be to miss the point, and to acquiesce in a false dichotomy between "cultural" and "physical" features. The real distinction is between features that are simple and context free on the one hand, and features that are extraordinarily complex and have many layers of context dependency on the other. The latter are indeed of major importance for explaining human behavior. But neither they, nor our capacity for recognizing them, is forever beyond a naturalistic understanding. For we can already understand, right here and now, how a system of many simple physical elements can come to represent them, and to respond to them, and to undergo dramatic conceptual development in the process. That is the prospect that a computational neuroscience holds out to us, and I think it would be a tragedy if antireductionist convictions should frustrate or slow our pursuit of this prospect. Such conservative convictions, to judge from the preceding discussion, may be based on true and important premises about human nature. But they underestimate the capacity of emerging science to provide a highly revealing and naturalistic *explanation* of those very same premises. And such explanation, after all, is what scientific reduction amounts to.

3   Conclusion

The plasticity of human consciousness is real, and precious, and theoretically important. Yet it is not beyond naturalistic explanation. The diffuse and culturally-constituted character of many of the features to which humans respond is also real and important. But those features are still a part of the natural world, and it is not impossible to understand either how they are constituted, or how a purely physical system is able to discriminate them. This conclusion does leave intact the idea that many of the important determinants of human behavior are to be found at the very high level of complexity that constitutes a culture. But that is all right. Perhaps a reductionist is bound to say that we are *composed* of simple things. But he is not bound to say that either we, or our environment, *are* simple things.

I close on a cautionary note. The story of the preceding pages has shown how a naturalistic approach to human consciousness is not automatically and fundamentally opposed to the explanatory categories of our existing culture. On the contrary, it may vindicate them by providing a naturalistic explanation of them. But it remains possible that this deeper understanding of our cognitive microstructure will frequently reveal mistakes and misconceptions in our commonsense categories. Indeed, given the great complexity of humans and human culture, it is only to be expected that our commonsense ideas concerning the dimensions of human consciousness and the springs of human action will turn out to be pinched and defective in various ways. And we may hope that fields such as connectionist AI and computational neurobiology will be a source of new and better ideas on these matters. I emphasize this point because, although I wish to concede the dynamical relevance of high-level culturally-embedded features, it remains an open scientific question which features at that level are the truly real and genuinely important ones. Perhaps folk psychology has a firm if partial grasp of them. And perhaps they remain largely to be discovered.

PART II

The Structure of Science

Chapter 8

The Ontological Status of Observables:
In Praise of the Superempirical Virtues

At several points in the reading of van Fraassen's book (1980), I feared I would no longer be a realist by the time I completed it. Fortunately, sheer doxastic inertia has allowed my convictions to survive its searching critique, at least temporarily, and as we address you today, van Fraassen and I still hold different views. I am a scientific realist, of unorthodox persuasion, and van Fraassen is a constructive empiricist, whose persuasions currently define the doctrine. I assert that global excellence of theory is the ultimate measure of truth and ontology at all levels of cognition, even at the observational level. Van Fraassen asserts that descriptive excellence at the observational level is the only genuine measure of any theory's truth, and that one's acceptance of a theory should create no ontological commitments whatever beyond the observational level.

Against his first claim I shall maintain that observational excellence or "empirical adequacy" is only one epistemic virtue among others, of equal or comparable importance. And against his second claim I shall maintain that the ontological commitments of any theory are wholly blind to the idiosyncratic distinction between what is and what is not humanly observable, and so should be our own ontological commitments. Criticism will be directed primarily at van Fraassen's *selective* skepticism in favor of observable ontologies over unobservable ontologies; and against his view that the superempirical theoretical virtues (simplicity, coherence, explanatory power) are merely pragmatic virtues, irrelevant to the estimate of a theory's truth. My aims are not merely critical, however. Scientific realism does need reworking, and there are good reasons for moving it in the direction of van Fraassen's constructive empiricism, as will be discussed in the

This paper first appeared in the *Pacific Philosophical Quarterly* 63 (1982), no. 3. As the prose suggests, it was first presented at a symposium on scientific realism (Halifax, 1981) that focused on my 1979 book and Bas van Fraassen's 1980 book.

closing section of this paper. But those reasons do not support the skeptical theses at issue.

1   How van Fraassen's Problem Collapses into Hume's Problem

Before pursuing our differences, it will prove useful to emphasize certain convictions that we share. Van Fraassen is already a scientific realist in the minimal sense that he interprets theories literally and he concedes them a truth value. Further, we agree that the observable/ unobservable distinction is entirely distinct from the nontheoretical/ theoretical distinction, and we agree as well that all observation sentences are irredeemably laden with theory.

Additionally, I absolutely reject many sanguine assumptions common among realists. I do not believe that on the whole our beliefs must be at least roughly true; I do not believe that the terms of "mature" sciences must typically refer to real things; and I very much doubt that the Reason of *Homo sapiens*, even at its best and even if allowed infinite time, would eventually encompass all and/or only true statements.

This skepticism is born partly from a historical induction: so many past theories, rightly judged excellent at the time, have since proved to be false. And their current successors, though even better founded, seem but the next step in a probably endless and not obviously convergent journey. (For a most thorough and insightful critique of typical realist theses, see the recent paper by Laudan [1981].)

Evolutionary considerations also counsel a healthy skepticism. Human reason is a hierarchy of heuristics for seeking, recognizing, storing, and exploiting information. But those heuristics were invented at random, and they were selected for within a very narrow evolutionary environment, cosmologically speaking. It would be miraculous if human reason were completely free of false strategies and fundamental cognitive limitations, and doubly miraculous if the theories we accept failed to reflect those defects.

Thus some very realistic reasons for skepticism with respect to any theory. Why, then, am I still a scientific realist? Because these reasons fail to discriminate between the integrity of observables and the integrity of unobservables. If anything is compromised by these considerations, it is the integrity of theories generally. That is, of *cognition* generally. Since our observational concepts are just as theory laden as any others, and since the integrity of those concepts is just as contingent on the integrity of the theories that embed them, our observational ontology is rendered *exactly as dubious* as our nonobservational ontology.

This parity should not seem surprising. Our history contains real examples of mistaken ontological commitments in both domains. For example, we have had occasion to banish phlogiston, caloric, and the luminiferous ether from our ontology—but we have also had occasion to banish witches, and the starry sphere that turns about us daily. These latter items were as "observable" as you please, and they were widely "observed" on a daily basis. We are too often misled, I think, by our casual use of 'observes' as a success verb: we tend to forget that, at any stage of our history, the ontology presupposed by our observational judgments remains essentially speculative and wholly revisable, however entrenched and familiar it may have become.

Accordingly, since the skeptical considerations adduced above are indifferent to the distinction between what is and is not observable, they provide no reason for resisting a commitment to unobservable ontologies *while allowing* a commitment to what we take to be observable ontologies. The latter appear as no better off than the former. For me, then, the "empirical success" of a theory remains a reason for thinking the theory to be true, and for accepting its overall ontology. The inference from success to truth should no doubt be severely tempered by the skeptical considerations adduced, but the inference to *unobservable* ontologies is not rendered *selectively* dubious. Thus, I remain a scientific realist. My realism is highly circumspect, but the circumspection is uniform for unobservables and observables alike.

Perhaps I am wrong in this. Perhaps we should be selectively skeptical in the fashion van Fraassen recommends. Does he have other arguments for refusing factual belief and ontological commitment beyond the observational domain? Indeed he does. In fact, he does not appeal to historical induction or evolutionary humility at all. These are *my* reasons for skepticism (and they will remain, even if we manage to undermine van Fraassen's). They have been introduced here to show that, while there are some powerful reasons for skepticism, those reasons do not place unobservables at a selective disadvantage.

Very well, what are van Fraassen's reasons for skepticism? They are very interesting. To summarize quickly, he does a compelling job of deflating certain standard realist arguments (from Smart, Sellars, Salmon, Boyd, and others) to the effect that, given the aims of science, we have no alternative but to bring unobservables (not just into our calculations, but) into our literal ontology. He also argues, rather compellingly, that the superempirical virtues, such as simplicity and comprehensive explanatory power, are at bottom merely pragmatic virtues, having nothing essential to do with any theory's truth. This leaves only empirical adequacy as a genuine measure of any theory's truth. Roughly, a theory is empirically adequate if and only if everything it says about *observable* things is true. Empirical adequacy is thus a necessary condition on a theory's truth.

However, claims van Fraassen, the truth of any theory whose ontology includes unobservables is always radically underdetermined by its empirical adequacy, since a great many logically incompatible theories can all be empirically equivalent. Accordingly, the inference from empirical adequacy to truth now appears presumptuous in the extreme, especially since it has just been disconnected from additional selective criteria such as simplicity and explanatory power, criteria which might have reduced the arbitrariness of the particular inference drawn. Fortunately, says van Fraassen, we do not need to make such wanton inferences, since we can perfectly well understand science as an enterprise that never really draws them. Here we arrive at his positive conception of science as an enterprise whose sole intellectual aims are empirical adequacy and the satisfaction of certain human intellectual needs.

The central element in this argument is the claim that, in the case of a theory whose ontology includes unobservables, its empirical adequacy underdetermines its truth. (We should notice that in the case of a theory whose ontology is completely free of unobservables, its empirical adequacy does not underdetermine its truth: in that case, truth and empirical adequacy are obviously identical. Thus van Fraassen's *selective* skepticism with respect to unobservables.) That is, for any theory T inflated with unobservables, there will always be many other such theories incompatible with T, but empirically equivalent to it.

In my view, the notions of "empirical adequacy" and its cognate relative term "empirically equivalent" are extremely thorny notions of doubtful integrity. If we attempt to explicate a theory's "empirical content" in terms of the observation sentences it entails (or entails if conjoined with available background information, or with possible future background information, or with possible future theories), we generate a variety of notions that are variously empty, context relative, ill defined, or flatly incompatible with the claim of underdetermination. Van Fraassen expresses awareness of these difficulties and proposes to avoid them by giving the notions at issue a model-theoretic rather than a syntactic explication. I am unconvinced that this improves matters decisively (on this issue, see Wilson 1980; also Musgrave 1985, Hooker 1985, Glymour 1985, and Wilson 1985). In particular, I think van Fraassen has not dealt at all adequately with the problem of how the so-called "empirical equivalence" of two incompatible theories remains *relative* to which background theories are added to the evaluative context, especially background theories that in some way revise our conception of what humans can observe. I intend to sidestep this issue for now, however, since the matter is complex and there is a much simpler objection to be voiced.

Let me approach my objection by first pointing out that the empirical adequacy of any theory is itself something that is radically underdetermined by any evidence conceivably available to us. Recall that, for a theory to be empirically adequate, what it says about observable things must be true—*all* observable things, in the past, in the indefinite future, and in the most distant corners of the cosmos. But since any actual data possessed by us must be finite in its scope, it is plain that we here suffer an underdetermination problem no less serious than that claimed above. This is Hume's problem, and the lesson is that even observation-level theories must suffer radical underdetermination by the evidence. Accordingly, theories about observables and theories about unobservables appear on a par again, so far as skepticism is concerned.

Van Fraassen thinks there is an important difference between the two cases, and one's first impulse is to agree with him. We are all willing to concede the existence of Hume's problem, the problem of justifying the inference to unobserv*ed* entities. But the inference to entities that are downright unobserv*able* appears as a different and *additional* problem.

The appearance is an illusion, as the following considerations will show. Consider some of the different reasons why entities or processes may go unobserved by us. First, they may go unobserved because, relative to our natural sensory apparatus, they fail to enjoy an appropriate spatial or temporal *position*. They may exist in the Upper Jurassic Period, for example, or they may reside in the Andromeda Galaxy. Second, they may go unobserved because, relative to our natural sensory apparatus, they fail to enjoy the appropriate spatial or temporal *dimensions*. They may be too small, or too brief, or too large, or too protracted. Third, they may fail to enjoy the appropriate *energy*, being too feeble, or too powerful, to permit useful discrimination. Fourth and fifth, they may fail to have an appropriate *wavelength*, or an appropriate *mass*. Sixth, they may fail to "feel" the relevant fundamental *forces* our sensory apparatus exploits, as with our inability to observe the background neutrino flux, despite the fact that its energy density exceeds that of light itself.

This list could be lengthened, but it is long enough to suggest that being spatially or temporally distant from our sensory apparatus is only one among many ways in which an entity or process can fall outside the compass of human observation, a way distinguished by no relevant epistemological or ontological features.

There is clearly some *practical* point in our calling a thing "*observable*" if it fails *only* the first test (spatiotemporal proximity), and "*unobservable*" if it fails any of the others. But that is only because of the contingent practical fact that humans generally have somewhat more *control* over the spatiotemporal perspective of their sensory systems than they have over their size, or reaction time, or mass, or wavelength sensitivity, or chemical constitution. Had we been less mobile than we are—rooted to the earth like Douglas firs, say—yet been more voluntarily plastic in our sensory constitution, the distinction between the "merely unobserved" and the "downright unobservable" would have been very differently drawn. It may help to imagine here a suitably rooted arboreal philosopher named (what else?) Douglas van Fiirrsen, who, in his sedentary wisdom, urges an antirealist skepticism concerning the spatially very *distant* entities postulated by his fellow trees.

Admittedly, for any distant entity one can in principle always change the relative spatial position of one's sensory apparatus so that the entity is observed: one can go to it. But equally, for any microscopic entity one can in principle always change the relative spatial *size* or *configuration* of one's sensory apparatus so that the entity is observed. Physical law imposes certain limitations on such plasticity, but so also does physical law limit how far one can travel in a lifetime.

To emphasize the importance of these considerations, let me underscore the structure of my objection here. Consider the distinction between

(1) things observed by some human (with unaided senses),

(2) things thus observable by humans, but not in fact observed,

(3) things not observable by humans at all.

Van Fraassen's position would exclude (3) from our rational ontology. This has at least some initial plausibility. But his position would not be at all plausible if it were committed to excluding both (3) *and* (2) from our rational ontology. No party to the present discussion is willing to restrict rational ontology to (1) alone. Van Fraassen's position thus requires a *principled* distinction between (2) and (3), a distinction *adequate* to the radical difference in epistemic attitude he would have us adopt toward them. The burden of my argument is that the distinction between (2) and (3), once it is unearthed, is only very feebly principled, and is wholly inadequate to bear the great weight that van Fraassen puts on it.

The point of all this is that there is no special or novel problem about inferences to the existence of entities commonly called "unobservables." Such entities are merely those that go unobserved by us for reasons *other* than their spatial or temporal distance from us. But whether the "gap" to be bridged is spatiotemporal, or one of the many other gaps, the logical/epistemological problem is the same in all cases: ampliative inference and underdetermined hypotheses. I therefore fail to see how van Fraassen can justify tolerating an ampliative inference when it bridges a gap of spatial distance, while refusing to tolerate an ampliative inference when it bridges a gap of, for example, spatial size. Hume's problem and van Fraassen's problem collapse into one.

Van Fraassen attempts to meet such worries about the inescapable ubiquity of speculative activity by observing that "It is not an epistemological principle that one may as well hang for a sheep as for a lamb" (1980, p. 72). Agreed. But it is a principle of *logic* that one may as well hang for a sheep as for a sheep, and van Fraassen's lamb (empirical adequacy) is just another sheep.

Simply to hold *fewer* beliefs from a given set is, of course, to be less adventurous, but it is not necessarily to be applauded. One might decide to relinquish all one's beliefs save those about objects weighing less than 500 kilograms, and perhaps one would then be logically safer. But in the absence of some relevant epistemic difference between one's beliefs about such objects and one's beliefs about other objects, that is perversity, not parsimony.

L t me summarize. As van Fraassen sets it up, and as the instrumentalists set it up before him, the realist looks more gullible than the nonrealist, since the realist is willing to extend belief beyond the observable, while the nonrealist insists on confining belief within that domain. I suggest, however, that it is really the nonrealists who are being the more gullible in this matter, since they suppose that the epistemic situation of our beliefs about observables is in some way superior to that of our beliefs about unobservables. But in fact, their epistemic situation is not superior. They are exactly as dubious as their nonobservational cousins. Their *causal history* is different (they are occasioned by activity in the sensory pathways), but the ontology they presuppose enjoys no privilege or special credibility.

2   The Primacy of the Superempirical Virtues

Let me now try to address the question of whether the theoretical virtues such as simplicity, coherence, and explanatory power are *epistemic* virtues genuinely relevant to the estimate of a theory's truth, as tradition says, or merely *pragmatic* virtues, as van Fraassen urges. His view promotes empirical adequacy, or evidence of empirical adequacy, as the only genuine measure of a theory's truth, the other virtues (insofar as they are distinct from these) being cast as purely pragmatic virtues, to be valued only for the human needs they satisfy. Despite certain compelling features of the account of explanation that van Fraassen provides, I remain inclined toward the traditional view.

My reason is simplicity itself. Since there is no way of conceiving or representing "the empirical facts" that is completely independent of speculative assumptions, and since we shall occasionally confront theoretical alternatives on a scale so comprehensive that we must also choose between competing modes of conceiving what the empirical facts before us *are*, it is clear that the epistemic choice between these global alternatives cannot be made by comparing the extent to which they are adequate to some common touchstone, "the empirical facts." In such a case, the choice must be made on the comparative global virtues of the two global alternatives, T_1-plus-the-observational-evidence-therein-construed, versus T_2-plus-the-observational-evidence-therein-(differently)-construed. That is, it must be made on superempirical grounds such as relative coherence, simplicity, and explanatory unity.

Van Fraassen has said that to "save the appearances" is to exhibit them as a fragment of a larger unity. With this I wholly agree. But I am here pointing out that it is a decision between *competing* larger unities that determines what we count as "the true appearances" in the first place. There is no independent way to settle that question. And if such global decisions can only be made on what van Fraassen calls "pragmatic" grounds, then it would seem to follow that any decision concerning what the *observable* world contains must be essentially "pragmatic" also. Inflationary metaphysics and "pragmatic" decisions begin, it seems, as soon as we open our eyes.

Global issues such as these are reminiscent of Carnap's "external" questions, and I think it likely that van Fraassen, like Carnap, does not regard them as decidable in any but a second-rate sense, since they can only be decided by second-rate (i.e., by pragmatic) considerations. If so, however, it is difficult to see how van Fraassen can justify a selectively realist attitude toward "observables," since, as we have seen, pragmatic considerations must attend their selection also. (These issues receive extended treatment in Churchland 1979, sections 2, 3, 7, and 10.) What all of this illustrates, I think, is the poverty of van Fraassen's crucial distinction between factors that are "empirical, and therefore truth-relevant," and factors that are "superempirical, and therefore *not* truth-relevant."

As I see it then, values such as ontological simplicity, coherence, and explanatory power are some of the brain's most basic criteria for recognizing information, for distinguishing information from noise. And I think they are even more fundamental values than is "empirical adequacy," since collectively they can overthrow an entire conceptual framework for representing the empirical facts. Indeed, they even dictate how such a framework is constructed by the questing infant in the first place. One's observational taxonomy is not read off the world directly; rather, one comes to it piecemeal and by stages, and one settles on that taxonomy which finds the greatest coherence and simplicity in the world, and the most and the simplest lawful connections.

I can bring together my protective concerns for unobservables and for the superempirical virtues by way of the following thought experiment. Consider a man for whom absolutely *nothing* is observable. All of his sensory modalities have been surgically destroyed, and he has no visual, tactile, or other sensory experience of any kind. Fortunately, he has mounted on top of his skull a microcomputer fitted out with a variety of environmentally-sensitive transducers. The computer is connected to his association cortex (or perhaps the frontal lobe, or Wernicke's area) in such a way as to cause in him a continuous string of singular beliefs about his local environment. These "intellectual intuitions" are not infallible, but let us suppose that they provide him with much the same information that our perceptual judgments provide us.

For such person, or for a society of such persons, the *observable* world is an empty set. There is no question, therefore, of their evaluating any theory by reference to its "empirical adequacy," as characterized by van Fraassen (i.e., isomorphism between some observable features of the world and some "empirical substructure" of one of the theory's models). But such a society is still capable of science, I assert. They can invent theories, construct explanations of the facts-as-represented-in-past-spontaneous-beliefs, hazard predictions of the facts-as-represented-in-future-spontaneous-beliefs, and so forth. In principle, there is no reason they could not learn as much as we have (compare Feyerabend 1969).

But it is plain in this case that the global virtues of simplicity, coherence, and explanatory unification are what *must* guide the continuing evolution of their collected beliefs. And it is plain as well that their ontology, whatever it is, must consist entirely of *unobservable* entities. To invite a van Fraassenean disbelief in unobservable entities is, in this case, to invite the suspension of all beliefs beyond tautologies! Surely reason does not require them to be so abstemious.

It is time to consider the objection that those aspects of the world that are successfully monitored by the transducing microcomputer should count as "observables" for the folk described, despite the lack of any appropriate field of internal sensory qualia to mediate the external circumstance and the internal judgment it causes. Their tables-and-chairs ontology, as expressed in their spontaneous judgments, could then be conceded legitimacy.

I will be the first to accept such an objection. But if we do accept it, then I do not see how we can justify van Fraassen's selective skepticism with respect to the wealth of "unobservable" entities and properties reliably monitored by *our* transducing measuring instruments (electron microscopes, cloud chambers, chromatographs, etc.). The spontaneous singular judgments of the working scientist, at home in his theoretical vocabulary and deeply familiar with the measuring instruments to which his conceptual system is responding, are not worse off, causally or epistemologically, than the spontaneous singular judgments of our transducer-laden friends. If skepticism is to be put aside above, it must be put aside here as well.

My concluding thought experiment is a complement to the one just outlined. Consider some folk who observe, not less of the world than we do, but more of it. Suppose them able to observe a domain normally closed to us: the microworld of virus particles, DNA strands, and large protein molecules. Specifically, suppose a race of humanoid creatures each of whom is born with an electron microscope permanently in place over his left eye. The scope is biologically constituted, let us suppose, and it projects its image onto a human-like retina, with the rest of their neurophysiology paralleling our own.

Science tells us, and I take it that van Fraassen would agree, that virus particles, DNA strands, and most other objects of comparable dimensions count as observable entities for the humanoids described. The humanoids, at least, would be justified in so regarding them and in including them in their ontology.

But we humans may not include such entities in our ontology, according to van Fraassen's position, since they are not observable with our unaided perceptual apparatus. We may not include such entities in our ontology even though we can construct, and even if we do construct, electron microscopes of identical function, place them over our left eyes, and enjoy exactly the same microexperience as the humanoids!

The difficulty for van Fraassen's position, if I understand it correctly, is that his position requires that a humanoid and a scope-equipped human must embrace *different* epistemic attitudes toward the microworld, even though their causal connections to the world and their continuing experience of it are identical: the humanoid is required to be a realist with respect to the microworld, and the human is required to be an antirealist (i.e., an agnostic) with respect to the microworld. But this distinction between what we and they may properly embrace as real seems to me to be highly arbitrary and radically undermotivated. For the only difference between the humanoid and a scope-equipped human lies in the *causal origins* of the transducing instruments feeding information into their respective brains. The humanoid's scope owes its existence to information coded in his genetic material. The human's scope owes its existence to information coded in his cortical material, or in technical libraries. I do not see why this should make any difference in their respective ontological commitments, whatever they are, and I must decline to embrace any philosophy of science which says that it must.

3   Toward a More Realistic Realism

I now turn from critic of van Fraassen's position to advocate. One of the most central elements in his view seems to me to be well motivated and urgently deserving of further development. As he explains in his introductory chapter, his aim is to reconceive the relation of theory to world, and the units of scientific cognition, and the virtue of those units when successful. He says, "I use the adjective 'constructive' to indicate my view that scientific activity is one of construction rather than discovery: construction of models that must be adequate to the phenomena, and not discovery of truth concerning the unobservable" (1980, p. 5).

The traditional view of human knowledge is that the unit of cognition is the sentence or proposition, and the cognitive virtue of such units is truth. Van Fraassen rejects this overtly linguistic guise for his empiricism. He invites us to reconceive a theory as a set of models (rather than as a set of sentences), and he sees empirical adequacy (rather than truth) as the principal virtue of such units.

Though I reject his particular reconception, and the selective skepticism he draws from it, I think the move away from the traditional conception is entirely correct. The criticism to which I am inclined is that van Fraassen has not moved quite far enough. Specifically, if we are to reconsider truth as the aim or product of cognitive activity, I think we must reconsider its applicability right across the board, and not just in some arbitrarily or idiosyncratically segregated domain of "unobservables." That is, if we are to move away from the more naive formulations of scientific realism, we should move in the direction of *pragmatism* rather than in the direction of a positivistic instrumentalism. Let me elaborate.

When we consider the great variety of cognitively active creatures on this planet—sea slugs and octopuses, bats, dolphins, and humans; and when we consider the ceaseless reconfiguration in which their brains or central ganglia engage—adjustments in the response potentials of single neurons made in the microsecond range, changes in the response characteristics of large systems of neurons made in the seconds-to-hours range, dendritic growth and new synaptic connections and the selective atrophy of old connections effected in the day-plus range; then van Fraassen's term 'construction' begins to seem highly appropriate. There is endless construction and reconstruction, both functional and structural. Further, it is far from obvious that truth is either the primary aim or the principal product of this activity. Rather, its function would appear to be the ever more finely tuned administration of the organism's *behavior*. Natural selection does not care whether a brain has or tends toward true beliefs, so long as the organism reliably exhibits reproductively advantageous behavior. Plainly, there is going to be *some* connection between the faithfulness of the brain's world model and the propriety of the organism's behavior. But just as plainly, the connection is not going to be direct.

While we are considering cognitive activity in biological terms and in all branches of the phylogenetic tree, we should note that it is far from obvious that sentences or propositions or anything remotely like them constitute the basic elements of cognition in creatures generally. Indeed, as I have argued at length elsewhere (1979, in chapters 1 and 5 above), it is highly unlikely that the sentential kinematics embraced by folk psychology and orthodox epistemology represents or captures the basic parameters of cognition and learning even in humans. That framework is part of a commonsense theory that threatens to be either superficial or false. If we are ever to understand the *dynamics* of cognitive activity, therefore, we may have to reconceive our basic unit of cognition as something other than the sentence or proposition, and reconceive its virtue as something other than truth.

Success of this sort on the descriptive-explanatory front would likely have normative consequences. Truth, as currently conceived, might cease to be an aim of science. Not because we had lowered our sights and reduced our epistemic standards, as van Fraassen's constructive empiricism would suggest, but because we had *raised* our sights, in pursuit of some epistemic goal even *more* worthy than truth. I cannot now elucidate such goals, but we should be sensible of their possible existence. The notion of truth, after all, is but the central element in a clutch of descriptive and normative *theories* (folk psychology, folk epistemology, folk semantics, classical logic), and we can expect conceptual progress here as appropriately as anywhere else.

The notion of truth is suspect on purely metaphysical grounds anyway. It suggests straightaway the notion of The Complete and Final True Theory: at a minimum, the infinite set of all true sentences. Such a theory would be, by epistemic criteria, the best theory possible. But nothing whatever guarantees the existence of such a unique theory. Just as there is no largest positive integer, it may be that there is no best theory. It may be that for any theory whatsoever, there is always an even better theory, and so ad infinitum. If we were thus unable to speak of *the* set of all true sentences, what sense could we make of truth sentence-by-sentence?

These considerations do invite a "constructive" conception of cognitive activity, one in which the notion of truth plays at best a highly derivative role. The formulation of such a conception, adequate to all of our epistemic criteria, is the outstanding task of epistemology. I do not think we shall find that conception in van Fraassen's model-theoretic version of "positivistic instrumentalism," nor do I think we shall find it quickly. But the empirical brain begs unraveling, and we have plenty of time.

Finally, there is a question put to me by Stephen Stich. If ultimately my view is even more skeptical than van Fraassen's concerning the relevance or applicability of the notion of truth, why call it scientific *realism* at all? For at least two reasons. The term 'realism' still marks the principal contrast with its traditional adversary, positivistic instrumentalism. Whatever the integrity of the notion of truth, theories about unobservables have just *as much* a claim to truth, epistemologically and metaphysically, as theories about observables. Second, I remain committed to the idea that there exists a world, independent of our cognition, with which we interact, and of which we construct representations: for varying purposes, with varying penetration, and with varying success. Lastly, our best and most penetrating grasp of the real is still held to reside in the representations provided by our best theories. Global excellence of theory remains the fundamental measure of rational ontology. And that has always been the central claim of scientific realism.

Chapter 9

On the Nature of Theories:

A Neurocomputational Perspective

1 The Classical View of Theories

Not long ago, we all knew what a theory was: it was a set of sentences or propositions, expressible in the first-order predicate calculus. And we had what seemed to be excellent reasons for that view. Surely any theory had to be *statable*. And after it had been fully stated, as a set of sentences, what residue remained? Furthermore, the sentential view made systematic sense of how theories could perform the primary business of theories, namely, prediction, explanation, and inter-theoretic reduction. It was basically a matter of first-order deduction from the sentences of the theory conjoined with relevant premises about the domain at hand.

Equally important, the sentential view promised an account of the nature of learning, and of rationality. Required was a set of formal rules to dictate appropriate changes or updates in the overall set of believed sentences as a function of new beliefs supplied by observation. Of course, there was substantial disagreement about which rules were appropriate. Inductivists, falsificationists, hypothetico-deductivists, and Bayesian subjectivists each proposed a different account of them. But the general approach seemed clearly correct. Rationality would be captured as the proper set of formal rules emerged from logical investigation.

Finally, if theories are just sentences, then the ultimate virtue of a theory is truth. And it was widely expected that an adequate account of rational methodology would reveal why humans must tend, in the long run, toward theories that are true.

Hardly anyone will now deny that there are serious problems with every element of the preceding picture, difficulties I shall discuss below. Yet the majority of the profession is not yet willing to regard

This essay was first published in C. W. Savage, ed., *The Nature of Theories*, Minnesota Studies in the Philosophy of Science, vol. 14 (Minneapolis: University of Minnesota Press, 1989).

them as fatal. I profess myself among the minority that does so regard them. In urging the poverty of "sentential epistemologies" for over a decade now (1975b, 1979, chapters 1 and 5), I have been motivated primarily by the *pattern* of the failures displayed by that approach. Those failures suggest to me that what is defective in the classical approach is its fundamental assumption that languagelike structures of some kind constitute the basic or most important form of representation in cognitive creatures, and the correlative assumption that cognition consists in the manipulation of those representations by means of structure-sensitive rules.

To be sure, not everyone saw the same pattern of failure, nor were they prepared to draw such a strong conclusion even if they did. For any research program has difficulties, and so long as we lack a comparably compelling *alternative* conception of representation and computation, it may be best to stick with the familiar research program of sentences and rules for their manipulation.

However, it is no longer true that we lack a comparably compelling alternative approach. Within the last five years, there have been some striking theoretical developments and experimental results within cognitive neurobiology and connectionist AI. These have provided us with a powerful and fertile framework with which to address problems of cognition, a framework that owes nothing to the sentential paradigm of the classical view. My main purpose in this essay is to make the rudiments of that framework available to a wider audience, and to explore its far-reaching consequences for traditional issues in the philosophy of science. Before turning to this task, let me prepare the stage by briefly summarizing the principal failures of the classical view and the most prominent responses to them.

2   *Problems and Alternative Approaches*

The depiction of learning as the rule-governed updating of a system of sentences or propositional attitudes encountered a wide range of failures. For starters, even the best of the rules proposed failed to reproduce reliably our preanalytic judgments of credibility, even in the artificially restricted or toy situations in which they were asked to function. Paradoxes of confirmation plagued the hypothetico-deductive accounts (Hempel 1965; Scheffler 1963). The indeterminacy of falsification plagued the Popperian accounts (Lakatos 1970; Feyerabend 1970; Churchland 1975b). Laws were assigned negligible credibility on Carnapian accounts (Salmon 1966). Bayesian accounts, like Carnapian ones, presupposed a given probability space as the epistemic playground within which learning takes place, and they could not account for the rationality of major shifts from one probability space to another, which is what the most interesting and important cases of learning amount to. The rationality of large-scale *conceptual change*, accordingly, seemed beyond the reach of such approaches. Furthermore, simplicity emerged as a major determinant of theoretical credibility on most accounts, but none of them could provide an adequate definition of simplicity in syntactic terms, or give a convincing explanation of why it was relevant to truth or credibility in any case. One could begin to question whether the basic factors relevant to learning were to be found at the linguistic level at all.

Beyond these annoyances, the initial resources ascribed to a learning subject by the sentential approach plainly presupposed the successful completion of a good deal of sophisticated learning on the part of that subject already. For example, reliable observation judgments do not just appear out of nowhere. Living subjects have to *learn* to make the complex perceptual discriminations that make perceptual judgments possible. And they also have to *learn* the linguistic or propositional system within which their beliefs are to be constituted. Plainly, both cases of learning will have to involve some procedure quite distinct from that of the classical account. For that account presupposes antecedent possession of both a determinate propositional system and a capacity for determinate perceptual judgment, which is precisely what, prior to extensive learning, the human infant lacks. Accordingly, the classical story cannot possibly account for all cases of learning. There must exist a type of learning that is prior to, and more basic than, the process of sentence manipulation at issue.

Thus are we led rather swiftly to the idea that there is a level of representation *beneath* the level of the sentential or propositional attitudes, and to the correlative idea that there is a learning dynamic that operates primarily on sublinguistic factors. This idea is reinforced by reflection on the problem of cognition and learning in nonhuman animals, none of which appear to have the benefit of language, either the external speech or the internal structures, but all of which engage in sophisticated cognition. Perhaps their cognition proceeds entirely without benefit of any system for processing sentencelike representations.

Even in the human case, the depiction of one's knowledge as an immense set of individually stored "sentences" raises a severe problem concerning the relevant retrieval or application of those internal representations. How is it one is able to retrieve, from the millions of sentences stored, exactly the handful that is relevant to one's current predictive or explanatory problem, and how is it one is generally able to do this in a few tenths of a second? This is known as the "frame problem" in AI, and it arises because, from the point of view of fast and relevant retrieval, a long list of sentences is an appallingly inefficient way to store information. And the more information a creature has, the worse its application problem becomes.

A further problem with the classical view of learning is that it finds no essential connection whatever between the learning of *facts* and the learning of *skills*. This is a problem in itself, since one might have hoped for a unified account of learning, but it is doubly a problem when one realizes that so much of the business of understanding a theory and being a scientist is a matter of the skills one has acquired. Memorizing a set of sentences is not remotely sufficient: one must learn to *recognize* the often quite various instances of the terms they contain; one must learn to *manipulate* the peculiar formalism in which they may be embedded; one must learn to *apply* the formalism to novel situations; one must learn to *control* the instruments that typically produce or monitor the phenomena at issue. As T. S. Kuhn first made clear (1962), these dimensions of the scientific trade are only artificially separable from one's understanding of its current theories. It begins to appear that even if we do harbor internal sentences, they capture only a small part of human knowledge.

These failures of the classical view over the full range of learning, both in humans and in nonhuman animals, are the more suspicious given the total disconnection of the classical view from any theory concerning the structure of the biological brain, and the manner in which it might *implement* the kind of representations and computations proposed. Making acceptable contact with neurophysiological theory is a long-term constraint on any epistemology: a scheme of representation and computation that cannot be implemented in the machinery of the human brain cannot be an adequate account of human cognitive activities.

The situation on this score used to be much better than it is now: it was clear that the classical account of representation and learning could easily be realized in typical digital computers, and it was thought that the human brain would turn out to be relevantly like a digital computer. But quite aside from the fact that computer implementations of sentential learning chronically produced disappointing results, it has become increasingly clear that the brain is organized along computational lines radically different from those employed in conventional digital computers. The brain, as we shall see below, is a massively parallel processor, and it performs computational tasks of the classical kind at issue only very slowly and comparatively badly. Loosely speaking, it does not appear to be designed to perform the tasks the classical view assigns to it.

I conclude this survey by returning to specifically philosophical matters. A final problem with the classical approach has been the failure of all attempts to explain why the learning process must tend, at least in the long run, to lead us toward *true* theories. Surprisingly, and perhaps distressingly, this Panglossean hope has proved very resistant to vindication (van Fraassen 1980; Laudan 1981). Although the history of human intellectual endeavor does support the view that over the centuries our theories have become dramatically *better* in many dimensions, it is quite problematic whether they are succes- sively "closer" to "truth." Indeed, the notion of truth itself has recently come in for critical scrutiny (Putnam 1981; Churchland, chapter 8 above; Stich 1989). It is no longer clear that there *is* any unique and unitary relation that virtuous belief systems must bear to the nonlinguistic world. Which leaves us free to reconsider the great many different dimensions of epistemic and pragmatic virtue that a cognitive system can display.

The problems of the preceding pages have not usually been pre- sented in concert, and they are not usually regarded as conveying a unitary lesson. A few philosophers, however, have been moved by them, or by some subset of them, to suggest significant modifications in the classical framework. One approach that has captured some adherents is the "semantic view" of theories (Suppe 1974; van Fraas- sen 1980; Giere 1988). This approach attempts to drive a wedge be- tween a theory and its possibly quite various linguistic formulations by characterizing a theory as a *set of models*, those that will make a first-order linguistic statement of the theory come out *true* under the relevant assignments. The models in the set all share a common ab- stract structure, and that structure is what is important about any theory, according to the semantic view, not any of its idiosyncratic linguistic expressions. A theory is true, on this view, just in case it includes the actual world, or some part of it, as one of the models in the set.

This view buys us some advantages, perhaps, but I find it to be a relatively narrow response to the panoply of problems addressed above. In particular, I think it strange that we should be asked, at this stage of the debate, to embrace an account of theories that has abso- lutely nothing to do with the question of how real physical systems might embody representations of the world, and how they might execute principled computations on those representations in such a fashion as to learn. Prima facie, at least, the semantic approach takes theories even farther into Plato's Heaven, and away from the buzzing brains that use them, than did the view that a theory is a set of sent- ences. This complaint does not do justice to the positive virtues of the semantic approach (see especially Giere 1988, whose version does make some contact with current cognitive psychology). But it is clear that the semantic approach is a response to only a small subset of the extant difficulties.

A more celebrated response is embodied in Kuhn's *Structure of Scientific Revolutions* (1962). Kuhn centers our attention not on sets of sentences, nor on sets of models, but on what he calls paradigms or exemplars, which are specific *applications* of our conceptual, mathematical, and instrumental resources. Mastering a theory, on this view, is more a matter of being able to perform in various ways, of being able to solve a certain class of problems, of being able to recognize diverse situations as relevantly similar to that of the original or paradigmatic application. Kuhn's view brings to the fore the historical, sociological, and psychological factors that structure our theoretical cognition. Of central importance is the manner in which one comes to perceive the world as one internalizes a theory. The perceptual world is redivided into new categories, and while the theory may be able to provide necessary and sufficient conditions for being an instance of any of its categories, the perceptual recognition of any instance of a category does not generally proceed by reference to those conditions, which often transcend perceptual experience. Rather, perceptual recognition proceeds by some inarticulable process that registers *similarity* to one or more perceptual *prototypes* of the category at issue. The recognition of new applications of the apparatus of the entire theory displays a similar dynamic. In all, a successful theory provides a prototypical beachhead that one attempts to expand by analogical extensions to new domains.

Reaction to this view has been deeply divided. Some applaud Kuhn's move toward naturalism, toward a performance conception of knowledge, and away from the notion of truth as the guiding compass of cognitive activity (Munevar 1981; Stich 1989). Others deplore his neglect of normative issues, his instrumentalism and relativism, and his alleged exaggeration of certain lessons from perceptual and developmental psychology (Fodor 1984). I shall address these issues later in this chapter.

A third and less visible reaction to the classical difficulties has simply rejected the sentential or propositional attitudes as the most important form of representation used by cognitive creatures, and has insisted on the necessity of empirical and theoretical research into *brain* function in order to answer the question of what *are* the most important forms of representation and computation within cognitive creatures. Early statements can be found in P. M. Churchland 1975b and Hooker 1975; extended arguments appear in P. M.

Churchland 1979 and chapter 1; and further arguments appear in P. S. Churchland 1980a and 1986; and in Hooker 1987.

While the antisentential diagnosis could be given some considerable support, as the opening summary of this section illustrates, neuroscience as the recommended cure was always more difficult to sell, given the functional opacity of the biological brain. Recently, however, this has changed dramatically. We now have some provisional insight into the functional significance of the brain's microstructure, and some idea of how it represents and computes. What has been discovered so far appears to vindicate the claims of philosophical relevance and the expectations of fertility in this area, and it appears to vindicate some central elements in Kuhn's perspective as well. This neurofunctional framework promises to sustain wholly new directions of cognitive research. In the sections below I shall try to outline the elements of this framework and its applications to some familiar problems in the philosophy of science. I begin with the physical structure and the basic activities of the brainlike systems at issue.

3   Elementary Brainlike Networks

The functional atoms of the brain are cells called neurons (figure 9.1). These have a natural or default level of activity, which can, however, be modulated up or down by external influences. From each neuron

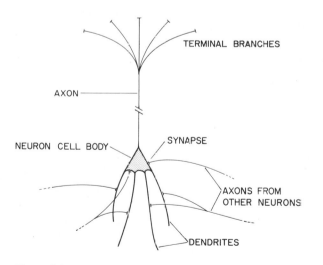

TERMINAL BRANCHES

AXON

NEURON CELL BODY

SYNAPSE

AXONS FROM OTHER NEURONS

DENDRITES

Figure 9.1
A schematic neuron

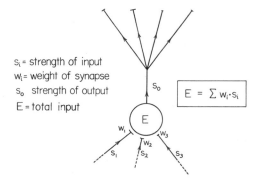

s_i = strength of input
w_i = weight of synapse
s_o strength of output
E = total input

$$E = \sum w_i \cdot s_i$$

Figure 9.2
A neuronlike processing unit

there extends a long, thin output fiber called an axon, which typically branches at the far end so as to make a large number of *synaptic connections* with either the central cell body or the bushy *dendrites* of other neurons. Each neuron thus receives inputs from a great many other neurons, which inputs tend to excite (or to inhibit, according to the type of synaptic connection) its normal or default level of activation. The level of activation induced is a function of the *number* of connections, of their size or *weight*, of their *polarity* (stimulatory or inhibitory), and of the *strength* of the incoming signals. Furthermore, each neuron is constantly emitting an output signal along its own axon, a signal whose strength is a direct function of the overall level of activation in the originating cell body. That signal is a train of pulses or *spikes*, as they are called, which are propagated swiftly along the axon. A typical cell can emit spikes along its axon at anything between 0 and perhaps 200 hertz. Neurons, if you like, are humming to one another, in basso notes of varying frequency.

The networks to be explored attempt to simulate natural neurons with artifical units of the kind depicted in figure 9.2. These units admit of various levels of activation, which I shall assume to vary between 0 and 1. Each unit receives input signals from other units via "synaptic" connections of various weights and polarities. These are represented in the diagram as small end plates of various sizes. For simplicity I dispense with dendritic trees: the "axonal" end branches from other units all make connections directly to the "cell body" of the receiving unit. The total modulating effect E impacting on that unit is just the sum of the contributions made by each of the connections. The contribution of a single connection is just the product of its weight w_i times the strength s_i of the signal arriving at that connec-

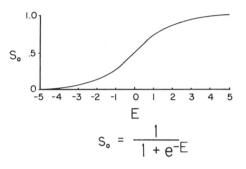

Figure 9.3
The sigmoid axonal output function

tion. Let me emphasize that if for some reason the connection weights were to change over time, then the unit would receive a quite different level of overall excitation or inhibition in response to the very same configuration of input signals.

Turn now to the output side of things. As a function of the total input E, the unit modulates its activity level and emits an output signal of a certain strength s_o along its "axonal" output fiber. But s_o is not a direct or *linear* function of E. Rather, it is an S-shaped function as in figure 9.3. The reasons for this small wrinkle will emerge later. I mention it here because its inclusion completes the story of the elementary units. Of their intrinsic properties, there is nothing left to tell. They are very simple indeed.

It remains to arrange them into networks. In the brain, neurons frequently consitute a population all of which send their axons to the site of a second population of neurons, where each arriving axon divides into terminal end branches in order to make synaptic connections with many different cells within the target population. Axons from cells in this second population can then project to a third population of cells, and so on. This is the inspiration for the arrangement of figure 9.4.

The units in the bottom or input layer of the network may be thought of as "sensory" units, since the level of activation in each is directly determined by aspects of the environment (or perhaps by the experimenter, in the process of simulating some environmental input). The activation level of a given input unit is designed to be a response to a specific aspect or dimension of the overall input stimulus that strikes the bottom layer. The assembled set of simultaneous activation levels in all of the input units is the network's *representation* of the input stimulus. We may refer to that configuration of stimulation levels as the *input vector*, since it is just an ordered set of numbers

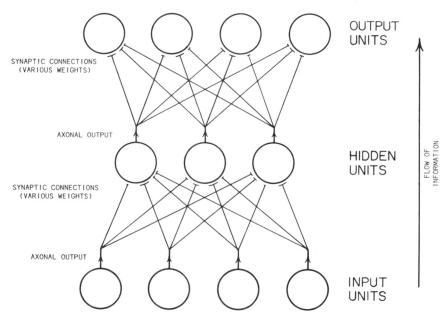

OUTPUT
UNITS

SYNAPTIC CONNECTIONS
(VARIOUS WEIGHTS)

AXONAL OUTPUT

HIDDEN
UNITS

FLOW OF
INFORMATION

SYNAPTIC CONNECTIONS
(VARIOUS WEIGHTS)

AXONAL OUTPUT

INPUT
UNITS

Figure 9.4
A simple network

or magnitudes. For example, a given stimulus might produce the vector < .5, .3, .9, .2>.

These input activation levels are then propagated upward, via the output signal in each unit's axon, to the middle layer of the network, to what are called the "hidden units." As can be seen in figure 9.4, any unit in the input layer makes a synaptic connection of some weight or other with every unit at this intermediate layer. Each hidden unit is thus the target of several inputs, one for each cell at the input layer. The resulting activation level of a given hidden unit is essentially just the sum of all of the influences reaching it from the cells in the lower layer.

The result of this upward propagation of the input vector is a set of activation levels across the three units in the hidden layer, called the "hidden unit activation vector." The values of that three-element vector are strictly determined by

(a) the makeup of the *input vector* at the input layer,
(b) the various values of the *connection weights* at the ends of the terminal branches of the input units.

What this bottom half of the network does, evidently, is convert or transform one activation vector into another.

The top half of the network does exactly the same thing, in exactly the same way. The activation vector at the hidden layer is propagated upward to the output (topmost) layer of units, where an *output vector* is produced, whose character is determined by

(*a*) the makeup of the activation vector at the hidden layer,

(*b*) the various values of the connection weights at the ends of the terminal branches of the hidden units.

Looking now at the whole network, we can see that it is just a device for transforming any given input-level activation vector into a uniquely corresponding output-level activation vector. And what determines the character of the global transformation effected is the peculiar set of values possessed by the many connection weights. This much is easy to grasp. What is not so easy to grasp, prior to exploring examples, is just how very powerful and useful those transformations can be. So let us explore some real examples.

4   Representation and Learning in Brainlike Networks

A great many of the environmental features to which humans respond are difficult to define or characterize in terms of their purely physical properties. Even something as mundane as the vowel sound /ā/, as in 'rain', resists such characterization, for the range of acoustical variation among acceptable and recognizable /ā/s is enormous. A female child at two years and a basso male at fifty will produce quite different sorts of atmospheric excitations in pronouncing this vowel, but each sound will be easily recognized as an /ā/ by other members of the same linguistic culture.

I do not mean to suggest that the matter is utterly intractable from a physical point of view, for an examination of the acoustical power spectrum of voiced vowels begins to reveal some of the similarities that unite /ā/s. And yet the analysis continues to resist a simple list of necessary and sufficient physical conditions on being an /ā/. Instead, being an /ā/ seems to be a matter of being *close enough* to a *typical /ā/* sound along a *sufficient* number of distinct *dimensions of relevance*, where each notion in italics remains difficult to characterize in a nonarbitrary way. Moreover, some of those dimensions are highly contextual. A sound type that would not normally be counted or recognized as an /ā/ when voiced in isolation may be unproblematically so counted if it regularly occurs, in someone's modestly accented speech, in all of the phonetic places that would normally be occupied by /ā/s. Evidently, what makes something an /ā/ is in part a matter of the entire linguistic surround. In this way do we very quickly ascend to the abstract and holistic level for even the simplest of culturally embedded properties.

What holds for phonemes holds also for a great many other important features recognizable by us: colors, faces, flowers, trees, animals, voices, smells, feelings, songs, words, meanings, and even metaphorical meanings. At the outset, the categories and resources of physics, and even neuroscience, look puny and impotent in the face of such subtlety.

And yet it is a purely physical system that recognizes such intricacies. Short of appealing to magic, or of simply refusing to confront the problem at all, we must assume that some configuration of purely physical elements is capable of grasping and manipulating these features, and by means of purely physical principles. Surprisingly, networks of the kind described in the preceding section have many of the properties needed to address precisely this problem. Let me explain.

Suppose we are submarine engineers confronted with the problem of designing a sonar system that will distinguish between the sonar echoes returned from explosive mines, such as might lie on the bottom of sensitive waterways during wartime, and the sonar echoes returned from rocks of comparable sizes that dot the same underwater landscapes. The difficulty is twofold: echoes from both objects sound indistinguishable to the casual ear, and echoes from each type show wide variation in sonic character, since both rocks and mines come in various sizes, shapes, and orientations relative to the probing sonar pulse.

Enter the network of figure 9.5. This one has thirteen units at the input layer, since we need to code a fairly complex stimulus. A given sonar echo is run through a frequency analyzer and is sampled for its relative energy levels at thirteen frequencies. These thirteen values, expressed as fractions of 1, are then entered as activation levels in the respective units of the input layer, as indicated in figure 9.5. From here they are propagated through the network, being transformed as they go, as explained earlier. The result is a pair of activation levels in the two units at the output layer. We need only two units here, for we want the network eventually to produce an output activation vector at or near $\langle 1, 0 \rangle$ when a mine echo is entered as input, and an output activation vector at or near $\langle 0, 1 \rangle$ when a rock echo is entered as input. In a word, we want it to *distinguish* mines from rocks.

It would, of course, be a miracle if the network made the desired discrimination immediately, since the connection weights that deter-

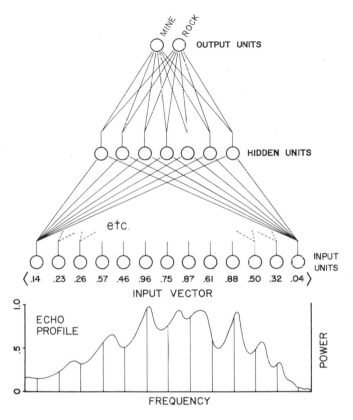

Figure 9.5
Perceptual recognition with a large network

mine its transformational activity are initially set at random values. At the beginning of this experiment, then, the output vectors are sure to disappoint us. But we proceed to *teach* the network by means of the following procedure.

We procure a large set of recorded samples of various (genuine) mine echoes, from mines of various sizes and orientations, and a comparable set of genuine rock echoes, keeping careful track of which is which. We then feed these echoes into the network, one by one, and observe the output vector produced in each case. What interests us in each case is the amount by which the actual output vector *differs* from what would have been the correct vector, given the identity of the specific echo that produced it. The details of that error, for each element of the output vector, are then fed into a special rule that computes a set of small changes in the values of the various synaptic weights in the system. The idea is to identify those weights most responsible for the error, and then to nudge their values in a direction that would at least reduce the amount by which the output vector is in error. The slighty modified system is then fed another echo from the training set, and the entire procedure is repeated.

This provides the network with a "teacher." The process is called "training up the network" and it is standardly executed by an auxiliary computer programmed to feed samples from the training set into the network, monitor its responses, and adjust the weights according to the special rule after each trial. Under the pressure of such repeated corrections, the behavior of the network slowly converges on the behavior we desire. That is to say, after several thousands of presentations of recorded echoes and subsequent adjustments, the network starts to give the right answer close to ninety percent of the time. When fed a mine echo, it generally gives something close to a <1, 0> output. And when fed a rock echo, it generally gives something close to a <0, 1>.

A useful way to think of this is captured in figure 9.6. Think of an

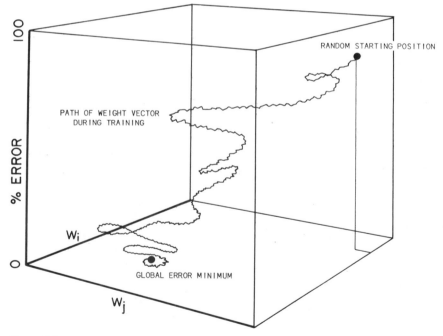

Figure 9.6
Learning: gradient descent in weight/error space. Axes are shown for only 2 of 105 synaptic weights

abstract space of many dimensions, one for each weight in the network (105 in this case), plus one dimension for representing the overall error of the output vector on any given trial. Any point in that space represents a unique configuration of weights, plus the performance error that that configuration produces. What the learning rule does is steadily nudge that configuration away from erroneous positions and toward positions that are less erroneous. The system inches its way down an "error gradient" toward a global error minimum. Once there, it responds reliably to the relevant kinds of echoes. It even responds well to echoes that are similar to mine echoes, by giving output vectors that are closer to <1, 0> than to <0, 1>.

There was no guarantee the network would succeed in learning to discriminate the two kinds of echoes, because there was no guarantee that rock echoes and mine echoes would differ in any systematic or detectable way. But it turns out that mine echoes do indeed have some complex of relational or structural features that distinguishes them from rock echoes, and under the pressure of repeated error corrections, the network manages to lock onto, or become "tuned" to, that subtle but distinctive weave of features.

We can test whether it has truly succeeded in this by now feeding the network some mine and rock echoes not included in the training set, echoes it has never encountered before. In fact, the network does almost as well classifying the new echoes as it does with the samples in its training set. The "knowledge" it has acquired generalizes quite successfully to new cases. (This example is a highly simplified account of some striking results from Gorman and Sejnowski 1988a, 1988b.)

All of this is modestly amazing, because the problem is quite a difficult one, at least as difficult as learning to discriminate the phoneme /ā/. Human sonar operators, during a long tour of submarine duty, eventually learn to distinguish the two kinds of echoes with some uncertain but nontrivial regularity. But they never perform at the level of the artificial network. Spurred on by this success, work is currently underway to train up a network to distinguish the various phonemes characteristic of English speech (Zipser and Elman 1987). The idea is to produce a speech-recognition system that will not be troubled by the acoustic idiosyncrasies of diverse speakers, as existing speech-recognition systems are.

The success of the mine/rock network is further intriguing because the "knowledge" the network has acquired, concerning the distinctive character of mine echoes, consists of nothing more than a carefully orchestrated set of connection weights. And it is finally intriguing because there exists a learning algorithm—the rule for adjusting the weights as a function of the error displayed in the output vector—that will eventually produce the required set of weights, given sufficient examples on which to train the network (Rumelhart et al. 1986b).

How can a set of connection weights possibly embody knowledge of the desired distinction? Think of it in the following way. Each of the thirteen input units represents one aspect or dimension of the incoming stimulus. Collectively, they give a simultaneous profile of the input echo along thirteen distinct dimensions. Now perhaps there is only one profile that is roughly characteristic of mine echoes; or perhaps there are many different profiles, united by a common relational feature (e.g., that the activation value of unit number 6 is always three times the value of unit number 12); or perhaps there is a disjunctive set of such relational features; and so forth. In each case it is possible to rig the weights so that the system will respond in a typical fashion, at the output layer, to all and only the relevant profiles.

The units at the hidden layer are very important in this. If we consider the abstract space whose seven axes represent the possible activation levels of each of the seven hidden units, then what the system is searching for during the training period is a set of weights that *partitions* this space so that any mine input produces an activation vector across the hidden units that falls somewhere within one large subvolume of this abstract space, while any rock input produces a vector that falls somewhere into the complement of that subvolume (figure 9.7). The job of the top half of the network is then the relatively easy one of distinguishing these two subvolumes into which the abstract space has been divided.

Vectors near the center of (or along a certain path in) the mine-vector subvolume represent *prototypical* mine echoes, and these will produce an output vector very close to the desired <1, 0>. Vectors nearer to the surface (strictly speaking, the hypersurface) that partitions the abstract space represent atypical or problematic mine echoes, and these produce more ambiguous output vectors, such as <.6, .4>. The network's discriminative responses are thus graded responses: the system is sensitive to *similarities* along all of the relevant dimensions, and especially to rough conjunctions of these subordinate similarities.

So we have a system that learns to discriminate hard-to-define perceptual features, and to be sensitive to similarities of a comparably diffuse but highly relevant character. And once the network is trained up, the recognition task takes only a split second, since the system processes the input stimulus in parallel. It finally gives us a dis-

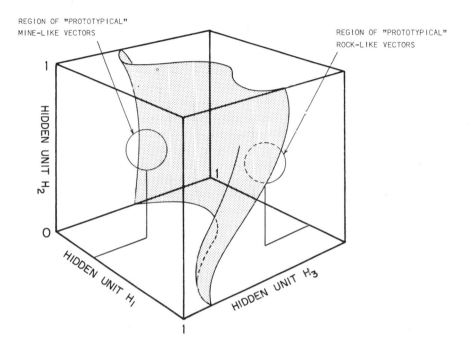

Figure 9.7
Learned partition on hidden-unit activation-vector space. Axes are shown for only three of seven hidden-unit activation levels

criminatory system that performs something like a living creature, both in its speed and in its overall character.

I have explained this system in some detail, so that the reader will have a clear idea of how things work in at least one case. But the network described is only one instance of a general technique that works well in a large variety of cases. Networks can be constructed with a larger number of units at the output layer, so as to be able to express not just two, but a large number of distinct discriminations.

One network, aptly called NETtalk by its authors (Rosenberg and Sejnowski 1987), takes vector codings for seven-letter segments of printed words as inputs and gives vector codings for phonemes as outputs. These output vectors can be fed directly into a sound synthesizer as they occur, to produce audible sounds. What this network learns to do is to transform printed words into audible speech. Though it involves no understanding of the words that it "reads," the network's feat is still very impressive, because it was given no rules whatever concerning the phonetic significance of standard English spelling. It began its training period by producing a stream of unintelligible babble in response to text entered as input. But in the course of many thousands of word presentations, and under the steady pressure of the weight-nudging algorithm, the set of weights slowly meanders its way to a configuration that reduces the measured error close to zero. After such training, it will then produce as output, given arbitrary English text as input, perfectly intelligible speech with only rare and minor errors.

This case is significant for a number of reasons. First, the trained network makes a large number of discriminations (79, in fact), not just a binary one. Second, it contains no explicit representation of any *rules*, however much it might seem to be following a set of rules. Third, it has mastered an input/output transformation that is notoriously irregular, and it must be sensitive to lexical context in order to do so. (Specifically, the phoneme it assigns to the center or focal letter of its seven-letter input is in large part a function of the identity of the three letters on either side.) And fourth, it portrays some aspects of a sensori*motor* skill, rather than a purely sensory skill: it is producing highly complex behavior.

NETtalk has some limitations, of course. Pronunciations that depend on specifically semantical or grammatical distinctions will generally elude its grasp—unless they happen to be reflected in some way in the corpus of its training words, as occasionally they are—since NETtalk knows neither meanings nor syntax. But such dependencies affect only a very small percentage of the transformations appropriate to any text, and they are in any case to be expected. To overcome them completely would require a network that actually understands the text being read. And even then mistakes would occur, for even humans occasionally misread words as a result of grammatical or semantic confusion. What is arresting about NETtalk is just how very much of the complex and irregular business of text-based pronunciation can be mastered by a simple network with only a few hundred neuronlike units.

Another rather large network (by Lehky and Sejnowski 1988a, 1988b) addresses problems in vision. It takes codings for smoothly varying gray-scale pictures as input; and after training, it yields as outputs surprisingly accurate codings for the curvatures and orientations of the physical objects portrayed in the pictures. It solves a form of the shape-from-shading problem long familiar to theorists in the field of vision. This network is of special interest because a subsequent examination of the receptive fields of the trained hidden units shows them to have acquired some of the same response properties as are displayed by cells in the visual cortex of mature animals. Specifically, they show a maximal sensitivity to spots, edges, and bars in specific orientations. This finding echoes the seminal work of Hubel and Wiesel (1962), in which cells in the visual cortex were discovered to have receptive fields of this same character. Results of this kind are very important, for if we are to take these artificial networks as models for how the brain works, then they must display realistic behavior not just at the macro level; they must also display realistic behavior at the micro level.

Enough examples. You have seen something of what networks of this kind can do and of how they do it. In both respects they contrast sharply with the kinds of representational and processing strategies that philosophers of science, inductive logicians, cognitive psychologists, and AI workers have traditionally ascribed to us (namely, sentencelike representations manipulated by formal rules). You can see also why this theoretical and experimental approach has captured the interest of those who seek to understand how the microarchitecture of the biological brain produces the phenomena displayed in human and animal cognition. Let us now explore the functional properties of these networks in more detail, and see how they bear on some of the traditional issues in epistemology and the philosophy of science.

5   Some Functional Properties of Brainlike Networks

The networks described above are descended from a device called the Perceptron (Rosenblatt 1959), which was essentially just a two-layer network as opposed to a three-layer network. Devices of this configuration could and did learn to discriminate a considerable variety of input patterns. Unfortunately, having the input layer connected directly to the output layer imposes very severe limitations on the range of possible transformations a network can perform (Minsky and Papert 1969), and interest in Perceptron-like devices was soon eclipsed by the much faster-moving developments in standard "program-writing" AI, which exploited the high-speed general-purpose digital machines that were then starting to become widely available. Throughout the seventies, research in artificial "neural nets" was an underground program by comparison.

It has emerged from the shadows for a number of reasons. One important factor is just the troubled doldrums into which mainstream or program-writing AI has fallen. In many respects, these doldrums parallel the infertility of the classical approach to theories and learning within the philosophy of science. This is not surprising, since mainstream AI was proceeding on many of the same basic assumptions about cognition, and many of its attempts were just machine implementations of learning algorithms proposed earlier by philosophers of science and inductive logicians (Glymour 1988). The failures of mainstream AI—unrealistic learning, poor performance in complex perceptual and motor tasks, weak handling of analogies, and snail-like cognitive performance despite the use of very large and fast machines—teach us even more dramatically than do the failures of mainstream philosophy that we need to rethink the style of representation and computation that we have been ascribing to cognitive creatures.

Other reasons for the resurgence of interest in networks are more positive. The introduction of additional layers of intervening or "hidden" units produced a dramatic increase in the range of possible transformations that the network could effect. As Sejnowski et al. describe it,

> Only the first-order statistics of the input pattern can be captured by direct connections between input and output units. The role of the hidden units is to capture higher-order statistical relationships and this can be accomplished if significant underlying features can be found that have strong, regular relationships with the patterns on the visible units. The hard part of learning is to find the set of weights which turn the hidden units into useful feature detectors. (1986, p. 264)

Equally important is the S-shaped, nonlinear response profile (figure 9.3) now assigned to every unit in the network. So long as this response profile remains linear, any network will be limited to computing purely linear transformations. (A transformation $f(x)$ is *linear* just in case $f(n \cdot x) = n \cdot f(x)$, and $f(x + y) = f(x) + f(y)$.) But a nonlinear response profile for each unit brings the entire range of possible nonlinear transformations within reach of three-layer networks, a dramatic expansion of their computational potential. Now there are *no* transformations that lie beyond the computational power of a large enough and suitably weighted network (Hornik et al. 1989).

A third factor was the articulation, by Rumelhart, Hinton, and Williams (1986a), of the *generalized delta rule* (a generalization, to three-layer networks, of Rosenblatt's original teaching rule for adjusting the weights of the Perceptron), and the empirical discovery that this new rule very rarely got permanently stuck in inefficient local minima on its way toward finding the best possible configuration of connection weights for a given network and a given problem. This was a major breakthrough, not so much because "learning by the back-propagation of error," as it has come to be called, was just like human learning, but because it provided us with an efficient technology for quickly training up various networks on various problems, so that we could study their properties and explore their potential.

The way the generalized delta rule works can be made fairly intuitive given the idea of an abstract weight space as represented in figure 9.6. Consider any output vector produced by a network with a specific configuration of weights, a configuration represented by a specific position in weight space. Suppose that this output vector is in error by various degrees in various of its elements. Consider now a single synapse at the ouput layer, and consider the effect on the output vector that a small positive or negative change in its weight would have had. Since the output vector is a determinate function of the system's weights (assuming we hold the input vector fixed), we can calculate which of these two possible changes, if either, would have made the greater improvement in the output vector. The relevant change is made accordingly. (For more detail, see Rumelhart et al. 1986b.)

If a similar calculation is performed over every synapse in the network, and the change in its weight is then made accordingly, what the resulting shift in the position of the system's overall point in weight space amounts to is a small slide down the steepest face of the local "error surface." Note that there is no guarantee that this incremental shift moves the system directly toward the global position of zero error (that is why perfection cannot be achieved in a single jump). On the contrary, the descending path to a global error minimum may be highly circuitous. Nor is there any guarantee that the system must eventually reach such a global minimum. On the contrary, the downward path from a given starting point may well lead to a merely local minimum, from which only a large change in the system's weights will afford escape, a change beyond the reach of the delta rule. But in fact this happens relatively rarely, for it turns out that the more dimensions (synapses) a system has, the smaller the probability of there being an intersecting local minimum in *every one* of the available dimensions. The global point is usually able to slide down some narrow cleft in the local topography. Empirically, then, the back-propagation algorithm is surprisingly effective at driving the system to the global error minimum, at least where we can identify that global minimum effectively.

The advantage this algorithm provides is easily appreciated. The possible combinations of weights in a network increases exponentially with the size of the network. If we conservatively assume that each weight admits of only 10 possible values, the number of distinct positions in weight space (i.e., the number of possible weight configurations) for the simple rock/mine network of figure 9.5 is already 10^{105}! This space is far too large to explore efficiently without something like the generalized delta rule and the back propagation of error to do it for us. But with the delta rule, administered by an auxiliary computer, researchers have shown that networks of the simple kind described are capable of learning some quite extraordinary skills, and of displaying some highly intriguing properties. Let me now return to an exploration of these.

An important exploratory technique in cognitive and behavioral neuroscience is to record, with an implanted microelectrode, the electrical activity of a single neuron during cognition or behavior in the intact animal. This is relatively easy to do, and it does give us tantalizing bits of information about the cognitive significance of neural activity (recall the results of Hubel and Wiesel mentioned earlier). Single-cell recordings give us only isolated bits of information, however, and what we would really like to monitor are the *patterns* of simultaneous neural activation across large numbers of cells in the same subsystem. Unfortunately, effective techniques for simultaneously recording from large numbers of adjacent cells are still in their infancy. The task is extremely difficult.

By contrast, this task is extremely easy with the artificial networks we have been describing. If the network is real hardware, its units are far more accessible than the fragile and microscopic units of a living brain. And if the network is merely being simulated within a standard computer (as is usually the case), one can write the program so that the activation levels of any unit, or set of units, can be read out on command. Accordingly, once a network has been successfully trained up on some skill or other, one can then examine the collective behavior of its units during the exercise of that skill.

We have already seen the results of one such analysis in the rock/mine network. Once the weights have reached their optimum configuration, the activation vectors (i.e., the patterns of activation) at the hidden layer fall into two disjoint classes: the vector space is partitioned in two, as depicted schematically in figure 9.7. But a mere binary discrimination is an atypically simple case. The reader NETtalk, for example, partitions its hidden-unit vector space into fully 79 subspaces. The reason is simple. For each of the 26 letters in the alphabet, there is at least one phoneme assigned to it, and for many letters there are several phonemes that might be signified, depending on the lexical context. As it happens, there are 79 distinct letter-to-phoneme associations to be learned if one is to master the pronunciation of English spelling, and in the successfully trained network a distinct hidden-unit activation vector occurs when each of these 79 possible transformations is effected.

In the case of the rock/mine network, we noted a similarity metric within each of its two hidden-unit subspaces. In the case of NETtalk, we also find a similarity metric, this time across the 79 functional hidden-unit vectors (by 'functional vector' I mean a vector that corresponds to one of the 79 desired letter-to-phoneme transformations in the trained network). Rosenberg and Sejnowski did a cluster analysis of these vectors in the trained network. Roughly, their procedure was as follows. They asked, for every functional vector in that space, What other such vector is closest to it? The answers yielded about 30 vector pairs. They then constructed a secondary vector for each such pair, by averaging the two original vectors, and asked, for every such secondary vector, What other secondary vector (or so far unpaired primary vector) is closest to it? This produced a smaller set of secondary-vector pairs, on which the averaging procedure was repeated to produce a set of tertiary vectors. These were then paired in turn, and so forth. This procedure produces a hierarchy of groupings among the original transformations, and it comes to an end with a grand division of the 79 original vectors into two disjoint classes.

As it happens, that deepest and most fundamental division within the hidden-unit vector space corresponds to the division between the consonants and the vowels! Looking further into this hierarchy, into the consonant branch, for example, we find that there are subdivisions into the principal consonant types, and that within these branches there are further subdivisions into the most similar consonants. All of this is depicted in the tree diagram of figure 9.8. What the network has managed to recover, from its training set of several thousand English words, is the highly irregular phonological significance of standard English spelling, plus the hierarchical organization of the phonetic structure of English speech.

Here we have a clear illustration of two things at once. The first lesson is the capacity of an activation-vector space to embody a rich and well-structured hierarchy of categories, complete with a similarity metric embracing everything within it. And the second lesson is the capacity of such networks to embody representations of factors and patterns that are only partially or implicitly reflected in the corpus of inputs. Though I did not mention it earlier, the rock/mine network provides another example of this, in that the final partition made on its hidden-unit vector space corresponds in fact to the objective distinction between sonar targets made of *metal* and sonar targets made of *nonmetal*. That is the true uniformity that lies behind the apparently chaotic variety displayed in the inputs.

It is briefly tempting to suggest that NETtalk has the concept of a hard *c*, for example, and that the rock/mine network has the concept

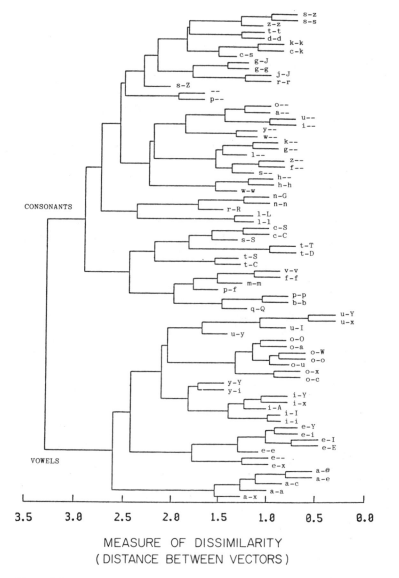

MEASURE OF DISSIMILARITY
(DISTANCE BETWEEN VECTORS)

Figure 9.8
Hierarchy of partitions on hidden-unit vector space of NETtalk

of metal. But this won't really do, since the vector-space representations at issue do not play a conceptual or computational role remotely rich enough to merit their assimilation to specifically human concepts. Nevertheless, it is plain that both networks have contrived a system of internal representations that truly corresponds to important distinctions and structures in the outside world, structures that are not explicitly represented in the corpus of their sensory inputs. The value of those representations is that they and only they allow the networks to "make sense" of their variegated and often noisy input corpus, in the sense that they and only they allow the network to respond to those inputs in a fashion that systematically reduces the error messages to a trickle. These, I need hardly remind, are the functions typically ascribed to *theories*.

What we are confronting here is a possible conception of knowledge or understanding that owes nothing to the sentential categories of current common sense. An individual's overall theory-of-the-world, we might venture, is not a large collection or a long list of stored symbolic items. Rather, it is a specific point in that individual's synaptic weight space. It is a configuration of connection weights, a configuration that partitions the system's activation-vector space(s) into useful divisions and subdivisions relative to the inputs typically fed the system. 'Useful' here means 'tends to minimize the error messages'.

A possible objection here points to the fact that differently weighted systems can produce the same, or at least roughly the same, partitions on their activation-vector spaces. Accordingly, we might try to abstract from the idiosyncratic details of a system's connection weights, and identify its global theory directly with the set of partitions they produce within its activation-vector space. This would allow for differently weighted systems to have the same theory.

There is some virtue in this suggestion, but also some vice. While differently weighted systems can embody the same partitions and thus display the same output performance on any given input, they will still *learn* quite differently in the face of a protracted sequence of new and problematic inputs. This is because the learning algorithm that drives the system to new points in weight space does not care about the relatively global partitions that have been made in activation space. All it cares about are the individual *weights* and how they relate to apprehended error. The laws of cognitive evolution, therefore, do not operate primarily at the level of the partitions, at least on the view of things here being explored. Rather, they operate at the level of the weights. Accordingly, if we want our "unit of cognition" to figure in the *laws* of cognitive development, the point in weight space seems the wiser choice of unit. We need only concede that different global theories can occasionally produce identical short-term behavior.

The level of the partitions certainly corresponds more closely to the "conceptual" level, as understood in common sense and traditional theory, but the point is that this seems not to be the most important dynamical level, even when explicated in neurocomputational terms. Knowing a creature's vector-space partitions may suffice for the accurate short-term prediction of its behavior, but that knowledge is inadequate to predict or explain the evolution of those partitions over the course of time and cruel experience. Knowledge of the weights, by contrast, *is* sufficient for this task. This gives substance to the conviction, voiced earlier in section 2, that explain the phenomenon of *conceptual change*, we need to unearth a level of subconceptual combinatorial elements within which different concepts can be articulated, evaluated, and then modified according to their performance. The connection weights provide a level that meets all of these conditions.

This general view of how knowledge is embodied and accessed in the brain has some further appealing features. If we assume that the brains of the higher animals work in something like the fashion outlined, then we can explain a number of puzzling features of human and animal cognition. For one thing, the speed-of-relevant-access problem simply disappears. A network the size of a human brain—with 10^{11} neurons, 10^3 connections on each, 10^{14} total connections, and at least 10 distinct layers of hidden units—can be expected, in the course of growing up, to partition its internal vector spaces into many billions of functionally relevant subdivisions, each responsive to a broad but proprietary range of highly complex stimuli. When the network receives a stimulus that falls into one of these classes, the network produces the appropriate activation vector in a matter of only tens or hundreds of milliseconds, because that is all the time it takes for the parallel-coded stimulus to make its way through only two or three or ten layers of the massively parallel network to the functionally relevant layer that drives the appropriate behavioral response. Since information is stored not in a long list that must somehow be searched, but rather in the myriad connection weights that configure the network, relevant aspects of the creature's total information are automatically accessed by the coded stimuli themselves.

A third advantage of this model is its explanation of the functional persistence of brains in the face of minor damage, disease, and the normal but steady loss of its cells with age. Human cognition degrades fairly gracefully as the physical plant deteriorates, in sharp contrast to the behavior of typical computers, which have a very low fault tolerance. The explanation of this persistence lies in the massively parallel character of the computations the brain performs, and in the very tiny contribution that each synapse or each cell makes to the overall computation. In a large network of 100,000 units, the loss or misbehavior of a single cell will not even be detectable. And in the more dramatic case of widespread cell loss, so long as the losses are more or less randomly distributed throughout the network, the gross character of the network's activity will remain unchanged. What happens is that the *quality* of its computations will be progressively degraded.

Turning now toward more specifically philosophical concerns, we may note an unexpected virtue of this approach concerning the matter of *simplicity*. This important notion presents two problems: it is robustly resistant to attempts to define or measure it, and it is not clear why it should be counted an epistemic virtue in any case. There seems no obvious reason, either a priori or a posteriori, why the world should be simple rather than complex, and epistemic decisions based on the contrary assumption thus appear arbitrary and unjustified. Simplicity, conclude some (van Fraassen 1980), is a merely pragmatic or aesthetic virtue, as opposed to a genuinely epistemic virtue. But consider the following story.

The rock/mine network of figure 9.5 displayed a strong capacity for generalizing beyond the sample echoes in its training set: it can accurately discriminate entirely new samples of both kinds. But trained networks do not always generalize so well, and it is interesting what determines their success in this regard. How well the training generalizes is in part a function of *how many* hidden units the system possesses, or uses to solve the problem. There is, it turns out, an optimal number of units for any given problem. If the network to be trained is given more than the optimal number of hidden units, it will learn to respond appropriately to all of the various samples in its training set, but it will generalize to new samples only very poorly. On the other hand, with less than the optimal number, it never really learns to respond appropriately to all of the samples in its training set.

The reason is as follows. During the training period the network gradually generates a set of internal representations at the level of the hidden units. One class of hidden-unit activation vectors is characteristic of rocklike input vectors; another class is characteristic of minelike input vectors. During this period the system is *theorizing* at the level of the hidden units, exploring the space of possible activation vectors, in hopes of finding some partition or set of partitions on it that the output layer can then exploit in turn, so as to draw the needed distinctions and thus bring the process of error-induced synaptic adjustments to an end.

If there are far too many hidden units, then the learning process can be partially subverted in the following way. The lazy system cheats: it learns a set of *unrelated* representations at the level of the hidden units. It learns a distinct representation for each sample input (or for a small group of such inputs) drawn from the very finite training set, a representation that does indeed prompt the correct response at the output level. But since there is nothing common to all of the hidden-unit rock representations, or to all of the hidden-unit mine representations, an input vector from outside the training set produces a hidden-unit representation that bears no relation to the representations already formed. The system has not learned to see *what is common* within each of the two stimulus classes, which would allow it to generalize effortlessly to new cases that shared that common feature. It has just knocked together an ad hoc "look-up table" that allows it to deal successfully with the limited samples in the training set, at which point the error messages cease, the weights stop evolving, and the system stops learning. (I am grateful to Terry Sejnowski for mentioning to me this wrinkle in the learning behavior of typical networks.)

There are two ways to avoid this ad hoc, unprojectible learning. One is to enlarge dramatically the size of the training set. This will overload the system's ability to just "memorize" an adequate response for each of the training samples. But a more effective way is just to reduce the number of hidden units in the network, so that it lacks the resources to cobble together such wasteful and ungeneralizable internal representations. We must reduce them to the point where it has to find a *single* partition on the hidden-unit vector space, a partition that puts all of the sample rock representations on one side, and all of the sample mine representations on the other. A system constrained in this way will generalize far better, for the global partition it has been forced to find corresponds to something *common* to each member of the relevant stimulus class, even if it is only a unifying dimension of variation (or set of such dimensions) that unites them all by a similarity relation. It is the generation of that similarity relation that allows the system to respond appropriately to novel examples. They may be new to the system, but they fall on a spectrum for which the system now has an adequate representation.

Networks with only a few hidden units in excess of the optimal number will sometimes spontaneously achieve the maximally simple "hypothesis" despite the excess units. The few unneeded units are slowly shut down by the learning algorithm during the course of training. They become zero-valued elements in all of the successful vectors. Networks will not always do this, however. The needed simplicity must generally be forced from the outside, by a progressive reduction in the number of available hidden units.

On the other hand, if the network has too few hidden units, then it lacks the resources even to express an activation vector that is adequate to characterize the underlying uniformity, and it will never master completely even the smallish corpus of samples in the training set. In other words, simplicity may be a virtue, but the system must command sufficient complexity at least to meet the task at hand.

We have just seen how forcing a neural network to generate a smaller number of distinct partitions on a hidden-unit vector space of fewer dimensions can produce a system whose learning achievements generalize more effectively to novel cases. *Ceteris paribus*, the simpler hypotheses generalize better. Getting by with fewer resources is, of course, a virtue in itself, though a pragmatic one, to be sure. But this is not the principal virtue here displayed. Superior generalization is a genuinely epistemic virtue, and it is regularly displayed by networks constrained, in the fashion described, to find the simplest hypothesis concerning whatever structures might be hidden in, or behind, their input vectors.

Of course, nothing guarantees successful generalization: a network is always hostage to the quality of its training set relative to the total population. And there may be equally simple alternative hypotheses that generalize differentially well. Yet from the perspective of the relevant microdynamics, we can see at least one clear reason why simplicity is more than a merely pragmatic virtue. It is an epistemic virtue, not principally because simple hypotheses avoid the vice of being complex, but because they avoid the vice of being ad hoc.

6   How Faithfully Do These Networks Depict the Brain?

The functional properties so far observed in these model networks are an encouraging reward for the structural assumptions that went into them. But just how accurate are these models, as depictions of the brain's microstructure? A wholly appropriate answer here is uncertain, for we continue to be uncertain about what features of the brain's microstructure are and are not functionally relevant, and we are therefore uncertain about what is and is not a "legitimate" simplifying assumption in the models we make. Even so, it is plain that the models are *in*accurate in a variety of respects. The point of the present section is to summarize and evaluate these failings. Let me

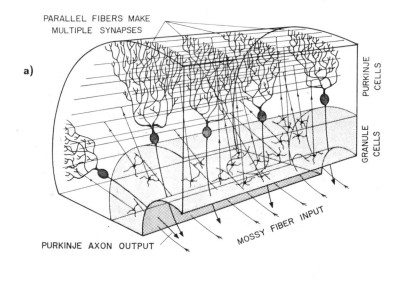

PARALLEL FIBERS MAKE
MULTIPLE SYNAPSES

a)

PURKINJE CELLS

GRANULE CELLS

MOSSY FIBER INPUT

PURKINJE AXON OUTPUT

b)

PARALLEL FIBER
INPUT

p_1 q_1 r_1 ← a

p_2 q_2 r_2 ← b

p_3 q_3 r_3 ← c

p_4 q_4 r_4 ← d

x   y   z

PURKINJE CELL OUTPUT

Figure 9.9
a) A schematic section of the cerebellum (cell population and fiber density reduced for clarity). *b*) Neural matrix

begin by underscoring the basic respects in which the models appear to be correct.

It is true that real nervous systems display, as their principal organizing feature, layers or populations of neurons that project their axons *en masse* to some distinct layer or population of neurons, where each arriving axon divides into multiple branches whose end bulbs make synaptic connections of various weights onto many cells at the target location. This description captures all of the sensory modalities and their primary relations to the brain; it captures the character of the various areas of the central brain stem; and it captures the structure of the cerebral cortex, which in humans contains at least six distinct layers of neurons, where each layer is the source and/or the target of an orderly projection of axons to and/or from elsewhere.

It captures the character of the cerebellum as well (figure 9.9*a*), a structure discussed in chapter 5 in connection with the problem of motor control. I there described the cerebellum as having the structure of a very large "matrix multiplier," as schematized in figure 9.9*b*. Following Pellionisz and Llinas 1982, I ascribed to this neural matrix the function of performing sophisticated transformations on incoming activation vectors. This is, in fact, the same function performed between any two layers of the three-layered networks described earlier, and the two cases are distinct only in the superficial details of their wiring diagrams. A three-layered network of the kind discussed earlier is equivalent to a pair of neural matrices connected in series, as is illustrated in figure 9.10. The only substantive difference is that in figure 9.10*a* the end branches synapse directly onto the receiving cell body itself, while in 9.10*b* they synapse onto some dendritic filaments extending out from the receiving cell body. The actual connectivity within the two networks is identical. The cerebellum and the motor

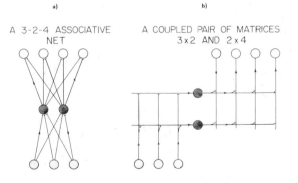

a)

A 3-2-4 ASSOCIATIVE
NET

b)

A COUPLED PAIR OF MATRICES
3 x 2 AND 2 x 4

Figure 9.10
The equivalence of nets and matrices

end of natural systems, accordingly, seem to be further instances of the gross pattern at issue.

But the details present all manner of difficulties. To begin with small ones, note that in real brains an arriving axon makes synaptic contact with only a relatively small percentage of the thousands or millions of cells in its target population, not with every last one of them as in the models. This is not a serious difficulty, since model networks with comparably pared connections still manage to learn the required transformations quite well, though perhaps not so well as a fully connected network.

More serious, real axons, so far as is known, have terminal end bulbs that are uniformly inhibitory, or uniformly excitatory, according to the type of neuron. We seem not to find a mixture of both kinds of connections radiating from the same neuron, nor do we find connections changing their sign during learning, as is the case in the models. Moreover, that mixture of positive and negative influences is essential to successful function in the models: the same input cell must be capable of inhibiting some cells down the line at the same time that it is busy exciting others. Further, cell populations in the brain typically show extensive "horizontal" cell-to-cell connections *within* a given layer. In the models there are none at all (see, e.g., figure 9.4). Their connections join units only to units in distinct layers.

These last two difficulties might conceivably serve to cancel each other. One way in which an excitatory end bulb might serve to *inhibit* a cell in its target population is first to make an excitatory connection onto one of the many small *interneurons* typically scattered throughout the target population of main neurons, which interneuron has made an inhibitory synaptic connection onto the target main neuron. Exciting the inhibitory interneuron would then have the effect of inhibiting the main neuron, as desired. And such a system would display a large number of short horizontal intralayer connections, as is observed. This is just a suggestion, however, since it is far from clear that the elements mentioned are predominantly connected in the manner required.

More serious still, there are several major problems with the idea that networks in the brain learn by means of the learning algorithm so effective in the models, the procedure of back propagating apprehended errors according to the generalized delta rule. That procedure requires two things: (1) a computation of the partial correction needed for each unit in the output layer, and via these corrections a computation of a partial correction for each unit in the earlier layers, and (2) a method of causally conveying these correction messages back through the network to the sites of the relevant synaptic connections in such a fashion that each weight gets nudged up or down accordingly. In a computer simulation of the networks at issue (which is currently the standard technique for exploring their properties), both the computation and the subsequent weight adjustments are easily done: the computation is done *outside* the network by the host computer, which has direct access to and control over every element of the network being simulated. But in the self-contained biological brain, we have to find some real source of adjustment signals and some real pathways to convey them back to the relevant units. Unfortunately, the empirical brain displays little that answers to exactly these requirements.

Not that it contains nothing along these lines: the primary ascending pathways already described are typically matched by reciprocal or "descending" pathways of comparable density. These allow higher layers to have an influence on affairs at lower layers. Yet the influence appears to be on the activity levels of the lower cells themselves, rather than on the myriad synaptic connections whose weights need adjusting during learning. There may be indirect effects on the synapses, of course, but it is far from clear that the brain's wiring diagram answers to the demands of the back-propagation algorithm.

The case is a little more promising in the cerebellum (figure 9.9a), which contains a second major input system in the aptly named *climbing fibers* (not shown in the diagram for reasons of clarity). These fibers envelop each of the large Purkinje cells from below in the same fashion that a climbing ivy envelops a giant oak, with its filamentary tendrils reaching well up into the bushy dendritic tree of the Purkinje cell, which tree is the locus of all of the synaptic connections made by the incoming parallel fibers. The climbing fibers are thus at least roughly positioned to do the job that the back-propagation algorithm requires of them, and they are distributed one to each Purkinje cell, as consistent delivery of the error message requires (Thompson 1986). Equally, they might serve some other quite different learning algorithm, as advocated by Pellionisz and Llinas (1985). Unfortunately, there is as yet no compelling reason to believe that the modification of the weights of the parallel-fiber-to-Purkinje-dendrite synapses is even within the causal power of the climbing fibers. Nor is there any clear reason to see either the climbing fibers in the cerebellum, or the descending pathways elsewhere in the brain, as the bearers of any appropriately computed error-correction messages appropriate to needed synaptic change.

On the hardware side, therefore, the situation does not support the idea that the specific back-propagation procedure of Rumelhart et al.

is the brain's central mechanism for learning. (Nor, it should be mentioned, did they claim that it is.) And it is implausible on some functional grounds as well. First, in the process of learning a recognition task, living brains typically show a progressive reduction in the reaction time required for the recognitional output response. With the delta rule, however, learning involves a progressive reduction in error, but reaction times are constant throughout. A second difficulty with the delta rule is as follows. A necessary element in its calculated apportionment of error is a representation of what would have been the *correct* vector in the output layer. That is why back propagation is said to involve a global *teacher*, an information source that always knows the correct answers and can therefore provide a perfect measure of output error. Real creatures generally lack any such perfect information. They must struggle along in the absence of any sure compass toward the truth, and their synaptic adjustments must be based on much poorer information.

And yet their brains learn. Which means that somehow the configuration of their synaptic weights must undergo change, change steered in some way by error or related dissatisfaction, change that carves a path toward a regime of decreased error. Knowing this much, and knowing something about the microstructure and microdynamics of the brain, we can explore the space of possible learning procedures with some idea of what features to look for. If the generalized delta rule is not the brain's procedure, as it seems not to be, there remain other possible strategies for back-propagating sundry error measures, strategies that may find more detailed reflection in the brain. If these prove unrealizable, there are other procedures that do not require the organized distribution of any global error measures at all; they depend primarily on local constraints (Hinton and Sejnowski 1986; Hopfield and Tank 1985; Barto 1985; Bear et al. 1987).

One of these is worthy of mention, since something along these lines does appear to be displayed in biological brains. *Hebbian learning* (so called after D. O. Hebb, who first proposed the mechanism) is a process of weight adjustment that exploits the temporal coincidence, on either side of a given synaptic junction, of a strong signal in the incoming axon and a high level of excitation in the receiving cell. When such conjunctions occur, Hebb proposed, some physical or chemical change is induced in the synapse, a change that increases its weight. Of course, high activation in the receiving cell is typically caused by excitatory stimulation from many other incoming axons, and so the important temporal coincidence here is really between high activation among certain of the incoming axons. Those whose high activation coincides with the activation of many others have their subsequent influence on the cell increased. Crudely, those who vote with winners become winners.

A Hebbian weight-adjusting procedure can indeed produce learning in artificial networks (Linsker 1986), although it does not seem to be as general in its effectiveness as is back propagation. On the other hand, it has a major functional advantage over back propagation. The latter has scaling problems, in that the process of calculating and distributing the relevant adjustments expands geometrically with the number of units in the network. But Hebbian adjustments are locally driven; they are independent of one another and of the overall size of the network. A large network will thus learn just as quickly as a small one. Indeed, a large network may even show a slight advantage over a smaller one, since the temporal coincidence of incoming stimulations at a given cell will be better and better defined with increasing numbers of incoming axons.

We may also postulate "anti-Hebbian" processes, as a means of reducing synaptic weights instead of increasing them. And we need to explore various possible flavors of each. We still have very little understanding of the functional properties of these alternative learning strategies. Nor are we at all sure that Hebbian learning, as described above, is really how the brain typically adjusts its weights. There does seem to be a good deal of activity-sensitive synaptic modification occurring in the brain, but whether its profile is specifically Hebbian is not yet established. Nor should we expect the brain to confine itself to only one learning strategy, for even at the behavioral level we can discern distinct types of learning. In sum, the problem of what mechanisms actually produce synaptic change during learning is an unsolved problem. But the functional success of the generalized delta rule assures us that the problem is solvable in principle, and other more plausible procedures are currently under active exploration.

While the matter of how real neural networks generate the right configuration of weights remains obscure, the matter of how they perform their various cognitive tasks once configured is a good deal clearer. If even small artifical networks can perform the sophisticated cognitive tasks illustrated earlier in this paper, there is no mystery that real networks should do the same or better. What the brain displays in the way of hardware is not radically different from what the models contain, and the differences invite exploration rather than disappointment. The brain is, of course, very much larger and denser than the models so far constructed. It has many layers rather than just two or three. It boasts perhaps a hundred distinct and highly specialized cell types, rather than just one. It is not a single n-layer network, but rather a large committee of distinct but parallel networks, interacting in sundry ways. It plainly commands many spaces of stunning complexity, and many skills in consequence. It stands as a glowing invitation to make our humble models yet more and more realistic, in hopes of unlocking the many secrets remaining.

7   Computational Neuroscience: The Naturalization of Epistemology

One test of a new framework is its ability to throw a new and unifying light on a variety of old phenomena. I will close this essay with an exploration of several classic issues in the philosophy of science. The aim is to reconstruct them within the framework of the computational neuroscience outlined above. In section 5 we saw how this could be done for the case of theoretical simplicity. We there saw a new way of conceiving of this feature, and found a new perspective on why it is a genuine epistemic virtue. The hope in what follows is that we may do the same for other problematic notions and issues.

A good place to begin is with the issue of foundationalism. Here the central bone of contention is whether our observation judgments must always be theory laden. The traditional discussion endures largely for the good reason that a great deal hangs on the outcome, but also for the less momentous reason that there is ambiguity in what one might wish to count as an "observation judgment" (an explicitly uttered sentence? a covert assertion? a propositional attitude? a conscious experience? a sensation?), and a slightly different issue emerges depending on where the debate is located.

But from the perspective of this essay, it makes no difference at what level the issue might be located. If our cognitive activities arise from a weave of networks of the kind discussed above, and if we construe a global theory as a global configuration of synaptic weights, as outlined in section 5, then it is clear that no cognitive activity whatever takes place in the absence of vectors being processed by some specific configuration of weights. That is, no cognitive activity whatever takes place in the absence of some theory or other.

This perspective bids us see even the simplest of animals and the youngest of infants as possessing theories, since they too process their activation vectors with some configuration of weights or other. The difference between us and them is not that they lack theories. Rather, their theories are just a good deal simpler than ours, in the case of animals. And their theories are much less coherent, less organized, and less informed than ours, in the case of human infants. Which is to say, they have yet to achieve points in overall weight space that partition their activation-vector spaces into useful and well-structured subdivisions. But insofar as there is cognitive activity at all, it exploits whatever theory the creature embodies, however useless or incoherent it might be.

The only place in the network where the weights need play no role is at the absolute sensory periphery of the system, where the external stimulus is transduced into a coded input vector for subsequent delivery to the transforming layers of weights. However, at the first occasion on which these preconceptual states have any effect at all on the downstream cognitive system, it is through a changeable configuration of synaptic weights, a configuration that produces one set of partitions on the activation-vector space of the relevant layer of neurons, one set out of millions of alternative possible sets. In other words, the very first thing that happens to the input signal is that it gets conceptualized in one of many different possible ways. At subsequent layers of processing, the same process is repeated, and the message that finally arrives at the linguistic centers, for example, has been shaped at least as much by the partitional constraints of the embedded conceptual system(s) through which it has passed as by the distant sensory input that started things off.

From the perspective of computational neuroscience, therefore, cognition is constitutionally theory laden. Presumptive processing is not a blight on what would otherwise be an unblemished activity; it is just the natural signature of a cognitive system doing what it is supposed to be doing. It is just possible that some theories are endogenously specified, of course, but this will change the present issue not at all. Innateness promises no escape from being theory laden, for an endogenous theory is still a *theory*.

In any case, the idea is not in general a plausible one. The visual system, for example, consists of something in the neighborhood of 10^{10} neurons, each of which enjoys better than 10^3 synaptic connections, for a total of at least 10^{13} weights each wanting specific genetic determination. That is an implausibly heavy load to place on the coding capacity of our DNA molecules. (The entire human genome contains only about 10^9 nucleotides.) It would be much more efficient to specify endogenously only the general structural principles of a type of learning network that is then likely to learn in certain standard directions, given the standard sorts of inputs and error messages that a typical human upbringing provides. This places the burden of steering our conceptual development where it belongs: on the external world, an information source far larger and more reliable than the genes.

It is a commonplace that we can construct endlessly different theories with which to explain the familiar facts of the observable world. But it is an immediate consequence of the perspective here adopted that that we can also apprehend the "observable world" itself in a similarly endless variety of ways. For there is no preferred set of partitions into which our sensory spaces must inevitably fall. It all depends on how the relevant networks are *taught*. If we systematically change the pattern of the error messages delivered to the developing network, then even the very same history of sensory stimulations will produce a quite differently weighted network, one that partitions the world into classes that cross-classify those of current common sense, one that finds perceptual similarities along dimensions quite alien to the ones we currently recognize, one that feeds its outputs into a very differently configured network at the higher cognitive levels as well.

In relatively small ways this phenomenon is already familiar to us. Specialists in various fields, people required to spend years mastering the intricacies of some domain of perception and manipulation, regularly end up being able to perceive facts and to anticipate behaviors that are wholly opaque to the rest of us. But there is no reason why such variation should be confined to isolated skills and specialized understanding. In principle, the human cognitive system should be capable of sustaining any one of an enormous variety of decidedly global theories concerning the character of its commonsense *Lebenswelt* as a whole. (This possibility, defended in Feyerabend 1965, is explored at some length via examples in Churchland 1979. For extended criticism of this general suggestion, see Fodor 1984. For a rebuttal and a counterrebuttal see chapter 12 below and Fodor 1988.)

To appreciate just how great is the conceptual variety that awaits us, consider the following numbers. With a total of perhaps 10^{11} neurons with an average of at least 10^3 connections each, the human brain has something like 10^{14} weights to play with. If we conservatively suppose that each weight admits of only 10 possible values, the total number of distinct possible configurations of synaptic weights (that is, distinct possible positions in weight space) is 10 for the first weight, times 10 for the second weight, times 10 for the third weight, etc., for a total of $10^{10^{14}}$, or $10^{100,000,000,000,000}$! This is the total number of (just barely) distinguishable theories embraceable by a human, given the cognitive resources we currently command. To put this number into some remotely adequate perspective, recall that the total number of elementary particles in the entire universe is only about 10^{87}.

In this way does a neurocomputational approach to perception allow us to reconstruct an old issue, and to provide novel reasons for the view that our perceptual knowledge is both theory laden and highly plastic. And it will do more. Notice that the activation-vector spaces that a matured brain has generated, and the prototypes they embody, can encompass far more than the simple sensory types such as phonemes, colors, smells, tastes, faces, and so forth. Given high-dimensional spaces, which the brain has in abundance, those spaces and the prototypes they embody can encompass categories of great complexity, generality, and abstraction, including those with a tem-poral dimension, such as harmonic oscillator, projectile, traveling wave, Samba, twelve-bar blues, democratic election, six-course din-ner, courtship, elephant hunt, civil disobedience, and stellar collapse. It may be that the input dimensions that feed into such abstract spaces will themselves often have to be the expression of some earlier level of processing, but that is no problem. The networks under dis-cussion are hierarchically arranged to do precisely this as a matter of course. In principle, then, it is no harder for such a system to repre-sent types of *processes*, *procedures*, and *techniques* than to represent the "simple" sensory qualities. From the point of view of the brain, these are just more high-dimensional vectors.

This offers us a possible means for explicating the notion of a *para-digm*, as used by T. S. Kuhn in his arresting characterization of the nature of scientific understanding and development (Kuhn 1962). A paradigm, for Kuhn, is a prototypical *application* of some set of mathe-matical, conceptual, or instrumental resources, an application ex-pected to have distinct but similar instances which it is the job of normal science to discover or construct. Becoming a scientist is less a matter of learning a set of laws than it is a matter of mastering the details of the prototypical applications of the relevant resources in such a way that one can recognize and generate further applications of a relevantly similar kind.

Kuhn was criticized for the vagueness of the notion of a paradigm, and for the unexplicated criterion of similarity that clustered further applications around it. But from the perspective of the neurocompu-tational approach at issue, he can be vindicated on both counts. For a brain to command a paradigm is for it to have settled into a weight configuration that produces some well-structured similarity space whose central hypervolume locates the prototypical application(s). And it is only to be expected that even the most reflective person will be incompletely articulate on what dimensions constitute this highly complex and abstract space, and even less articulate on what metric distributes examples along each dimension. A complete answer to these questions would require a microscopic examination of the per-son's brain. That is one reason why exposure to a wealth of examples is so much more effective in teaching the techniques of any science than is exposure to any attempt at listing all the relevant factors. We are seldom able to articulate them all, and even if we were able, listing them is not the best way to help a brain construct the relevant internal similarity space.

Kuhn makes much of the resistance typically shown by scientific communities to change or displacement of the current paradigm. This stubbornness here emerges as a natural expression of the way in which networks learn, or occasionally fail to learn. The process of learning by gradient descent is always threatened by the prospect of a purely *local* minimum in the global error gradient. This is a position where the error messages are not yet zero, but where every *small* change in the system produces even larger errors than those currently encountered. With a very high-dimensional space the probability of there being a simultaneous local minimum in every dimension of the weight space is small: there is usually some narrow cleft in the canyon out which the configuration point can eventually trickle, thence to continue its wandering slide down the error gradient and toward some truly global minimum. But genuine local minima do occur, and the only way to escape them, once caught, is to introduce some sort of random noise into the system in hopes of bouncing the system's configuration point out of such tempting cul-de-sacs. Furthermore, even if a local quasi minimum does have an escape path along one or more dimensions, the error gradient along them may there be quite shallow, and the system may take a very long time to find its way out of the local impasse.

Finally, and just as important, the system can be victimized by a highly biased "training set." Suppose the system has reached a weight configuration that allows it to respond successfully to all of the examples in the (narrow and biased) set it has so far encountered. Subsequent exposure to the larger domain of more diverse examples will not necessarily result in the system's moving any significant distance away from its earlier configuration, unless the relative frequency with which it encounters those new and anomalous examples is quite high. For if the encounter frequency is low, the impact of those examples will be insufficient to overcome the gravity of the false minimum that captured the initial training set. The system may require "blitzing" by new examples if their collective lesson is ever to "sink in."

Even if we do present an abundance of the new and diverse examples, it is quite likely that the delta rule discussed earlier will force the system through a sequence of new configurations that perform very poorly indeed when re-fed examples from the original training set.

This temporary loss of performance on certain previously "understood" cases is the price the system pays for the chance at achieving a broader payoff later, when the system finds a new and deeper error minimum. In the case of an artificial system chugging coolly away at the behest of the delta rule, such temporary losses need not impede the learning process, at least if the frequency of new examples is sufficiently high. But with humans the impact of such a loss is often more keenly felt. The new examples that confound the old configuration may simply be ignored or rejected in some fashion, or they may be quarantined and made the target of a distinct and disconnected learning process in some adjacent network. Recall the example of sublunary and superlunary physics.

This raises the issue of explanatory unity. A creature thrown unprepared into a complex and unforgiving world must take its understanding wherever it can find it, even if this means generating a disconnected set of distinct similarity spaces each providing the creature with a roughly appropriate response to some of the more pressing types of situation it typically encounters. But far better if it then manages to generate a single similarity space that unifies and replaces the variation that used to reside in two entirely distinct and smaller spaces. This provides the creature with an effective grasp on the phenomena that lay *between* the two classes already dealt with, but which were successfully comprehended by neither of the two old spaces. These are phenomena that the creature had to ignore, or avoid, or simply endure. With a new and more comprehensive similarity space now generating systematic responses to a wider range of phenomena, the creature has succeeded in a small piece of conceptual unification.

The payoff here recalls the virtue earlier discovered for simplicity. Indeed, it is the same virtue, namely, superior generalization to cases beyond those already encountered. This result was achieved, in the case described in section 5, by reducing the number of hidden units, which forced the system to make more efficient use of the representational resources remaining. This more efficient use is realized when the system partitions its activation-vector space into the minimal number of distinct similarity subspaces consistent with reducing the error messages to a minimum. When completed, this process also produces the maximal *organization* within and among those subspaces, for the system has found those enduring dimensions of variation that successfully unite the diversity confronting it.

Tradition speaks of developing a single "theory" to explain everything. Kuhn (1962) speaks of extending and articulating a "paradigm" into novel domains. Kitcher (1981, 1989) speaks of expanding the range of application of a given "pattern of argument." It seems to me that we might unify and illuminate all of these notions by thinking in terms of the evolving structure of a hidden-unit activation-vector space, and its development in the direction of representing all input vectors somewhere within a single similarity space.

This might seem to offer some hope for a Convergent Realist position within the philosophy of science, but I fear that exactly the opposite is the case. For one thing, nothing guarantees that we humans will avoid getting permanently stuck in some very deep but relatively local error minimum. For another, nothing guarantees that there exists a possible configuration of weights that would reduce the error messages to *zero*. A unique global error minimum relative to the human neural network there may be, but for us and for any other finite system interacting with the real world, it may always be nonzero. And for a third thing, nothing guarantees that there is only *one* global minimum. Perhaps there will in general be many quite different minima, all of them equally low in error, all of them carving up the world in quite different ways. Which one a given thinker reaches may be a function of the idiosyncratic details of its learning history. These considerations seem to remove the goal itself—a unique truth—as well as any sure means of getting there. Which suggests that the proper course to pursue in epistemology lies in the direction of a highly naturalistic and pluralistic form of pragmatism. For a running start on precisely these themes, see Munevar 1981 and Stich 1989.

8   Concluding Remarks

This essay opened with a survey of the problems plaguing the classical or "sentential" approach to epistemology and the philosophy of science. I have tried to sketch an alternative approach that is free of all or most of those problems, and has some novel virtues of its own. The following points are worth noting. Simple and relatively small networks of the sort described above have already demonstrated the capacity to learn a wide range of quite remarkable cognitive skills and capacities, some of which lie beyond the reach of the older approach to the nature of cognition (e.g., the instantaneous discrimination of subtle perceptual qualities, the effective recognition of similarities, and the real-time administration of complex motor activity). While the specific learning algorithm currently used to achieve these results is unlikely to be the brain's algorithm, it does provide an existence proof: by procedures of this general sort, networks can indeed learn with fierce efficiency. And there are many other procedures awaiting our exploration.

The picture of learning and cognitive activity here painted encompasses the entire animal kingdom. Cognition in human brains is fundamentally the same as cognition in brains generally. We are all of us processing activation vectors through artfully weighted networks. This broad conception of cognition puts cognitive theory firmly in contact with neurobiology, which adds a very strong set of constraints on the former, to its substantial long-term advantage.

Conceptual change is no longer a problem. It happens continuously in the normal course of all cognitive development. It is sustained by many small changes in the underlying hardware of synaptic weights, which changes gradually repartition the activation-vector spaces of the affected population of cells. Conceptual *simplicity* is also clearer when viewed from a neurocomputational perspective, both in its nature and in its epistemological significance.

The old problem of how to retrieve relevant information is transformed by the realization that it does not need to be "retrieved." Information is stored in brainlike networks in the global pattern of their synaptic weights. An incoming vector activates the relevant portions, dimensions, and subspaces of the trained network by virtue of its own vectorial makeup. Even an incomplete version of a given vector (that is, one with several elements missing) will often provoke essentially the same response as the complete vector by reason of its relevant similarity. For example, the badly whistled first few bars of a familiar tune will generally evoke both its name and the rest of the entire piece. And it can do this in a matter of milliseconds, because even if the subject knows thousands of tunes, there are still no lists to be searched.

It remains for this approach to comprehend the highly discursive and linguistic dimensions of human cognition, those that motivated the classical view of cognition. We need not pretend that this will be easy, but we can see how to start. We can start by exploring the capacity of networks to manipulate the structure of existing language, its syntax, its semantics, its pragmatics, and so forth. But we might also try some novel approaches, such as allowing each of two distinct networks, whose principal concerns and activities are nonlinguistic, to try to learn from scratch some systematic means of manipulating, through a proprietary dimension of input, the cognitive activities of the other network. What system of mutual manipulation—what *language*—might they develop?

The preceding pages illustrate some of the systematic insights that await us if we adopt a more naturalistic approach to traditional issues in epistemology, an approach that is grounded in computational neuroscience. However, a recurring theme in contemporary philosophy is that normative epistemology *cannot* be "naturalized" or reconstructed within the framework of any purely descriptive scientific theory. Notions such as "justified belief" and "rationality," it is said, cannot be adequately defined in terms of the nonnormative categories to which any natural science is restricted, since "ought" cannot be derived from "is." Conclusions are then drawn from this to the principled autonomy of epistemology from any natural science.

While it may be true that normative discourse cannot be replaced without remainder by descriptive discourse, it would be a distortion to represent this as the aim of those who would naturalize epistemology. The aim is rather to enlighten our normative endeavors by reconstructing them within a more adequate conception of what cognitive activity consists in, and thus to free ourselves from the burden of factual misconceptions and tunnel vision. It is only the *autonomy* of epistemology that must be denied.

Autonomy must be denied because normative issues are never independent of factual matters. This is easily seen for our judgments of instrumental value, as these always depend on factual premises about causal sufficiencies and dependencies. But it is also true of our most basic normative concepts and our judgments of intrinsic value, for these have factual presuppositions as well. We speak of *justification*, but we think of it as a feature of *belief*, and whether or not there are any beliefs and what properties they have is a robustly factual matter. We speak of *rationality*, but we think of it as a feature of *thinkers*, and it is a substantive factual matter what thinkers are and what cognitive kinematics they harbor. Normative concepts and normative convictions are thus always hostage to some background factual presuppositions, and these can always prove to be superficial, confused, or just plain wrong. If they are, then we may have to rethink whatever normative framework has been erected upon them. The lesson of the preceding pages is that the time for this has already come.

Chapter 10

On the Nature of Explanation: A PDP Approach

Neural network models of sensory processing and associative memory provide resources that allow us to state a new theory of what explanatory *under-standing consists in. That theory finds the theoretically important factors to reside not at the level of propositions and the relations between them, but at the level of the activation patterns across large populations of neurons. This theory portrays* explanatory understanding *and* perceptual recognition *as being different instances of the same more general sort of cognitive achieve-ment:* prototype *activation. It thus purports to effect a unification of the theory of explanation and the theory of perception. It also finds a systematic and revealing unity among the wide diversity of types of explanation (causal, functional, mathematical, intentional, reductive, etc.), a diversity that has been a chronic problem for older theories of explanation.*

1 Introduction

The notion of explanation has figured centrally in most contemporary accounts of scientific knowledge and rational belief. Explanation is usually cited, along with prediction, as one of the two principal func-tions of our factual beliefs. And the rationality of such beliefs is com-monly said to be measured, at least in part, by the relative range or quality of the explanations they make possible. If something like this is correct, then it is important for us to try to understand what explanation is, and what distinguishes a good explanation from a poor one.

Several existing accounts attempt to meet this challenge. They will be addressed below. The present paper proposes a new account of the matter—the *prototype activation model*—an account distinguished, for starters, by its being grounded in a novel and unorthodox concep-tion of what cognition consists in. That conception derives from cur-rent research in cognitive neurobiology and from parallel distributed processing (PDP) models of brain function. (See Rumelhart et al. 1986a, 1986b; Churchland 1986a, 1989.) These PDP models are noteworthy for many reasons, but first among them in the present context is their almost complete dissociation from the *sentential* or *propositional* conception of what knowledge consists in, and from the conception of human information processing as *rule-governed inference*. Those venerable conceptions play a central role in all of the older accounts of explanation, and in orthodox accounts of cognition generally. They will play almost no role in the account to be proposed.

This is not to say that the older accounts of explanation are entirely without integrity. On the contrary, from the PDP perspective we can see why each of them has the appeal it does, and also why that appeal is to some degree genuine. That is to say, the prototype activation model successfully reduces/explains the major features of its competitors. It is also free from most of their celebrated defects. I will try to illustrate these claims as we proceed.

The prototype activation model is focused first and foremost on what it is to have *explanatory understanding* of a problematic thing, event, or state of affairs. The linguistic expression, exchange, or production of such understanding, should there be any, is an entirely secondary matter. I shall approach the topic with the aims of an empirical scientist rather than with the aims of a logician or conceptual analyst. The goal is to outline a substantive empirical theory of what explanatory understanding really is, rather than to provide an analysis of the concept of explanation as it currently is used or ideally should be used. Normative issues will certainly be addressed, and some unexpected insights will emerge, but normative concerns are not the prime focus of the present chapter. Rather, what concerns us is the nature of the cognitive process that takes place inside the brain of the creature for whom explanatory understanding suddenly dawns, and in whom it is occasionally reactivated.

On the prototype-activation (PA) model, a close approximation to this process is the process of *perceptual recognition*, as when one suddenly recognizes an indistinct outline as the face of a close friend, or as when one finally recognizes the faint motion under the hedge as a foraging mouse. On the PA model, essentially the same kind of computational achievement underlies both perceptual recognition and explanatory understanding. The latter is distinguished primarily by being a response to a wider variety of cognitive situations: it is not limited to sensory inputs.

A close connection between perception and explanation is by now a familiar theme in both psychology and philosophy. One's perceptual judgments, and perhaps even one's perceptual experiences themselves, have often been portrayed as the perceiver's best *explanatory* account of the peripheral stimuli (Gregory 1966, 1970a; Rock 1983). In this tradition the notion of explanation is used in hopes of explicating the phenomenon of perception. The strategy of the present chapter will reverse the order of things somewhat: I shall exploit a novel PDP account of perceptual recognition in hopes of explicating the phenomenon of explanatory understanding. I remain faithful to the earlier tradition, however, since my basic aim will be to show that both phenomena are fundamentally the same.

Let me open the discussion by trying to motivate the search for a new account of explanation, and for trying to launch it in the specific directions indicated. We may begin by recalling the covering-law or deductive-nomological (D-N) model (Hempel 1965), since so many of the current models are just artful restrictions or generalizations of that basic and very elegant idea. While much attention has been paid to the *logical* virtues and vices of this model, relatively little has been paid to its shortcomings when evaluated from a *psychological* point of view.

In fact, the D-N model is psychologically unrealistic in several important ways. If someone has just come to understand why a is F, the D-N model typically requires that we ascribe to that person knowledge of some universally quantified conditional statement having Fx as its consequent, plus knowledge of a series of initial conditions adequate to discharge the conjuncts in the antecedent of that conditional, plus the successful deduction of Fa from this assembled information, or at least the appreciation that the deductive relation exists.

However, while people have an explanatory understanding of much of what goes on around them on a minute-by-minute and even a second-by-second basis, people are decidedly and regularly inarticulate when asked to voice either the general law on which their understanding is presumably based, or the set of initial conditions that tie that law to the explanandum then at issue. What premises people are typically able to supply, when queried, often falls dramatically short of the full requirements of the D-N model. Moreover, the logical acumen ascribed to people on this account is often substantially in excess of what university students with formal training in logic can display.

Furthermore, the assembly of relevant factual premises and the search for relevant deductive relations is a process that takes time, often a good deal of time. All of this sits poorly with the great speed with which explanatory understanding is commonly achieved. It is often achieved almost instantaneously, as when one understands at a glance why one end of the kitchen is filled with smoke: the toast is burning! Such swiftness is not confined to mundane cases. If one has the relevant conceptual skills, the same speed is also displayed in more esoteric cases, as when one appreciates at a glance why Jupiter is an oblate spheroid: it is a plastic object spinning rapidly; or as when one appreciates at a glance why some red giant star in a close binary system has the shape of an egg pointed at its more compact blue companion: it is a very large object free-falling in a gravitational field.

At the other end of the spectrum, nonhuman animals provide a further illustration of these difficulties. Animals too display behavior that indicates the achievement of explanatory understanding, as when a frustrated coyote bites and paws at the leg trap whose jaws have captured its mate. The coyote understands why its mate cannot leave. Animals too can anticipate elements of the future and understand elements of the present and past, often in some detail. But the assembly of discursive premises and the execution of formal inferences is presumably beyond their capacities, especially at the speeds that faithfulness to their insight and behavior requires.

These particular criticisms of the D-N model are unusual in being empirical and psychological rather than logical in character. Even so, they are highly general. They will apply to all of the accounts of explanation that require, as the original D-N model requires, extensive propositional knowledge, relevant retrieval of same, and keen deductive insight. For it is precisely these features that give rise to the difficulties. Is there some alternative way of characterizing the way knowledge is represented in living creatures, and the way it is deployed or accessed in specific cases to provide local explanatory understanding? Yes, there is.

2   Conceptual Organization in PDP Networks

Recent years have seen an upswell of research into the functional properties of "neural" networks. These are artificial networks that simulate or model certain salient features of the neuronal organization of the brain. What is interesting is that even simple versions of these networks have shown themselves capable of some very striking computational achievements, and they perform these computations in a fashion that recalls important features of animal cognition.

A primary feature of neuronal organization is abstractly depicted in the "neural" network of figure 10.1a. The circles in the bottom row of the network represent a population of sensory neurons. Each of these units projects a proprietary axonal fiber toward a second population of neuronlike units. The axon there divides into a fan of terminal branches, so as to make a synaptic connection with every unit in the second population. Real cells are not quite so exhaustive in their

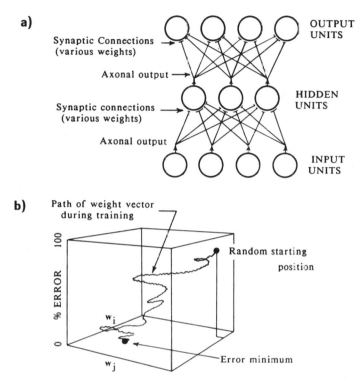

Figure 10.1
a) A simple network. *b*) Learning: gradient descent in weight/error space. Axes are shown for only 2 of 24 synaptic weights

connectivity, but a typical axon can make many thousands or even hundreds of thousands of connections.

This arrangement allows any unit at the input layer to have an impact on the activation levels of all of the units at the second or "hidden" layer. An input stimulus produces some activation level in a given input unit, which then conveys a signal of proportional strength along its axon and out the end branches to the many synaptic connections onto the hidden units. These connections stimulate or inhibit the hidden units as a function of the strength of the signal, the size or "weight" of each synaptic connection, and its polarity. A given hidden unit simply sums the effects incident from its many input synapses. The global effect is that a *pattern of activations* across the set of input units produces a distinct *pattern of activations* across the set of hidden units. Which pattern gets produced, for a given input, is strictly determined by the configuration of synaptic weights meeting the hidden units.

The units in the second layer project in turn to a third population of units, there to make another set of synaptic connections. In real brains this pattern is typically iterated through many layers (roughly, $5 < n < 50$) before the chain concludes in a population of motor or other output neurons, but for purposes of illustration, a network of just three layers will suffice.

In this upper half too, the global effect is that an activation pattern across the hidden units produces a distinct activation pattern across the output units. As before, exactly what pattern-to-pattern trans-formation takes place is fixed by the configuration of synaptic weights meeting the output units. All told, this network is a device for trans-forming any one of a great many possible input vectors (i.e., activa-tion patterns) into a uniquely corresponding output vector. It is a device for computing a specific function, and which function it computes is fixed by the global configuration of its synaptic weights.

Now for the payoff. There are various procedures for adjusting the weights so as to yield a network that computes almost any function— that is, any vector-to-vector transformation—that we might desire. In fact, we can even impose on it a function we are *unable to specify*, so long as we can supply a modestly large set of examples of the desired input-output pairs. This process is called "training up the network." It typically proceeds by entering a sample input vector at the lowest layer, noting the erroneous vector this produces at the topmost layer, calculating the difference between this actual output and the desired output, and then feeding this error measure into a special rule, the generalized delta rule (Rumelhart et al. 1986a). That rule then makes a small adjustment in the antecedent configuration of all of the synaptic weights in the network. Repeating this procedure many times, over the many examples, forces the network to slide down an error gradient in the abstract space that represents its possible synaptic weights (see figure 10.1b). The adjustments continue until the net-work has finally assumed a configuration of weights that does yield the appropriate outputs for all of the inputs in the training set.

To give a real example, suppose we want the network to discrimi-nate sonar echoes returned from large metallic objects, such as explo-sive mines, from sonar echoes returned from large submarine rocks. The discrimination of such echoes poses a serious problem because they are effectively indistinguishable by the human ear, and they vary widely in character even within each class. We begin by record-ing fifty different mine echoes and fifty different rock echoes, a fair sample of each. We then digitize each echo with a frequency analyz-er, and feed the resulting vector into the bank of input units (figure 10.2a). We want the output units to respond with appropriate activa-

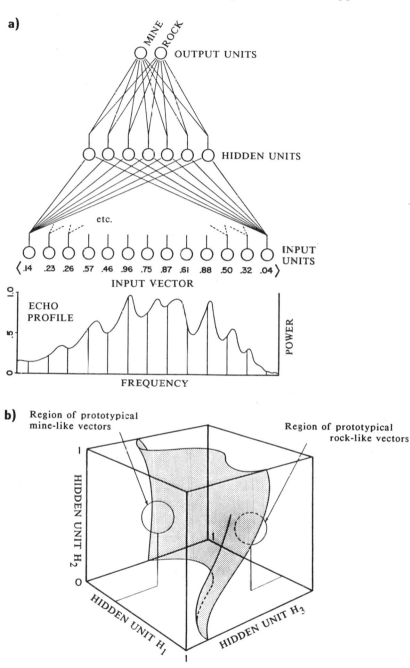

Figure 10.2
a) Perceptual recognition with a large network. b) Learned partition on hidden-unit activation-vector space. Axes are shown for only three of seven hidden-unit activation levels

tion levels (specifically, <1, 0> for a mine, <0, 1> for a rock) when fed an echo of either kind.

The network's initial verdicts are chaotic, since its synaptic weights were set at random values. But under the pressure of the weight-nudging algorithm, it gradually learns to make the desired distinction. And after it has mastered the echoes in the training set, it will generalize: it will reliably identify mine and rock echoes from outside its training set, echoes it has never heard before. Mine echoes, it turns out, are indeed united by some subtle weave of features, to which weave the network has become tuned during the training process. The same is true for rock echoes. (See Gorman and Sejnowski 1988.)

Here we have a binary discrimination between a pair of diffuse and very hard-to-define acoustic properties. Indeed, *we never did define them*! It is the network that has generated an appropriate internal characterization of each type of sound, fueled only by examples. If we now examine the behavior of the hidden units during discriminatory acts in the trained network, we discover that the training process has partitioned the space of possible activation vectors across the hidden units. (See figure 10.2b. Note that this space is not the space of figure 10.1b. Figure 10.1b depicts the space of possible synaptic weights. Figure 10.2b depicts the space of possible activation vectors across the middle layer.) The training process has generated a *similarity gradient* that culminates in two "hot spots"—two rough regions that represent the range of hidden-unit vector codings for a *prototypical* mine and a *prototypical* rock. The job of the top half of the network is then just the relatively simple one of discriminating these two subvolumes of that vector space.

Several features of such networks beg emphasis. First, the output verdict for any input is produced very quickly, for the computation occurs in parallel. The global computation at each layer of units is distributed among many simultaneously active processing elements: the weighted synapses and the summative cell bodies. Hence the expression 'parallel distributed processing'. Most striking, the speed of processing is entirely independent of both the number of units involved and the complexity of the function executed. Speed is determined solely by the number of distinct *layers* in the network. This makes for very swift processing indeed. In a living brain, where a typical information-processing pathway has something between five and fifty layers, and each pass through that hierarchy takes something between ten and twenty milliseconds per layer, we are looking at overall processing times, even for complex recognitional problems, of between one-twentieth of a second and one second. Empirically, this is the right range for living creatures.

Second, such networks are functionally persistent. They degrade gracefully under the scattered destruction of synapses or units. Since each synapse supplies such a small part of any computation, its demise leaves the network essentially unchanged. Third, and very important for our purposes, the network will regularly render correct verdicts given only a degraded version or a smallish part of a familiar input vector. This is because the degraded or partial vector is relevantly *similar* to a prototypical input, and the internal coding strategy generated in the course of training is exquisitely sensitive to such similarities among possible inputs.

And exactly which similarities are those? They are whichever similarities meet the joint condition that they unite some significant portion of the examples in the training set, and the network managed to become tuned to them in the course of training. The point is that there are often many overlapping dimensions of similarity being individually monitored by the trained network: individually they may be modest in their effects, but if several are detected together their impact can be decisive. Here we may recall Wittgenstein's description of how humans can learn, by ostension, to detect "family resemblances" that defy easy definition. PDP networks recreate exactly this phenomenon.

Finally, such networks can learn functions far more complex than the one illustrated, and make discriminations far beyond the binary example portrayed. In the course of learning to pronounce English text, Rosenberg and Sejnowski's NETtalk (1987) partitioned its hidden-unit vector space into fully 79 subspaces, one for each of the 79 letter-to-phoneme transformations that characterize the phonetic significance of English spelling. Since there are 79 distinct phonemes in English speech, but only 26 letters in the alphabet, each letter clearly admits of several different phonetic interpretations, the correct one being determined by context. Despite this ambiguity, the network also learned to detect which of several possible transforms is the appropriate one, by being sensitive to the various letters that flank the target letter inside the word. All of this is a notoriously irregular matter for English spelling, but the "rules" were learned by the network even so.

Other networks have learned to recognize the complex configuration and orientation of curved surfaces, given only gray-scale pictures of those surfaces as input. That is, they solve a version of the classic shape-from-shading problem in visual psychology. Still others learn to divine the grammatical elements of sentences fed as input, or to predict the molecular folding of proteins given amino-acid sequences as input. These networks perform their surprising feats of learned categorization and perceptual recognition with only the smallest of "neuronal" resources—usually much less than 10^3 units. This is only one hundred millionth of the resources available in the human brain. With such powerful cognitive effects being displayed in such modest artificial models, it is plausible that they represent a major insight into the functional significance of our own brain's microstructure. That, in any case, is the assumption on which the following discussion will proceed.

3   Recognition and Understanding

Let me now try to highlight those functional features of PDP networks that will lead us back toward the topic of explanation. The first feature I want to emphasize is the partitioning, in a suitably trained network, of its hidden-unit activation-vector space into a system of prototype representations, one for each of the general categories to which the network has been trained (see again figure 10.2*b* for the simplest sort of case). Any prototype representation is in fact a specific vector (that is, a pattern of activations) across the network's hidden units, but we may conceive of it more graphically as a specific point or small volume in an abstract state space of possible activation vectors, since that portrayal highlights its geometrical relations with representations of distinct prototypes, and with activation vectors that are variously close to (that is, similar to) the prototype vector.

The second point to emphasize is that a single prototypical point or activation vector across the hidden units represents a wide range of quite different possible sensory activation patterns at the input layer: it represents the extended family of relevant (but individually perhaps nonnecessary) features that collectively unite the relevant class of stimuli into a single kind. Any member of that diverse class of stimuli will activate the entire prototype vector at the hidden units. Also, any input-layer stimulus that is relevantly *similar* to the members of that class, in part or in whole, will activate a vector at the hidden units that is fairly close, in state space, to the prototype vector.

In dynamical terms, the prototype position is called an "attractor." We may think here of a wide-mouthed funnel that will draw a broad but delicately related range of cases into a single narrow path. This process is instanced in your ability to recognize a friend's face in any of a wide variety of expressions, positions, and conditions of viewing. Or in your ability to recognize a horse in almost any posture and from almost any perspective. These are exactly the sorts of capabilities displayed by suitably trained PDP networks.

A third point is to emphasize again that PDP networks are extraordinarily fast. Once trained, they achieve the "recognitions" at issue in a matter of milliseconds. And they will make distinct recognitions, one after another, as fast as you can feed them appropriately distinct stimuli.

Turn now to the units at the output layer. In the stick-figure account of cognition I am trying to outline, these are to be conceived as driving or initiating some specific motor activity: perhaps something relatively simple, as in NETtalk, where the output vector codes a phoneme and actually produces, via a speech synthesizer, an audible sound. In a living creature, however, the output will typically be more complex, as when a dog's sudden olfactory recognition of a gopher initiates a routine of rooting and digging at the favored location; or as when a bird's sudden visual recognition of a stalking cat prompts it to initiate a sequence of wing motions that launch it into the air.

The picture I am trying to evoke, of the cognitive lives of simple creatures, ascribes to them an organized "library" of internal representations of various prototypical perceptual situations, situations to which prototypical *behaviors* are the computed output of the well-trained network. The prototypical situations include feeding opportunities, grooming demands, territorial defense, predator avoidance, mating opportunities, offspring demands, and other similarly basic situations, to each of which a certain broad class of behaviors is appropriate. And within the various generic prototype representations at the appropriate level of hidden units, there will be subdivisions into more specific subprototypes whose activation prompts highly specific versions of the generic form of behavior. (Is the mouse eating sesame seeds? Or hickory nuts? Is it avoiding a cat? Or a hawk?) These various prototypes are both united and distinguished by their relative positions in the hidden-unit vector space. They are all close together, but they differ slightly in their positions along one or more of the relevant axes. These differences evoke relevantly different responses at the output layer.

As just outlined, this picture will inevitably recall memories of behaviorism, for the perceptual environment is here portrayed as the fundamental control of motor behavior, and the link between the two will appear very stimulus-responsish to many eyes. But that construal of the basic character of the mechanisms at issue is oversimple and deeply misleading, as I shall try briefly to explain.

The simple networks of figures 10.1a and 10.2a fail to portray some obvious augmentations that living brains clearly use. Real brains boast many successive layers of hidden units rather than just one—

perhaps as many as a hundred layers along some pathways. Further, real brains divide into many distinct processing hierarchies working side by side on different problems. A brain is not a single network, but a committee of many cooperating networks—perhaps over a thousand of them in a typical mammalian brain. And most important for the present issue, the input to a given bank of hidden units comes not *just* from the sensory periphery, but from elsewhere in the brain itself. The brain is a *recurrent* network. The all-up input to any layer will almost always include some "current context" information that derives from earlier processing elsewhere in the brain.

Unlike the models in the figures, almost any layer of units in the brain will receive some "descending" axonal projections returning from the next layer of units upward in its hierarchy, and it will often receive "horizontal" projections from layers within the many adjacent networks working on related informational tasks. Accordingly, which prototype vectors get activated within a given layer is generally a function of diverse inputs, some of which arrive unvarnished from the sensory periphery, but many of which reflect concurrent activity elsewhere in the brain.

This frees the brain from the knee-jerk style of operation that worried us a few moments ago. Its ultimate behavior is a function of factors so many and so subtle, factors that interact in such highly volatile ways, that the brain's behavior has become predictable only in its broadest outlines and only for very short periods into the future. Moreover, the factors controlling behavior reside within the brain itself as much as in the external environment.

To return to the basic issue, we can now see how the brain can command a large and sophisticated repertoire of prototype activation vectors, each one representing some complex prototypical situation in the external world. We have seen how such vectors can be activated by the perceptual apprehension of even a small portion of the relevant external situation, and how those vectors can activate in turn behaviors appropriate to the entire external situation, and not to just the small part that was initially coded in perception.

I wish to suggest that those prototype vectors, when activated, constitute the creature's recognition and concurrent *understanding* of its objective situation, an understanding that is reflected in the creature's subsequent behavior. Of course, a creature may *fail* to recognize/understand its current perceptual or cognitive situation. The vector activated at the relevant layer of hidden units may fall well outside any of the prototypical volumes of the relevant state space, and the behavior subsequently produced will therefore not be drawn from its well-honed repertoire. The resulting behavior may be just confused.

Or it may be a default routine of flight from the unknown. Or perhaps it will be a default routine of stumbling *exploration*, one that may finally find either a physical or a cognitive perspective from which the situation suddenly does activate one of the creature's many prototype vectors. It may find, that is, a perspective from which the situation suddenly does make sense.

By way of whatever learning algorithm governs synaptic adjustments, such failures and subsequent successes, especially in quantity, will modify the character and state-space location of the creature's internal prototype representations, so that situations of the puzzling kind just solved will successfully activate a prototype vector more readily in future.

4   Prototype Activation: A Unified Theory of Explanation

The aim of the preceding sections was to illustrate the initial plausibility of a novel conception of cognitive activity, a conception in which vector coding and vector-to-vector transformation constitute the basic forms of representation and computation, rather than sentential structures and inferences made according to structure-sensitive rules. Let us assume, for the sake of argument, that this conception is basically accurate even for human brains. If so, then we must immediately be impressed by the range of conceptual resources such systems can command, given the neuronal machinery available.

With roughly 10^{11} nonsensory neurons, the human brain commands a global state space of fully 10^{11} dimensions. Each brain subsystem will typically be operating with something like one-thousandth of that number, which gives a typical specialized state space approximately 10^8 proprietary dimensions to play with. This will allow for some stunningly complex and fine-grained representations, since a single vector with 10^8 elements can code the contents of an entire book. A state space of 10^8 dimensions will also allow for a similarly stunning variety of coding vectors. If we assume that each neuron admits of only 10 distinct levels of activation (a serious under-estimation), then that typical specialized state space must have at least 10^{10^8} or $10^{100,000,000}$ functionally distinct positions within it. This is the number of distinct possible *activation vectors*. To appreciate the magnitude of this number, recall that the total number of elementary particles in the entire physical universe, photons included, is only about 10^{87}. And recall that, on the above assumptions, your brain commands something like a thousand of these specialized state spaces.

Of course, the vectors themselves represent nothing, save in the context of the global configuration of synaptic weights that produced them, and which dictate their effects on subsequent layers of neurons. Here again we have a superastronomical range of possibilities. In a given subsystem of 10^8 neurons, a typical neuron will have at least 10^3 synaptic connections arriving from other neurons, for a total of 10^{11} distinct synapses within that subsystem. If each synapse admits of only 10 distinct weights, then we have $10^{10^{11}}$ or $10^{100,000,000,000}$ distinct possible configurations of *weights* for that subsystem alone.

Overall, and crudely speaking, this means that a typical subsystem will have a lexicon of 10^{10^8} possible representations, each of which has 10^8 elements, and each of which could have any one of $10^{10^{11}}$ possible "meanings." We should not balk, therefore, at the premise of the following discussion, which regards it as unproblematic that the brain should command intricate prototype representations of such things as stellar collapse, cell meiosis, positron-positron collision, redox reaction, gravitational lens, oceanic rift, harmonic oscillator, intentional action, and economic depression. Such phenomena, intricate though they are, are not beyond reach of the representational resources described.

The discussion to this point has all been preamble to the following suggestion: Explanatory understanding consists in the activation of a specific prototype vector in a well-trained network. It consists in the apprehension of the problematic case as an instance of a general type, *a type for which the creature has a detailed and well-informed representation*. Such a representation allows the creature to anticipate aspects of the case so far unperceived, and to deploy practical techniques appropriate to the case at hand (see figure 10.3, *a* and *b*). Given the preceding discussion, this idea has some plausibility already. It is my aim in the remainder of this chapter to illustrate how much illumination and unity this suggestion can bring to a wide range of cognitive phenomena.

Let me open my exposition by responding to a possible objection, which will allow me to emphasize an important feature of the vectorial representations here at issue. "What you have outlined," runs the objection, "may be a successful account of spontaneous *classification*, but explanatory *understanding* surely involves a great deal more than mere classification."

The objection evokes a process of mere "labeling," a process that puts the apprehended situation into a featureless pigeonhole, a process in which most of the complex information contained in the input is lost in its reduction to a canonical neural response. Yet this

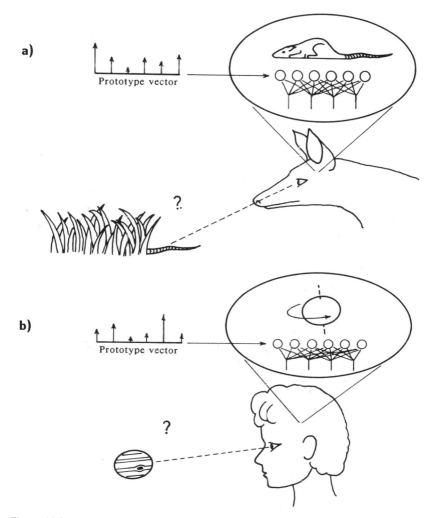

Figure 10.3
Explanatory understanding as the activation of a prototype vector. *a*) Ampliative activation of *desert rat* vector. *b*) ampliative activation of *rotating plastic body* vector

is precisely the wrong way to view the process of recognition and the character of the representation activated.

What we must remember is that the prototype vector embodies an enormous amount of information. Its many elements—perhaps as many as 10^8 elements was our earlier guess—each constitute one dimension of a highly intricate portrait of the prototypical situation. That vector has structure, a great deal of structure, whose function is to represent an overall *syndrome* of objective features, relations, sequences, and uniformities. Its activation by a given perceptual or other cognitive circumstance does not represent a loss of information. On the contrary, it represents a major and speculative *gain* in information, since the portrait it embodies typically goes far beyond the local and perspectivally limited information that may activate it on any given occasion. That is why the process is useful: it is quite dramatically ampliative. On each such occasion, the creature ends up understanding (or perhaps *mis*understanding) far more about the explanandum situation than was strictly presented in the explanandum itself. What makes this welcome talent of ampliative recognition possible is the many and various examples the creature has already encountered, and its successful generation of a unified prototype representation of them during the course of training.

This view entails that different people may have different levels or degrees of explanatory understanding, even though they classify a given situation in what is extensionally the same way. The reason is that the richness of their respective prototype representations may differ substantially. This is a welcome consequence, since explanatory understanding does indeed come in degrees. On the present view, its measure is just the richness and accuracy of the creature's prototype.

With these points in hand, let us now turn to a larger issue. One prominent fact, ill addressed by any existing account of explanation, is the variety of different *types* of explanation. We have causal explanations, functional explanations, moral explanations, derivational explanations, and so forth. Despite some procrustean analytical attempts, no one of these seems to be the basic type to which all of the others can be assimilated. On the prototype-activation model, however, we can unify them all in the following way. Explanatory understanding is the same thing in all of these cases: what differs is the character of the prototype that is activated.

4.1 Property-cluster prototypes   I begin with what is presumably the simplest, most common, and most superficial kind of explanatory understanding, and with the simplest and most superficial kind of prototype: the cluster of typically cooccurrent properties. Think of the typical cluster of features that constitutes a cat, or a cookie, or a tree, or a bird. These prototypes comprehend the vast majority of one's conceptual population, and they are activated on a regular basis in the course of one's mundane affairs. Because of their familiarity to everyone, cases involving them are seldom puzzling to anyone. But the explicit questions of inquiring children reflect the background explanatory role these prototypes continue to play for all of us. "Why is its neck so long, Daddy?" "It's a *swan* dear; swans have very long necks." "Why is he all spotted, Mommy?" "He's a *leopard* dear; leopards are always spotted, except when they're young."

4.2 Etiological prototypes   These are what lie behind *causal* explanations. An etiological prototype depicts a typical temporal *sequence* of event types, such as the cooking of food upon exposure to heat, the deformation of a fragile object during impact with a tougher one, the escape of liquid from a tilted container, and so on. These sequences contain prototypical elements in a prototypical order, and they make possible our explanatory understanding of the temporally extended world. We apparently command a very large repertoire of such prototypes, much of it organized into an elaborate hierarchy of species and subspecies.

Note that the temporal inverse of an etiological prototype is generally *not* an etiological prototype as well. This means that causal explanations are generally asymmetric in character. The height of a flagpole and the altitude of the sun may jointly explain the length of the pole's shadow. But the length of the pole's shadow will serve to explain neither of the other two facts. That asymmetry, a major problem for other accounts of explanation, is a natural consequence of the present account.

Some may complain here that I have simply helped myself to an unexplicated notion of "causal process" or "etiology" in order to sustain a particular analysis of explanation, one that takes "cause" as a primitive. This charge misses my purpose. I am not attempting to provide an analytic definition of the notion of explanation. I am trying to provide a revealing and unifying characterization of the sorts of brain events that constitute explanatory understanding. Those events, I suggest, are prototype activations. An important subclass of activated prototypes represent typical temporal sequences or processes. These, I observe, appear to underwrite what philosophers have called causal explanations.

Now just what intricacies constitute a genuine etiological prototype, and how the brain distinguishes between real causal processes and mere pseudoprocesses, are secondary matters I shall leave for a future occasion. We have, at a minimum, a novel set of resources with which to address that old problem. It is sufficient for present purposes to observe that, within the framework of the PA model, we can immediately reconstruct, at least to a first approximation, the major types of antecedently recognized explanation. To this task I now return.

4.3 Practical prototypes These, I suggest, are what lie behind *functional* explanations. One thing humans understand very well, being agents in the world, is complex means-end relations between possible situations realizable by us and expectable consequences thereof that may be desirable to us. To portray any temporal configuration of actual or potential situations in this means-end way is to make graphic or salient for us certain of the causal relations that unite them. It is a way of portraying a causal structure in the world in the guise of an actual or figurative practical problem, with the explanandum event or feature as its practical solution.

Practical prototypes, like etiological prototypes, also depict sequences of event types or feature dependencies, but in the case of practical prototypes the explanandum *begins* the explanatory sequence, whereas in etiological prototypes the explanandum *concludes* the explanatory sequence. Thus, a functional explanation does provide some entirely objective information, as in "His peripheral blood vessels all contracted in order to protect his central organs from the gathering cold." But sometimes they ring very hollow, as in "Supernova 1987A collapsed on itself in order to spread photons and neutrinos throughout the physical universe." Just when functional explanations are appropriate and when they are not is a delicate issue that I shall bypass on this occasion.

4.4 Superordinate prototypes Some explanations, typically those in science, logic, and mathematics, concern not singular facts but *general* truths. Why do planets move on ellipses? Why are the theorems of the sentential calculus all tautologies? Why do the interior angles of any triangle always sum to exactly one straight angle? Here the objects of puzzlement are not singular situations; they are prototypical syndromes themselves. Even so, explanatory understanding seems to consist in the apprehension of the subordinate prototype as being an instance of some superordinate prototype.

The puzzle about triangles will illustrate the point. Why is the sum always the same? And why is it exactly 180°? Consider the prototypical situation depicted in figure 10.4a, namely, two parallel lines cut by a third. A prototypical feature of that situation is the equality of the

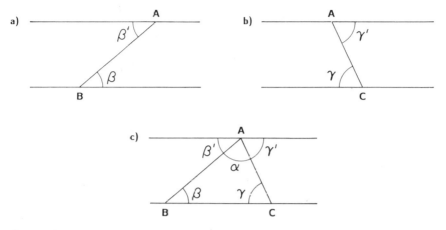

Figure 10.4
Understanding a subordinate prototype as one instance of a superordinate prototype

angles β and β'. (As it happens, this captures the substance of Euclid's famous parallel postulate.) Another depiction of that same prototype appears in figure 10.4b, a feature of which is the equality $\gamma = \gamma'$. Now imagine these two figures superimposed, as in figure 10.4c, to form the triangle ABC. The sum $\alpha + \beta' + \gamma'$ is evidently a straight angle. And given the two equalities noted earlier, it is evident that $\alpha + \beta + \gamma$ must equal the very same value. This prototypical feature of triangles can now be seen as just another instance of a yet more general prototype. Once the latter has been relevantly activated, as in figure 10.4c, the former is no longer puzzling.

Explanations of this subordinate-superordinate kind are typically displayed in intertheoretic reductions, where one theory is subsumed in whole or in part by a more general theory. They are also displayed when our scattered understanding in some domain is successfully axiomatized, which on the present view is just another instance of the same process.

Axiomatizations, in this century's experience, are ruthlessly syntactic affairs. The D-N model was right at home in accounting for explanations within that general context. But axiomatization was not always thus. I have used an example from geometry here in order to suggest that the successful systematization of theoretical understanding can be pictorial or graphical, as well as occasionally syntactic. As with many others, I acquired my conception of axiomatization as a student of formal logic and of the philosophy of science and mathematics in the mid sixties. Within that tradition, axiomatization was *essentially* a syntactic affair. When subsequently I looked through

Euclid's original *Elements*—acclaimed as the first great axiomatization in history—I was therefore struck by how very *un*syntactic and how vividly diagrammatic the whole affair was.

This was standardly put down to the sloppiness of Euclid's presentation. I can no longer entirely believe that. Though quite real, syntactic systematization now appears as only one of several modes of cognitive systematization, perhaps of relatively minor importance. The basic mode of systematization is the reconfiguration of the similarity metric across the relevant vector space, so that previously diverse and unrelated cases are now rerepresented as being relevantly similar to each other, as being slightly different instances of the same more general prototype. This reconfiguration can happen in two ways: within the space that contains the relevant prototypes, so that they come to occupy closely proximate positions; or in the next layer up, so that they are seen as instances of a higher prototype located in a subsequent layer of hidden units.

This more encompassing view of conceptual unification is of course entirely compatible with the idea of syntactic unification through axiomatization. It merely subsumes that mode of organization under a more general mode. The presented "axioms" of formal systems, you will recall, are almost always axiom *schemata*, having a potential infinity of distinct but recognizable instances. And the rules of inference are inference schemata as well, whose diverse applications must be mastered by the person using them. Thus do we learn to discriminate *proofs*. What unites the class of theorems is that each is the last line of some proof or other. In this way, evidently, can prototype-trained PDP networks handle the combinatorial and generative aspects of cognition. Their capacity for discriminating relevant structure and principled iteration may be limited, of course. But then, so is ours (see Bechtel and Abrahamson, forthcoming).

There is a great deal more to be said about explanatory unification, but for now let us move on.

4.5   Social-interaction prototypes   These underwrite *ethical, legal,* and *social-etiquette* explanations, a class of explanations unaddressed, to my knowledge, by any prior account of explanation. This is faintly surprising, since they are both real and familiar. "Why shouldn't I disperse this bunch of troublemakers?" asks the redneck cop approaching a so-far peaceful demonstration. "Because that would be a case of violating their constitutional right to peaceful assembly" is an explanatory reply. "Why shouldn't I discuss Mary's marital problems with Doris?" asks the gossip. "Because that would be violating a confidence" is an explanatory reply. "Aw, why can't I go play outside in the rain?" asks the seven-year-old boy. "Because you have your new clothes on, and company will be here for Thanksgiving dinner in half an hour" is an explanatory reply. Here we appeal to various prototypical misbehaviors—denying a constitutional right, betraying a confidence, being inappropriately turned out for a family fete—of which the contemplated behavior is claimed to be an instance. Acquiring a legal, moral, or social sensibility is a matter of mastering a large system of such social-interaction prototypes, and of coming to perceive the social world from within that framework. (Since writing this paper, I have learned that moral explanations have indeed been recognized and discussed. Sturgeon [1985], for example, assimilates them to the D-N pattern.)

4.6 Motivational prototypes   These underwrite our familiar folk-psychological explanations of intentional actions. By rights, such explanations should not be assigned a separate category in the present list, since motivational prototypes are properly just a special subclass of the etiological prototypes discussed in section 4.2 above. They are, I believe, causal explanations (chapters 1 and 6). But I did not wish to break the flow of exposition in section 4.2 by addressing a disputed case. On the other hand, I do not wish to leave this important class entirely unmentioned.

Motivational prototypes depict typical configurations of desires, beliefs, and preferences as the antecedents of intelligent behavior. The explanations they underwrite are distinct from the functional explanations described in section 4.3, since the elements in the causal sequence of a functional explanation are typically external to any agent's body and temporally later than the action to be explained. With action explanations, by contrast, the initial elements in the explanatory sequence are always internal to the agent—his desires, beliefs, and deliberative activities—and they are always prior to the behavior to be explained.

Motivational prototypes are but a subclass of a large family of affective, deliberative, and cognitive prototypes, those that collectively make up folk psychology. A perennial objection to the idea that our self conception has the character of a theory has been its apparent requirement that each of us command many thousands of universally quantified conditionals—the "laws" of folk psychology. From the PDP perspective, this is no longer a requirement. As a picture is worth a thousand words, so a few hundred complex prototypes can do the work of many thousands of laws. And unlike laws, a prototype is activated directly by the apprehended situation it may serve to explain. The access problem largely evaporates. To be sure, inappropriate prototypes will often be activated, conflicts with further experience will thus ensue, and the puzzling explanandum will then have to be readdressed from within a more informed context. But the prototype vectors, whether appropriate or inappropriate, will typically be activated within a second or so.

The upshot for the dispute about folk psychology is that it is still a theory, just like any other theory. What has changed, and changed for the better, is our conception of how theoretical knowledge is both stored and accessed in cognitive creatures.

Though I very much doubt it is complete, I shall now bring this catalog of prominent kinds of prototypes to a close. You can see how they allow the prototype-activation model to account in a unified fashion for the most familiar and widely discussed types of explanatory understanding, and for some previously undiscussed types as well.

5   Inference to the Best Explanation

The idea of prototype activation throws some much-needed light on the popular idea of "inference to the best explanation," a process that has often been invoked to account for the fixation of many of our beliefs, even our observational beliefs (see, for example, Harman 1965, 1973). That idea is appealing, since it does seem to address what distinguishes the beliefs we do acquire from the many we might have acquired: the former have better explanatory power relative to the overall circumstance that occasioned them.

But the idea is also problematic, since it suggests a choice made from a range of considered alternatives. As a matter of psychological fact, alternatives are rarely even present. And in any case, our beliefs are typically fixed so swiftly that there is no time for the comparative evaluation of complex matters such as the relative explanatory power of each of a range of alternatives.

On the PDP approach, we can begin to explicate the crude notion of "inference to the best explanation" with the more penetrating notion of "activation of the most appropriate prototype vector." Activating the most appropriate available prototype is what a well-trained network does as a matter of course, and it does it directly, in response to the input, without canvassing a single alternative vector. In the end, the process is not one of "inference" at all, nor is its outcome generally a sentence. But the process is certainly real. It just needs to be reconceived within the more penetrating framework of cognitive neurodynamics. When it is, both the alternatives problem and the speed problem disappear.

C. S. Peirce, who called the process "abduction," found the former problem especially puzzling. Peirce, one of the pioneers of modern formal logic, appreciated very early that for any set of observations there is a literal infinity of possible hypotheses that might be posed in explanation. But how can we possibly search a space of infinite size? Indeed, how can we even *begin* to search it effectively when its elements are not well ordered? Peirce marveled that human scientists are able so regularly to produce, from this infinite sea of mostly irrelevant and hopeless possible candidates, hypotheses that are both relevant and stand some nontrivial chance of being true. From the sentential perspective, Peirce was right to marvel. But from the neurocomputational perspective, the situation is not so mysterious.

We do not search an infinite space of possible explanations. In general, we do not search at all: in familiar cases a suitable prototype is activated directly. And if the novelty of the case foils our waiting categories and thus forces us into search mode, then we search only the comparatively tiny space comprising the set of our own currently available prototype vectors. Even here the search is mostly blind and probably stops at the first success. If one's initial encounter with the problematic explanandum fails to activate directly a familiar and subsequently successful prototype vector, then one repeatedly reenters the problematic input in a variety of different cognitive contexts, in hopes of finally activating some prototype vector or other, or some vector close enough to an existing prototype to give one at least some handle on the problem (see chapter 11).

Since the range of concurrently possible understandings is closed under the relation "is at least within hailing distance of an existing prototype," then *of course* any element from that range will appear both relevant and potentially true. Peirce, and we, are the victims of a perspectival effect. Our hypotheses will look at least passably hopeful to us because they are drawn from a source that collectively defines what will be found plausible by us. We should thus be wary of assuming, as Peirce seems to have assumed, that we have any special nose for truth.

I have raised Peirce's worry here for a further reason: the process just described illustrates the role of *analogy* in the discovery of new explanatory hypotheses. So many of our best theories have had their origins in a provocative initial analogy, perhaps strained in some dimensions, that subsequently proved to be a fruitful vehicle of understanding (see Hesse 1966; Kuhn 1962). The process finds a ready depiction within the present framework. A prototype vector whose activation has hitherto been confined to one empirical domain subsequently comes to be activated with profit in a new domain.

More accurately, the new domain activates a vector that is *close* to the old prototype, close enough to evoke at least some of its cognitive and behavioral consequences. An analogy between two domains has been discovered and exploited. (On this, see also chapter 11, section 3.)

Unfortunately, talk of analogy has always been hobbled by our inability to say anything very specific about what constitutes the relevant kind of similarity. We are now in a position to be entirely specific. Analogy, or similarity, consists in the close proximity of the respective prototype representations, activated by the two empirical domains, in the relevant hidden-unit activation-vector space. And the constituting dimensions of that very high-dimensional similarity are given by the response properties of each neuron in the relevant hidden layer. This means that any analogy is a complex and highly subtle matter, easily recognized, perhaps, even though it will typically transcend effective verbal description. Most important, it is no longer a mystery why both of these things should be so. The many dimensions of the relevant vector space are *used* by us, but they are not generally *known* to us.

The title of this section refers to the "best" explanation. But how, on this PDP approach to explanation, are competing modes of understanding to be evaluated? What makes one explanation better than another? Here we must answer carefully, since we are denied the usual semantic vocabulary of reference, truth, consistency, entailment, and so forth. The cognitive kinematics here being explored does not have sentences or propositions as its basic elements; the basic elements are activation vectors. The various dimensions of epistemic virtue will therefore have to be reconceived in terms that are grounded in this new conception of what cognitive activity consists in.

That will be no small task, and I cannot pretend seriously to undertake it here. What I shall do is illustrate how some aspects of the problem can be addressed, and how the network approach supplies unexpected insight into at least some perennial problems.

At the simplest level, it is easy enough to describe the differential virtue that two distinct prototype vectors A and B can have as a response to a problematic situation. If we assume that we are dealing with a well-trained network, and that the integrity of the two prototypes is not in question, then it may be a just criticism to say that A is simply the *wrong* prototype for the problematic situation at hand. It may be wrong because the situation confronted is not a member of the class of situations that will reliably activate A from almost any perspective, even though it happened to activate A on this occasion.

This can occur if the agent apprehended only a misleading part of the problematic situation, a part that led to the activation of A because that unusual part was relevantly similar to A's typical activators. Unfortunately for the agent, however, the problematic situation is such that, if addressed from any one of many slightly different perceptual or cognitive points of view and then reentered into the network, it would reliably activate B in almost every case. In this statistical sense, A *misrepresents* the situation, whereas B does not.

Correlatively, the behavioral consequences typically activated in turn by A may be highly, even lethally, inappropriate to the problematic situation in question, in contrast to those activated by B. A real example of both failures would be a coyote's faulty understanding of the nature of a small tapered appendage disappearing into a tuft of long grass. The hungry coyote understands it as the tail of a retreating desert rat and acts accordingly. In fact, the problematic item is the tail of a poisonous snake, which coyotes generally avoid (see again figure 10.3a).

Pragmatic and statistical considerations can thus provide a fairly robust distinction between appropriate and inappropriate prototypes, at least for simple cases. We can even reconstruct the distinction between the *correctness* of a prototype on a given occasion, and its *warrant* on that occasion. High warrant is a matter of low ambiguity in the input. We need to ask, Is the input vector closely similar to any other possible input vector that would activate a different prototype? If so, then the ambiguity of the current input is high and the warrant of the prototype vector activated is correspondingly low. If the input is not remotely similar to any activationally diverse input, then its ambiguity is low and the warrant of its activated prototype is high. Similarity among input vectors is measured as usual: by their geometrical proximity within the activational state space for the relevant input layer.

The evaluation of occasion-specific explanations is one thing, but what of evaluating the propriety of an entire class of explanations? How do we evaluate, that is, the integrity of the prototypes, and systems of prototypes, themselves? It is difficult to provide much of an answer to this question, since the answer must draw on some general story of how to evaluate the global cognitive configurations of neural networks. It must draw, that is, on some analog of a general account of "theoretical virtue."

We are as yet in no position even to sketch such an account. But it is clear that there may be gold in these hills. The cognitive behavior of quite simple networks displays an unexpected connection between representational economy, conceptual unification, and the capacity for successfully generalizing past experience to novel cases. Very briefly, the story is this. Suppose we wish a network to discriminate *F*s. And suppose we train that network to a high level of success on some training set (the rock/mine network, for example). Despite its success at recognizing *F*s drawn from the training set, the network will do very poorly at recognizing new examples of *F* drawn from outside the training set if the number of hidden units in the network is very much larger than a certain optimal number. The reason is that, with so many hidden units to exploit, the lazy network will tend to learn a distinct and unrelated prototype for each of the distinct and slightly different examples of *F* in its training set. These unrelated prototypes will sustain appropriate responses at the output layer, and with the error messages thus reduced to nothing, the system will cease any further learning. In particular, nothing forces it to generate a *single* prototype (at the center of a *unitary* similarity gradient) as its response to the entire range of relevantly similar examples of *F* in the training set.

The cost of such laziness comes due when the network is presented with a new example from the relevant class of stimuli, an example drawn from outside its training set. That example will be similar to all of the others, but the network is in a relatively poor position to see that similarity, since it has not learned to see *what is common* to all of the relevant examples in the original training set. To be sure, it will do better than chance at recognizing new examples, since it does have some scattered grasp of the class at issue. But still, it performs poorly.

By contrast, a network that is denied a surplus of hidden units, a network given too few resources to permit such ad hoc and unprojectible learning, is a network that is forced to continue learning until it finds a single prototype region, a region at the center of a unified similarity gradient, a region near which to code every example of *F* in its training set. A *unified* solution to the recognition problem is the only solution for which it has adequate resources. After being forced by circumstance to find such a solution, the network will subsequently recognize a wide range of novel examples of *F* almost as reliably as those it was trained on, since it possesses a similarity gradient adequate to catch almost all of them. (For a more detailed discussion, see P. M. Churchland 1989b or chapter 9.)

Conceptual unification, evidently, is a cognitive virtue of enormous importance, at least as conceived on the present model of cognition. It is important for the very good reason that cognitive configurations having that virtue do much better at generalizing their past experience to new cases. It is therefore reasonable to regard explanations that involve prototypes embedded in a unified cognitive configuration as superior to those that involve prototypes not so embedded. Here is a further dimension in which explanations can be evaluated.

All told, then, we can evaluate them as follows. A virtuous mode of explanatory understanding (that is, an activated prototype vector) should be a *rich* portrait of the general type at issue; it should be strongly *warranted* (that is, have low ambiguity in the input that occasions it); it should be *correct* (relative to the library of currently available alternative prototypes); and it should be part of the most *unified* cognitive configuration possible. Evidently, normative epistemology is not essentially tied to a propositional-attitude conception of cognitive activity. It is robustly possible within the framework here being explored. And on the specific matter of conceptual unity—what it is, and why it is a virtue—the new framework can already claim a proprietary success, a success where the old framework has been a chronic failure.

6   *Comparison with Earlier Models*

Let us begin with the venerable D-N model. It was correct in insisting that explanatory understanding requires the deployment of some information that is general in character. Beyond this insight, almost nothing is correct. The model's commitment to a sentential or propositional mode of knowledge representation renders it unable to account for explanatory understanding outside of that narrow context, and it generates a host of problems even within that context. Slow access, inarticulation of laws, and deductive inappreciation were discussed at the beginning of this essay. To these we may add the problems of explanatory asymmetry (Bromberger 1966; Teller 1974), irrelevant explanation (Salmon 1970), and accidental universals (E. Nagel 1961).

None of these difficulties attend the prototype-activation model. Concerning the matter of access, relevant understanding is usually accessed in milliseconds. Concerning our inability to articulate laws, the PA model does not even suggest that we should be able to articulate them. For what gets accessed is not a stored universal conditional, but a complex prototype. Similarly, while our deductive incompetence is a problem for the D-N view, on the PA model deductive inference typically plays no role at all in the process of prototype activation. Moreover, as noted in section 4, etiological prototypes are in general temporally asymmetric. Explanatory asymmetries are thus only to be expected. Irrelevant explanations (such as appealing to "hexed salt" in order to explain a sample's dissolving in

224 The Structure of Science

water) appeal to strictly nonexistent prototypes. And finally, what moves us to reject an impotent explanatory premise as a merely accidental universal is that fact that, despite its truth, it fails to express any of our learned prototypes.

What a well-turned deductive-nomological argument certainly can do is successfully *evoke* explanatory understanding in the hearer by provoking activation of the relevant prototype with some well-structured and highly salient verbal stimuli. D-N arguments are therefore entirely appropriate things to exchange in a great many explanatory contexts, especially in complex contexts. But they do not embody or account for the understanding itself.

Some of the attempts made to patch the D-N model can be seen as well-motivated but opaque attempts to bridge the gap between the cognitive weakness of universally quantified conditionals and the cognitive muscle of genuine learned prototypes. In response to some of the standard difficulties, Brody (1972) suggested imposing a "causal relation" condition and/or an "essential feature" condition in addition to the usual D-N requirements. On the prototype activation model, the relevant difficulties are handled by something rather similar: the existence within the creature of learned etiological prototypes and property-cluster prototypes. This may explain the appeal of Brody's proposals. However, these two kinds of prototypes constitute only two of five or six different kinds commonly deployed in explanation. It is a shortcoming of Brody's account that it encompasses only these two kinds of explanation. Also, his account remains a restricted version of the D-N model. It is fundamentally sentential in character, and it does not escape the empirical objections voiced in section 1.

An important alternative to the D-N model is the *statistical relevance* or SR model (Salmon 1971). Perhaps the most salient and appealing feature of this model is its rejection of the requirement that the explanandum be inevitable or even probable in light of the explanans. Rather, understanding consists in grasping the statistics of the explanandum situation correctly, whatever those probabilities happen to be. Thus, it is said, one may properly explain my having the flu by pointing to my week of nursing a pair of flu-infected children, even though the probability of the former on the latter is less than 10 percent in an adult.

Though many have contrary intuitions, I think this is a welcome modification. The explanans in such a case does throw light on the explanandum: one's understanding of the situation is significantly improved, despite the low probability at issue. In many domains, probabilities far below unity is all that the world ever provides. Explanatory understanding then appears on the thin side, but it does not disappear entirely.

For better or for worse, the prototype activation model seems committed to the same view. A prototype is by definition "general," in the same sense in which a property is general: it has many instances. But that is the only sense in which it need be general. A prototype vector is not just a cluster of universally quantified conditionals in neural disguise. A prototype, you will recall, can represent a wide range of diverse examples. There need be no feature that is universal, or even nearly universal, to all examples in the class. The statistical distribution of relevant features, across the class comprehended by the prototype, may have almost any profile. But whatever that distribution is, it will be represented in the *salience* accorded each relevant feature in the similarity space configured at the relevant layer of hidden units. And it will likely be reflected in the subsequent cognitive and motor behavior that has been learned by the network. Activation of that vector, nonuniform though its portrait of the class may be, still represents the network's understanding of the input.

Though all of this may be true, I do not think it accounts for more than a small part of the explanatory appeal of the remark "I nursed two flu-infected children for a week," relative to the question "Why do you have the flu?" Rather, that explanans has the clout it does because it activates an etiological prototype concerning the typical transmission of viral infections, a prototype whose warrant in this case may be extremely high, despite the general low probability of adult illness given exposure to infected children. The warrant may be high because infection from those two children may be the only serious opportunity for infection you encountered, and we do demand some infective etiology for every case of flu. The importance of causal structures is also a major theme of Salmon's more recent work within the statistical perspective (1978, 1984). From the PDP perspective, this represents a welcome recognition of the importance of etiological prototypes for explanatory understanding.

Overall, however, it also represents a vision of explanation that is confined to only the second of the five or six important kinds of prototypes outlined in section 4. Causal structures are relevant to some kinds of explanations, but certainly not to all: think of explaining mathematical facts. And despite its sharing some important commitments with the prototype activation model, the SR model remains firmly lodged within the sentential framework of folk psychology, and thus is heir to all of the empirical and psychological problems discussed in section 1.

A different and increasingly popular approach to explanation abandons hope of finding anything very interesting, well defined, and unitary about what counts as an explanation. Van Fraassen (1977, 1980) has urged that whatever reduces someone's puzzlement can count, in that context, as an explanation, and it is evident that a considerable diversity of things can be expected to meet this vague and ultimately pragmatic condition. Here our attention is shifted away from understanding itself and is focused instead on the large variety of verbal or other acts that might, in context, produce it.

It is a consequence of the prototype-activation model that the variety of things that can finally prompt a relevant prototype in a situation of puzzlement is endlessly various. There is nothing canonical about inputs that fail to activate a prototype, and there is nothing canonical about what subtle modifications or augmentations of those inputs will finally make them do so. A one-word hint, a salient gesture, an accidental analogy, almost *anything*, in context, might augment the available input so as finally to trip the activation of some appropriate prototype. "Why is everyone so tense around here this morning?" asks the office manager of a random employee. A rolling of the eyes and a flicker of a glance toward the desk of the office troublemaker tells him all he needs to know.

Well and good. But endless variety in the immediate causal antecedents of explanatory understanding is wholly consistent with unity in the basic nature of understanding itself. The case for seeing such unity is detailed throughout this essay. The variety van Fraassen finds in explanatory contexts is entirely real, but I suggest it properly belongs only to the pragmatics of explanation.

Of course, van Fraassen's account *is* first and foremost an account of the pragmatics of explanation. But it directly suggests a correlative account of what explanatory understanding consists in. If we take his story at face value, explanatory understanding would presumably consist in the possession of an acceptable answer to a topic question, "Why P?" where the answer is acceptable because it entails or otherwise satisfactorily singles out the explanandum "P" from its local "contrast class" of relevant alternatives.

I think this has to be wrong. Explanatory understanding is an ubiquitous phenomenon, an almost continuously unfolding feature of the bulk of any cognitive creature's ongoing conscious experience. It is not a specific answer that singles out a unique member from a specific contrast class of possible alternatives, contextually posed. Nor is it generally an answer to any *question*, explicit or implicit, at all. It is nothing remotely so linguistic, so stylized, or so occasional. In general, explicit questions arise only when explanatory understanding, for some reason or other, temporarily fails or eludes us. If we confine attention to such atypical cases, then van Fraassen's account of the pragmatics of such occasional "cognitive recovery" may begin to look plausible. Yet even in these atypical cases it is plausible only for language-using humans. Puzzlement and its resolution in nonhuman animals (that is, in most of the cognitive creatures on the planet) is not plausibly portrayed in van Fraassen's terms. And not surprisingly. They are the same terms that got the D-N model in trouble. They portray knowledge as essentially propositional in character.

Accordingly, what van Fraassen has given us is, at most, an account of the structure and rules of a certain game, an essentially linguistic game, a game that is occasionally played by the older members of a single species of animal on those exceptional occasions when explanatory understanding for some reason eludes them. It does not provide, nor does it imply, a satisfactory account of explanatory understanding itself.

Perhaps because of his general commitment to constructive empiricism—which sees bare descriptive empirical adequacy as the only genuine epistemic virtue—van Fraassen despaired too quickly of finding anything unitary, interesting, and *epistemologically significant* in the general topic of explanation. On the prototype-activation model, however, explanatory understanding emerges as being on a cognitive continuum with perceptual recognition, a genuinely epistemological matter if ever there was. Additionally, as we saw at the end of the preceding section, explanatory unification is an important and understandable determinant of how successfully one is able to generalize past experience to new cases, which is also an epistemological rather than a merely pragmatic matter. Let us look more deeply into this topic.

I have made conceptual unification an important element of the account proposed. But the present account is not the only one that accords a central importance to explanatory unification. Friedman (1974) and Kitcher (1981, 1989) have both urged that the virtue of an explanation is a function of whether it is, or promises to be, an element or instance of a unified account of a broad range of phenomena. Explanatory virtue, according to them, is not just a matter of the relation between the local explanans and the local explanandum. It is also a matter of the global virtues of the framework of which the local explanans is but one application. While each offers a different account of what the explanatory unification of our knowledge consists in, they are agreed in making participation in such unity the dominant virtue of any explanation.

On the view of explanation here being defended, they are almost certainly right. Some will resist the elevation of unity to this level of importance, arguing that explanatory unity is a purely aesthetic or pragmatic virtue, valued by humans, perhaps, but strictly irrelevant to truth (van Fraassen 1980). Yet we have already seen in section 5 how a "superempirical" virtue like conceptual unity has inevitable consequences for the "empirical adequacy" of a cognitive configuration, as displayed in its ability to discriminate correctly novel instances of a learned category. The lesson here repeats an earlier lesson (urged in chapter 8): we should be very reluctant to assent, as van Fraassen does, to any distinction drawn between the "genuinely empirical" and hence "truth-relevant" virtues of a theory, and its "merely superempirical" and hence "truth-irrelevant" virtues. The distinction is without integrity.

We can push the general lesson of section 5 even farther. If perceptual recognition and explanatory understanding are really instances of the same form of cognitive achievement, as I have suggested repeatedly in this essay, then it is proper to regard perceptual recognition itself as being just a case of *explanatory understanding at the sensory periphery*. On this view, the factors that make for worthy modes of explanatory understanding are the very same factors that make for worthy modes of perceptual apprehension of the world in the first place.

This vital point is the motivating theme of my 1979 book. The insight derives ultimately from C. S. Peirce, who explicitly voices the position on perceptual recognition here being defended: "Perceptual judgment is the limiting case of abductive judgment" (Hartshorne and Weiss 1935, vol. 5, para. 186). We can now sustain Peirce's insight (and Gregory's and Rock's) with a revealing and neurally grounded account of what "abductive judgment" really consists in. It consists in prototype activation. With choices at the empirical periphery thus hopelessly hostage to explanatory values, we can now see that the virtue of explanatory unity must play a dominant role in any adequate epistemology. It cannot be demoted to a merely pragmatic status, as it is in the austere ideology of constructive empiricism.

The PDP perspective also allows us to say something useful about the conflict between the Gibsonian "ecological" approach to perception and the "new look" approach to the same topic. The first point to make is that the Gibsonians appear to be right on the following matter. Perceptual processing is impressively fast and direct: inference appears to play no role at all. On the other hand, the new-look theorists appear to be right on the following point. Our perceptual processing is profoundly theory laden, in that it is dictated largely by the accumulated knowledge—the configuration of weights—acquired in the course of past experience. There is no longer any conflict between these two convictions. They are both a part of the PDP perspective.

A notable view that does suffer, however, is Fodor's view (1984), which attempts to embrace the worst of both positions. Fodor and Pylyshyn (1981) have argued against the Gibsonians that the perceptual process is extensively inferential, and Fodor (1984) has argued against me (1979), and other New Look sympathizers, that nevertheless the process is basically theory neutral. For a better insight on these issues, see Hatfield 1989.

Let us return to Kitcher's account of explanation. It does more than compellingly portray unity as the preeminent cognitive and explanatory virtue that it is. It also discovers and profitably deploys the idea of prototypes. Kitcher takes an important step away from the traditional D-N picture by introducing the notion of an abstract *argument pattern*. These are highly abstract logical structures characteristic of the particular scientific theory being exploited, structures that will yield a great variety of relevantly specific arguments when instantiated to suit a specific explanatory problem. One is reminded here of Kuhn 1962. But unlike Kuhn, Kitcher explains the matter in great detail and shows how an impressive amount of light can be thrown on many chronic problems if we adopt his point of view.

From the PDP perspective, Kitcher's achievement must be judged genuine. The deployment of prototypes is what is central to explanatory understanding, and for maximal virtue it is vital that they be part of a unified cognitive configuration. The problem with Kitcher's story is that it is still much too narrowly *linguistic* in its conception of knowledge representation, and it encompasses only a small subset of the full range of different types of explanation. These are serious defects in the story. Even so, I would much rather highlight its equally prominent virtues, since I would like to claim that the PA account successfully reduces it. The incorporation of the general features of Kitcher's story further illustrates the conceptual unity that the prototype-activation model brings to the topic of explanation.

If the conceptual unity it brings is genuine, then it ought to permit the recognition and understanding of hitherto unrecognized types of explanation. There is some sign of this. The belated recognition of legal, moral, and social-etiquette explanations was a novel experience for me, I am somewhat embarrassed to say, and one might suggest aesthetic explanation as a further category. Perhaps others will see more.

Finally, let me close this essay by adverting to a highly general virtue of the prototype-activation model. I am compelled to cite it, since, as I look back over this essay, I am distressed at how fragile is the account proposed, and how sketchy are the few details provided. What makes me hopeful in the face of this is the fact that the prototype-activation model of explanation meets its own primary condition of virtue, a condition of independent and antecedent plausibility. Specifically, the model brings a welcome and revealing unity into a stubborn diversity of explanation types, and the model is itself an integral part of a highly unified background conception of cognitive activity, one that encompasses with some success the general structure and activity of biological brains, and the structure and cognitive behavior of a new class of artificial computing systems. For this reason, if no other, we should be moved to explore it further.

Chapter 11
Learning and Conceptual Change

---

1 Introduction

To cognitive creatures, the world is a highly ambiguous place. Not just in the ambiguity it presents to our sensory systems, where the initial coding is typically consistent with a diversity of external circumstances, but more profoundly in the ambiguity it presents to our *conceptual* systems. Any conceptual framework, no matter how robust or natural its categories may seem to us, is but a single point in a practically infinite space of alternative possible frameworks, each with a comparable a priori claim on our commitment. Some of the frameworks in this vast and almost entirely unexplored volume will be closely similar to our current scheme, but countless others will be so distant and alien as to escape intelligibility to us, short of a long period of reeducation.

This talk of a vast space of alternatives is not merely romantic. Each of us has a history of conceptual diversity already. For you were not born with your adult framework. You came to it slowly, through a long period of development. There is indeed a space, through which each of us has a complex journey already completed.

An individual's conceptual history is represented by a specific trajectory through this vast space of conceptual alternatives. That trajectory is traced by a point that changes its position swiftly and dramatically in the early stages of life, more slowly in later childhood, and only very slowly throughout the adult years. Fortunately, sheer determination can extend the capacity for continued exploration of the vast space available, at least in some individuals, and this makes possible an ongoing tradition of institutionalized scientific research.

Talk of conceptual "space" may seem metaphorical still, but as outlined in the two preceding chapters, recent research has shown us how to make literal and very useful sense of it. If we assume that the human brain is a multilayered network of interconnected units, we can uniquely specify its current position in conceptual space by specifying the individual strengths or weights of its myriad synaptic connections (figure 11.1*b*). That configuration of weights can be directly represented by a specific point in a multidimensional space, a space with a distinct axis for each of the brain's 10^{14} synaptic connections (figure 11.1*a*). For a human brain, therefore, this "weight space," as it is called, will have fully 10^{14} dimensions with at least 10 possible positions along each. Its volume is almost unimaginably vast—at least $10^{10^{14}}$ functionally distinct positions—as our guiding metaphor suggested.

And there is a second space to consider here, comparable in its vastness: the space of possible *activation patterns* across the brain's 10^{11} neurons (figure 11.1*c*). This "activation-vector space," as it is called, has a distinct axis for each *neuron*, an axis that measures the level of that neuron's activity. As outlined in the earlier chapters, a specific configuration of synaptic weights will partition the activation space of a given neuronal layer into a taxonomy of distinct *prototypes* or *"universals"* (figure 11.1*c* depicts a simple binary partition). To specify that global configuration of weights is thus to specify the global conceptual framework currently in use by the relevant individual. To change any of those weights is to change, however slightly, the conceptual framework they dictate. To trace a creature's actual path through the space of possible synaptic configurations would be to trace its conceptual history (figure 11.1*a*). And to understand what factors induce changes in those weights would be to understand what drives conceptual change.

The present chapter continues the exploration of this view. I wish to address four problems in particular. The first concerns the phenomenon of multiple conceptual competence. The second concerns an important distinction between genuine conceptual change and mere conceptual redeployment. The third problem concerns the factors that drive these two kinds of change. And the fourth concerns the recently apprehended vastness of cognitive space, and the need to automate not just the experimental but also the theoretical aspects of the scientific enterprise, if we are ever to explore that space effectively.

I begin by reraising a problem addressed in chapter 9. Should we identify one's conceptual framework with the configuration of synaptic *weights* in one's brain? Or with the *partitions* they effect across the activation vector space of the assembled neurons to which they connect? Or perhaps with the overall input-output *function* that the network comes to instantiate? The weights uniquely dictate both the partitions and the function, but despite the functional primacy of the weights, there are good reasons for identifying the partitions, and the

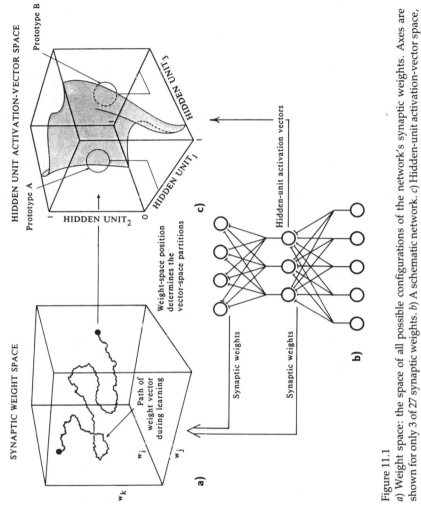

Figure 11.1

a) Weight space: the space of all possible configurations of the network's synaptic weights. Axes are shown for only 3 of 27 synaptic weights. *b*) A schematic network. *c*) Hidden-unit activation-vector space, the space of all possible activation vectors across the population of hidden units function they serve, as reflecting most directly the antecedent notion of a "conceptual framework."

While the weights are of essential importance for understanding long-term learning and fundamental conceptual change, the partitions across the activation space, and the prototypical hot-spots they harbor, are much more useful in reckoning the cognitive and behavioral similarities across individuals in the short term. People react to the world in similar ways not because their underlying weight configurations are closely similar on a synapse-by-synapse comparison, but because their *activation spaces* are similarly partitioned. Like trees similar in their gross physical profiles, brains can be similar in their gross functional profiles, while being highly idiosyncratic in the myriad details of their fine-grained arborization (compare Quine 1960, p. 8).

Thus, a perfect identity of weight configurations will indeed produce a perfect identity of partitions on the activation space, but one can also achieve almost identical partitions with a large variety of quite different weight configurations. Synaptic contrasts in one place may compensate for further synaptic contrasts in another place, so that the functional profile of two brains may end up practically the same. At least for now, therefore, let us adopt the partitions and the functions they serve as the closest available neural analog of what the philosophical tradition conceives as our "conceptual framework."

(We could insist on the point in weight-space as the more profound analog, as I earlier recommended [p. 177], and we may yet find reason to do so. But if we do, a vital similarity measure across the weight configurations will still advert to the partitional and functional factors at issue.)

2   Multiple Conceptual Competence

Humans have the occasional capacity to apprehend the same thing in one of two or more quite different ways, often at will. Examples range from the simple case of being able to see a familiar curve as now a duck and now a rabbit, to the more unusual and global case of apprehending natural phenomena now in an Aristotelian fashion, now in a Newtonian fashion, and now in an Einsteinian fashion. How is it possible, on the network models at issue, for a single individual to do this? How is it possible for one to bring distinct conceptual resources alternatively to bear on one and the same problem? How could one train a network to have this capacity?

The problem is that to train a network to any sort of competence is to impose a function on it. A function delivers a unique output for any given input. But the situation at issue seems to require that the network sometimes deliver a different output given the same input. These demands are incompatible, and the solution is to recast the problem so that the relevant inputs are not strictly identical after all. With the inputs distinguished, we can then train the network to joint competence on two functions with nonoverlapping domains.

An example will illustrate. Suppose we wish to train a network to give as output the *sum* of any two single-digit numbers entered as input. A typical input would be <2, 5>, and the desired output <7>. The relevant function is thus a smallish set of ordered pairs, each pair being an input and its proper output. Now suppose we also wish to train the network to give as output the *product* of any two single-digit numbers entered as input. A typical input would be <2, 5>, and the desired output <10>. We are now asking the impossible, unless we make it possible for the network somehow to discriminate inputs on which addition is to be performed from inputs on which multiplication is to be performed.

This is easily done. Add to each input a "context-fixing" element, so that we enter <2, 5, +> when we want addition performed, and we enter <2, 5, ×> when we want multiplication performed. With the sets of input elements from each function now completely disjoint, the union of the two functions desired will be a legitimate function also. We then train the network on that larger function (i.e., on that larger set of input/output examples), and the result is that it learns both to add and to multiply. Intriguingly, the typical result of such training is the partitioning of the hidden-unit activation space into two distinct subspaces, one in which the various multiplicative transformations are all coded, and the other in which the various additive transformations are all coded. What trips these different cognitive behaviors is the appearance of one of the context-fixing elements, "+" or "×", as part of each input.

This simple example illustrates a general strategy. A network can learn to deal with the "same" class of inputs in a variety of different ways according to which context-indicating elements accompany those inputs. Those context fixers can and often will be supplied by the external environment. But that is not their only possible source. The only firm requirement is that the context-fixing information somehow reaches the hidden units along with the rest of the input information. This requirement is consistent with the context fixers having their origins somewhere else within the network itself, especially if we are dealing with a complex network like the brain, which has many layers and many distinct processing pathways. The idea is that the total input to the relevant layer of hidden units includes either "descending" or "horizontal" projections from one or more distinct layers elsewhere in the larger network. In figure 11.1b, this could be visualized by imagining some additional axons coming in from the side to form synaptic connections onto the hidden units over and above the connections already arriving there from the sensory periphery.

This yields a network where the manner in which the sensory input is processed is both variable and under the control of the network itself. Such a network can process a given perceptual input in any one of several different ways. It can "see" a figure as either a duck or a rabbit, as it were, depending on which of its activational subspaces (conceptual resources) it has kicked into gear with the relevant context-fixing inputs. This is true not only at the level of perceptual processing, but at higher levels as well. A situation drawn from memory, or contemplated in imagination, or apprehended from a printed description can also be understood in a variety of different ways, depending on what contextual information accompanies its apprehension at the relevant population of processing units. It is not mysterious, then, on the model of cognition here being explored, that one can learn to perceive/understand the world in an Aristotelian fashion, and in a Newtonian fashion, and in an Einsteinian fashion, and then use each framework (each subvolume of the activation space) by turns, to suit either aesthetic whim or practical occasion.

3 Conceptual Change versus Conceptual Redeployment

A possible problem for the vector-processing model of cognition concerns the time course of conceptual change. On the face of it, the unique determinant of a network's conceptual resources (activation-space partitions) is the network's configuration of synaptic weights, and the only way to change the former is to change the latter. But changes in the weight of any given synaptic connection happen only in small increments. Accordingly, the learning network's global trajectory through weight space (figure 11.1a) must always approximate a continuous path. But conceptual change is a process that at least occasionally displays dramatic *dis*continuities. Scales fall from the eyes, the light dawns, the structure is suddenly apparent, and so forth, sometimes on a time scale of seconds. How to reconcile the apparent conflict?

There are several ways we might approach this problem. First, we might highlight the recent evidence indicating that changes in the number and/or surface area of synaptic connections meeting a given cell can, at least in some circumstances, take place on a time scale of minutes (Desmond and Levy 1983). A related line of evidence concerns the long-term potentiation (LTP) of neuronal response in some cells, a process also occurring in the one-minute range (Desmond and Levy 1986). While this evidence is encouraging, it remains unclear whether such changes are either large enough or fast enough to solve the problem at issue.

A second approach points out that the functional relation between the weight configurations on the one hand, and the resulting partitions on the activation space on the other, is a highly nonlinear and occasionally volatile relation (see p. 172). Relatively small changes in the weights can occasionally produce large and sudden changes in the partitions across the conceptual space. This fact could mitigate the problematic lethargy shown by the point in weight space.

A third approach might attempt to play down the discontinuities claimed for our conceptual behavior, by arguing that historical and autobiographical descriptions of the relevant shifts have been chronically exaggerated. Here we would attempt to deny, or play down, the phenomena we had originally hoped to explain. Some combination of these points, perhaps, will constitute a solution to the problem.

Perhaps they may. Fortunately, the discussion of the preceding section makes available to us immediately a quite different and rather less strained solution. There is a way to account even for large-scale conceptual shifts, on a time scale as short as milliseconds, that requires no motion from the weight-space point whatsoever. The crucial idea is the idea of *conceptual redeployment*, a process in which a conceptual framework that is already fully developed, and in regular use in some other domain of experience or comprehension, comes to be used for the first time in a new domain.

Examples are many and familiar. Consider Huygen's seventeenth-century realization that optical phenomena, previously grasped via the ray traces of geometrical optics, could be more comprehensively understood as instances of wave phenomena. Here the theory of waves in mechanical media—a theory already well-formed in Huygen's mind in connection with sound waves and water waves—was applied in a domain hitherto unaddressed by that framework, and with systematic success. There was no need for Huygens to effect a global reconfiguration of his synaptic weights to achieve this conceptual shift. He had only to apprehend a familiar class of phenomena in a new cognitive context, one supplied largely by himself, in order to have the inputs activate vectors in an area of his conceptual space quite different from the areas they had previously activated. The difference was the context fixers brought to the problem. And the result was a radically new understanding of optical phenomena. The novelty, however, consisted in the unusual redeployment of old resources, not the creation from scratch of new ones. No new resources were created; nor were any old resources destroyed.

A second example is provided in the various seventeenth-century attempts to apply the conceptual resources of *terrestrial* mechanics to the case of motions in the superlunary heavens, a domain long thought to be governed by distinct and divine principles. From the rectilinear perspective of the recently developed mechanics, the circular motion of the planets around the Sun—which constitutes a centripetal acceleration *toward* the Sun—clearly asked for a *force* on the planets directed toward the Sun. It could be a push from the outside or a pull from the inside, but from the new perspective it had somehow to be there. Descartes' vortex theory tried to fill out the story in the first way; Newton's gravitational theory tried, with more striking success, to fill it out in the second. But in both cases, existing conceptual resources were being reapplied in a new domain. Contemplation of the heavens was now activating, on a regular basis, prototype vectors that were initially provoked only in response to terrestrial situations.

A third and very striking example is the systematic reconception of optical phenomena as *electromagnetic* phenomena, a shift that spread quickly throughout the scientific community of the late 1800s. James Maxwell's beautiful summary of the relations between electric and magnetic fields entailed the existence of a wavelike electromagnetic disturbance, spreading out from any oscillating charge, with a velocity of $(\mu \times \epsilon)^{-1/2}$, where μ and ϵ represent the magnetic permeability and the electric permittivity of the surrounding medium. (These features are a measure of how much an electric or magnetic field is "diluted" when it passes through the medium in question.) For the atmosphere these two values were well known. A quick calculation yielded a velocity of roughly 3.0×10^8 m/s for such spreading electromagnetic disturbances, a velocity indistinguishable from the measured velocity of light. This extraordinary coincidence invited an attempt to see further optical phenomena as facets of oscillatory electromagnetic phenomena.

As it developed, this electromagnetic reincarnation of Huygen's much simpler vision immediately displayed all of the virtues of its antecedent, plus an unexpected cornucopia of further virtues. Electromagnetic (EM) waves were transverse, and thus were polarizable, just as light had proved to be. Unfamiliar features of transparent substances, such as their permittivity (ϵ) and permeability (μ), suddenly became salient, since it is they that dictate the differing velocities of EM waves in the relevant substances, and it is those relative velocities that dictate the refractive index of any substance. The refractive indexes for transparent substances were already well known, and the systematic agreement with the predictions of the new theory was striking. These various indexes suddenly emerged as transparent instances of the electric and magnetic properties of matter.

Here again a familiar domain was ambiguous and proved to be understandable in more than one way. When addressed with the appropriate context-fixing inputs (perhaps no more than the admonition "Any ray of light *is* a train of EM waves!"), optical phenomena began systematically to activate vectors in an unexpected subvolume of conceptual space, a subvolume that was initially partitioned by its extensive training on entirely nonoptical phenomena. Moreover, after extended practice at approaching the old phenomena with the new subvolume in gear, one clearly did better at understanding things than one did with the old framework. And finally, a major virtue of this shift, a virtue displayed in both of preceding examples as well, is that one now had a *unified* understanding of what initially appeared as disjoint empirical domains.

It is clear from these three examples that conceptual change is regularly a matter of conceptual redeployment, as opposed to fundamental conceptual novelty. It is also clear that such shifts can initially take place, in a given individual, on a time scale of seconds or less, although the full exploration of the novel use of old resources may well take years. Indeed, so many of the historical examples fit this redeployment mold that one may begin to wonder if history contains *any* examples of real conceptual novelty. I believe that it does—Faraday's conception of a "field of force" comes quickly to mind—but I also suspect that such cases are relatively rare. The bulk of the conceptual discontinuities displayed in the history of science are clearly cases of conceptual redeployment.

These can often be cases of learning, however, in the deeper sense and beyond the making of the shift itself. The redeployed resources seldom survive extended contact with the new domain entirely unchanged, and the process of shaping and refocusing those resources is a process in which the relevant subvolume of one's activation space is now subject to a new regime of training examples. This will often lead to a yet more subtle articulation of the antecedent partitions, a process of learning that is comparatively slow and thus easily explained in terms of the gradual motion of one's weight-space position.

What we have to acknowledge is that the notion of "learning" is starting to fragment in interesting ways. Beyond the basic but comparatively slow process of synaptic adjustment, there is the more short-term process whereby one learns how to deal with a puzzling new situation by repeatedly reapprehending it in conjunction with various context-fixing auxiliary inputs, in hopes of eventually activating some robust prototype vector within a subvolume that is already well trained. The ten-year old takes apart the old alarm clock and after a half-hour's pondering sees how it all works. The math student puzzles over a homework problem and after several false starts suddenly sees the path through it. The physician confronts a confusing set of symptoms and, several failed tests and incoherent diagnoses later, finally lights on a successful one. These are all paradigm cases of learning, in the sense of "coming to understand," but the underlying process here is quite different from the slow process that partitions one's activation spaces in the first place.

The frequency and importance of conceptual redeployment requires us to acknowledge a further divergence, which I have been suppressing to this point, between the partitions across one's activation space(s) and the input-output function one instantiates. Plainly it is possible for two people to have closely similar partitions, but widely divergent deployments: they may command essentially the same conceptual resources, but apply them to quite different domains. Two physicists (Newton and Huygens, say) may have a comparable command of both projectile mechanics and wave mechanics, and yet one chronically understands light as the high-speed ballistic motion of tiny corpuscles, while the other chronically understands light as a train of compression waves in the ether. The same sensory inputs produce different conceptual responses in each, and thus different behavior from each, since particles and waves often call for different techniques of manipulation and behave differently in many circumstances. Because of their different applications, the two physicists will have a different input-output function, despite commanding identical conceptual resources.

A more familiar case concerns the domain of application of the resources of folk psychology. We all share a more or less common conception of intentional agents, and yet some of us, the devoutly religious, chronically find intentional significance in a wide range of phenomena that are perfectly natural to the rest of us. The interpretation of natural disasters and natural blessings, both large and small, as the deliberate punishments, rewards, and messages of a hidden intentional agent (God) who has specific expectations of us is an interpretation still embraced by a large portion of the contemporary population. Not surprisingly, their behavior is often quite different from those who deploy the relevant resources more narrowly: they display prayer, sacrifice, penance, resignation, and so forth. Here again we have common resources differently applied, with a quite different global input-output function as the result.

Such cases give us reason to regard a person's trajectory through weight space as capturing only a part of what we would normally regard as one's conceptual evolution. The repeated redeployment of existing conceptual resources can produce some profound changes in one's cognitive and practical life, with only minimal changes in the configuration of one's synaptic weights and in the activation-space partitions that they produce. If we want to know what drives conceptual change, then, we must address both the dynamics of the moving point in weight space and the more superficial but still vitally important dynamics of conceptual redeployment.

4   What Drives Conceptual Change?

We may begin by asking the narrower question of what drives conceptual redeployment. Here there are several factors, the first of which is blind *luck*. That Maxwell's EM theory should have yielded a velocity for EM waves exactly equal to the known velocity of light was the sheerest serendipity. That Newton's analysis of bodies falling under an inverse-square law should have yielded Kepler's well-known ellipses was another stroke of sheer good fortune. Other theories (Huygen's) and other analyses (Descartes') were not nearly so fortunate. But perhaps these are factors that pull rather than push. What factors positively drive conceptual redeployment?

Frustration with the poor performance of older frameworks figures prominently. Recall Kuhn's analysis of gathering anomalies, crisis science, and the resulting radiation in conceptual approaches to old problems. Individuals show an increasing willingness to explore, and the scientific community shows an increasing willingness to tolerate, unorthodox conceptions of recalcitrant phenomena. Old inputs are repeatedly reentered into one's already trained network, with a variety of increasingly unusual context fixers, in hopes of activating some antecedently-developed prototype vector in a subvolume of activation space hitherto devoted to other phenomena entirely. Should success be achieved, the (hyper)distance between the old and new prototype vectors is a measure of how great the conceptual change effected.

Though gathering anomalies are perhaps the most common force behind such explorations, they are clearly not *necessary* for conceptual exploration of this kind. The simple desire for *theoretical unity* can drive a systematic search for new ways of comprehending old phenomena, even when the old ways are functioning quite nicely. Here the only defect that need be felt in one's current conceptual resources is the fact that they are still diverse rather than unitary.

Examples are common enough. Classical, or "phenomenological," thermodynamics was enormously successful (it helped to produce the industrial revolution), but this did not dissuade the tradition of Bernoulli, Joule, Kelvin, and Boltzmann from repeatedly trying to reconceive thermal phenomena within the broader framework of kinetic and corpuscular theories. Newtonian mechanics had conquered motion at both the astronomical and the human scales. One had to wonder if it also held true at the submicroscopic scale. The possibility of apprehending heat as mechanical energy at the molecular level was therefore very inviting.

An unusual sensitivity to failures of unity seems to have driven the greater part of Einstein's theoretical work. Special relativity was an attempt to bring mechanics and electrodynamics together under a common and internally coherent roof. General relativity was an attempt to unify the physics of both accelerated and unaccelerated reference frames. In both cases the new conceptual perspective was provided by four-dimensional geometry with nonstandard metrics. But in neither case was the search for this more unitary perspective driven by any prominent experimental failing in any of the older views. His later search for a unified field theory is a further instance of the same general yearning.

This impulse toward unity is vitally important in any cognitive creature, an impulse coequal with sensitivity to the data, for reasons we can now understand (see chapter 9, section 5). It is curious that the relative strengths of these two impulses seem so variable across individuals. A major imbalance in either direction yields a familiar pathology. Valuing unity at the radical expense of local empirical success yields a castle-in-the-air fantasy world for its victim to live in. And valuing local empirical success at the radical expense of synoptic unity traps its victim in a disconnected set of small and windowless rooms: it yields a hidebound and narrow vision that will not generalize successfully to unfamiliar cases.

Finally, conceptual redeployment is occasionally prompted by some fortunate novelty in one's experience. Ampère's observation that a cylindrical coil of current-carrying wire produced a bipolar magnetic field moved him to reconceive the long-familiar case of magnetized iron bars as having circular currents somehow flowing inside of them as well, just as in the coil. Fresnel's striking demonstration of concentric circles of light at the center of a tiny circular shadow moved many thinkers to foresake Newtonian corpuscles and to set about reconceiving light on a wave model. And Einstein's much later observation of the curious photoelectric effect moved him to re-conceive light waves as quantized after all. In such cases, the striking new phenomenon discovered in a familiar domain is capable, all by itself and without arduous context fixing, of activating specific vectors in some heterodox portion of one's activation space. Here the phenomena themselves have the salient character necessary to activate an unusual interpretation directly.

Conceptual shifts of the kind under discussion constitute perhaps the greater portion of our scientific development, but they seem superficial relative to the prior and deeper learning process by which our activation spaces are partitioned in the first place, and by which they must be readjusted. What factors drive change at this most fundamental level? What forces the weight-space point to move? This remains an open question. The best I can do on this occasion is briefly to summarize the dynamical alternatives salient both in network modeling and in physiological research. (A more comprehensive survey of the former is available in Hinton, forthcoming.)

Supervised Learning
This class of learning algorithms requires a suitable number of ordered pairs, drawn from the function to be learned, for presentation to the network. Of crucial importance is the availability of the correct output for any of the given inputs. The most popular algorithm of this kind is currently the *back-propagation* procedure described in chapter 9, section 5. Here the desired output vector is compared element-by-element with the actual output vector produced by the student network in response to a training input. The difference between the two outputs is then used to compute a small and proprietary adjustment for each weight in the entire network. That change is such as to nudge the network's global point in weight space a small distance down the steepest slope of the local "error surface." The path of repeated nudgings, produced by repeated presentations of the input-output pairs in the training set, is a path that eventually leads to a position of low error or accurate performance on all of the training examples.

This learning procedure is highly effective, but it does have several severe shortcomings, both as an account of how biological brains learn, and even as a technology for training artifical nets. First, the requirement that the correct output be available to the learning network in every case is clearly unrealistic. After failing to solve a problem, real brains do not generally get to look at the correct answers at the back of the book. Second, the brain shows no plausible mechanisms for computing and distributing such globally informed adjustments to its myriad weights. And third, the back-propagation procedure scales upward to large networks only very poorly. The number of weights increases exponentially with the number of neuronal units in the network, and thus so does the task of computing a proprietary adjustment for each, especially when the procedure requires thousands of repetitions. Even for artificial nets, this will impose a ceiling on the size of the nets we can train in acceptable time with the back-propagation algorithm. The training of networks approaching 10^3 units already poses a serious strain on the best existing machines.

Boltzmann learning procedures offer some improvements over back propagation, although they bring defects of their own. Let us address the same kind of three-layer network discussed above, and the same problem of training it up on a given set of input-output vector pairs. Here we take an input-output pair and "clamp" each onto the input and output units respectively. Suppressing nicities, we may describe the Boltzmann procedure for synaptic adjustment as follows. Each synapse is sensitive to the level of activity it receives from its own axon, and to the level it finds in the unit to which it connects. Under Boltzmann learning, its weight will be driven up or down to conform with these local constraints; that is, they will tend to assume local values that would tend to produce the local output given the local input.

Given that the vectors across the input and output layers are temporarily *fixed*, and that the input vector is repeatedly propagated upward through a network whose synaptic weights are set at random values, there will inevitably be failures of fit between the activity levels of the fixed output vector and the summed synaptic activity that reaches it from below. These clashes produce changes in the weights of the synapses meeting the final, or output, layer of units. Similarly, a whole hidden unit whose output synapses are under uniform pressure to shrink (or expand) is a unit whose internal activation level is put under pressure to shrink (or expand). This pressure is released by appropriate reductions (increases) in the weights of its input synapses.

Overall, and in response to these multiple constraints, the network's weights have a tendency to settle gradually into a final configuration that is consistent with the overall constraints, and especially with the constraints imposed by the fixed output vector. This is a configuration that would *yield* a real output vector that is similar to the training output vector, if the network were suddenly unclamped and presented again with the relevant input. (With back propagation, by contrast, the presentation of each training pair produces only a tiny change in the weight-space position and only a tiny improvement in the network's performance.)

In order to lubricate this process, and to free it from getting caught in purely local error minima of poor final performance, each weight is repeatedly subjected to random increases and decreases during the course of settling. These random changes are of significant size at the beginning of the settling process, but are slowly reduced to zero as it proceeds. It is as if the network's critical elements were heated up at the beginning and slowly allowed to cool in the process of finding their minimally stressful mutual accomodation of weights. This process is called "simulated annealing." In all, the system is evolving toward the more probable of its possible configurations relative to the clamped constraints. That is why the process is called "Boltzmann learning."

The process described constitutes only one training cycle. The modified net must now be clamped with the next input-output pair, and the process repeated. And so with all of the pairs in the training set. The second cycle may well obliterate many or most of the gains made in the first, but the overall process eventually drives the weight-space point to an error minimum that is *common* to all of the training pairs. The weight-space point thus follows a more lengthy and adventurous path than it does under back propagation, but the result is much the same.

There are advantages to this procedure. For one, it does not require a globally computed error, nor any global system to distribute it. Global information about error filters across the whole network, but by means of many purely *local* effects computed locally, independently, and simultaneously. For this reason, Boltzmann learning scales up to large networks rather better than does back propagation. The local character of the teaching may also be more plausible from a biological point of view.

On the other hand, Boltzmann learning is still slow for very large networks, since they can take a long time to settle to equilibrium, and a distinct settling cycle must be done for each training pair. This difficulty can be circumvented with artifical networks, since the settling process can be automated to exceptionally high speeds in electronic analog systems. But it remains a prima facie problem for the procedure as an account of learning in biological brains. Further, learning cannot take place unless the correct answers (outputs) are somehow supplied. Boltzmann learning, as described above, still depends on having the answers at the back of the book.

Reinforced learning

We can escape the unreality of an omniscient teacher by exploring learning procedures in which the error messages are less well informed. Indeed, we can use either of the two procedures just described, with the difference that the output vectors to which they are trained are variously *degraded* versions of the desired output vectors: they are partial, or they are distorted by random influences. Surprisingly, this can actually improve the quality of learning in some cases, since adding a very small amount of noise to the teaching signals can smooth out the misleading idiosyncracies of the examples in a given training set (Zipser and Elman 1987). On the whole, however, degrading the teaching signals produces a proportional (or worse) degradation in the learning process. For the most part, the weight-space point is still being nudged down an error gradient, but it is no longer taking the steepest path available at each step. It thus takes longer to find the relevant error minimum. We buy a greater realism at the expense of slower learning.

Neither the back-propagation nor the Boltzmann procedure is necessary for reinforced learning, however. Any procedure that sets the weight-space point in motion, perhaps even in random motion, and then modifies that motion in response to some measure of success or failure, counts as an instance of reinforced learning. This will include a wide range of possibilities.

Unsupervised learning (Hebb rules)

It is a surprising fact that some learning algorithms will allow a network to learn a good deal about its environment with no error messages concerning its output performance whatever: all they need is a large sample of inputs. What networks do when developing under such algorithms is to evolve processing strategies that (*a*) maximize their capacity for identifying salient information in the set of input vectors, (*b*) convey such information from layer to layer in efficiently coded forms, and (*c*) find similarities among the inputs so that they are taxonomized into potentially useful groupings. Such algorithms partition the relevant spaces so that diversity is recognized, information is usefully compressed and transmitted, and prototypes are developed.

The learning rules that perform these surprising feats are called "Hebb rules," after D. O. Hebb (1949). The basic form of synaptic adjustment is as follows. If a given synapse is the site of both a strong presynaptic signal and a highly activated postsynaptic cell, then the weight of that synapse is increased. This procedure is thus sensitive to the *correlations* among the diverse elements of the input signals arriving at a given cell, and it modifies the network's processing behavior so as to magnify them.

The qualitative description just given admits of a wide variety of quantitative realizations, and the many possible "flavors" of Hebbian learning yield an unexpected variety of cognitive results. For some settings of the relevant parameters, a Hebbian learning procedure will produce units that show the same response properties found in biological neurons. In one striking experiment (Linsker 1986), the input units are arranged in a two-dimensional layer so as to simulate a retina. Even if this network is fed a series of inputs that represent sheer *noise*, a Hebbian algorithm will modify the response properties of the hidden units so that their "receptive fields" (i.e., that pattern of activations across the *input* units which produces a maximal response in the hidden unit at issue) show the on-center/off-surround pattern, or the oriented bar pattern, found in real cortical cells (Hubel and Weisel 1962).

A different flavor of the Hebb rule produces a partitioning of the hidden-unit vector space such that the many inputs are grouped into distinct *similarity* classes. A further flavor yields a network that performs a "principal-component analysis" on the set of its inputs. That is, it spontaneously finds a set of axes of representation such that variation across the set of input vectors is maximized: the network becomes tuned to the important *differences* among the input vectors. (See Linsker 1986, 1988.) This variety of results is exciting because Hebb rules hold real promise of biological reality. It is already known that variation in synaptic weights is driven by a Hebbian dynamic for a central class of cells in the hippocampus (Kelso, Ganong, and Brown 1986). And there is evidence for a negative Hebb rule—one that *de*creases the weights of previously potentiated synapses—in other cells in the same area (Stanton and Sejnowski, in preparation). Furthermore, Hebbian adjustments are locally driven and occur independently throughout the network. This allows global adjustments in the weight-space position to happen quickly and without the guidance of any global "teacher."

With unsupervised learning, however, we are not training the network to instantiate a specific input-output function. What function it does come to instantiate is dictated solely by the statistical properties of the set of inputs, the connectivity of the network, and the flavor of the Hebb rule that governs synaptic adjustments. This limitation is not as severe as one might have guessed, perhaps, but a creature must have some way of subjecting its output vectors to external criticism if it is to learn the many intricacies of the world in general. The problem here is with *completely* unsupervised learning, however, rather than with Hebb rules themselves. For Hebb rules can perfectly well subserve learning in supervised as well as in unsupervised networks. The Boltzmann procedure described earlier, for example, uses principles of local synaptic adjustment that are already one instance of a Hebb rule. Such rules also scale very well to large networks. All told, Hebb rules appear to buy us speed, biological reality, and functional fecundity.

That functional fecundity remains largely unexplored, however, and few lessons can yet be drawn concerning the character of learning and rational methodology in science. Even so, one or two very general lessons emerge from the preceding discussion. They are worth noting.

The first lesson concerns the character of the factors that drive synaptic adjustment and conceptual change. Are they exhausted by considerations of mere "professional interest," as some theorists have argued (see Pickering 1981, 1984), or does the world itself exert a robust influence on the process? In the many network models that have appeared in the research program under discussion, it is clear that it is the world itself that is driving the learning process, whether by means of back propagation of measured error, by means of the progressive reduction of cognitive dissonance with imposed output vectors, or by means of a progressive accomodation to the objective statistical distribution among inputs.

It must immediately be admitted, of course, that these networks are not functioning in a complex *social* world, as is a real scientist. And it must also be admitted that for a network as complex and sensitive as a human brain, the pressure to instantiate socially acceptable functions can often be overwhelming. But while the character of social pressures will have a vital role to play in any adequate account of learning in scientific communities, there is no reason whatever to regard them as *exhausting* the dynamical pressures. We know that in nonsocial cases of learning (artificial networks, simple animals), it is the nonsocial world itself that is the instructor, a relentless and often highly successful instructor. And unless institutionalized science somehow represents a total *corruption* of a process that shows systematic integrity elsewhere, there is no reason to embrace the extremely skeptical, antirealist social determinism suggested above. On the contrary, science has outperformed those purer but simpler creatures.

On the other hand, from the perspective of the present chapter, the naturalism of the "strong program" in the sociology of knowledge (Bloor 1976) appears entirely justified. Throughout this chapter we have been exploring causal accounts of the learning process—

accounts, moreover, that are uniform for successful and unsuccessful cognitive configurations alike. And we have found it neither necessary nor useful to fall back on the language of observation statements, logical inferences, rational beliefs, or truth. However, the alternative to these antiquarian notions need not be a skeptical account of knowledge, as so many fear. Rather, one hopes, it will simply be a better account of knowledge.

The second major lesson I wish to draw, from the picture of cognition explored in this chapter, concerns the appalling vastness of the conceptual space in which we find ourselves. I am reminded here of the shock that must have confronted Greek thinkers when Aristarchos of Samos first put a realistic metric on the dimensions of the physical universe. While scholars of the period where quite prepared to believe that the heavens were very large, Aristarchos' crude but well-conceived calculations caught them quite unprepared for just *how* large. To a community used to thinking of the scale of the heavens in terms of thousands of miles at most, Aristarchos brought compelling geometrical reasons for extending the yardstick to hundreds of thousands of miles in the case of the Moon, millions of miles in the case of the Sun, and many thousands of millions of miles in the case of the stars. An expansion of this magnitude changes one's perspective on things.

I believe we are now confronting a similar lesson. Contemporary scholars, with a few notable exceptions (e.g., Davidson 1973), are prepared to concede the possibility of alternative conceptual schemes, perhaps a great many of them. But the reckoning of the true extent of the space of alternatives that arises from the point-in-weight-space model of human knowledge is one that catches us unprepared, however liberal our prior sentiments. $10^{100,000,000,000,000}$ (just-barely discriminable) alternatives is not a number one would have picked, and yet that is a minimum reckoning (see again chapter 9, section 7).

The significance of this number will be clearer if we note the following points. Simple networks have already been trained up on a wide range of dramatically different problems: phoneme recognition, shape discrimination, multiplication tables, music composition, loan-application evaluation, hand-eye coordination, text reading, and so on. Each of these trained skills represents what we would call a "dramatically different conceptual configuration" of the network. The number of such dramatically distinct skills already produced by various researchers, many of which are now available for sale, is in the thousands and is still climbing. But nearly all of them are achieved in networks of less than 10^3 units. This means that any one of them is a skill that a standard 10^3-unit network could have; it needs only to be weighted properly.

As we noted, such a network commands, at a bare minimum, a thousand dramatically different possible conceptual configurations, and it has this capacity with only 10^3 units and something like $(10^3)^2$ or 10^6 synaptic connections. Assuming, as before, 10 distinct possible values for each synaptic weight, such a system has 10^{10^6} distinct possible weight configurations. This is a very large number indeed, but it is a paltry fraction of the figure for a human brain. In principle, our combinatorial options are greater than the small artificial network's by a factor of $10^{10^{14}}/10^{10^6} = 10^{(10^{14}-10^6)} = 10^{99,999,999,999,000,000}$. The number of "dramatically different conceptual configurations" open to us should therefore be greater than the small network's by the same factor.

One's excitement at the extent of the opportunities available here is quickly joined by a dismay at the problem of how to explore that space effectively. If we suppose that one could make an arbitrary change in each one of one's synaptic weights 10 times every second and did so for every second of one's life (10^{10} updates), one would still have visited a total of only $1/10^{(100,000,000,000,000-10)}$th portion of the functional positions available. Figures like this, and those in the preceding paragraphs, change one's perspective on things, for they begin to put a recognizable metric on the space. A maximal reckoning of any possible human cognitive excursion comprehends but an infinitesimal part of a minimally reckoned cognitive space.

As with astronomical space, it is clear that the effective exploration of cognitive space will require major instrumental help. We cannot run fast enough, jump high enough, or see far enough to explore the heavens without technological augmentation of our native resources. We need manned spacecraft, unmanned probes, and optical and radio telescopes. The same is true for the exploration of cognitive space. Our native resources are inadequate to the task, by many orders of magnitude. But we need not be limited by our native resources. Let us discuss the possibilities.

5   Automated Science

The advent of artificial neural nets, and of automated procedures for teaching them, opens the possibility of automating aspects of the scientific enterprise itself. Computers, of course, have been helping us to assemble, organize, and filter *data* for decades. But teachable networks promise returns far in excess of these humble duties. For they promise to do something *conceptual* with the data, something similar to what intelligent creatures do with it. They promise the possibility of effectively automating, for the first time, the *theoretical* part of the scientific enterprise.

The prospects here cover a wide range of possible achievements. Let us begin with some of the simplest. "Expert systems" are now a part of the marketplace. These are carefully written programs, typically diagnostic in their practical applications, that attempt to encapsulate and to exploit the expert knowledge available in some domain. They are regularly good enough to be useful, but chronically they are poor enough to be frustrating. Part of the problem is that such programs inevitably represent someone's attempt to *articulate* the available wisdom in the relevant domain. Such reconstructions typically fall well short of the detailed expertise of a skilled professional, though in programmed form they do display the virtues of tirelessness, speed, and uniformity of treatment. They fall short because much of an expert's wisdom is *inarticulate*: it consists of knowledge that is not stored in linguistic form and is difficult both to recover from the expert and to recast in the idiom of a programming language (see Dreyfus 1979; Dreyfus and Dreyfus 1986).

From the perspective of knowledge representation in neural nets, these difficulties are not surprising. One's capacities for discriminating subtle and complex patterns typically resides in a very high-dimensional representation space, a space whose individual dimensions each codify some intricate feature of the input space (remember that each hidden unit receives weighted inputs from thousands of sensory units). Recovering all of this information from a living expert is effectively impossible, and exploiting all of it effectively in a serial machine might take too much time even if it could be recovered.

The solution is to forget the task of trying to articulate the desired knowledge within a set of explicit rules. Instead, train up an artificial neural network on the same data set that trained the human expert. For example, if medical diagnosis is the expertise being modeled, then what is needed is a large number of pairs in which the input is the profile of metabolic parameters and pathological symptoms of a real patient, and the output is the correct diagnosis as to his disease. Here no attempt is made to articulate rules that will connect complex symptoms to specific diseases. The network is left to generate its own "rules" in response to the patterns implicit in the large data set. We do, of course, exploit the human expert's knowledge to provide the diagnoses on which the network is trained, but it is the many examples that do the work: no attempt is made to articulate that knowledge. We wish only to re-create it—and perhaps to exceed it in speed, range, and reliability—in the trained artificial network.

Once that expertise has been achieved, we can read out the configuration of weights that sustains it and then fix those values immediately into any number of new networks. The expertise can thus be mass-produced without further training. More importantly, we can also read out the partitions effected across the various activation spaces of the various layers of hidden units, in order to discover what taxonomic strategies were found by the network as its solution to the general problem set it. Perhaps its taxonomies will parallel our own, and perhaps they will not. The network may find new groupings of old cases, and it may identify, as diagnostically important, features that went unnoticed by human experts. In this way might artificial networks provide us with new insights into the taxonomy and causal structure of the world, even in domains we already command.

This approach is repeatable in a wide variety of contexts: psychological, chemical, geological, economic, meteorological, and industrial. And no doubt it will be, since PDP expert systems will offer real advantages over the conventional programmed expert systems available today. Instead of struggling to equal human expertise in a specific domain, they promise to exceed it in almost every respect.

Yet these minor prognostications are not what motivate this closing section. They serve only to introduce the shape of the larger project. What we need to address is the problem of training networks to a useful understanding of domains where human experts have no understanding, or none that is satisfactory. This will require that our artificial networks use learning strategies that place negligible reliance on antecedent knowledge and expert teachers, beyond what instruction the world itself can provide. If we can construct genuinely parallel *hardware* realizations of the large networks that will be needed, and if we can automate such learning procedures so that they will take place many orders of magnitude faster than they do now, either in serial machines or in human brains, then we can turn such systems loose on existing data sets like stellar and galactic surveys, the behavior of national economies, the properties of millions of chemical compounds, and the varieties of psychological dysfunction. Presentation of the data must be automated as well, to exploit the network's great speed. We can then examine with interest what order our artificial networks manage to find in such complex and teeming domains. For they will be able to explore the space of cognitive possibilities— large subspaces of it, anyway—far more swiftly and extensively than we can ever hope to explore it without their help.

What sort of symbiotic relationships may emerge here, between existing human brains on the one hand, and very large and fast neural nets on the other, is an engaging question that invites the imagination for a ride. Making a network equal in all respects to the human brain, but just faster, seems still much too hard a job to be completed in the near future. So we must not expect to have something to which we can simply *talk*. If we are willing to settle for less familiar kinds of interactions, however, then networks large and fast enough to be useful seem designable and buildable right here and now. The difficulty will lie in making *accessible* to us the cognitive achievements we may expect them to make. The goods will always lie in the structured partitions that emerge, in the course of learning, within the hidden-unit activation spaces. But as the networks get larger and the dimensionality of those spaces goes up, it will be progressively harder to display in accessible ways, and to make sense of, the structures that develop within them. For we can expect them, after all, to develop conceptual resources that are alien to us. Internalizing a penetrating new framework may thus take some time, even if it is handed to us on a platter.

Even if we can develop such turbocharged versions of, or adjuncts to, our native cognitive capacities, the space confronting us remains abyssal. An electronic or optical realization of the neural organization of the human brain will have transmission velocities 10^7 times faster than axonal velocities, and this may allow the artificial system to learn 10^7 times faster than a human brain. This would be an impressive gain. But the conceptual space it could explore in a lifetime would still comprise but a miniscule portion of the space available: it would discharge less than a single zero in the exponent of the denominator of the tiny fraction discussed earlier. There is little prospect, therefore, that a "final, true theory of the cosmos" is something we can ever expect to discover. Nothing guarantees that *any* point in human cognitive space is such as to yield a network with zero error on every performance. And should such a point exist, which I very much doubt, it would still be a needle in a monumental haystack.

And yet, if there is no real prospect of an end to our cognitive journey, there is every prospect that our conceptual frameworks can continue to get better and better, ad infinitum, especially since we can always artificially expand the number of neuronal units and synaptic connections available to a given thinker, and thus expand the conceptual space to be searched. In the long run, this may be a more effective incentive to intellectual progress than the prospect of a final resting place could ever be.

Chapter 12

Perceptual Plasticity and Theoretical Neutrality: A Reply to Jerry Fodor

The doctrine that the character of our perceptual knowledge is plastic, and can vary substantially with the theories embraced by the perceiver, has been criticized in a recent paper by Fodor. His arguments are based on certain experimental facts and theoretical approaches in cognitive psychology. My aim in this paper is threefold: (1) to show that Fodor's views on the impenetrability of perceptual processing do not secure a theory-neutral foundation for knowledge; (2) to show that his views on impenetrability are almost certainly false; and (3) to provide some additional arguments for, and illustrations of, the theoretical character of all observation judgments.

The idea that observational knowledge always and inevitably involves some theoretical presuppositions or prejudicial processing is an idea that has provoked much discussion in recent years, for its consequences are profound. If observation cannot provide a theory-neutral access to at least some aspects of reality, then our overall epistemic adventure contains both greater peril, and greater promise, than we might have thought. The first and perhaps the most important consequence is that we must direct our attention away from foundational epistemologies, and toward epistemologies that tell a more global story of the nature of theoretical justification and rational belief. A second consequence is that our current observational ontology is just one such ontology out of an indefinitely large number of alternative observational ontologies equally compatible with our native sensory apparatus. And a third consequence is that, since some theoretical frameworks are markedly superior to others, the quality of our observational knowledge is in principle improvable. If the conceptual framework in which our perceptual responses to the world

This paper first appeared in *Philosophy of Science* 55, no. 2 (June 1988). It is here expanded by some new material on neuroscience added to section 1.2 and some material on meaning added to section 2.2.

are habitually framed were to be replaced by a more accurate and penetrating conception of physical reality, then our newly-framed perceptual judgments could be significantly more revealing of the structural properties and the dynamical details of our perceptual environment.

The motivation for such a view is not purely philosophical. Perceptual psychology provides supporting evidence in the form of experiments designed to illustrate both the inevitable ambiguity of perceptual situations and the cunning resolution of those ambiguities at the hands of general assumptions imposed by "higher" cognitive centers (Gregory 1970a, 1974; Bruner 1973; Rock 1983). These "New Look" ideas, however, have recently come under interesting attack from within cognitive and computational psychology itself. The complaint is that these ideas have exaggerated the extent to which perceptual processing is under the control of the higher cognitive centers. And the counterclaim is that the job of reducing ambiguity is conducted largely or entirely by peripheral "modules" whose activities are insulated from, and quite insensitive to, the fickle content of human belief.

It is here that Jerry Fodor enters the debate. In a recent paper (Fodor 1984), he marshalls the alleged modularity of our perceptual systems in criticism of various claims made by Hanson (1961), Kuhn (1962), Churchland (1979), and others concerning the theory-laden character of perceptual knowledge and the holistic nature of the human epistemic enterprise. My principal aim in this chapter is to show that Fodor's specific claims about the psychology of human perception are mostly irrelevant to the epistemological issues at stake here. His discussion serves more to muddy the waters than to clarify them, for even if the modularity/encapsulation thesis is correct—which almost certainly it is not—it contains no significant message concerning the traditional epistemological issues. It is, in short, a red herring. In what follows, I shall try to defend and expand on the specific claims, listed in my opening paragraph, against the several criticisms directed at them in Fodor's paper.

There are three principal ways in which any perceptual belief may fail of theoretical neutrality: in its causal history or *etiology*, in its *semantics*, and in the purely *extensional structure* of the ontology it presupposes. In his 1984, Fodor has much to say on the first topic, a little on the second, and he does not discuss the third. Since he does not address what I have called "extensional bias" (Churchland 1975a), and space does not permit its exploration here, I shall merely emphasize its existence and move on. What follows will be focused on the first two loci of epistemic prejudice.

1   The Etiology of Perceptual Belief

1.1   Does encapsulated processing buy us theory-neutral perceptions?

I shall pass over Fodor's opening discussion in order to address immediately what he describes as his main point (p. 35). Fodor, of course, is quite aware that early perceptual processing very likely does involve many elements that resemble or correspond to general empirical "assumptions" about the world (e.g., the three-dimensionality of space, the spatial and temporal continuity of common objects, the sharp change of luminance at a body's boundaries, color constancy through changing environments, the occlusion of distant bodies by proximate ones, etc.), and to "inferences" drawn or "hypothesis selections" made in accordance with a system of such default assumptions. On this view, the etiology of perceptual beliefs looks highly, even dramatically, theoretical in character, as Fodor himself remarks (p. 34).

But Fodor's view, to a first approximation at least, is that (a) the assumptions involved in early processing are endogenously fixed in all of us, and (b) the processing in which they play a role is insulated from any contrary assumptions or theories—indeed, from any *additional* assumptions whatever—that the perceiver may subsequently come to believe. Our perceptual processing is thus encapsulated; it delivers outputs to the higher cognitive centers, but it is impenetrable to any inputs from them. The result, according to Fodor, is that all humans are fated to share a common perceptual experience, an experience whose character is not subject to change as a function of any theories we may come to embrace. There is therefore an important sense, he concludes, in which human perception is neutral vis-à-vis the rough and tumble of competing theories. There is an unchanging perspective, on at least some parts of reality, that all human theorists must share in common.

The evidence in support of these claims is twofold. First, Fodor cites a number of experimental facts that illustrate, not the plasticity of perception, but rather the occasional rigidity of our perceptual deliverances (e.g., the persistence of certain illusions, such as the Muller-Lyer illusion) even in cases where we know them to be mistaken. Second, he claims that if perception is to be theory dependent in any epistemologically interesting sense, then the perceptual modules must have "*access to* ALL *(or anyhow, arbitrarily much) of the background information at the perceiver's disposal*" (p. 35). Given the rigidity just cited, however, he concludes that the modules at issue lack such access, and hence that perception is not theory dependent in any interesting sense.

Let us suppose, for the moment, that our perceptual modules are indeed informationally isolated in the fashion claimed. That is, they embody a systematic set of endogenous or genetically implanted assumptions about the world, whose influence on perceptual processing is unaffected by any additional or contrary information.

Now this may be a recipe for a certain limited *consensus* among human perceivers, but it is hardly a recipe for theoretical *neutrality* and it is plain misleading to use this latter term to describe what encapsulation might secure. As conceived within the relevant dialectical tradition, an observation judgment is *theory neutral* just in case its truth is not contingent upon the truth of any general empirical assumptions, that is, just in case it is free of potentially problematic presuppositions. If an observation judgment does have such presuppositions, its theory-laden character will in no way be reduced by hardwiring those presuppositions into the process by which the judgment is produced, and by closing the process to all contrary information.

If everyone is a hopeless slave of the same hardwired theory, then what we have is a universal dogmatism, not an innocent Eden of objectivity and neutrality. The alleged cognitive impenetrability of our perceptual processing does nothing to reduce the extent to which the truth of our perceptual beliefs is contingent upon the truth of those background empirical assumptions or theories in which they are semantically embedded. Encapsulation does nothing to ensure the truth of our perceptual beliefs, not even their "truth in general" or their "truth under normal circumstances." Nor does it ensure their epistemological integrity relative to competing interpretations of our sensory input. It merely dooms us to a single point of view, a point of view that is epistemologically just as problematic as any of the infinity of other sets of empirical assumptions that might have been hardwired into us instead.

Fodor's premises, therefore, do not buy him anything like the theoretical neutrality of our perceptual judgments. An unchangeable set of prejudicial empirical assumptions is still a set of prejudicial empirical assumptions.

Fodor's premises may seem to solve, at least, the problem of incommensurability, by guaranteeing some effective communication, at the observation level, between ideologically diverse human theorists. But as we shall see at the end of this section, they fail to guarantee this also, since rigidity in our early perceptual processing is entirely consistent with plasticity at the level of conceptual apprehension and discursive judgment. And despite a popular misconception on this point, communication was never the real problem anyway. The epistemological problem of incommensurable alternatives arises most clearly and forcefully within a *single* individual, one who is "bitheoretical." Putting Fodor aside for a moment, consider someone who has internalized two competing theories, and has learned two correspondingly different ways of perceiving the relevant aspects of the world, but is torn over which of these two global packages to choose. It is not communication that is the problem here (he can perfectly well understand himself); the problem is theoretical evaluation and rational choice in the absence of a neutral touchstone.

I am not arguing at this point that Fodor's encapsulation thesis is false, only that it would not secure for us any theory-neutral foundation for knowledge, even were it true. Fodor's hardwired consensus is a sham neutrality: it mistakes the presumed universality of our prejudice for the absence of any prejudice. And hardwired or no, that consensus would last only until the first mutant or alien comes along, to confront us with a different perceptual point of view.

In fact, we begin to become such mutants or aliens ourselves when we change our sensory modalities by augmenting them with unusual instruments, such as phase-contrast microscopes, deep-sky telescopes, long-baseline stereoscopes, infrared scopes, and so forth. And the metamorphosis is completed when, after years of professional or amateur practice, we learn to see the world appropriately and efficiently with these new senses. This learning requires both that we suppress certain habits of processing "natural" to the naked eye and to the familiar world of middle-sized material objects, and that we learn to process the retinal data in novel ways, ways that are appropriate to the unfamiliar features one perceives by these novel means (e.g., interference patterns, diffraction rings, dark nebulae, fusion planes, temperature gradients, etc.). Reflections such as these do begin to challenge Fodor's factual claim of encapsulation or impenetrability. Let us therefore focus on the evidence he cites in support of that claim.

1.2 Is the impenetrability thesis correct?

Visual illusions are good illustrations of the assumptions involved in early processing, since the illusion is often the result of the persistent operation of some assumption that is appropriate for most situations, but which is inappropriate for the particular situation at issue. Fodor cites the stubborn persistence of various visual illusions, even when we know that we are being misled, and even where we have the information about the inappropriate assumptions responsible for the illusory experience. Why, Fodor asks, doesn't *this* information affect the way we see the world, and thereby undo the illusion? His answer is that our perceptual processing is guided by mechanisms or

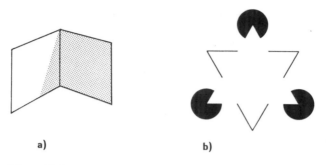

Figure 12.1
a) Schematic preparation for illusory color contrast. *b*) Illusory contours and brightness contrast

assumptions that cannot be successfully overridden by contrary assumptions imposed from the outside.

A first response is just to point out the great many illusions and visual effects whose character shows that our visual modules are indeed penetrable by higher cognitive assumptions. Consider the wide range of ambiguous figures, such as the duck/rabbit, the old/young woman, the Necker cube, and the vase/faces. Such examples are ambiguous with respect to orientation, or scale, or perspective, or figure/ground, or any of a variety of other dimensions. But in all of these cases one learns very quickly to make the figure flip back and forth at will between the two or more alternatives, by changing one's assumptions about the nature of the object or about the conditions of viewing. At least some aspects of visual processing, evidently, are quite easily controlled by the higher cognitive centers.

One such reversible illusion is striking in that it extends even to changes in perceived *color*. Take a monochromatic birthday card or similar folded rectangle. Place it upright and oriented to the light so that one of the inside faces is in a very slight shadow relative to the other inside face. (Figure 12.1*a* illustrates the relevant configuration, but only a real card will support the illusion.) Despite this slight shadow, the two faces of the card will be perceived as having the same objective color. Now, closing one eye to defeat stereoscopic orientation cues, treat the object as a Necker cube and deliberately invert its orientation—in thought—so that the middle fold appears closer to you than the two outside edges. This will produce an obvious distortion in the perceived shape of the card: it will no longer look like a folded rectangle. And it will also produce a change in the perceived color of the shadowed and unshadowed areas of the card. In its original appearance, the slight contrast in luminance is suppressed by the visual system as a mere shadow effect. But in the card's inverted configuration, the slight contrast in luminance is no longer consistent with a shadow hypothesis, and the contrast between the two areas is robustly interpreted as a sharp difference in their intrinsic colors. (I owe this example to Richard Gregory.)

Illusory contours provide a similar but contrasting example. The white background in figure 12.1b is, of course, entirely uniform. But most of us can see a slightly brighter triangular figure interposed between us and the three black circles, a figure with distinct rectilinear contours marked by a sharp change in luminance, even in the gap between the black circles. Here the eye-brain conjures up luminance differences where in reality there are none. And again, the illusion is penetrable and reversible. Tell yourself that the circles have wedges cut out of them; see the elements of the diagram as six independent objects artfully arranged against a uniform background; center your attention on the two prongs of any V; and the illusory contours disappear.

These assembled examples compile a wide range of elements central to visual perception—contour, contrast, color, orientation, distance, size, shape, figure versus ground—all of which are cognitively penetrable. Collectively, they constitute a strong case against Fodor's claims of impenetrability for our perceptual processing.

But perhaps I am gathering evidence selectively or aiming it at an exaggerated version of Fodor's view. Perhaps many other elements of perceptual processing, even the dominant share, are *impenetrable*, despite these examples of a contrary cast. What examples does Fodor cite, then, in support of such a claim?

Only one, the Muller-Lyer illusion (figure 12.2a), though the class he has in mind is clear enough (it will include the Ponzo illusion, the Hering illusion, and similarly persistent illusions). The Muller-Lyer, however, is an odd example for Fodor to be using, because the "textbook story" on how it works (a story apparently endorsed by Fodor, p. 33) explains it as the effect of our having *learned*, in judging absolute size, to make automatic corrections for the variation of an object's angular size with distance (fig. 12.2b.) That is, the illusion exists in the first place only because the relevant processing module is the well-trained victim of some substantial prior education—that is, of some penetration by cognitive activity. The Ponzo and the Hering illusions may have a similar origin. Accordingly, they are all of them poor examples on which to base a general claim of impenetrability.

Now I will grant that, its cognitive origins aside, the Muller-Lyer illusion cannot be overridden by any casual, fleeting, "voluntary"

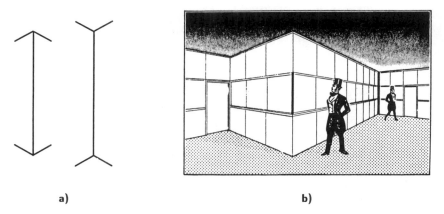

a)   **b)**

Figure 12.2
a) The Muller-Lyer illusion. *b*) The Muller-Lyer illusion in a realistic setting (bold, vertical lines)

attempt to modify the character of one's visual experience. By itself, however, this means relatively little, for the issue is not whether visual processing is in general very *easily* or *quickly* penetrated by novel or contrary information; the issue is whether in general it is penetrable at all, where the acceptable means of penetration can include long regimes of determined training, practice, or conditioning. If the Muller-Lyer illusion is an incidental consequence of a long period of perceptual training on certain typical kinds of perceptual problems, then presumably a long period of training in an environment of a quite different perceptual character would produce a subject free from that particular illusion. Fodor, it seems to me, is in no position to insist otherwise, especially given examples of the following kind, which are not speculative, but real.

Recall the effects of chronically worn inverting lenses on the visual perception of normal humans. Such lenses have the effect of inverting the orientation of all visual information relative to the body's tactile and motor systems. In short, they turn the visual world upside down. (Kottenhoff [1957] provides a useful summary of this research.)

The initial effect is profoundly disorienting, but with little more than a week's practice, subjects adjust to the new perceptual regime. The subjects are not confined to a chair or bed for the duration of the experiment, but are forced by practical necessity to continue to interact with familiar objects and to engage in the normal forms of motor behavior. The result is that the subjects slowly manage to recoordinate their vision with the rest of their sensory and motor systems, and the illusion of the world's being upside down is said to fade away, all on a time scale of roughly a week.

When the lenses are first put on and the world is made to appear upside down, the subjects are of course quite aware of what the lenses are doing. They may even know how they do it. But the illusion is not banished by the mere possession of this information. It would clearly be wrong, however, to draw from this any conclusion about the impenetrability of our visual processors. A few weeks of steady practice and experience penetrates them quite nicely. And the degree to which that penetration is successful is further revealed when the lenses are finally removed: for a short time thereafter, the subjects suffer a disorientation illusion very much like that encountered when the lenses were first put on. Their visual processing, reconfigured by training to compensate for the lenses, continues to "compensate" after the lenses are gone.

In similar experiments on animals, training produces a reversal in the character of what one might have presumed to be endogenously specified reflexes, such as the vestibulor-ocular reflex, which directs one's eyes, when fixated on a target, to move an appropriate amount to the left or right in order to compensate for head movements in the opposite direction. Here the brain seems literally to rewire the relevant neural mechanism under the pressures imposed by left-right inverting lenses. (see Gonshor and Jones 1976.)

Cases like these are important, for they reflect the plasticity of some very deep "assumptions" implicit in visual processing, such as the specific orientation of the visual world relative to one's other sense modalities and to one's motor systems. If assumptions as deep as these can be reshaped in a week or two, then our perception begins to look very plastic and very penetrable indeed.

I expect Fodor to object, however, that examples such as these, dramatic though they may be, are not cases of the *cognitive* penetration of our peripheral modules. These perceptual changes are wrought not by the simple acquisition of certain beliefs, nor by reflecting on them in the relevant perceptual circumstances. Rather, they are wrought by some form of training, practice, or conditioning, often lengthy.

One way to turn this objection aside is to attack the integrity of the highly questionable dichotomy between "cognitive penetrability" and other forms of penetrability (see the commentaries on Pylyshyn 1980 in that work). But I shall not pursue this path here. There is a simpler and more direct response: Who ever claimed that the character of a scientist's perception is changed simply and directly by his embracing a novel belief? None of the theorists cited in Fodor's paper have defended such an unrealistic view. And all of us, at some point or other, have emphasized the importance of long familiarity with the novel idiom, of repeated practical applications of its principles, and of socialization within a like-minded group of researchers.

Kuhn is quite explicit (1962, chapters 5 and 10) that the enveloping paradigm that shapes the scientist's perception is not constituted solely by a set of explicit laws, but by an entire disciplinary matrix that includes standard ways of applying and using the resources of the paradigm, skills acquired during a long apprenticeship. And my own discussion of the plasticity of perception (1979, chapter 2) has the relevant community learning their nonstandard observational vocabulary from birth, in an ongoing *practical* setting where no other idiom is even contemplated.

I confess to having used one example where a temporary shift in perception can be made fairly swiftly: the example of reperceiving the organization of the solar system in a heliocentric rather than a geocentric fashion (1979, pp. 30–34). This case is rather closer to the Necker cube in character than to the case of the inverting lenses. But even here it was emphasized that simply having the relevant Copernican beliefs is not enough; one must learn how to see the changing heavens as an unfolding instance of the Copernican organization, as viewed from our peculiar perspective within it. Having the relevant beliefs is one thing: we are all of us Copernicans, after all. Reshaping one's perception is quite another.

The point is a general one. A physics student does not come to see the motions of common objects in a new way simply by memorizing Newton's three laws. Most freshman physics students do memorize those laws, but relatively few have their perceptions much altered. The few who do are distinguished by having *practiced* the skills of applying those laws in a wide variety of circumstances. They do come to perceive a common pattern in the behavior of moving bodies that was hitherto invisible to them, but memorizing the laws was only the first step in a fairly lengthy process. There are sudden flashes of insight, to be sure, as when one first grasps how the pattern is instantiated in some typical case. But on the whole, the process of reshaping one's perception takes time, and it requires more than the mere adoption of a belief or three.

To summarize these points, if Fodor is attacking the view that perceptual processing always (or even usually) responds directly and immediately to changes in one's theoretical commitments, then he is attacking a straw man. This is not a view that anyone has defended. On the other hand, if Fodor is denying that perceptual processing is plastic in the face of more comprehensive and protracted kinds of pressures, such as the forced practical *use* of some novel perspective, then the empirical facts are against him. For by these means, even very basic aspects of visual processing can be overturned and reconfigured, as we saw with the visual-inversion experiments.

Some degree of "diachronic" penetrability is grudgingly conceded by Fodor (p. 39), since the alternative is to hold that *all* of our adult perceptual capacities are *endogenously* specified. We know that they are not, since the development of so-called "normal" perception itself plainly involves a great deal of learning on the part of the growing infant. Our perceptual, practical, and social environment shapes our perceptual capacities mightily, especially in their early stages of development, and this suggests that different courses of learning would produce interestingly different perceptual capacities. Fodor attempts to play down this concession, however, by suggesting that the range of possible variation in perceptual development might be quite narrow.

Why he thinks this is left unexplained. The claim needs arguing, the facts suggest otherwise, and one need not turn to academic journals for shining examples. To see the nonstandard perceptual capacities that our native modalities can acquire, think of the following. In recent centuries most humans have learned to perceive speech not just auditorally but visually: we have learned to read. And some have learned to perceive speech by touch: they read Braille. And some of us have learned not just to hear music, but to see it: we have learned to sight-read musical notation. Now, neither the eyes nor the fingers were evolved for the instantaneous perception of those complex structures and organizations originally found in auditory phenomena, but their acquired mastery here illustrates the highly sophisticated and decidedly supernormal capacities that learning can produce in them. And if these capacities, why not others? Diachronic penetration, I assert, is not only possible and actual; it is commonplace.

Finally, there is neurophysiological evidence that suggests the systematic penetrability of the peripheral modules by the higher cognitive centers. Cell-staining techniques have allowed us to trace out a gross "wiring diagram" for many parts of the brain. When introduced into a neuronal body, certain chemical stains—notably, horseradish peroxidase—are transported down the entire length of its long fiber-like axon. This marks the axons visually, and the paths they trace through successive sections or slices of the brain can then be followed with an optical microscope. In the case of vision, for example, the dominant nervous pathway starts at the retina, and proceeds via the optic nerve to the lateral geniculate nucleus (LGN), and stepwise from there by other pathways to the primary visual cortex, to the secondary visual cortex, and from there to a variety of other areas even higher in the processing hierarchy.

But these "ascending" pathways are almost invariably matched by "descending" pathways that lead us stepwise back through the intermediate brain areas and all the way out to the earliest processing systems at the retina. The descending projections from the visual cortex back to the LGN, for example, are even greater in number than those in the ascending direction. And though the claim is not well established, there is some evidence that fully 10 percent of the axonal fibers in the human optic nerve are descending projections from the LGN back out to the retinal surface itself, the very first transducer in the processing hierarchy (Wolter 1965; Wolter and Lund 1968; Sacks and Lindenberg 1969).

There are similar chains of descending pathways—from the various areas topmost in the information-processing hierarchy, down through all of the intermediate processing stages, and all the way out to the periphery—for all of the other sensory modalities as well. This organizational pattern is typical in mammals and also in birds (Livingston 1978, pp. 45–49). Prima facie, the function of these descending pathways is "centrifugal control." They allow for the modulation of lower level neural activity as a function of the demands sent down from levels higher in the cognitive hierarchy. Experimentation on their functional significance is so far limited, but lesions confined to the descending optic nerve pathways (from LGN to retina) are known to cause perceptual deficits in birds, even though the descending fibers in their case constitute only 1 percent of the optic nerve total. Lesioned birds are less able than intact birds to distinguish edible seeds from other minute objects in dim light (Rogers and Miles 1972).

If such descending pathways were always sharply confined close to the sensory periphery, or if they were to be found scattered only here and there in the information-processing hierarchy, then we might have some realistic hope of dismissing any backward loop as an element of what is still an "encapsulated module" from a functional point of view. But descending pathways are the rule in the processing hierarchy of the brain, not the exception. They appear to connect the upper levels in the hierarchy to most and perhaps to all of the lower ones, in each and every one of the sensory modalities. In sum, the wiring of the brain relative to its sensory periphery certainly does not suggest the encapsulation and isolation of perceptual processing. As with the psychological data discussed earlier, it strongly suggests exactly the opposite arrangement.

[Added in 1989: Two new pieces of neuroscientific evidence have recently emerged that bear on the questions of both plasticity and theory-ladenness. The first piece of evidence is theoretical and derives from the new connectionist models of information processing in the brain. Those models identify the general knowledge acquired by any organism with the acquired configuration of its myriad synaptic weights. Since on this model all cognitive processing, including perceptual processing, consists in vector transformations at the hands of those modifiable and much instructed weights, it would seem that all perceptual processing is inescapably laden with the legacy of general knowledge shaped by past experience. (For a more detailed discussion, see chapter 9, section 7.)

The second piece of evidence is experimental and concerns the functional plasticity of auditory cortex. Sur et al. (1988) induced the axons in the optic nerve of neonate ferrets to project into the animals' auditory pathway (the medial geniculate nucleus or MGN) instead of to their normal visual pathway (the LGN). The result is an animal whose auditory cortex is now driven exclusively by information sent from the eyes. Such animals do develop significant visual function as they mature, and recordings from cells in the "auditory" cortex of adult animals show the cells to have developed the same directional sensitivity, orientation selectivity, and capacity for edge detection displayed by cells in the visual cortex of normal animals. This striking result suggests that the processing characteristics peculiar to our adult sensory systems are not endogenously specified, as Fodor's picture invites us to suppose, but rather are developed over time in a highly plastic system that is shaped by the long-term characteristics of the sensory input they receive from the periphery. This does not sit at all well with a picture of endogenously specified assumptions unique to each modality. This result is also exactly what one should expect if the connectionist models of learning and information processing just mentioned have any integrity.]

1.3 Is the encapsulation thesis relevant?

Before concluding this section on the etiology of perceptual judgments, I wish to address a further and vitally important point. Let us suppose, for the sake of argument, that perceptual processing is entirely rigid and impenetrable up to the contents of one's visual (auditory, tactile, etc.) manifold; rigid, that is, up to the character of one's sensations. Even if, as now seems very unlikely, visual processing is thus rigid, the outputs of that system are still capable of driving in turn an enormous variety of quite different *conceptual* frameworks. The point here is that sensations themselves are not yet truth-valuable or semantically-contentful states: they are still a stage, though perhaps a late stage, in the processing that leads to specific perceptual judgments or beliefs. Now (and this is a point that I have made explicitly before in 1979, pp. 38–39), however rigid that prior processing might be, there are indefinitely many different possible mappings from the domain of sensations to the domain of propositions (judgments, beliefs), and which of these many mappings comes to characterize your own perceptual activity is a function of which of the indefinitely many conceptual frameworks you have learned as the framework of spontaneous response to the contents of your sensory manifold.

Accordingly, the plasticity of perceptual judgment defended by me in earlier writings does not require that we "penetrate" the peripheral perceptual modules in any case. We need only *connect* the outputs of those modules to whatever system of conceptual activity governs our discursive thinking. Further, if two people have learned radically different frameworks, then they will have a severe communication problem despite the rigidity of their peripheral processing. Thus my earlier observation (section 1.1) that encapsulation fails to solve the problem of incommensurability.

That our *conceptual* system is plastic I regard as obvious. That we can successfully connect different conceptual systems to one and the same sensory system I regard as only slightly less obvious. The doctrine of the plasticity of human perceptual judgment requires no premises beyond these.

A few words, then, in support of the less obvious of the two premises. Consider the conceptual framework used for describing pitch in musical theory. It begins with the chromatic scale: C, C♯, D, D♯, E, F, F♯, G, G♯, etc. This is not just a list of names. The sequence has a periodic character (octaves), an absolute position in auditory space, and a well-defined metric of various intervals. In fact, the chromatic scale and its various properties form the foundation of musical theory. Clearly, however, this conceptual framework is not innate to our auditory processing, nor is it a part of ordinary language. But people are regularly trained to use it in auditory perception. In time, the better students master what we call a sense of absolute pitch ("That's a middle C, . . . and that's the A above middle C").

More intricate yet, there is the domain of musical chords, and of harmonious sequences of chords. Chords are structured sets of simultaneously sounded notes, sets that fall into an organized matrix of different types (majors, minors, sevenths, ninths, diminisheds, augmenteds, etc.). These too can be directly recognized, by ear, by one suitably practised in the relevant theory and vocabulary. Such a person perceives, in any composition whether great or mundane, a structure, development, and rationale that is lost on the untrained ear.

We are contemplating a musical example not because it is the only empirical example one can cite, but because it is an unproblematic example. Everyone knows that the "ear can be trained," as we say, to sustain these remarkable and nonstandard perceptual capabilities. But the example of trained musical perception is a straightforward existence proof for the possibility of theoretically-transformed perception in general. What wants appreciating is that this example is repeatable in a great many other domains. What is required is learning the relevant theory, and extended practice in using it.

We may begin to see some of the endless possibilities by noting that one can just as easily learn to recognize sounds under their dominant *frequency* descriptions as under their music-theoretic descriptions ("That is an oscillation of 262 hertz, . . . and that's one of 415 hertz"). Equally possible, one can learn to recognize them under their *wavelength* descriptions ("That has a wavelength of 1.19 meters, . . . and that has a wavelength of 0.75 meters"). The payoff is that one's spontaneous perceptual judgments then put one in a position to anticipate, manipulate, and exploit the details of such auditory phenomena as interference effects, standing waves, doppler shifts, intensities, and so forth. One requires only a facility with a few elementary laws of wave propagation. (For example, recall the sound made by a moving car as heard by the pedestrian it passes: ZEEEEEEYowwwwwww. Suppose you can hear that the dominant frequency of its approaching hum (ZEEEEEE) is 262 hertz (a middle C), and that its receding hum (Yowwwwww) is 220 hertz (a lower A). In such a case you may safely infer that its unshifted, or intrinsic, frequency must be roughly halfway between the heard extremes, or about 241 hertz. Since the heard frequency is Doppler-shifted from this value by about 21 hertz, which is about 9 percent of the intrinsic frequency (241 hertz), then the velocity of the car must also be about 9 percent of the velocity of sound (740 mph), or about 65 mph. So, if you learn to recognize sounds under their frequency descriptions, then the velocities of unseen objects are often but a quick inference away. Examples like this can be multiplied indefinitely.)

I conclude this section with an instructive fable. Consider the imaginary community, discussed at length in my 1979, whose members all have the unquestioned assumption that physical objects contain an observable fluid substance, called "caloric," that is confined in common objects under a variety of different pressures. According to everyone's "commonsense" convictions, caloric is produced or released in great quantities by fires and by friction; it always flows from high-pressure bodies to low-pressure bodies; a sufficiently high pressure causes the boiling of water; a sufficiently low pressure causes water to freeze; and so forth.

Most important, all members of this community regard the pressure of caloric as an observable feature of the world: where you, upon touching a simmering kettle, have the spontaneous perceptual belief *that this kettle is hot*, they have the spontaneous perceptual belief *that this kettle has a high caloric fluid pressure*. In sum, we have here a community using the conceptual framework of early classical thermodynamics as a commonsense *observation* framework for that same range of phenomena commonly addressed by us with "folk thermodynamics"—the familiar framework of hot and cold. The virtues of this caloric framework, and its persistence in the face of criticism, will not be repeated here, but they are considerable.

I cite this example because the people of this community are making spontaneous "observational" judgments that are obviously laden with theory. Moreover, the theory at issue is known by us to be false, and so the prejudicial character of all of their perceptual beliefs in this area is made even more dramatic. Consider now a philosopher of this society, Jerry Caloric, who argues as follows.

"Consider the illusion produced when one's left hand is allowed to rest in a bucket of water at high caloric pressure, and one's right hand in a bucket at low caloric pressure, and then both hands are immersed in a bucket at an intermediate caloric pressure. If you judge with the left hand, this water has a low caloric pressure; if you judge with the right, it has a high caloric pressure.

"Of course, both we and Granny know how this illusion is produced. The nerves of the two hands become differently fatigued by the extreme caloric pressures in the first two buckets, and thus each gives a different and false response to the intermediate pressure of the third bucket. But notice that possession of this information does absolutely nothing to dispel the illusion.

"We may conclude, therefore, that our peripheral modules are cognitively impenetrable. Accordingly, our perceptual judgments about the *caloric-fluid pressures* of common objects are in an important sense theory neutral. The theories we embrace have no effect on caloric perception, and all humans with normal perceptual systems will thus perceive the world in exactly this same way."

I have here recreated the form of Fodor's argument in a setting where the conclusion is clearly false. The point is to highlight some of the ways his argument fails in its original setting. The first lesson is that Fodor, like the philosopher just quoted, fails to appreciate the highly systematic and speculative character of his own observational idioms, a character they will have quite independently of any rigidity in our peripheral modules. And the second lesson is that Fodor never takes seriously the possibility that, even given the rigidity of perceptual processing up to the character of our sensations, one can still train oneself to use, in spontaneous "observational" mode, conceptual frameworks radically different from those we learned at mother's knee.

2   The Semantics of Observation Predicates

Implicit in the preceding remarks is the view that the meaning of an observation term derives not primarily, nor even perhaps at all, from the typical etiology of its observational application, but rather from the network of general beliefs and assumptions in which it is embedded. Because the contents of such embedding networks can vary substantially, so also can the meaning of our observation terms. Fodor correctly identifies this approach to meaning as a major element in my argument for the theory-laden character of perceptual judgment (I call it "the conceptual-role theory of meaning" or "the network approach"; he calls it "meaning holism"). The argument is simple and quickly stated.

(1) Any judgment consists in the application of *concepts* (e.g., *a* is *F*).

(2) Any concept is a node in a *network* of concepts whose connecting threads are sentences, and its meaning or semantic identity is determined by its peculiar place in that network. (This, in stick-figure form, is the theory of meaning referred to.)

(3) Any network of concepts is a *theory*, minimally, a theory as to some of the classes into which nature divides itself, and some of the relations that hold between them.

∴ (4) Any judgment presupposes a theory.

∴ (5) Any *observation* judgment presupposes a theory.

The theory-ladenness of observation terms thus emerges as a consequence, not of their having some special and regrettable disease, but simply as a consequence of their being meaningful terms at all.

2.1   Objections to the network approach: Fodor's reductio
The defect Fodor finds in an unqualified network approach to meaning is that it allows too much leeway in what an observation sentence

might mean. "So Churchland holds, on holistic grounds, that an observation sentence might mean *anything* depending upon theoretical context. I emphasize that this conclusion is equivalent to the claim that *anything might be an observation sentence* depending upon theoretical context; or, in material mode, that *anything might be observed* depending upon theoretical context" (Fodor 1984, p. 28). This tracing of presumed equivalences overextends itself. I do not hold that, given normal human senses, *anything* might be observed by us. We cannot observe what does not exist, and we cannot observe (without instrumental help) what is beyond any physical detection by our native senses. On the other hand, I do assert that almost any predicate could function as the vehicle of spontaneous perceptual judgment for someone trained to conceive of things in the relevant way. But whether his "observation" judgments constitute genuine cases of veridical perception will be a function of whether the feature he takes himself to be observing really exists, and whether his sensory system has some reliable discriminatory response to the occurrence of that feature. Failing either of these conditions, his "observation" judgments will be systematically mistaken, as in the case of the Friends of Caloric. But while mistaken, those judgments may still be highly successful, both from a practical and from a theoretical point of view.

In sum, my position entails that we can observe many features of the world quite different from the features we are used to observing, and that we might not really be observing some of the features that we think we are. But it does not entail that we can observe everything.

2.2 Belief networks versus causal connections

The preceding is not Fodor's main worry, however, and what looked like an attempt at a *reductio* may be just a rhetorical flourish. What he really seems to object to is the idea that the meaning of observation terms might have nothing to do with the objective features of the world that typically elicit or *cause* their spontaneous use. And he cites the possibility that at least some of an observation term's semantic properties might be determined *non*holistically, perhaps by the causal connections just alluded to. He then concludes, "In light of this, I propose simply not to grant that all the semantic properties of sentences/beliefs are determined by their theoretical context. And Granny proposes not to grant that too" (p. 30).

This is not good enough, for two reasons. We do not require Fodor's concession that *all* of the semantic properties of sentences or beliefs are determined by their theoretical context. So long as *some* of the semantic properties of any observation sentence are inevitably determined in that fashion, such sentences will still be stuck with a significant burden of prejudicial theory. To achieve a truly theory-neutral foundation for knowledge, Fodor needs a class of sentences, or terms, *none* of whose semantic properties is dependent on theory.

Second, there are decisive reasons in support of the claim that at least some of any observation term's semantic properties must be determined by the network of beliefs that embeds it. Consider the following argument.

If a term 'F' is to be a meaningful observation term, then its predication in 'Fa' must have some material *consequences*: it must imply some further sentences, it must be incompatible with some others, and so forth. The sentence 'Fa' will clearly have this property if it is asserted in a context where general sentences such as '$(x)(Fx \supset Gx)$', '$(x)((Fx \ \& \ Hx) \supset {\sim}Kx)$', and so forth, are already assumed. 'Fa' will then imply 'Ga', be incompatible with '$(Ha \ \& \ Ka)$', and so forth.

But if 'F' figures in no such background beliefs or assumptions whatsoever, then 'Fa' will be entirely without consequence or significance for anything. It will have no bridges to link its assertion or denial with the assertion or denial of any other sentence. It will be a wheel that turns nothing, a coin weightless in every balance, an assertion empty by any measure. Less figuratively, its assertion will be *computationally inert*. It will be without computational significance for the very cognitive system that asserts it.

Meaningful observation terms, therefore, will always be embedded within some set of assumptions. And since there is no analytic/synthetic distinction, those assumptions will always be speculative and corrigible. Meaningful observation terms, we seem bound to conclude, will always be laden with theory.

It will be pointed out, of course, that, even in the absence of any background assumptions, 'Fa' will have a host of purely *formal* consequences, such as '$Pv{\sim}P$', '$Q \supset Fa$', and so on. But the pattern of these trivial consequences is exactly the *same* for 'Fa' as it is for any other putative observation sentence: 'Ga', 'Ha', etc. These consequences thus cannot serve to bestow any distinct significance on 'Fa'. It is the *material* consequences of 'Fa' (i.e., the ones that flow from substantive, or nonformal, background assumptions) that do that. Which is another way of stating the central claim of the network theory: what determines the meaning of any term is the peculiar cluster of beliefs in which the term figures, and the peculiar pattern of inferences they make possible.

Given the clear inevitability of an ideological component in the meaning of any observation term, one may begin to wonder at the relative contribution of that component as against another possible component of meaning, a causal component. I have criticized causal accounts of meaning elsewhere (Churchland and Churchland 1983; Churchland 1986e), so I shall here restrict myself to some brief remarks and illustrations.

Consider again the Friends of Caloric discussed earlier. In their spontaneous use of the vocabulary of caloric theory, they are responding to exactly the same feature of the objective world to which we respond with the vocabulary of 'hot', 'cold', etc. But our respective observation sentences—'That is hot' versus 'That has a high caloric-fluid pressure'—certainly do not mean the same thing. They are committed to radically different ontologies and to systematically different behaviors. The alien's understanding of "thermal phenomena" is very different from ours. What we have, then, is two expressions that are typically elicited by the *same* cause, but which differ widely in their meaning.

We can also argue for the complementary conclusion. Consider the meaning of the "observation" vocabulary of the Friends of Caloric, as used by them (1) in this world, and (2) in a different possible world in which there really is a fluid substance that answers to their collected beliefs, a fluid whose changing pressure causes all the familiar sensations in them, a world, in short, at which the theory of caloric-fluid is *true*. Now, in our world the spontaneous application of their term 'high caloric-fluid pressure' is typically caused by the high mean molecular kinetic energy of the object felt. In the other possible world, its application is typically caused by a high caloric-fluid pressure. But that expression, along with the entire theory that embeds it, means exactly the same thing in that world as it does in this. The only difference is that in the other world the Friends of Caloric are more fortunate: in that world their beliefs about caloric—*the very same, or semantically identical, beliefs*—are all true!

Two paragraphs ago, we had the same cause of spontaneous application, but different meanings. In the last paragraph, we have the same meanings, but different causes of spontaneous application. Moreover, what covaries with meaning in the first case is the surrounding network of beliefs. And what is coconstant with meaning in the second case is the surrounding network of beliefs. The meaning of an observation term, I therefore conclude, has nothing whatever to do with the typical cause of its spontaneous application. Its meaning is fixed by other factors entirely: specifically, by the surrounding network of beliefs.

This maximal claim that ideology completely exhausts meaning is not needed to resist Fodor's position, but I am strongly inclined to defend the claim in any case. The argument just given forms part of the reason. The robust causal connection between a high mean molecular kinetic energy and the alien's application of the term 'high caloric-fluid pressure' contributes nothing that I can discern to the semantic content of the quoted expression. Neither does it provide a reference for that expression (it is quite empty of reference), nor does it guarantee the truth of any of its typical applications (they are all false). All that causal connection does is prompt the aliens spontaneously to *deploy* the expression at issue. Its meaning, its reference, and the truth of its applications (to the extent they have any) arise from other sources entirely.

Another reason for looking skeptically at causal accounts of meaning arises from their regular failure to assign semantic contents that are consistent with the ideology of the speaker. The bronze-age report 'Thor is hurling heavenly fire and pounding his hammer' may be a reliable indicator that (i.e., have the *calibrational content* that) there is a sudden large-scale flux of electrons with accompanying atmospheric shock wave. But this latter description would radically misrepresent the meaning of the bronze-age native's report. That meaning is fixed by the assembled beliefs about Thor, fire, and so forth, embraced by the native. The point here is just the obvious one that we can systematically *miscon*ceive what we *perc*eive, a fact that causal accounts of meaning are constitutionally inclined to suppress.

A further reason that causal accounts of meaning are suspect is that, on such accounts, semantic content becomes computationally impotent. One's computational economy has access to the formal and structural features of one's observation judgments or reports, but it has no access to their distal causal antecedents. The computational or inferential consequences of an observation judgment, therefore, will be *independent* of its "content," if semantic content is assigned according to distal causal antecedents.

A final problem with causal accounts is the ambiguity of their assignments of meaning. An utterance typically has a unique meaning, at least given context, but an utterance is always the last member of a long *sequence* of internal and external causal antecedents. Which of the many causal antecedents that make up the chain supplies the "real" meaning of the utterance, and on what principle is the selection made?

Part of the initial appeal of causal accounts of meaning derives from the fact that, when we translate or assign content to the observation reports of another speaker, we typically expect his observation reports, as translated by us, to be roughly reliable indicators of the world around him as perceived by us. Thus the impulse to assign content on a causal/calibrational basis. But while quite reasonable in pedestrian circumstances, this translational policy ignores the possibility that the speaker has a systematically different, and perhaps systematically mistaken, conception of observational reality. Translating his utterances according to their external causes *as reckoned by us* will thus amount to a systematic misrepresentation of the alien's meaning, a "Whig translation," as it were. Worse yet, this policy ignores or precludes the possibility that *we too* might be systematically mistaken in our observational conceptions. It is therefore amusing that a causal approach to meaning should be advanced in criticism of the claim that observation is plastic and theory laden, for the causal theory was initially plausible only to the degree that it *ignored* the theoretical commitments implicit in our observation judgments, and *suppressed* the possibility of systematic falsehood in our observational conceptions. Such factors must inevitably return to haunt causal accounts. And they do. Judgmental error emerges as the single greatest problem for causal accounts of meaning, even in their *loci classici*: Dretske 1981; Fodor 1988a.

This concludes my discussion of causal approaches to meaning. To the extent, often very limited, that our terms do find real referents or extensions in the world, it is because of the global structure and the global virtues of the framework that embeds those terms. Crudely, there must exist an assignment of individuals to our singular terms, and an assignment of extensions to our general terms, such that a significant proportion of the beliefs or assumptions embedding those terms are true on that assignment. What counts as "significant" will here go unexplored, but pragmatic considerations surely dominate.

This view is consistent, we should note, with a fierce skepticism about the ultimate integrity of the notion of reference. Nothing guarantees that a system of beliefs will always, or ever, determine a *unique* set of relations between its terms and elements in the world (see Putnam 1975, 1981). If genuine reference must be unique, then very likely it is chronically underdetermined by the structural properties of sets of beliefs. Some will see in this a motive for trying to add in a causal component to the theory of meaning in order to take up the slack left by unaided networks of belief. For example, the 1985 Putnam succumbed to this impulse; the 1981 Putnam did not. But I suggest that the real lesson of the Twin Earth cases, and of the later arguments inspired by the Skolem-Löwenheim theorem, is quite different and rather more sobering. The real lesson is that the folk-semantical notion of "reference" is without any real integrity. Reference is uniquely fixed neither by networks of belief, nor by causal relations, nor by anything else, because there *is no* single and uniform relation that connects each descriptive term to the world in anything like the fashion that common sense supposes.

These last remarks touch on themes that cannot be pursued here (see chapter 13 and Stich 1989). Happily, reference is not at the center of the debate over theory-ladenness. It is meaning-as-understanding that occupies that position. My aim in this section has been to reestablish the strong presumption that any observation term, to the extent that it is meaningful at all, must be embedded in a network of corrigible assumptions.

2.3   *Sensational plasticity versus conceptual plasticity*

One possible way to defend Fodor would be to concede the theory-dependent character of our observational concepts and judgments, and try to insist on no more than the theory-independent character of our *sensations*. Fodor himself seems to be sketching a position of this sort late in his paper when he urges the rigidity of "the look of things" versus the penetrability and plasticity of "how things are judged to be" (p. 40).

But this defense will not take us any distance at all. For one thing, if all Fodor wishes to insist on is uniformity in the character of our sensations through changes in our doxastic commitments, then his argument is largely an *ignoratio*. It fails to address the major epistemological tradition at issue, whose central theme has always been the theory-laden character, not of our sensations, but of our observational concepts and observational judgments.

And there is a very good reason for the centrality of that theme. Thinkers in the tradition at issue (Popper, Feyerabend, Hanson, etc.) have been primarily concerned with the refutation or corroboration of theories. But sensations themselves neither confirm nor refute any theory. Sensations belong to the wrong logical space: it is only an observation *judgment*, or *belief*, or *report* that can be logically consistent or inconsistent with any theory (Popper 1959). Thus the chronic concern, throughout the positivist and postpositivist periods, with the possibility of a theory-neutral observation *vocabulary*. Whether sensations themselves might be infected or modified by theory was rarely, if ever, an issue.

My own 1979 position, to cite one target of Fodor's, simply assumes the generally constant character of our sensory responses to the environment. The plasticity that excited me there was confined to the conceptual frameworks within which we make our judgmental responses to the passing contents of our sensory manifold. Accordingly, if rigidity in the character of our sensations is all Fodor is concerned to defend, then I do not understand his objection to, and dismissal of (pp. 28–29), the alternative perceptual possibilities sketched in my 1979 (p. 30). For that sketch makes no assumptions about the plasticity of our sensations. It is *conceptual* plasticity that is there at issue.

To be sure, sensational plasticity would constitute an *additional* argument for the plasticity of perception. At least one author has cautiously advanced a claim of this kind (Kuhn 1962, pp. 120–121). And I, for another, am now willing to defend it vigorously (recall the examples in figure 12.1). So there is a genuine point to attacking it, as Fodor does. But it is wrong to represent or regard this attack, successful or otherwise, as aimed at the principal arguments in favor of theory-ladenness. Those arguments have typically been based on other grounds entirely: on the plasticity of our conceptual responses to sensory activity.

3   Conclusion

I shall spare the reader a reprise of the various conclusions already reached. Instead, let me try to evoke a general picture of the situation. The central issue of this paper is not an argument about the obscure etiology of a certain class of beliefs or the arcane semantics of a certain class of terms. The real disagreement is about the fundamental character of the human epistemic situation and the long-term possibilities for the evolution of the human spirit.

Our epistemic situation I assert, is one in which even the humblest judgment or assertion is always a speculative leap, not just in its assertion over its denial, but also in the background conceptual framework in which that judgment is constituted, in preference to the infinity of other conceptual frameworks that one might have used instead. In the case of perceptual judgments, what the senses do is cause the perceiver to activate some specific representation from the antecedent system of possible representations—that is, from the conceptual framework—that has been brought to the perceptual situation by the perceiver. A perceptual judgment, therefore, can be no better, though it can be worse, than the broad system of representation in which it is constituted.

This means that perceptual judgments are evaluable at two distinguishable levels. The first concerns the propriety of the judgment as evaluated by the local standards of the framework that embeds it (Was the observer in a position to make it? Was the observation carelessly made? Is it inconsistent with information already in hand?). These correspond to what Carnap (1956) has called "internal questions." The second level concerns the adequacy of the embedding framework overall, as a system adequate to represent the range of nomologically possible configurations that the objective world might assume. These correspond roughly to what Carnap has called "external questions" (Do the categories of my framework capture the objective divisions in reality? Do the basic generalizations of my framework express genuine laws of nature?).

External questions are rather daunting. Local standards of evaluation are both inapplicable and question begging, and global standards are vague and elusive. Good positivist that he was, Carnap reacted by denying that such questions are factual in character, claiming that the decision to use a given conceptual framework is ultimately just a practical question, to be decided on pragmatic grounds. But Carnap was mistaken in seeing a fundamental difference between the two kinds of questions, and between two kinds of grounds for acceptance. So-called "external questions" are just large-scale theoretical questions, to be decided on empirical and systematic grounds like anything else. And so-called "pragmatic" considerations attend epistemic decisions at every level of inquiry, even the most humble and mundane.

In fact, external questions are confronted by humans and dealt with on a daily basis, by scientists inventing and evaluating new frameworks for understanding this or that domain, and also by infants and children, who must evolve a conceptual framework adequate to conduct a life in the *Lebenswelt* of concurrent human society. This means that our conceptual frameworks can and regularly do undergo *change*, both within the lifetime of an individual and in society as a whole, over historical periods. To use a Hegelian figure, the journey of the human spirit is essentially the story of our evolving conception of the world, and of our own place within it. Our eyes are little different from a baboon's or a chimpanzee's, but our perceptual knowledge is profoundly superior to theirs. Our motor systems are little different from those of any other primate, but our practical capabilities and intentional actions encompass universes quite closed to them. The main difference lies in the dramatically superior conceptual frameworks we have evolved epigenetically, and not without misadventure, over the course of the last 500,000 years.

If we have come this far, must the journey end here? Manifestly not. The long awakening is potentially endless. The human spirit will continue its breathtaking adventure of self-reconstruction, and its perceptual and motor capacities will continue to develop as an integral part of its self-reconstruction. But only if we try hard to see new opportunities, and only if we work hard at leaving old frameworks behind.

Chapter 13

Conceptual Progress and Word-World Relations: In Search of the Essence of Natural Kinds

The problem of natural kinds forms a busy crossroads where a number of larger problems meet: the problem of universals, the problem of induction and projectibility, the problem of natural laws and *de re* modalities, the problem of meaning and reference, the problem of intertheoretic reduction, the question of the aim of science, and the problem of scientific realism in general. Nor do these exhaust the list. Not surprisingly then, different writers confront a different "problem of natural kinds," depending on which background issue is for them the principal issue at stake. The issues of essentialism, meaning, and reference, for example, have tended to dominate recent discussions of natural kinds (Kripke 1972; Putnam 1975, 1981; Mellor 1977; Churchland 1979; Shapere 1982). But evidently these issues are only part of the puzzle.

The present paper outlines in fairly broad strokes a view of natural kinds, and of our semantic access to them, that contrasts fairly sharply with the recently popular view associated with Putnam and Kripke, wherein the terms of natural language can be and generally are firmly attached to real, natural classes of objects, even where we might hold systematically false beliefs about those objects. This view, it seems to me, has had a largely retrograde effect on discussions concerning the relation(s) between language and the world, and there is need to reconceive the matter from a broader and more naturalistic perspective.

I propose to be skeptical here about two things in particular. First, I shall criticize the idea that there is a theory-neutral or intension-independent relation that connects words to unique natural sections of the world. And second, I shall argue that on the best available account of natural kinds, most of the kinds we regard as natural kinds are not natural kinds at all, but merely "practical" kinds. The set of

This paper first appeared in the *Canadian Journal of Philosophy* 15, no. 1 (March 1985).

genuinely natural kinds contains at most a tiny elite of very basic physical properties, and may indeed be empty entirely. The positive upshot of the discussion is that we need to reappraise our conception of the human medium of cognitive representation and its relation to the world, and we need to reconsider our conception of the most basic aims of rational cognition. I shall try to address these issues as we proceed.

1   Natural Kinds and Scientific Progress: The Putnam-Kripke View

What wants rejecting in the Putnam-Kripke story is not just the specific models of how the extensions of natural-kind terms are secured (by a demonstrative ostension or dubbing ceremony, plus some recursive device), but also the background vision of the aims of science, and of the nature of scientific progress, in which that claim is made. Their choice of examples is significant: gold, water, and heat dominate the discussion. These are all kinds that are well entrenched in the common vocabulary, and all have enjoyed a relatively smooth reduction to some category provided by microtheory. Water is H_2O molecules, gold is Au atoms, and heat is molecular kinetic energy.

The picture we get, if we generalize innocently from these examples, is one of a stable antecedent taxonomy of reality, a framework of commonsense terms each in firm referential contact with an objectively real class, where the advance of science provides us with nothing more than a new and more penetrating account of what *unites* that already palpated class. The aim of science emerges as the *explication* of natural classes already secured, rather than as the *discovery* of novel classes that finally do display natural integrity, classes that may well fail to correspond, even roughly, to the specious categories we antecedently embraced.

This conservative picture tends to suppress the important fact that the antecedent taxonomy provided by common sense is as richly theoretical, conjectural, and provisional as are the more obviously "theoretical" taxonomies that may, or may *not*, reduce it. And it tends to suppress the fact that the "manifest" taxonomy of common sense has neither a better, nor a firmer, nor even a *different* handle on the hidden natural kinds than do the novel theoretical taxonomies that aspire to replace it.

Since all knowledge is conjectural and theoretical, any framework of commonsense terms at any stage of our history will have the same tenuous sort of claim to have as extensions the real natural classes. That claim will have the same sort of grounding at any stage, namely, the explanatory and theoretical success of the current taxonomic framework. And each stage must anticipate being superseded, sooner or later, by a quite different taxonomy of natural kinds, with greater explanatory and predictive success. This means that a central aim of science is to find out *which* of the infinite range of possible natural-kind taxonomies is truly the *right* taxonomy. To make the "explication" of *current* categories a fundamental aim of science is to claim for those categories an integrity that they may not possess.

The fluidity and fragility of commonsense taxonomy can be seen even in the relatively stable examples at issue. The "gold" of the late medieval period included rather more than we countenance as gold today, since "gold" was then conceived primarily in phenomenological terms that admitted sundry alloys and ersatzes of gold into the class. This was not simply a mistake on the part of our ancestors. As they conceived of things, "gold" was something that came in various *grades*, which trailed off smoothly into the baser metals. And from the point of view of alchemical theory, this was only to be expected, since the hidden principle responsible for the characteristics of high-grade "gold" was thought to be a spirit that displayed varying degrees of maturity, a spirit that was wed in varying degrees of harmony with the other spirits that ensoul a metal. Conceived within medieval commonsense, the extension of their term was wider than ours. Conceived within alchemical theory, it had no extension at all. In neither case did it have the same extension as our term "gold."

The extension of the term "water" has presumably undergone a similar evolution, as very primitive peoples came to experience phase transitions, came to see the poverty in a notion of "water" that holds wetness to be an essential feature, and came to a broader notion of water that included ice and steam as variant forms of the stuff. More recently, the extension of this term has expanded again, to include more than just H_2O, since we have learned that deuterium will form a compound, heavy water, that is distinct from, but strikingly similar to, the more common compound formed from hydrogen.

The case of commonsense heat and temperature provides us with a more dramatic example. As I have argued elsewhere (1979, pp. 23-24) the commonsense notions of hot, warm, and cold are empirically incoherent, in that they attempt to impose a one-dimensional continuum of properties where nature supplies three distinct and divergent continua—*degree* of heat energy, *amount* of heat energy, and *rate of flow* of heat energy—none of which corresponds adequately to the commonsense conception. Our commonsense terms here are not just different in extension from the thermodynamic terms that displace them; they are entirely empty of extension, despite their usefulness in our quotidian affairs, since nothing in nature *answers* to the collected laws of "commonsense thermodynamics."

I am keenly aware that this claim is initially implausible, but I stand by it. Rather than enter again upon the intricacies of its defense, however, let me here address what *makes* it an upsetting claim. It upsets because it holds up the prospect that entire domains of our commonsense observational vocabulary might be utterly without reference or extension. It holds up the specter of large chunks of language, even an entire language, *unconnected* to the world by way of the reference of its singular terms and the extension of its general terms. This is not only shocking to contemplate; it leaves it a mystery how any language could function in such a disconnected predicament.

Shocking or no, let us contemplate it. (We will address the mystery of how a language can function in that predicament in a moment.) Without impugning anything that currently passes for commonsense, we can easily appreciate the possibility of such massive referential disconnection if we imagine a radically false scientific theory taught and used as an observation framework by ordinary people. To take an easy example, suppose we were to use the framework of *caloric fluid* to conceptualize and talk about thermal phenomena. (This possibility is explored at length in my 1979, pp. 16–25.) More specifically, suppose that we were trained to express our spontaneous *observation* judgments and reports in the vocabulary of caloric theory, e.g., "This porridge has a high-caloric fluid pressure, Mommy." Since you are antecedently convinced that caloric fluid does not exist and that the vocabulary of caloric theory is empty of reference and extension, you will agree that such a linguistic regime would meet the conditions at issue: a vocabulary functioning in an "observational" mode, but wholly without reference or extension.

There is no question that the vocabulary of caloric theory could function smoothly in the role described. (In fact, it would function even more smoothly than our current commonsense conceptions.) And the reason it could do so is that, while it would be disconnected from the world referentially, it would remain richly connected to the world *causally*, by way of our conceptual and linguistic responses to sensory input, and by way of our motor responses to our deliberational output. The primary connection between any language and the world is thus a *causal* one, and successful functioning requires only that the language constitute a useful subsystem of our sensorimotor pathways. If a language also enjoys referential connections with the world, that is a fortunate and a secondary achievement, one that relatively few linguistic frameworks can boast. Massive referential disconnection, therefore, is a real possibility, even in a smoothly functional vocabulary, and this remains true whatever we decide about the specific case of commonsense temperature.

So it is not unthinkable that our current commonsense conceptions of hot and cold are empty of extension. However, let us suppose that my earlier judgment against our commonsense thermal concepts is too harsh; let us suppose that some principle of charity bids us count thermodynamic temperature (*degree* of heat energy) as the real referent of our earlier usage of 'hot' and 'cold'. The irony is that *thermodynamic* temperature has turned out to enjoy no *uniform* essence in any case. Temperature is mean molecular KE, in a gas. But in a classical solid, temperature is mean maximum molecular KE. In a plasma it is a complex mix of differently embodied energies (ions, electrons, photons), depending on just how high the temperature is. And in a vacuum it is a specific wavelength distribution among the electromagnetic waves coursing through that vacuum. (These different instances of "temperature" form a coherent family because diverse instantiations can nevertheless be in mutual energetic equilibrium.) A familiar property has fragmented again, and discovers new and confusing instances. Even a *vacuum* can have a temperature! Our taxonomies form, dissolve, and reform, even as we watch.

Reflecting on conceptual changes of the magnitude we have been discussing may produce the occasional spell of vertigo, but the preceding examples illustrate that powerful conceptions can function and flourish despite massive referential disconnection, that competing theories need not be talking about "the same things," and that rational choices between theories can be made, and rational progress can be achieved, even though there is no sameness or continuity of reference, either synchronically across competing theories or diachronically across successive theories.

The competing idea that our commonsense terms *do* enjoy stable and objective natural classes as their extensions, by way of a Putnamean indexical/recursive formula, despite confusion or systematic falsehood in our beliefs about them, is perhaps an appealing idea, since it seems to make reference to real classes an easy matter in a difficult world. But it makes it far *too* easy for it to bear much scrutiny. To see this, consider a seventeenth-century incarnation of Putnam, intoning the following formula over a small fire:

> "Phlogiston is whatever bears the 'same-spirit' relation to the phlogiston right *here*" (speaker points to the vaporous outpourings above the fire).

Whether this secures anything at all in the way of a natural extension will be a function of the theoretical integrity of the notions of "phlogiston" and "is the same spirit as." As it happens, neither notion has any genuine integrity, and so nothing at all is secured. The same is true of other examples:

> "Caloric fluid is whatever bears the 'same substance' relation to the caloric I feel right *here*" (speaker holds up a warm coffee cup).
>
> "Heavenly crystal is whatever bears the 'same-substance' relation to the crystal up *there*" (speaker points to the crystal sphere that divides the superlunary from the sublunary realms).
>
> "Party drink is whatever bears the 'same-liquid' relation to the party drink in my hand" (speaker holds up a glass of grandma's randomly concocted pink party punch).

Putnam's formula, evidently, provides no guarantee that its intonation secures a natural class for an extension, nor that it secures anything at all for an extension. Nor should this be surprising. As Wittgenstein taught us, conceptually unaided pointing singles out nothing. But once we include a specific conceptual surround, the secured extension is partly a function of our intensions, our general assumptions, our *theories*. A similar point holds for the recursive clause of Putnam's formula. Expressions such as 'same substance' and 'same spirit' are obviously laden with theory, and the sameness relation there invoked will vary from one period of scientific history to another. Putnam's formula, therefore, does not constitute a non-intensional or theory-neutral means of securing a natural class as an extension for a given term, nor need it succeed in securing any natural class at all.

We can and must agree that Putnam sentences occasionally play some role in delineating the extension of some terms. The sentences that collectively make up any term's intension are usually general sentences, but singular sentences occasionally acquire a comparable importance (see Churchland 1979, pp. 72–73). For example, the sentence, 'The stuff in our lakes, rivers, and oceans is water' is a semantically important sentence. That sentence thus plays some role in determining the extension of our term 'water'. It provides a (corrigible) sufficient condition for being water. But the semantic role of such singular indexical sentences is in no way *privileged*: though they may play *a* role in fixing the extension of a given term, they are just further elements in the intension of that term. (Indeed, the example just cited has lost some of its semantic importance as a result of the expansion of chemical theory during the last three centuries.) Whether a term has a nonempty extension remains conditional on whether the collected assumptions that constitute its intension are, at least for the most part, *true*. And exactly which extension gets secured is a function of just what those collected assumptions are.

Since a term's intension (the set of semantically important sentences in which that term figures) may occasionally include indexical or demonstrative sentences, it must be conceded that exactly what extension gets secured will be determined in part by where, and in whose brain, that intension is asked to function as part of an ongoing cognitive economy. Extension is determined by intension plus context. If this is a concession to Putnam, then I think we must make it.

However, none of this implies that our natural-kind terms enjoy a firm and stable referential connection to a natural class of objects independently of the intensions that govern the use of those terms. None of this guarantees that our terms have a nonempty extension. None of this implies that the extensions of our terms do not differ as they appear in competing theories. And none of this implies that the extensions of our terms do not change as we change which theories we embrace.

Accordingly, we must learn to live, after all, with a roughly Fregean conception of the relation between intensions and extensions, even in the case of natural kinds. There is no royal road to securing natural classes as extensions for our terms. Our science must achieve reference the old-fashioned way: it must earn it, by slow plodding through a variety of very different conceptions of the world, in hopes of *finding* a theory that successfully carves nature at her systematic joints, a theory which displays that success in its unexcelled explanatory and predictive powers. Our referential access to natural kinds is by way of the corrigible systems of sentences we accept, and of what answers to them in the world. This does make our access to natural kinds fluid, uncertain, and problematic. But that is as it should be. The extensions of our terms are stably fixed neither by analytic truths, as in the orthodox empiricist tradition, nor by indexical/recursive pointings, as in the Putnam-Kripke alternative. They are not stably fixed by anything, since they are not stably fixed at all.

This concludes my discussion of our access to natural kinds. Let me now address the question of the essence of natural kinds. What are natural kinds? What distinguishes them from less substantial kinds of kinds?

2   *Natural Kinds as Law-Bound Kinds: Some Virtues, Consequences, and Difficulties*

Commonsense and Putnam's and Kripke's discussion examples suggest a conception of natural kinds as any kind with a hidden microessence that unites all of its instances. But that conception is parochial and ill considered, because it invites one to think of natural kinds as successfully revealed only or primarily in smooth intertheoretic reductions, in which commonsense or antecedent categories survive by reason of finding close analogues in the micro realm.

A better view conceives natural kinds as just kinds comprehended by genuine laws of nature. That is, the natural kinds are the *law-bound* kinds. This view sees natural kinds as revealed primarily when a new taxonomy displaces an older scheme entirely. (Such displacement can occasionally include a reduction of the old by the new, but it need not.) The identification of natural kinds remains a basic aim of science, on this view, but that is because identifying the laws of nature is a basic aim of science, and because the taxonomy of kinds and their embedding laws must emerge from inquiry together.

This conception of natural kinds is appealing in its simplicity, but it does present serious puzzles of its own. Most of these concern the notion of a natural law and the matter of their hierarchical relations. It is all very well to say that a natural law is a spatiotemporally unrestricted, counterfactual-supporting, explanation-sustaining universal conditional. But when it comes to cases, confusion gathers swiftly. We can all agree that the sentence

(1)   Any mass free of net forces moves, if at all, in a straight line with constant velocity

is a law of nature, and hence that *mass, force,* and *velocity* are natural kinds or properties. But now consider the sentence

(2)   Any chair free of net forces moves, if at all, in a straight line with constant velocity.

Is this a law of nature? Is *chair* thus a natural kind? If it is, then a lot of things are going to count as laws, and a lot of kinds are going to be natural: toothbrushes, spaceships, toasters, etc. Surely *chair* is not a natural kind. But how do we deny natural-law status to (2)? Sentence (2) follows from (1) and

(3)   Any chair is a mass used for sitting on.

We can all agree that (3), though true, is not a natural law, and perhaps here lies the key to denying natural-law status to (2).

Suppose we identify some natural laws as *basic* laws, on grounds of their relative inexplicability, and then stipulate that nothing else counts as a genuine natural law unless it is a purely logical consequence of some one or more basic laws. This will rule out (2) as a natural law, since it is neither basic, nor a consequence of purely natural laws alone: the nonnatural "law" (3) is also required for its deduction. This solution has independent plausibility. To explain a specific chair's rectilinear motion through space, one does not point to the fact that it is a chair, and then cite (2).   Rather, one points out that it has *mass*, and then one appeals to (1). It seems to be (1) that carries the explanatory clout, not (2).

This accommodation with the problem has considerable appeal, but if we buy it, we must be prepared to live with its consequences. Specifically, natural kinds turn out to constitute a very small and exclusive company, much smaller than one might have thought initially. Let me approach this claim by way of some examples.

In learning elementary mechanics, one learns to deduce lawlike expressions for the rotational inertia of various kinds of bodies. Starting from the relatively basic law that the rotational inertia I of a point particle of mass m at a distance r from the axis of rotation is mr^2, one can deduce general expressions for the rotational inertia of bodies with a more complex configuration. If M is the mass of the body, and R and L the relevant radius and length, we have, variously,

> For any hoop, $I = MR^2$
> For any solid cylinder, $I = MR^2/2$
> For any thin rod, $I = ML^2/12$
> For any solid sphere, $I = 2MR^2/5$
> For any dumbbell, $I = 2MR^2/5 + ML^2/4$
> For any hollow spherical shell with a thin rod stuck through it transversely, $I = 2MR^2/3 + ML^2/12$

and so forth (see figure 13.1).

Evidently, there are an indefinite variety of shapes, and for any specified shape a putative law can be deduced, using only the "definition" of the relevant shape or configuration of point masses, the basic inertial law cited, and the summative/integrative laws of mathematics. If the universally quantified sentences listed above are genuine natural laws, then *hoop, dumbbell, hollow spherical shell with thin rod stuck through it transversely*, and an unlimited number of other inelegant kinds are all going to count as natural kinds. Fortunately, these generalizations do *not* follow from basic laws alone: they all require a definition or stipulation of the form

(4)   A spherical shell is a set of point masses uniformly distributed an equal distance R from a center point,

(5)   A dumbbell is a set of point masses concentrated in two solid spheres of radii R a fixed distance L apart,

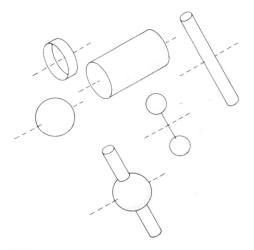

Figure 13.1
Rotating bodies and axes of rotation

etc. And it is plausible to insist that no such stipulation constitutes a natural law. According to the view being defended, then, the above generalizations are not genuine natural laws, and so the kinds they comprehend need not be natural kinds.

Well and good. Even so, generalizations such as those listed, and the kinds they comprehend, are not to be sniffed at. They constitute the bulk of our general and practical knowledge, and they can be extremely useful. Let us therefore call such universal statements, as follow from the conjunction of a genuine law with some stipulative definitions, a *practical law*. And let us call the kinds that figure in them *practical kinds*. These will be kinds constituted or recognized by us because their instances are very common in the environment, or because they have some practical relevance for us. In the same spirit, we might even speak of *practical explanations* as those which are sustained by practical laws and which concern the behavior of practical kinds of objects. These will not be genuine explanations, but, where they apply, a genuine explanation will be hidden in the wings.

So far our intuitions have not been unduly strained. But they will be seriously strained when it is appreciated that most of what are traditionally counted as natural kinds are merely practical kinds. Tigers, elms, apples, roses, perhaps even water and gold—all turn out not to be natural kinds, as characterized above. The reason is that all of them turn out to be of a piece with hoops, rods, spheres, and dumbbells. All of them are more or less arbitrary configurations of smaller or more basic bits. None of the generalizations in which they figure is a genuine law of nature. None of them, fairly clearly, is a *basic* law. Moreover, none of them, I emphasize, can even be deduced from basic laws save in conjunction with a nonlawlike stipulation specifying how instances of that kind (tigers, elms, etc.) are constituted from more basic elements of reality.

Take the natural kind *tiger*, for instance. And let us suppose that the following is as close as we can get to a genuine natural law about tigers.

(6)   Any live, adult tiger burns up at least 1000 Kcal per day.

This "practical" law is not beyond explanation. From a specification of the general physical and biochemical constitution of a tiger, one can deduce from basic thermodynamical laws that a system of that constitution will use energy at such a rate. But the specification of the general physical and biochemical constitution of a tiger is on all fours with the specification of the distribution of point masses in a spherical shell with a thin rod stuck through it transversely. Neither specification is a natural law; both specify only one configuration out of an infinite number of equally possible configurations of more basic elements, each of which configurations would have its own peculiar physical properties, equally a consequence of basic law as applied to that arbitrary case.

One does not naturally think of biological species as being as arbitrary as I am here insisting, since our world presents us with only a fixed subset of the infinite number of possible species. But that subset is an accident of evolutionary history. We could have had a completely different set of species, any one of countless other sets, just as we can have countless bodies differently configured so as to have different rotational inertias.

If the kinds *tiger*, *elm*, and *apple* turn out to be merely practical kinds, so also, it seems, do *water* and even *gold*. An instance of either substance is only one among endlessly many possible configurations of more basic elements, and its physical properties are determined by the laws governing those more basic elements. From a specification such as

(7)   Any H_2O molecule consists of two hydrogen atoms valence bonded to one oxygen atom,

in conjunction with electrodynamical laws, one can perhaps deduce,

(8)   Any volume of H_2O molecules is transparent to light.

But (7) seems to be of a piece with (4) and (5), and thus (8) emerges as a merely practical law about a merely *practical* kind: H_2O *molecule.* The same sorts of considerations, repeated at the subatomic level, reveal *Au atom* as a merely practical kind also. And so for all chemical compounds and all of the chemical elements.

In sum, the only genuine natural kinds appear to be those comprehended by absolutely the most basic laws of our science. On the view here outlined, *mass, length, duration, charge, color, energy, momentum,* and so forth all turn up safely as natural kinds or properties. But precious little else does. This austere result might move us to try to liberalize the conditions on natural kinds, but any attempt to do so threatens to let back in such kinds as *hoop, chair, dumbbell,* and *sphere with a stick through it.*

A briefly plausible suggestion here is importantly mistaken. What discriminates the chemical and elemental kinds from these arbitrary inertial configurations, we might suppose, is that under natural conditions the subatomic particles spontaneously form themselves into the elements, and under natural conditions those elements spontaneously form themselves into the chemical compounds. They can thus count as natural kinds after all.

Despite an initial appeal, this does not draw the desired distinction. Whether and which elements get formed is highly sensitive to the details of the environment: temperature, pressure, relative abundances of different particles, and so forth. There is nothing inevitable about the kinds that dominate our environment. Were the whole universe under the same gravitational squeeze that grips the matter of a neutron star, none of the familiar chemical elements would exist. Our world would be a symphony of purely nuclear chemistry rather than of electron chemistry. Equally important, under appropriate environmental circumstances, matter *will* form itself spontaneously into hoops (Saturn's rings), thin rods (sticks), spheres (planets), or even dumbbells (close binary stars). In general, if you specify a shape, I can concoct an environment adequate for its spontaneous formation. Either all of these are natural kinds then, or none of them are. I tentatively conclude that none of them are. Save only the elect few from the most basic physics, *all* kinds are merely "practical" kinds.

For my own part, I could rest content with this view. I might even end my discussion here. But two residual worries preclude peace of mind. The first concerns the basis and the integrity of the distinction between laws and nonlaws. And the second concerns the existence of basic or ultimate natural laws.

The first and lesser worry stems from the fact that natural laws differ tangibly from other true, unrestricted universal conditionals only in their functional and relational properties: they support explanations, counterfactuals, and modal statements; they are confirmed by their instances; they are, or turn out to be, an integrated part of a system of other laws. On these differences we can agree, but there seems to be nothing in the *world* that we can point to as the distinguishing feature of lawful regularities.

One approach to this problem locates the distinguishing feature of laws in their relations to things *other* than the real world—in their relations to each member of the set of nomically *possible* worlds, for example. Laws are distinguished by being true in all of them, while accidental universals are true only in some.

If this approach is to avoid putting the cart before the horse, then we must be *realists* with respect to the "set of nomically possible worlds." This appeals to me hardly at all. Solving the problem of the semantics of lawlike generalizations seems insufficient motivation for expanding our ontology by a factor of at least aleph-1 additional worlds. Better to take the view that this world, the real one, itself contains objective necessities and possibilities, which are reflected in the course of actual events, but are logically underdetermined by those events. This need not be a hopelessly mysterious view. It may be that some objective features of the real world find expression only in certain *global* features of our system of beliefs, in the coagulation of laws into coherent *systems* of laws. But I will not insist on such an account. Indeed, I remain deeply puzzled about the distinction between nomic and nonnomic universals, and about the modalities in general. Not puzzled enough to give up the notion of natural kinds, however.

The second worry is more serious. The account of natural kinds defended above uses the notion of "basic" laws of nature. It makes the tacit assumption that there exists some final, uniquely true theory whose laws express the basic regularities in the universe and whose predicates denote its most basic kinds. It was not supposed that we will ever possess such a utopian theory; only that our currently best theories give us our current best shot at reality's basic laws and basic kinds. And that basic laws and kinds *are there* to be aimed at.

This assumption is highly problematic. I do not know how to defend it, nor, I suggest, do you. Reflection will reveal its possible falsity, as follows. First, consider the possibility that, for any level of order discovered in the universe, there always exists a deeper taxonomy of kinds and a deeper level of order in terms of which the lawful order at the antecedent level can be explained. It is, as far as I can see, a wholly empirical question whether or not the universe is like this, like an "explanatory onion" with an infinite number of concentric explanatory skins. If it is like this, then then are no basic or ultimate laws to which all successful investigators must inevitably be led, and according to the account of natural kinds defended above, there are no natural kinds at all. All kinds are merely practical kinds.

According to my account then, it is an empirical question whether there are any natural kinds at all. It depends on whether the universe is or is not an infinitely layered explanatory onion. This too I can live with. But the worries do not end here. Even if the world is not an explanatory onion, there is still no guarantee that there exists a unique and final theory (that is, a set of sentences) flawlessly adequate to its complete description. On the contrary, it may be that the cognitive medium of human natural language suffers certain fundamental structural limitations in its capacity for representing the intricacies of the universe. And it may be that a wholly new medium of representation will be required if the human race is ever to make cognitive progress past a certain level of comparatively paltry apprehension.

This seems very likely to me, since I think it would be a *miracle* if evolution had already fitted us out with cognitive equipment that is structurally adequate to representing the deepest mysteries and subtlest intricacies of the cosmos. (On this point I differ substantially with David Lewis, who is inclined toward the contrary position that, give or take a few residual wrinkles, the Final Theory will be in our hands within a century. Not only do I not share his optimism here, I think that the idiosyncratic linguistic structures we call theories, and even the idiosyncratic neural systems we call brains, will prove to have fundamental shortcomings *qua* media for models of reality.) I think it is far more likely that we shall have to contrive major physical changes in, and enhancements to, our current cognitive equipment, if we are to transcend its inherent limitations. This might leave us with a medium or system of representation in which nothing *answers* to the notion of a universal generalization or the notion of a predicate. What science would then be pursuing, I cannot say. But I assume it would no longer be pursuing natural laws and natural kinds. Which leads me to suspect the ultimate integrity of these notions, right here and now.

A pair of examples may help to underscore the point just made. Despite what one might think, the particular cluster of cognitive talents found in us need not characterize any or all intelligent species. We tend think of the ability to manipulate linguistic structures, and perhaps mathematical structures, as being almost definitive of high-grade cognition. But even within our own species there are humans, of otherwise exemplary cognitive talents, who are wholly unable to engage in such activities. Victims of *global aphasia* are utterly unable to use or to comprehend language, and this is not a motor or a sensory deficit, but a specifically cognitive deficit. And yet they live among us without much assistance, and display an intelligence that is undiminished in most other respects. Victims of *acalculia* show a parallel global deficit with regard to the capacity to manipulate numbers, even to *count* in the single-digit range or to make the most elementary numerical judgments of less than or greater than. And yet such people get by with surprising and cunning compensations: one congenital acalculia victim became a millionaire in the real estate business, using an acute eye for promising property and a set of mutually isolated accountants to do his figures and banking for him. All of which illustrates that it is possible for a being to be highly intelligent and yet have no capacity *at all* for manipulating language or mathematics. This suggests in turn that there may be important and fundamental cognitive talents for which *we* are genetically unequipped and of which *we* are totally unaware, talents we must acquire if we hope to understand more deeply the universe around us.

To summarize, our access to natural kinds is fluid, conceptually mediated, and uncertain. The familiar multitude of putative natural kinds embraced by common sense, and by the many derivative sciences, are at best merely practical kinds. Genuine natural kinds form a very small, aristocratic elite among kinds in general, being found only in the most basic laws of an all-embracing physics. And if there are no such laws, or if the human cognitive medium should turn out to be a representational cripple, then perhaps there are no natural kinds at all.

Chapter 14

Moral Facts and Moral Knowledge

---

1 The Epistemology and Ontology of Morals

Moral knowledge has long suffered from what seems an unflattering contrast with scientific or other genuinely "factual" forms of knowledge. It is not hard to appreciate the appearance. One has no obvious sense organ for moral facts, as one does for so many of the facts displayed in the material world, and so there is an immediate epistemological problem about moral facts. How does one apprehend them? Connected to this epistemological problem is an ontological problem. For empirical statements, one typically finds an objective configuration of objects or properties to which the statement, if true, corresponds. For statements of moral truth, such as 'One ought to keep one's promises', one seems not to find comparable objective configurations, lying in obliging correspondence. And even if one rejects the correspondence conception of truth implicit in this objection, the widely accepted principle that "ought" cannot be derived from "is" would seem to leave the truth of moral statements grounded in something other than the way the material universe happens to be configured.

This appearance has tended to provoke one of two possible reactions. On the one hand, we have a long history of noncognitivist and other deflationary or overtly skeptical accounts of moral "knowledge." And on the other, we have a long history of inflationary accounts that try to locate the ground of moral truth in abstract general principles that are somehow certified by *reason* as opposed to empirical fact. This rough division does not capture every approach: utilitarianism, perhaps, is both nondeflationary and nonrationalist. But the division captures a good deal. My own inclination is to resist the appearance that tends to produce these two reactions, and thus to avoid the motivation for both pathologies. Moral truths, I shall argue, are roughly as robust and objective as other instances of truth, but this objectivity is not secured by their being grounded in pure reason or in some other nonempirical support. It is secured in something very like the way in which the objectivity of scientific facts is secured.

What motivates this suggestion is the novel account of knowledge and conceptual development emerging from neural-network models of cognitive function (see chapters 5 and 9 to 11, especially chapters 9 and 10). These models provide a portrait of knowledge in which most of the old epistemological concepts and contrasts, the ones used to characterize moral knowledge in particular as "nonfactual," have simply disappeared. The grammatical and semantic differences that appear to distinguish moral from factual propositions no longer loom large, because propositions no longer appear as the primary means of knowledge representation in any case. On these neurocomputational models, knowledge acquisition is primarily a process of learning *how*: how to recognize a wide variety of complex situations and how to respond to them appropriately. The quality of one's knowledge is measured not by any uniform correspondence between internal sentences and external facts, but by the quality of one's continuing performance. From this perspective, moral knowledge does not automatically suffer by contrast with other forms of knowledge. To the contrary, *praxis* now appears primary. It is *theoria* that stands in need of explanation.

My aim in this brief chapter is to sketch a view of moral, social, and political knowledge that locates it correctly in the epistemological and ontological scheme of things. It is an essay in metaethics, but the view proposed will allow us to make some observations about the character of the principal substantive moral theories and about the nature of the conflicts between them. Certainly it has consequences concerning the nature and the possibility of moral progress. Let me begin modestly, however, by sketching a view of the development of moral knowledge in children, a view motivated by the neural-network models at issue. My aim at this stage is only to suggest that (*a*) a child's acquisition of an elementary moral consciousness is not primarily a matter of his internalizing a set of discursive principles, and (*b*) such acquisition is a genuine case of learning something about the objective world. I shall aspire to bolder claims toward the end of this essay.

2   Moral Prototypes and Moral Development

As is evident from the workings of multilayered feed-forward networks, the discrimination and recognition of certain features of the perceptual environment may require the presence of one or more layers of "hidden" units, layers that intervene between the initial layer of transducing input units and the output layer where the desired discrimination is finally coded. Without one or more such intervening layers, a network's discriminative capacities will be limited to only the simplest of environmental features (see chapter 9, section 5). This means that, for many properties in the world, it is the entire network that manages to make the relevant discriminations: the job is not done by the units of the input layer alone.

Let us turn now to biological brains. It has become evident that very few, if any, of the properties we commonly regard as observational are distinguished by the peripheral cells alone. Most of them involve the activity of several subsequent layers in the processing hierarchy. And this is certainly true of relatively subtle properties. Consider your observing that the sky is threatening, that a banana is ideally ripe, that the car's engine is still cold, that Mary is embarrassed, that the lamb chops on the grill are ready, that the class is bored, that an infant is overtired, and so forth. These are the sorts of immediate and automatic discriminations that one learns to make, and on which one's practical life depends. To be sure, they are ampliative discriminations relative to the often meager peripheral stimulation that triggers them, and they are highly corrigible for that very reason. But they are not the result of applying abstract general principles, nor the result of drawing covert discursive inferences, at least in a well-trained individual. They represent the normal and almost instantaneous operation of a massively parallel network that has been trained over time to be sensitive to a specific range of environmental features.

The discrimination of social and moral features is surely an instance of the same process, and it is made possible by training of a similar kind. Children learn to recognize certain prototypical kinds of social situations, and they learn to produce or avoid the behaviors prototypically required or prohibited in each. Young children learn to recognize a distribution of scarce resources such as cookies or candies as a *fair* or *unfair distribution*. They learn to voice complaint in the latter case, and to withhold complaint in the former. They learn to recognize that a found object may be *someone's property*, and that access is limited as a result. They learn to discriminate *unprovoked cruelty*, and to demand or expect punishment for the transgressor and comfort for the victim. They learn to recognize a *breach of promise*, and to howl in protest. They learn to recognize these and a hundred other prototypical social/moral situations, and the ways in which the embedding society generally reacts to those situations and expects them to react.

How the learning child subsequently reacts to a novel social situation will be a function of which of her many prototypes that situation activates, and this will be a matter of the relative similarity of the new situation to the various prototypes on which she was trained. This means that situations will occasionally be ambiguous. One and the same situation can activate distinct prototypes in distinct observers. What seems a case of unprovoked cruelty to one child can seem a case of just retribution to another. Moral argument then consists in trying to reduce the exaggerated salience of certain features of the situation, and to enhance the salience of certain others, in order to change which prototype gets activated. The stored prototypes themselves regularly undergo change, of course, as experience brings ever new examples and the child's social/moral consciousness continues to develop.

What the child is learning in this process is the *structure of social space* and *how best to navigate one's way through it*. What the child is learning is practical wisdom: the wise administration of her practical affairs in a complex social environment. This is as genuine a case of learning about objective reality as one finds anywhere. It is also of fundamental importance for the character and quality of any individual's life, and not everyone succeeds equally in mastering the relevant intricacies. On these points I expect little disagreement. What is problematic is whether this process amounts to the learning of genuine Moral Truth, or to mere socialization. We can hardly collapse the distinction, lest we make moral criticism of diverse forms of social organization impossible. We want to defend this possibility, since, as Nietzsche would be the first to point out, the socialization described above can occasionally amount to a cowardly acquiescence in an arbitrary and stultifying form of life. Can we specify under what circumstances it will amount to something more than this?

3   Praxis, Theoria, and Progress

We may begin to answer this question by noting that an exactly parallel problem arises with regard to the learning of Scientific Truth. In school and university we are taught to recognize a panoply of complex prototypical situations—falling bodies, forces at equilibrium, oxidation, nuclear fission, the greenhouse effect, bacterial infection, etc.—and we are taught to anticipate the prototypical elements and effects of each. This is unquestionably a process of learning. On this there will be little disagreement. But it is just as clearly a process of socialization, a process of adopting the conceptual machinery of an antecedent society, thereafter to function smoothly within it. What is problematic is whether this process amounts to the learning of genuine Scientific Truth, or to mere socialization. We dare not collapse the distinction, lest we make scientific criticism of diverse theories impossible. We wish to defend that possibility, since, as history records, such socialization can amount to a myopic acquiescence in a foolish and impotent world view. Can we specify under what circumstances it will amount to something more than this?

We must be careful not to set our hurdle too high here. A decade of scrutiny has found the traditional forms of scientific realism to be very *un*realistic in their optimistic expectations of universal convergence on a unique set of Final Truths (Laudan 1981). The lessons of scientific history, the collapse of naive arguments, and the lessons of cognitive neurobiology (chapter 9, section 7) all invite a different accounting of the prospects of the scientific enterprise. A certain amount of conceptual *radiation*, rather than convergence, seems the more likely and the more healthy long-term fate of science. For the enterprise may have no unique final goal, just as biological evolution has no unique final goal. Moreover, the evaluation of our cognitive resources and commitments at any given time will have to look beyond such parochial virtues as Tarskian truth, since that is a feature unique to the parochial elements of human language, which is a peripheral medium of representation even for human cognition. It is unlikely to be of any fundamental significance in evaluating cognitive activity in creatures generally.

The radical character of these recent views aside, there remains every reason to think that the normal learning process, as instanced both in individuals and in the collective enterprise of institutional science, involves a reliable and dramatic increase in the amount and the quality of the information we have about the world. How to *recharacterize* our cognitive virtues is still an unsettled question, but the neurocomputational framework discussed in the earlier chapters shows us how to begin, and it leaves the existence of high-grade learning, intricate world modeling, and fertile cognitive futures in no serious doubt.

When such powerful learning networks as humans are confronted with the problem of how best to perceive the social world, and how best to conduct one's affairs within it, we have equally good reason to expect that the learning process will show an integrity comparable to that shown on other learning tasks, and will produce cognitive achievements as robust as those produced anywhere else. This expectation will be especially apt if, as in the case of "scientific" knowledge, the learning process is collective and the results are transmitted from generation to generation. In that case we have a continuing society under constant pressure to refine its categories of social and moral perception, and to modify its typical responses and expectations. Successful societies do this on a systematic basis. A body of legislation accumulates, with successive additions, deletions, and modifications. A body of case law accumulates, and the technique of finding and citing relevant precedents (which are, of course, *prototypes*) becomes a central feature of adjudicating legal disputes.

Just what are the members of the society learning? They are learning how best to organize and administer their collective and individual affairs. What factors provoke change and improvement in their typical categories of moral perception and their typical forms of behavioral response? That is, what factors drive moral learning? They are many and various, but in general they arise from the continuing social experience of conducting a life under the existing moral framework. That is, moral learning is driven by social experience, often a long and painful social experience, just as theoretical science is driven by experiment. Moral knowledge thus has just as genuine a claim to objectivity as any other kind of empirical knowledge. What are the principles by which rational people adjust their moral conceptions in the face of unwelcome social experience? They are likely to be exactly the same "principles" that drive conceptual readjustment in science or anywhere else, and they are likely to be revealed as we come to understand how empirical brains actually do learn (see chapter 11).

From what little we already know about learning in neural networks, we can already see that "superempirical" virtues such as simplicity and conceptual unity play a role that is comparable in importance to adequately comprehending the data of experience. We may, therefore, expect the same to be true in the domain of moral knowledge, and this expectation is born out by the character of the most prominent substantive moral theories. Just as scientific theories do, substantive moral theories attempt to find or impose a *unity* on the scattered concepts and convictions that make up one's moral consciousness. They attempt to account for the full range of our moral understanding in terms of a small number of allegedly more fundamental concepts, either moral or nonmoral.

This impulse to unity was discussed briefly in chapter 10, in the context of intertheoretic reduction and conceptual unification. There the process was characterized as the search for a *superordinate* prototype, of which the target prototypes can be usefully seen as various instances. That same character is evident in existing moral theories. One of the most primitive attempts at providing an explanatory unity to one's moral understanding portrays all moral imperatives as the commands of a stern (but loving) supernatural father. The *stern father* prototype is one that almost everyone possesses. It has certain salient features that make it appealing to many millions of people. And it provides a moral content they can understand. If we are all His children, for example, then every man is your brother and every woman your sister. This activates the "sibling" prototype most of us possess, which demands better treatment for siblings than one accords to non-family members, and so forth. In these ways, and others, one is invited to reconceive one's society as being an instance of a family, with all of the perceptions and impulses that come with that domestic prototype.

Less primitive attempts at explanatory understanding appeal to different prototypes. A more arresting account bids one reconceive one's relation to society as being an instance of the prototype, *party to a contract*, with all that that suggests. A different but closely related account bids one conceive all of one's moral decisions under the prototype, *maximizing private benefit under collective constraints*. A third attempts to unify all of one's moral precepts by seeing them as instances of *universalizable rules*. A fourth claims unity for them as *maximizing general utility*. And so on. This impulse to unity is entirely healthy, in our moral understanding as well as in our scientific understanding. The virtue of unified theories here, as elsewhere, is that they help to deepen our understanding and help us to deal better with novel social situations. It remains an open question, on which I shall not here tender comment, as to which of the superordinate prototypes just mentioned effects the deepest and most lasting unification of our understanding.

My point by now is clear, or as clear as I can make it in short compass, and I shall bring exploration of these parallels to a close. The approach of this chapter does not tell us anything substantive about which moral theory is correct. But it does indicate that moral knowledge is as genuine as knowledge elsewhere, and that moral progress is possible. There is no reason why our moral consciousness and moral understanding should not continue to improve and deepen indefinitely, just as our nonsocial perception and our theoretical science may do so. For in fact we do have an organ for understanding and recognizing moral facts. It is called the brain.

References

Allman, J. M., et al. 1981. "Visual Topography and Function." In C. N. Woolsey, ed., *Cortical Sensory Organization*, vol. 2. Clifton, N.J.: Humana Press.

Arbib, M., and Amari, S. 1985. "Sensorimotor Transformations in the Brain." *Journal of Theoretical Biology* 112:123–155.

Ballard, D. H. 1986. "Cortical Connections and Parallel Processing: Structure and Function." *Behavior and Brain Sciences* 9, no. 1: 67–90.

Barto, A. G. 1985. "Learning by Statistical Cooperation of Self-Interested Neuron-like Computing Elements." *Human Neurobiology* 4:229–256.

Bartoshuk, L. M. 1978. "Gustatory System." in R. B. Masterton, ed., *Handbook of Behavioral Neurobiology*, vol. 1, *Sensory Integration*, pp. 503–567. New York: Plenum Press.

Bear, M. F., Cooper, L. N., and Ebner, F. F. 1987. "A Physiological Basis for a Theory of Synapse Modification." *Science* 237, no. 4810.

Bechtel, W., and Abrahamsen, A. Forthcoming. *Connectionism and the Mind: An Introduction to Parallel Distributed Processing*. Oxford: Basil Blackwell.

Block, N. 1978. "Troubles with Functionalism." In C. W. Savage, ed., *Perception and Cognition: Issues in the Foundations of Psychology*, Minnesota Studies in the Philosophy of Science, vol. 9, pp. 261–325.

Block, N., and Fodor, J. 1972. "What Mental States Are Not." *Philosophical Review* 81:159–181.

Bloor, D. 1976. *Knowledge and Social Imagery*. Boston: Routledge & Kegan Paul.

Brandt, R., and Kim, J. 1967. "The Logic of the Identity Theory." *Journal of Philosophy* 64, no. 17: 515–537.

Brody, B. A. 1972. "Towards an Aristotelian Theory of Scientific Explanation." *Philosophy of Science* 39:20–31.

Bromberger, S. 1966. "Why-Questions." In R. Colodny, ed., *Mind and Cosmos*, pp. 86–111. Pittsburgh: Pittsburgh University Press.

Bruner, J. 1973. "On Perceptual Readiness." In J. Anglin, ed., *Beyond the Information Given*, pp. 7–42. New York: W. W. Norton & Co.

Campbell, K. 1983. "Abstract Particulars and the Philosophy of Mind." *Australasian Journal of Philosophy* 61, no. 2: 129–141.

Carnap, R. 1956. "Empiricism, Semantics, and Ontology." In R. Carnap, *Meaning and Necessity*, 2d edition, pp. 205–221. Chicago: University of Chicago Press.

Churchland, P. M. 1970. "The Logical Character of Action Explanations." *Philosophical Review* 79, no. 2: 214–236.

Churchland, P. M. 1975a. "Two Grades of Evidential Bias." *Philosophy of Science* 42, no. 3: 250–259.

Churchland, P. M. 1975b. "Karl Popper's Philosophy of Science." *Canadian Journal of Philosophy* 5, no. 1: 145–156.

Churchland, P. M. 1979. *Scientific Realism and the Plasticity of Mind*. Cambridge: Cambridge University Press.

Churchland, P. M. 1980. "Plasticity: Conceptual and Neuronal," *Behavior and Brain Sciences* 3, no. 1: 133–134.

Churchland, P. M. 1981a. "Eliminative Materialism and the Propositional Attitudes." *Journal of Philosophy* 78, no. 2: 67–90.

Churchland, P. M. 1981b. "Functionalism, Qualia, and Intentionality." *Philosophical Topics* 12, no. 1: 121–145.

Churchland, P. M. 1982. "Is *Thinker* a Natural Kind?" *Dialogue* 21, no. 2: 223–238.

Churchland, P. M. 1984. *Matter and Consciousness*. Cambridge: MIT Press.

Churchland, P. M. 1985a. "The Ontological Status of Observables: In Praise of the Superempirical Virtues." In P. M. Churchland, and C. A. Hooker, eds., *Images of Science*, pp. 35–47. Chicago: University of Chicago Press.

Churchland, P. M. 1985b. "Reduction, Qualia, and the Direct Introspection of Brain States." *Journal of Philosophy* 82, no. 1: 8–28.

Churchland, P. M. 1986a. "Some Reductive Strategies in Cognitive Neurobiology." *Mind* 95, no. 379: 279–309.

Churchland, P. M. 1986b. "On the Continuity of Science and Philosophy." *Mind and Language* 1, no. 1: 5–14.

Churchland, P. M. 1986c. "Firewalking and Physics." *The Skeptical Inquirer* 10, no. 3: 284–285.

Churchland, P. M. 1986d. "Cognitive Neurobiology: A Computational Hypothesis for Laminar Cortex." *Biology and Philosophy* 1, no. 1: 25–51.

Churchland, P. M. 1986e. "Semantic Content: In Defense of a Network Approach." *The Behavioral and Brain Sciences* 9, no. 1: 139–140.

Churchland, P. M. 1988a. "Folk Psychology and the Explanation of Human Behavior." *Proceedings of the Aristotelian Society*, suppl. 62:209–221.

Churchland, P. M. 1988b. "Perceptual Plasticity and Theoretical Neutrality: A Reply to Jerry Fodor." *Philosophy of Science* 55, no. 2: 167–187.

Churchland, P. M. 1989a. "On the Nature of Theories: A Neurocomputational Perspective." In C. W. Savage, ed., *The Nature of Theories*, Minnesota Studies in the Philosophy of Science, vol. 14. Minneapolis: University of Minnesota Press.

Churchland, P. M. 1989b. "Simplicity: The View from the Neuronal Level." In N. Rescher, ed., *Aesthetic Values in Science*. Forthcoming.

Churchland, P. M., and Churchland, P. S. 1983. "Content: Semantic and Information-Theoretic." *The Behavioral and Brain Sciences* 6, no. 1: 67–68.

Churchland, P. M., and Hooker, C. A., eds. 1985. *Images of Science: Essays on Realism and Empiricism*. Chicago: University of Chicago Press.

Churchland, P. S. 1978. "Fodor on Language Learning." *Syntheses* 38, no. 1: 149–159.

Churchland, P. S. 1980a. "A Perspective on Mind-Brain Research." *Journal of Philosophy* 77, no. 4: 185–207.

Churchland, P. S. 1980b. "Language, Thought, and Information Processing." *Noûs* 14:147–169.

Churchland, P. S. 1980c. "Neuroscience and Psychology: Should the Labor Be Divided?" *Behavioral and Brain Sciences* 3, no. 1: 133.

Churchland, P. S. 1981. "Is Determinism Self-Refuting?" *Mind* 90:99–101.

Churchland, P. S. 1986. *Neurophilosophy: Toward a Unified Understanding of the Mind-Brain*. Cambridge: MIT Press.

Cynader, M., and Berman, N. 1972. "Receptive Field Organization of Monkey Superior Colliculus." *Journal of Neurophysiology* 35:187–201.

Davidson, D. 1973. "On the Very Idea of a Conceptual Scheme." *Proceedings and Addresses of the American Philosophical Association* 47.

Dennett, D. C. 1971. "Intentional Systems." *Journal of Philosophy* 68, no. 4: 87–106. Reprinted in D. C. Dennett, *Brainstorms*, pp. 3–22 (Montgomery, Vt.: Bradford Books, 1978).

Dennett, D. C. 1975. "Brain Writing and Mind Reading." In K. Gunderson, ed., *Language, Mind, and Knowledge, Minnesota Studies in the Philosophy of Science*, vol. 7, pp. 403–415. Minneapolis: University of Minnesota Press.

Dennett, D. C. 1981. "Three Kinds of Intentional Psychology." In R. Healey, ed., *Reduction, Time, and Reality*, pp. 37–61. Cambridge: Cambridge University Press. Reprinted in D. C. Dennett 1987.

Dennett, D. C. 1987, *The Intentional Stance*. Cambridge: MIT Press.

Desmond, N., and Levy, W. 1983. "Synaptic Correlates of Associative Potentiation/ Depression: An Ultrastructural Study in the Hippocampus." *Brain Research* 265:21– 30.

Desmond, N., and Levy, W. 1986. "Changes in the Numerical Density of Synaptic Contacts with Long-Term Potentiation in the Hippocampal Dentate Gyrus." *Journal of Comparative Neurology* 253:466–475.

Dretske, F. 1981. *Knowledge and the Flow of Information*. Cambridge: MIT Press.

Dreyfus, H. 1979. *What Computers Can't Do*. New York: Harper & Row.

Dreyfus, H., and Dreyfus, S. 1986. *Mind over Machine*. New York: Macmillan.

Fales, E. 1982. "Natural Kinds and Freaks of Nature." *Philosophy of Science* 49, no. 1: 67–90.

Feyerabend, P. K. 1963a. "Materialism and the Mind-Body Problem." *Review of Metaphysics* 17:49–66. Reprinted in C. V. Borst, ed., *The Mind/Brain Identity Theory*, pp. 142–156. Toronto: Macmillan, 1970.

Feyerabend, P. K. 1963b. "How to Be a Good Empiricist." In B. Baumrin, ed., *Philosophy of Science*, vol. 2, pp. 3–19. New York: Interscience Publications. Reprinted in H. Morick, ed., *Challenges to Empiricism* (Belmont, California: Wadsworth, 1972), pp. 164–193.

Feyerabend, P. K. 1965. "Reply to Criticism: Comments on Smart, Sellars, and Putnam." In M. Wartofsky, ed., *Boston Studies in the Philosophy of Science*. New York: Reidel. Reprinted in P. K. Feyerabend, *Realism, Rationalism and Scientific Method*, Philosophical Papers, vol. 1 (Cambridge: Cambridge University Press, 1981), pp. 104–131.

Feyerabend, P. K. 1969. "Science without Experience." *Journal of Philosophy* 66, no. 22: 791–794.

Feyerabend, P. K. 1970. "Against Method: Outline of an Anarchist Theory of Knowledge." In Radner and Winokur, eds., *Analyses of Theories and Methods of Physics and Psychology. Minnesota Studies in the Philosophy of Science*, vol. 4, pp. 17–130. Minneapolis: University of Minnesota Press.

Feyerabend, P. K. 1980. "Consolations for the Specialist." In I. Lakatos, and A. Musgrave, eds., *Criticism and the Growth of Knowledge*. Cambridge: Cambridge University Press: 197–230.

Fodor, J. A. 1968. *Psychological Explanation*. New York: Random House.

Fodor, J. A. 1975. *The Language of Thought*. New York: Crowell.

Fodor, J. A. 1984. "Observation Reconsidered." *Philosophy of Science* 51, no. 1: 23–43.

Fodor, J. A. 1988a. *Psychosemantics: The Problem of Meaning in the Philosophy of Mind*. Cambridge: MIT Press.

Fodor, J. A. 1988b. "A Reply to Churchland's 'Perceptual Plasticity and Theoretical Neutrality.'" *Philosophy of Science* 55, no. 2: 188–194.

Fodor, J. A. and Pylyshyn, Z. 1981. "How Direct Is Visual Perception? An Examination of Gibson's 'Ecological Approach.'" *Cognition* 9, no. 2: 139–196.

Friedman, M. 1974. "Explanation and Scientific Understanding." *Journal of Philosophy* 71, no. 1: 5–18.

Gazzaniga, M. S., and LeDoux, J. E. 1975. *The Integrated Mind*. New York: Plenum Press.

Giere, R. 1988. *Explaining Science: A Cognitive Approach*. Chicago: University of Chicago Press.

Glymour, C. 1988. "Artificial Intelligence Is Philosophy." In J. Fetzer, ed., *Aspects of Artificial Intelligence*. Dordrecht, Holland: D. Reidel.

Glymour, C. 1985. "Explanation and Realism." In P. M. Churchland, and C. A. Hooker, eds., *Images of Science*, pp. 99–117. Chicago: University of Chicago Press.

Goldberg, M., and Robinson, D. L. 1978. "Visual System: Superior Colliculus." in R. Masterson, ed., *Handbook of Behavioral Neurobiology*, vol. 1, pp. 119–164. New York: Plenum Press.

Goldman, A. Forthcoming. "Interpretation Psychologized." *Mind and Language*.

Gonshor, A., and Jones, G. M. 1976. "Extreme Vestibulo-Ocular Adaptation Induced by Prolonged Optical Reversal of Vision." *Journal of Physiology* 256:381–414.

Gordon, B. 1973. "Receptive Fields in Deep Layers of Cat Superior Colliculus." *Journal of Neurophysiology* 36:157–178.

Gordon, R. 1986. "Folk Psychology as Simulation." *Mind and Language* 1, no. 2: 158–171.

Gorman, R. P., and Sejnowski, T. J. 1988a. "Learned Classification of Sonar Targets Using a Massively-Parallel Network." *IEEE Transactions: Acoustics, Speech, and Signal Processing*.

Gorman, R. P., and Sejnowski, T. J. 1988b. "Analysis of Hidden Units in a Layered Network Trained to Classify Sonar Targets." *Neural Networks* 1:75–89.

Gregory, R. 1966. *Eye and Brain*. London: McGraw Hill.

Gregory, R. 1970a. *The Intelligent Eye*. New York: McGraw Hill.

Gregory, R. 1970b. "The Grammar of Vision." *Listener* 83, no. 2133: 242–246. Reprinted in Gregory 1974.

Gregory, R. 1974. *Concepts and Mechanisms of Perception*. New York: Charles Scribners and Sons.

Grover, D., Camp, J., and Belnap, N. 1975. "A Prosentential Theory of Truth." *Philosophical Studies* 27, no. 2: 73–125.

Haldane, J. 1988. "Understanding Folk." *Proceedings of the Aristotelian Society*, suppl. 62:222–246.

Hanson, N. R. 1961. *Patterns of Discovery*. Cambridge: Cambridge University Press.

Harman, G. 1965. "Inference to the Best Explanation." *Philosophical Review* 74:88–95.

Harman, G. 1973. *Thought*. Princeton: Princeton University Press.

Hartshorne, C., and Weiss, P. 1935. *Collected Papers of Charles Sanders Peirce*. Cambridge: Harvard University Press.

Hatfield, G. 1989. "Computation, Representation, and Content in Noncognitive Theories of Perception." In S. Silvers, ed., *Representation*, pp. 255–288. Dordrecht: Kluwer.

Hebb, D. O. 1949. *The Organization of Behavior*. New York: Wiley.

Hempel, C. 1965. "Studies in the Logic of Confirmation." In C. Hempel, *Aspects of Scientific Explanation*, pp. 3–52. New York: Free Press.

Hesse, M. 1966. *Models and Analogies in Science*. Notre Dame: Notre Dame University Press.

Hinton, G. E. Forthcoming. "Connectionist Learning Procedures." *Artificial Intelligence*.

Hinton, G. E., and Sejnowski, T. J. 1986. "Learning and Relearning in Boltzmann Machines." in D. E. Rumelhart, J. McClelland, and the PDP Research Group, *Parallel Distributed Processing: Explorations in the Microstructure of Cognition*. Cambridge: MIT Press.

Hooker, C. A. 1975. "The Philosophical Ramifications of the Information Processing Approach to the Mind-Brain." *Philosophy and Phenomenological Research* 36:1–15.

Hooker, C. A. 1981. "Towards a General Theory of Reduction." *Dialogue* 20:38–59, 201–236, 496–529.

Hooker, C. A. 1985. "Surface Dazzle, Ghostly Depths: An Exposition and Critical Evaluation of van Fraassen's Vindication of Empiricism against Realism." In P. M. Churchland, and C. A. Hooker, eds., *Images of Science*, pp. 153–196. Chicago: University of Chicago Press.

Hooker, C. A. 1987. *A Realistic Theory of Science.* Albany: State University of New York Press.

Hopfield, J. J., and Tank, D. 1985. "'Neural' Computation of Decisions in Optimization Problems." *Biological Cybernetics* 52:141–152.

Hornik, K., Stinchcombe, M., and White, H. 1989. "Multi-Layer Feedforward Networks Are Universal Approximators." *Neuronetworks* 2, forthcoming.

Hubel, D. H., and Livingstone, M. S. 1987. "Segregation of Form, Color, and Stereopsis in Primate Area 18." *Journal of Neuroscience* 7:3378–3415.

Hubel, D. H., and Wiesel, T. N. 1962. "Receptive Fields, Binocular Interactions, and Functional Architecture in the Cat's Visual Cortex." *Journal of Physiology* 160:106–154.

Huerta, M. F., and Harting, J. K. 1984. "Connectional Organization of the Superior Colliculus." *Trends in Neuroscience* 7, no. 8: 286–289.

Jackson, F. 1982. "Epiphenomenal Qualia." *Philosophical Quarterly* 32, no. 127: 127–136.

Jackson, F. 1986. "What Mary Didn't Know." *Journal of Philosophy* 83, no. 5: 291–295.

Kanaseki, T., and Sprague, J. M. 1974. "Anatomical Organization of Pretectal Nuclei and Tectal Laminae in the Cat." *Journal of Comparative Neurology* 158:319–337.

Kelso, S. R., Ganong, A. H., and Brown, T. H. 1986. "Hebbian Synapses in Hippocampus." *Proceedings of the National Academy of Sciences* 83:5326–5330.

Kitcher, P. 1981. "Explanatory Unification." *Philosophy of Science* 48, no. 4: 507–531.

Kitcher, P. 1989. "Explanatory Unification and the Causal Structure of the World." In P. Kitcher, ed., *Scientific Explanation*, Minnesota Studies in the Philosophy of Science, vol. 13.

Konishi, M. 1986. "Centrally Synthesized Maps of Sensory Space." *Trends in Neuroscience* 9, no. 4: 163–168.

Kottenhoff, H. 1957. "Situational and Personal Influences on Space Perception with Experimental Spectacles." *Acta Psychologica* 13:79–97.

Kripke, Saul. 1972. "Naming and Necessity." In D. Davidson and G. Harman, eds., *Semantics of Natural Language*, pp. 253–355. Dordrecht, Holland: D. Reidel.

Kuhn, T. S. 1962. *The Structure of Scientific Revolutions.* Chicago: University of Chicago Press.

Lakatos, I. 1970. "Falsification and the Methodology of Scientific Research Programmes." In I. Lakatos and A. Musgrave, eds., *Criticism and the Growth of Knowledge.* Cambridge: Cambridge University Press.

Lakoff, G. 1987. *Women, Fire, and Dangerous Things.* Chicago: University of Chicago Press.

Land, E. 1977. "The Retinex Theory of Color Vision." *Scientific American*, December, 108–128.

Laudan, L. 1981. "A Confutation of Convergent Realism." *Philosophy of Science* 48, no. 1: 19–49.

Lehky, S., and Sejnowski, T. J. 1988a. "Computing Shape from Shading with a Neural Network Model." In E. Schwartz, ed., *Computational Neuroscience.* Cambridge: MIT Press.

Lehky, S., and Sejnowski, T. J. 1988b. "Network Model of Shape-from-Shading: Neural Function Arises from Both Receptive and Projective Fields." *Nature* 333 (June 2): 452–454.

Leikind, B. J., and McCarthy, W. J. 1985. "An Investigation of Firewalking." *The Skeptical Inquirer* 10, no. 1: 23–35.

Lewis, D. 1983. "Postscript to 'Mad Pain and Martian Pain.'" *Philosophical Papers*, vol. 1. New York: Oxford.

Linsker, R. 1986. "From Basic Network Principles to Neural Architecture: Emergence of Orientation Columns." *Proceedings of the National Academy of Sciences* 83:8779–8783.

Linsker, R. 1988. "Self-Organization in a Perceptual Network." *Computer*, March.

Livingstone, R. B. 1978. *Sensory Processing, Perception, and Behavior.* New York: Raven Press.

Livingstone, M. S., and Hubel, D. H. 1987. "Psychophysical Evidence for Separate Channels for the Perception of Form, Color, Movement, and Depth." *Journal of Neuroscience* 7:3416–3468.

Llinas, R. 1975. "The Cortex of the Cerebellum." *Scientific American*, January, 56–71.

Llinas, R. 1986. "'Mindness' as a Functional State of the Brain." In C. Blakemore and S. Greenfield, eds., *Mind and Matter.* Oxford: Blackwell.

Lycan, W. G. 1985. "Tacit Belief." In R. J. Bogdan, ed., *Belief.* Oxford: Oxford University Press.

Margolis, J. 1978. *Persons and Minds.* Dordrecht: Reidel.

Mays, L. E., and Sparks, D. L. 1980. "Saccades Are Spatially, Not Retinocentrically, Coded." *Science* 208:1163–1165.

McIlwain, J. T. 1975. "Visual Receptive Fields and Their Images in the Superior Colliculus of the Cat." *Journal of Neurophysiology* 38:219–230.

McIlwain, J. T. 1984. *Abstracts: Society for Neuroscience* 10, part 1: 268.

McKloskey, M. 1983. "Intuitive Physics." *Scientific American*, April, 122–130.

Mellor, D. H. 1977. "Natural Kinds." *British Journal for the Philosophy of Science* 28:229–312.

Meredith, M. A., and Stein, B. E. 1985. "Descending Efferents from the Superior Colliculus Relay Integrated Multisensory Information." *Science* 227, no. 4687: 657–659.

Merzenich, M., and Kaas, J. 1980. "Principles of Organization of Sensory-Perceptual Systems in Mammals." *Progress in Psychobiology and Physiological Psychology* 9:1–42.

Minsky, M. 1981. "A Framework for Representing Knowledge." In J. Haugeland, ed., *Mind Design.* Cambridge: MIT Press.

Minsky, M., and Papert, S. 1969. *Perceptrons.* Cambridge: MIT Press.

Mooney, R. D., et al. 1984. "Dendrites of Deep Layer, Somatosensory Superior Collicular Neurons Extend Into the Superficial Layer." *Abstracts: Society for Neuroscience* 10, part 1: 158.

Munevar, G. 1981. *Radical Knowledge.* Indianapolis: Hackett.

Musgrave, A. 1985. "Realism versus Constructive Empiricism." In P. M. Churchland and C. A. Hooker, eds., *Images of Science*, pp. 197–221. Chicago: University of Chicago Press.

Nagel, E. 1961. *The Structure of Science.* New York: Harcourt, Brace & World.

Nagel, T. 1974. "What Is It like to Be a Bat?" *Philosophical Review* 83, no. 4: 435–450.

Nemirow, L. 1980. Review of Thomas Nagel, *Mortal Questions. Philosophical Review* 89, no. 3: 473–477.

Pellionisz, A. 1984. "Tensorial Aspects of the Multi-Dimensional Approach to the Vestibulo-Oculomotor Reflex." In A. Berthoz and E. Melvill-Jones, eds., *Reviews in Oculomotor Research.* Elsevier.

Pellionisz, A., and Llinas, R. 1979. "Brain Modelling by Tensor Network Theory and Computer Simulation: The Cerebellum, Distributed Processor for Predictive Coordination." *Neuroscience* 4:323–348.

Pellionisz, A., and Llinas, R. 1982. "Space-Time Representation in the Brain: The Cerebellum as a Predictive Space-Time Metric Tensor." *Neuroscience* 7, no. 12: 2949–2970.

Pellionisz, A., and Llinas, R. 1985. "Tensor Network Theory of the Metaorganization of Functional Geometries in the Central Nervous System." *Neuroscience* 16, no. 2: 245–274.

Pfaff, D. W., ed. 1985. *Taste, Olfaction, and the Central Nervous System*. New York: Rockefeller University Press.

Pickering, A. 1981. "The Hunting of the Quark." *Isis* 72:216–236.

Pickering, A. 1984. *Constructing Quarks: A Sociological History of Particle Physics*. Chicago: University of Chicago Press.

Popper, K. 1959. *The Logic of Scientific Discovery*. New York: Harper & Row.

Popper, K. 1972. *Objective Knowledge*. New York: Oxford University Press.

Popper, K., and Eccles, J. 1978. *The Self and Its Brain*. New York: Springer Verlag.

Putnam, H. 1964. "Robots: Machines or Artificially Created Life?" *Journal of Philosophy* 61, no. 11: 668–691.

Putnam, H. 1970. "Is Semantics Possible?" In H. Kiefer, and M. Munitz, eds., *Languages, Belief, and Metaphysics*. Albany: State University of New York Press. Reprinted in H. Putnam, *Mind, Language and Reality*, pp. 139–152 (Cambridge: Cambridge University Press).

Putnam, H. 1971. "The Nature of Mental States." In D. Rosenthal, ed., *Materialism and the Mind-Body Problem*. New Jersey: Prentice-Hall. Reprinted in H. Putnam, *Mind, Language, and Reality*, pp. 429–440 (Cambridge: Cambridge University Press).

Putnam, H. 1975. "The Meaning of 'Meaning.'" In K. Gunderson, ed., *Language, Mind and Knowledge*, Minnesota Studies in the Philosophy of Science, vol. 7. Reprinted in H. Putnam, *Mind, Language and Reality*, pp. 215–271 (Cambridge: Cambridge University Press).

Putman, H. 1981. *Reason, Truth, and History*. Cambridge: Cambridge University Press.

Pylyshyn, Z. 1980. "Computation and Cognition: Issues in the Foundation of Cognitive Science." *Behavioral and Brain Sciences* 3, no. 1: 111–134.

Quine, W. V. O. 1960. *Word and Object*. Cambridge: MIT Press.

Quine, W. V. O. 1969. "Natural Kinds." In W. V. O. Quine, *Ontological Relativity and Other Essays*. New York: Columbia University Press.

Randi, J. 1982. *Flim-Flam! Psychics, ESP, Unicorns, and Other Delusions*. Buffalo, N.Y.: Prometheus Books.

Risset, J. C., and Wessel, D. L. 1982. "Exporation of Timbre by Analysis and Synthesis." In D. Deutsch, ed., *The Psychology of Music*. New York: Academic Press.

Robinson, D. A. 1972. "Eye Movements Evoked by Collicular Stimulation in the Alert Monkey." *Vision Research* 12:1795–1808.

Robinson, H. 1982. *Matter and Sense*. New York: Cambridge University Press.

Rock, I. 1983. *The Logic of Perception*. Cambridge: MIT Press.

Rogers, L. J., and Miles, F. A. 1972. "Centrifugal Control of Avian Retina: Effects of Lesions of the Isthmo-Optic Nucleus on Visual Behaviour." *Brain Research* 48:147–156.

Rorty, R. 1965. "Mind-Body Identity, Privacy, and Categories." *Review of Metaphysics* 19:24–54.

Rosch, E. 1981. "Prototype Classification and Logical Classification: The Two Systems." In E. Scholnick, ed., *New Trends in Cognitive Representation: Challenges to Piaget's Theory*. New Jersey: Lawrence Erlbaum.

Rosenberg, C. R., and Sejnowski, T. J. 1987. "Parallel Networks That Learn to Pronounce English Text." *Complex Systems* 1:145–168.

Rosenblatt, F. 1959. *Principles of Neurodynamics*. New York: Spartan Books.

Rumelhart, D. E., Hinton, G. E., and Williams, R. J. 1986a. "Learning Representations by Back-Propagating Errors." *Nature* 323:533–536.

Rumelhart, D. E., Hinton, G. E., and Williams, R. J. 1986b. "Learning Internal Representations by Error Propagation." In D. E. Rumelhart, J. L. McClelland, and the PDP Research Group, *Parallel Distributed Processing: Explorations in the Microstructure of Cognition*, vol. 1. Cambridge: MIT Press.

Sacks, J. G., and Lindenberg, R. 1969. "Efferent Nerve Fibers in the Anterior Visual Pathways in Bilateral Congenital Cyctic Eyeballs." *American Journal of Opthalmology* 68:691–695.

Salmon, W. 1966. *The Foundations of Scientific Inference*. Pittsburgh: University of Pittsburgh Press.

Salmon, W. 1970. "Statistical Explanation." In R. Colodny, ed., *The Nature and Function of Scientific Theories*, pp. 173–231. Pittsburgh: Pittsburgh University Press.

Salmon, W. 1971. *Statistical Explanation and Statistical Relevance*. Pittsburgh: Pittsburgh University Press.

Salmon, W. 1978. "Why Ask, 'Why'?" *Proceedings and Addresses of the American Philosophical Association* 51:683–705.

Salmon, W. 1984. *Scientific Explanation and the Causal Structure of the World*. Princeton: Princeton University Press.

Sayre, K. M. 1986. "Intentionality and Information Processing: An Alternative Model for Cognitive Science." *Behavioral and Brain Sciences* 9, no. 1: 121–138.

Schank, R., and Abelson, R. 1977. *Scripts, Plans, Goals, and Understanding*. New Jersey: John Wiley and Sons.

Scheffler, I. 1963. *The Anatomy of Inquiry*. New York: Knopf.

Schiller, P. 1984. "The Superior Colliculus and Visual Function." In I. Darian-Smith, ed., *Handbook of Physiology*, vol. 3, pp. 457–504.

Schiller, P., and Sandell, J. H. 1983. "Interactions between Visually and Electrically Elicited Saccades before and after Superior Colliculus and Frontal Eye Field Ablations in the Rhesus Monkey." *Experimental Brain Research* 49:381–392.

Schiller, P., and Stryker, M. 1972. "Single-Unit Recording and Stimulation in Superior Colliculus of the Alert Rhesus Monkey." *Journal of Neurophysiology* 35:915–924.

Searle, J. 1980. "Minds, Brains, and Programs." *Behavioral and Brain Sciences* 3, no. 3: 417–457.

Sejnowski, T. J., Kienker, P. K., and Hinton, G. E. 1986. "Learning Symmetry Groups with Hidden Units: Beyond the Perceptron." *Physica D* 22D:260–275.

Sellars, W. 1956. "Empiricism and the Philosophy of Mind." In H. Feigl and M. Scriven, eds., *The Foundations of Science and the Concepts of Psychology and Psychoanalysis*, Minnesota Studies in the Philosophy of Science, vol. 1. Minneapolis: University of Minnesota Press. Reprinted in W. Sellars, *Science, Perception and Reality*, pp. 127–196 (London: Routledge and Kegan Paul, 1963).

Shapere, Dudley. 1982. "Reason, Reference, and the Quest for Knowledge." *Philosophy of Science* 49, no. 1: 1–23.

Shoemaker, S. 1975. "Functionalism and Qualia." *Philosophical Studies* 27:291–315.

Smith, D. V. et al. 1983. "Coding of Taste Stimuli by Hamster Brain Stem Neurons." *Journal of Neurophysiology* 7:541–558.

Stanton, P. K., and Sejnowski, T. J. In preparation. "Associative Long-Term Depression in the Hippocampus: Evidence for Anti-Hebbian Synaptic Plasticity."

Stein, B. E. 1984. "Development of the Superior Colliculus." In W. M. Cowan, ed., *Annual Review of Neuroscience* 7:95–126.

Stich, S. P. 1983. *From Folk Psychology to Cognitive Science: The Case against Belief*. Cambridge: MIT Press.

Stich, S. P. 1989. *The Fragmentation of Reason*. Cambridge: MIT Press.

Strawson, P. F. 1958. "Persons." In H. Feigl, M. Scriven, and G. Maxwell, eds., *Concepts, Theories, and the Mind-Body Problem*, Minnesota Studies in the Philosophy of Science, vol. 2, pp. 330–353. Minneapolis: University of Minnesota Press.

Sturgeon, N. 1985. "Moral Explanation." In D. Copp, and D. Zimmerman, eds., *Morality, Reason, and Truth. Southern Journal of Philosophy*, suppl. to vol. 24.

Suppe, F. 1974. *The Structure of Scientific Theories*. Chicago: University of Illinois Press.

Sur, M., Garraghty, P., and Roe, A. 1988. "Experimentally Induced Visual Projections into Auditory Thalamus and Cortex." *Science* 242, no. 4884: 1437–1441.

Taylor, C. 1970. "Mind-Body Identity: A Side Issue?" In C. V. Borst, ed., *The Mind/Brain Identity Theory*, pp. 231–241. Toronto: Macmillan.

Taylor, C. 1987. "Overcoming Epistemology." In K. Baynes, J. Bohman, T. McCarthy, eds., *After Philosophy: End or Transformation?* pp. 464–488. Cambridge: MIT Press.

Teller, P. 1974. "On Why-Questions." *Noûs* 8:371–380.

Thompson, R. F. 1986. "The Neurobiology of Learning and Memory." *Science* 233:941–947.

Van Essen, D. C., and Maunsell, J. 1983. "Hierarchical Organization and Functional Streams in the Visual Cortex." *Trends in Neuroscience* 6:370–375.

Van Fraassen, B. 1977. "The Pragmatics of Explanation." *American Philosophical Quarterly* 14:143–150.

Van Fraassen, B. 1980. *The Scientific Image*. Oxford: Oxford University Press.

Van Fraassen, B. 1981. Critical Notice of Paul Churchland, *Scientific Realism and the Plasticity of Mind. Canadian Journal of Philosophy* 11, no. 3: 555–567.

Wilkes, K. 1981. "Functionalism, Psychology, and the Philosophy of Mind." *Philosophical Topics* 12, no. 1.

Wilkes, K. 1984. "Pragmatics in Science and Theory in Common Sense." *Inquiry* 27, no. 4: 339–361.

Wilson, M. 1980. "The Observational Uniqueness of Some Theories." *Journal of Philosophy* 77, no. 4: 208–232.

Wilson, M. 1985. "What Can Theory Tell Us about Observation?" In P. M. Churchland and C. A. Hooker, eds., *Images of Science*, pp. 222–242. Chicago: University of Chicago Press.

Wolter, J. R. 1965. "The Centrifugal Nerves in Human Optic Tract, Chiasm, Optic Nerve, and Retina." *Transactions of the American Opthalmological Society* 63:678–707.

Wolter, J. R., and Lund, O. E. 1968. "Reaction of Centrifugal Nerves in the Human Retina." *American Journal of Opthalmology* 66:221–232.

Zeki, S. 1980. "The Representation of Colours in the Cerebral Cortex." *Nature* 284:412–418.

Zeki, S. 1983. "Colour Coding in the Cerebral Cortex: The Reaction of Cells in Monkey Visual Cortex to Wavelengths and Colours." *Neuroscience* 9, no. 4: 741–765.

Zipser, D., and Elman, J. D. 1987. "Learning the Hidden Structure of Speech." *Journal of the Acoustical Society of America* 83, no. 4: 1615–1626.

Index